The Interpersonal Metafunction in 1 Corinthians 1–4

Linguistic Biblical Studies

Series Editors

Stanley E. Porter
Jesús Peláez
Jonathan M. Watt

VOLUME 19

This series, Linguistic Biblical Studies, is dedicated to the development and promotion of linguistically informed study of the Bible in its original languages. Biblical studies has greatly benefited from modern theoretical and applied linguistics, but stands poised to benefit from further integration of the two fields of study. Most linguistics has studied contemporary languages, and attempts to apply linguistic methods to study of ancient languages requires systematic re-assessment of their approaches. This series is designed to address such challenges, by providing a venue for linguistically based analysis of the languages of the Bible. As a result, monograph-length studies and collections of essays in the major areas of linguistics, such as syntax, semantics, pragmatics, discourse analysis and text linguistics, corpus linguistics, cognitive linguistics, comparative linguistics, and the like, will be encouraged, and any theoretical linguistic approach will be considered, both formal and functional. Primary consideration is given to the Greek of the New and Old Testaments and of other relevant ancient authors, but studies in Hebrew, Coptic, and other related languages will be entertained as appropriate.

The titles published in this series are listed at *brill.com/lbs*

The Interpersonal Metafunction in 1 Corinthians 1–4

The Tenor of Toughness

By

James D. Dvorak

BRILL

LEIDEN | BOSTON

Library of Congress Cataloging-in-Publication Data

Names: Dvorak, James D., author.
Title: The interpersonal metafunction in 1 Corinthians 1–4 : the tenor of
    toughness / by James D. Dvorak.
Description: Leiden ; Boston : Brill, [2021] | Series: Linguistic biblical
    studies, 1877–7554 ; volume 19 | Includes bibliographical references and
    index. | Summary: "In The Interpersonal Metafunction in 1 Corinthians
    1–4, James D. Dvorak offers a linguistic-critical discourse analysis of
    1 Cor 1–4 utilizing Appraisal Theory, a model rooted in the modern
    sociolinguistic paradigm known as Systemic-Functional Linguistics. This
    work is concerned primarily with the interpersonal meanings encoded in
    the text and how they pertain to the act of resocialization. Dvorak pays
    particular attention to the linguistics of appraisal in Paul's language
    to determine the values with which Paul expects believers in Christ to
    align. This book will be of great value to biblical scholars and
    students with interests in biblical Greek, functional linguistics,
    appraisal theory, hermeneutics, exegesis, and 1 Corinthians"— Provided
    by publisher.
Identifiers: LCCN 2021003367 (print) | LCCN 2021003368 (ebook) | ISBN
    9789004453791 (hardback) | ISBN 9789004453814 (ebook)
Subjects: LCSH: Bible. Corinthians, 1st, I–IV—Language, style. | Bible.
    Corinthians, 1st, I–IV—Criticism, interpretation, etc. | Discourse
    analysis. | Greek language, Biblical—Discourse analysis. |
    Functionalism (Linguistics) | Systemic grammar.
Classification: LCC BS2675.52 .D86 2021 (print) | LCC BS2675.52 (ebook) |
    DDC 227/.2066—dc23
LC record available at https://lccn.loc.gov/2021003367
LC ebook record available at https://lccn.loc.gov/2021003368

Typeface for the Latin, Greek, and Cyrillic scripts: "Brill". See and download: brill.com/brill-typeface.

ISSN 1877-7554
ISBN 978-90-04-45379-1 (hardback)
ISBN 978-90-04-45381-4 (e-book)

Copyright 2021 by James D. Dvorak. Published by Koninklijke Brill NV, Leiden, The Netherlands.
Koninklijke Brill NV incorporates the imprints Brill, Brill Hes & De Graaf, Brill Nijhoff, Brill Rodopi,
Brill Sense, Hotei Publishing, mentis Verlag, Verlag Ferdinand Schöningh and Wilhelm Fink Verlag.
Koninklijke Brill NV reserves the right to protect this publication against unauthorized use. Requests for
re-use and/or translations must be addressed to Koninklijke Brill NV via brill.com or copyright.com.

This book is printed on acid-free paper and produced in a sustainable manner.

Contents

Acknowledgements VII
List of Figures and Tables VIII
Abbreviations IX

1 **The Interpersonal Metafunction and Interpersonal Discourse Analysis** 1
  1   Introduction 1
  2   Theory: Key Tenets and Presuppositions 8
      2.1   *Language as Social Semiotic* 8
      2.2   *Stratification* 12
      2.3   *Metafunction, Register, and Genre* 13
      2.4   *Ideology* 35
      2.5   *Text* 40
  3   Conclusion 44

2 **"What's Your Take?" A Model for the Analysis of Intersubjective Stance in Written Discourse** 45
  1   Introduction 45
  2   Modeling APPRAISAL 47
      2.1   *The System of ATTITUDE* 47
      2.2   *The System of ENGAGEMENT* 67
      2.3   *The System of GRADUATION* 82
  3   Analytical Procedure 90

3 **"Tell Us How You Really Feel, Paul!" (Part 1)**
  An Appraisal Analysis of 1 Cor 1:1–2:16 94
  1   Introduction 94
  2   To Corinth with Love: The Letter Opening and Thanksgiving (1 Cor 1:1–9) 94
      2.1   *The Letter Opening (1 Cor 1:1–3)* 94
      2.2   *Thanksgiving (1 Cor 1:4–9)* 101
  3   Is Christ Divided? The Problem of Coteries in Corinth (1 Cor 1:10–4:21) (Part I) 107
      3.1   *Σχίσματα and Ἔριδες: Symptoms of a Deeper Problem (1 Cor 1:10–17)* 108
      3.2   *The Great Reversal I: The "Foolishness" of the Cross Supplants the "Wisdom" of the World (1 Cor 1:18–25)* 117

3.3 *The Great Reversal II: The Undeserving Receive What They Do Not Deserve (1 Cor 1:26–31)* 127

3.4 *The Great Reversal III: Power Is Delivered through Weakness (1 Cor 2:1–5)* 133

3.5 *Wisdom from Above (1 Cor 2:6–16)* 136

4 Conclusion 145

4 "Tell Us How You Really Feel, Paul!" (Part 2)
An Appraisal Analysis of 1 Cor 3:1–4:21 148

1 Is Christ Divided? The Problem of Coteries in Corinth (1 Cor 1:10–4:21) (Part 2) 148

1.1 *"Your Actions Prove Otherwise" (1 Cor 3:1–4)* 148

1.2 *The Great Reversal (Reprise) (1 Cor 3:5–9)* 155

1.3 *Consider Carefully How You Build (1 Cor 3:10–17)* 161

1.4 *"All Things Belong to the Wise" (1 Cor 3:18–23)* 167

1.5 *"Only My Master Judges Me" (1 Cor 4:1–5)* 171

1.6 *True Humility Exemplified by the Apostles (1 Cor 4:6–13)* 175

1.7 *Maintain the Family's Honor by Imitating Me (1 Cor 4:14–21)* 184

2 Conclusion 190

5 Conclusion 195

Appendix: Survey of the Literature on the Study of 1 Corinthians 199

Bibliography 213

Name Index 237

Scripture Index 241

Acknowledgements

This book is a revised version of my Ph.D. dissertation, which I wrote under the mentorship of Dr. Stanley E. Porter and Dr. Cynthia Long Westfall at McMaster Divinity College, Hamilton, ON, Canada. I successfully defended the dissertation in the spring of 2012. I wish to thank Stanley E. Porter, Jesús Peláez, and Jonathan M. Watt for inviting me to submit my research to such an erudite series as LBS.

It is impossible in this limited space to thank everyone who helped this work come to be; so many of my family and friends prayed on my behalf, encouraged me, and, in those moments when I was nearly consumed by doubt, gave me the "pep talks" I needed to see the project to its completion. Yet, there are a number of people who, because of their intimate involvement with this project, I must thank here.

I offer my sincerest gratitude to Dr. Stanley E. Porter, my doctoral supervisor, mentor, and friend during my studies at McMaster Divinity College. His mastery and passion for Biblical Greek and Linguistics, his expert teaching, his emphasis on excellence in scholarship, and his graciousness made my learning experience both worthwhile and extremely fulfilling. Dr. Cynthia Long Westfall, also at McMaster Divinity College (and the second reader on my dissertation committee) played a pivotal role in helping me complete this project. Her expertise in Greek and Linguistics as well as her keen biblical-theological insights made my work better. I am very grateful to her for giving me excellent advice leading up to my defense. I also wish to thank Dr. Mark J. Boda, Dr. Michael P. Knowles, Dr. Gordon L. Heath, and Dr. Lois K. Fuller Dow.

I absolutely could not have completed this task without the unwavering support of my family. My parents, Phil and Ellen, have been a constant source of love, support, and encouragement for all of my endeavors, especially this one. My brother, Jeff, and my sister, Susan, made sure that I worked hard but also took time to have some fun. My in-laws, Bob and Janet, Travis and Kelly, and Kelsey and Lisa often rearranged their families' lives to accommodate my writing schedule. I am, however, most grateful to my immediate family. My daughter and son, Sydney and Hagan, showed amazing flexibility, patience, and grace through the whole experience of moving from Oklahoma to Ontario and back, as well as during my intense times of research and writing (which required me to "hide"). Finally and most importantly, I am forever grateful to my lovely and loving wife, Celeste Joy, who held our family together—indeed, held me together—from the beginning of this journey to its end. I cannot thank you enough, Celeste. I love you so very much!

Figures and Tables

Figures

1 Stratification of social activity, discourse, and grammar 13
2 Stratification of context and language 14
3 Stratification including register 24
4 Dimensions of variation in field 25
5 Dimensions of variation in tenor 27
6 Dimensions of variation in mode 28
7 Stratification including genre 33
8 A basic overview of the APPRAISAL network 47
9 The ATTITUDE system network 67
10 An overview of ENGAGEMENT 69
11 The system of ENGAGEMENT 82
12 Preliminary network of GRADUATION 83
13 The system of GRADUATION 91

Tables

1 Particulate structure (experiential meaning) 16
2 Prime and Subsequent analysis of clauses from 1 Cor 3:18 17
3 Halliday's and Martin's views of register compared 23
4 AFFECT—(un)happiness 56
5 AFFECT—(in)security 56
6 AFFECT—(dis)satisfaction 58
7 JUDGMENT—social esteem 60
8 JUDGMENT—social sanction 60
9 Examples of APPRECIATION 62
10 Examples of isolating INTENSIFICATION 87
11 Attitudinal lexis with tentative clines of INTENSIFICATION 88
12 DENY–COUNTER pairs in 1 Cor 1:26–28 131
13 Attitudinal analysis of 1 Cor 4:9–13 178
14 Concede (CONCUR) + counter pairs in 1 Cor 4:10 182
15 Concede (CONCUR) + counter Pairs in 1 Cor 4:12c–13 183

Abbreviations

AB	Anchor Bible
ABD	*Anchor Bible Dictionary*. 6 vols. Edited by David Noel Freedman. New York: Doubleday, 1992
ANLEX	Timothy Friberg, Barbara Friberg, and Neva F. Miller. *Analytical Lexicon of the Greek New Testament*. Grand Rapids: Baker, 2000
AYB	Anchor Yale Bible
BAGD	Bauer, Walter, William F. Arndt, F. Wilbur Gingrich, and Frederick W. Danker. *Greek-English Lexicon of the New Testament and Other Early Christian Literature*. 2nd ed. Chicago: University of Chicago, 1979
BAGL	*Biblical and Ancient Greek Linguistics*
BBR	Bulletin of Biblical Research
BDAG	Danker, Frederick W., Walter Bauer, William F. Arndt, and F. Wilbur Gingrich. *Greek-English Lexicon of the New Testament and Other Early Christian Literature*. 3rd ed. Chicago: University of Chicago, 2000
BDF	Blass, Friedrich, Albert Debrunner, and Robert W. Funk. *A Greek Grammar of the New Testament and Other Early Christian Literature*. Chicago: University of Chicago Press, 1961
BECNT	Baker Exegetical Commentary on the New Testament
BETL	Bibliotheca Ephemeridum Theologicarum Lovaniensium
BibInt	*Biblical Interpretation*
BJRL	*Bulletin of the John Rylands Library*
BLG	Biblical Languages: Greek
BNTC	Black's New Testament Commentary
BT	*Bible Translator*
BZNW	Beihefte zur Zeitschrift für die Neutestamentliche Wissenschaft
CBET	Contributions to Biblical Exegesis and Theology
CBQ	*Catholic Biblical Quarterly*
CBR	*Currents in Biblical Research*
CPNIVC	The College Press NIV Commentary
ConcC	Concordia Commentary
CTJ	*Calvin Theological Journal*
CTL	Cambridge Textbooks in Linguistics
CurTM	*Currents in Theology and Mission*
CWMAKH	Collected Works of M. A. K. Halliday
DASK	Duisburger Arbeiten zur Sprach- und Kulturwissenschaft

DNTB	*Dictionary of New Testament Background.* Edited by Craig A. Evans and Stanley E. Porter. Downers Grove, IL: InterVarsity, 2000
DPL	*Dictionary of Paul and His Letters.* Edited by Gerald F. Hawthorne and Ralph P. Martin. Downers Grove, IL: InterVarsity Press, 1993
ECC	Eerdmans Critical Commentary
EDNT	*Exegetical Dictionary of the New Testament.* Edited by Horst Balz and Gerhard Schneider. ET. 3 vols. Grand Rapids: Eerdmans, 1990–1993
EGGNT	Exegetical Guide to the Greek New Testament
EKKNT	Evangelisch-Katholischer Kommentar zum Neuen Testament
EQ	*Evangelical Quarterly*
FF	Foundations & Facets
FFF	*Foundations and Facets Forum*
FN	*Filología Neotestamentaria*
GBS	Guides to Biblical Scholarship
GTA	Göttinger theologischer Arbeiten
HBSV	*Handbook of Biblical Social Values.* Edited by John J. Pilch and Bruce J. Malina. Matrix: The Bible in Mediterranean Context 10. Eugene, OR: Wipf and Stock, 2016
HNTC	Harper's New Testament Commentaries
HTS	Harvard Theological Studies
IAL	*Issues in Applied Linguistics*
ICC	International Critical Commentary
IESS	*International Encyclopedia of Social Sciences.* Edited by David L. Sills and Robert K. Merton. New York: Macmillan, 1968–
IFG3	M. A. K. Halliday and C. M. I. M. Matthiessen. *An Introduction to Functional Grammar.* London: Arnold, 2004
Int	*Interpretation*
JAAR	*Journal of the American Academy of Religion*
JBL	*Journal of Biblical Literature*
JEAP	*Journal of English for Academic Purposes*
JETS	*Journal of the Evangelical Theological Society*
JGRChJ	*Journal of Greco-Roman Christianity and Judaism*
JLIABG	*Journal of the Linguistics Institute of Ancient and Biblical Greek*
JPL	*Journal of Philosophic Logic*
JSNT	*Journal for the Study of the New Testament*
JSNTSup	Journal for the Study of the New Testament Supplement Series
JSOTSup	Journal for the Study of the Old Testament Supplement Series
JTS	*Journal of Theological Studies*
KEK	Kritisch-exegetischer Kommentar über das Neue Testament
LBRS	Lexham Bible Reference Series

ABBREVIATIONS

LCBI	Literary Currents in Biblical Interpretation
LCL	Loeb Classical Library
LEC	Library of Early Christianity
LENT	Linguistic Exegesis of the New Testament
LLL	Longman Linguistics Library
L&N	*Greek-English Lexicon of the New Testament Based on Semantic Domains.* Edited by J. P. Louw and E. A. Nida. New York: UBS, 1989
LNTS	Library of New Testament Studies
LSJ	H. G. Liddell, R. Scott, and H. S. Jones. *A Greek-English Lexicon.* 9th ed. Oxford: Oxford University Press, 1995
MNTC	Moffatt New Testament Commentary
MTSS	McMaster Theological Studies Series
NAB	New American Bible
NAC	New American Commentary
NASB	New American Standard Bible
NCBC	New Cambridge Bible Commentary
NET	New English Translation
NICNT	New International Commentary on the New Testament
NICOT	New International Commentary on the Old Testament
NIDNTT	*New International Dictionary of New Testament Theology.* Edited by C. Brown. 4 vols. Grand Rapids: Zondervan, 1975–1985
NIGTC	New International Greek Testament Commentary
NIV	New International Version
NIVAC	NIV Application Commentary
NovT	*Novum Testamentum*
NovTSup	Supplements to Novum Testamentum
NRSV	New Revised Standard Version
NTL	New Testament Library
NTM	New Testament Monographs
NTS	*New Testament Studies*
OBC	Oxford Bible Commentary
PAST	Pauline Studies
PNTC	Pillar New Testament Commentary
RelSRev	*Religious Studies Review*
RQ	*Restoration Quarterly*
SBG	Studies in Biblical Greek
SBLDS	Society of Biblical Literature Dissertation Series
SBLMS	Society of Biblical Literature Monograph Series
SBLRBS	Society of Biblical Literature Resources for Biblical Studies
SBLSS	Society of Biblical Literature Symposium Series

SE	*Studia evangelica*
SHBC	Smyth and Helwys Bible Commentary
SNTG	Studies in New Testament Greek
SNTSMS	Society for New Testament Studies Monograph Series
SP	Sacra Pagina
SSEJC	Studies in Scripture in Early Judaism and Christianity
ST	*Studia Theologica*
TDNT	*Theological Dictionary of the New Testament.* Edited by Gerhard Kittel and Gerhard Friedrich. Translated by Geoffrey W. Bromiley. 10 vols. Grand Rapids: Eerdmans, 1964–1976
TJ	*Trinity Journal*
TLNT	Ceslas Spiq. *Theological Lexicon of the New Testament.* Translated and edited by James D. Ernest. 3 vols. Grand Rapids: Eerdmans, 1994
TNIV	Today's New International Version
TUGAL	Texte und Untersuchungen zur Geschichte der altchristlichen Literatur
WBC	Word Biblical Commentary
WTJ	*Westminster Theological Journal*
ZNW	*Zeitschrift für die neutestamentliche Wissenschaft und die Kunde der älteren Kirche*

CHAPTER 1

The Interpersonal Metafunction and Interpersonal Discourse Analysis

1 Introduction

In 1993, Wayne Meeks published *The Origins of Christian Morality* in which he argues convincingly that the formation and maintenance of moral norms is inextricably bound up with the processes of community forma-tion and maintenance—and this, he demonstrates, was the case for the early Christians.[1] Community formation and maintenance and, thus, moral forma-tion and maintenance are social phenomena that may be described, as Meeks appropriately does, under the rubric of *resocialization*.[2] As one enters the Christian community through *conversion*—a simultaneous "transfer of loyalty and sense of belonging from one set of social relations to another, quite differ-ent set"[3]—the convert accepts and agrees to live within the moral boundaries of the community. Stepping beyond these boundaries would require further resocialization (e.g., gentle correction, stern warning, harsh rebuke).

---

1 Wayne A. Meeks, *The Origins of Christian Morality: The First Two Centuries* (New Haven: Yale, 1993), 5.

2 Resocialization is the process whereby a person willingly sets aside or alters certain beliefs, value positions, and behaviors and accepts new or modified ones as part of some form of social transformation (see Robert T. Shaefer and Robert P. Lamm, *Sociology*, 4th ed. [New York: McGraw Hill, 1992], 113; Orville G. Brim, "Adult Socialization," *IESS* 14:556; Peter L. Berger and Thomas Luckmann, *The Social Construction of Reality: A Treatise in the Sociology of Knowledge* [Garden City, NY: Doubleday, 1966], 129–63), though, as Meeks points out else-where, no one can ever completely efface their primary socialization (Wayne A. Meeks, *The Moral World of the First Christians*, LEC 6 [Philadelphia: Westminster, 1986], 13). In *You Belong to Christ: Paul and the Formation of Social Identity in 1 Corinthians 1–4* (Eugene, OR: Pickwick, 2010), J. Brian Tucker frames the discussion in terms of *identity formation*.

3 Meeks, *Origins of Christian Morality*, 31. Here the distinction between adhesion and conver-sion made by Nock in his classic work on conversion becomes apparent. According to Nock, adhesion involves the acceptance of religious rites as "useful supplements and not as substi-tutes, as they did not involve taking of a new way of life"; however, conversion involves "the reorientation of the soul of an individual, his deliberate turning from indifference or from an earlier form of piety to another, a turning which implies a consciousness that a great change is involved, that the old was wrong and the new is right" (Arthur D. Nock, *Conversion: The Old and the New in Religion from Alexander the Great to Augustine of Hippo* [Baltimore: John Hopkins, 1998], 7; see also Meeks, *Origins of Christian Morality*, 26–31).

© JAMES D. DVORAK, 2021 | DOI:10.1163/9789004453814_002

2   CHAPTER 1

The significance of Meeks's argument for the current study has to do with the vital role that language plays in the resocialization process. Meeks alludes to this in the discussion leading up to his thesis statement:

> Almost without exception, the documents that eventually became the New Testament ... are concerned with the way converts to the movement ought to behave. *These documents ... have among their primary aims the maintenance and growth of those communities.* In those documents we can see, though not always very clearly, the very formation of a Christian moral order, of a set of Christian moral practices.[4]

In other words, the texts of the New Testament—more precisely, *the instances of language that express the social and interpersonal meanings intended by the writers*—played a central role in the resocialization of the early Christians.[5] In fact, although Meeks utilizes ethnographic rather than sociolinguistic methodology,[6] he nevertheless acknowledges the instrumental role of language in the creation and maintenance of the community's moral order when he examines "the language [the community used] to provide explicit action guides for one another" and the "moral talk" used to reify their symbolic moral universe.[7]

---

4 Meeks, *Origins of Christian Morality*, 5 (italics added). See also Meeks, *Moral World*, 11–17.

5 On the primacy of language in (re-)socialization or the construction of shared reality, see Elinor Ochs, "Socialization Through Language and Interaction," *IAL* 2 (1991): 143; M. A. K. Halliday, *Language as Social Semiotic* (Baltimore: University Park Press, 1978), 213–16; Richard A. Hudson, *Sociolinguistics*, CTL (Cambridge: Cambridge University Press, 1980), 101–3; Berger and Luckmann, *Social Construction of Reality*, 152–54; Cate Poynton, *Language and Gender: Making the Difference*, 2nd ed. (Oxford: Oxford University Press, 1989), 11–16; Meeks, *Moral World*, 15; Tucker, *You Belong to Christ*, 55–58. Of course, other media/means and semiotic systems besides language may be used, such as shunning or removal from the group (see 1 Cor 5:1–13) (see Michel Foucault, *The Archaeology of Knowledge*, trans. Alan Sheridan [New York: Pantheon, 1972], 230–32; Pierre Bourdieu, *Logic of Practice*, trans. Richard Nice [Stanford, CA: Stanford University Press, 1990], 52–65; Elizabeth A. Castelli, *Imitating Paul: A Discourse of Power*, LCBI [Louisville: Westminster John Knox, 1991], 53–57; Norman Fairclough, *Discourse and Social Change* [Cambridge: Polity, 1992], 37–61; Jay L. Lemke, *Textual Politics* [London: Taylor & Francis, 1995], 28–36).

6 See Meeks, *Origins of Christian Morality*, 8–11.

7 Meeks, *Origins of Christian Morality*, 14–15. The linguistic nature of these formulations is made apparent by the headings under which Meeks discusses them: "The Language of Belonging," "The Language of Separation," "The Language of Obligation," and "The Grammar of Christian Practice." The first two headings are from Wayne A. Meeks, *The First Urban Christians: The Social World of the Apostle Paul* (New Haven: Yale University Press, 1983), 85 and 94; the second pair are from Meeks, *Origins of Christian Morality*, 66 and 91. See also the section "The Grammar of Christian Morals" in Meeks, *Moral World*, 124.

It is on this topic that the current work seeks to enter the scholarly discussion. Adopting a model that is distinctly sociolinguistic, the current project focuses upon the apostle Paul's use of language for the ideological (re-)positioning of the putative readers of canonical 1 Corinthians. It seeks to discover what discourse semantic resources are called upon to define or to redefine the chief criteria Paul and the Corinthians used to determine, explain, and legitimate the collective needs and wants, interests, and goals—in short, the values—of the Christian community at Corinth.[8] A key purveyor of ideology and its structures (e.g., values, judgments, experiences, perspectives) and the focal point of this study is *evaluation. Evaluation* refers to "the expression of [a] speaker or writer's attitude or stance towards, viewpoint on, or feelings about the entities or propositions that he or she is talking [or writing] about."[9] *Stance* has to do with what Martin and White call "bonding," that is "the investiture of attitude in activity, the resonance of attitude with events and things (abstract or concrete), around which shared reverberations [people] align into communing sympathies of kinship, friendship, collegiality and other of the many kinds of affinity and affiliation."[10] In short, stance is about creating community around shared values, where "value"

> describes some general quality and direction in life that human beings are expected to embody in their behavior. A value is a general, normative orientation of action in a social system. It is an emotionally anchored commitment to pursue and support certain directions or types of actions.[11]

---

8   On this view of ideology, see below. See also John H. Elliott, *What Is Social-Scientific Criticism?* GBS (Minneapolis: Fortress, 1993), 130.

9   Susan Hunston and Geoff Thompson, *Evaluation in Text: Authorial Stance and Construction of Discourse* (Oxford: Oxford University Press, 1999), 5. See Peter R. R. White, "Evaluative Semantics and Ideological Positioning in Journalistic Discourse: A New Framework for Analysis," in *Mediating Ideology in Text and Image*, ed. Inger Lassen, Jeanne Strunck and Torben Vestergaard (Amsterdam: John Benjamins, 2006), 38. Susan Hunston, "Evaluation and Ideology in Scientific Writing," in *Register Analysis: Theory and Practice*, ed. Mohsen Ghadessy, Open Linguistics Series (London: Pinter, 1993) 57–58: "Evaluation may be defined as anything which indicates the writer's attitude to the value of an entity in the text."

10 James R. Martin and Peter R. R. White, *The Language of Evaluation: Appraisal in English* (New York: Palgrave, 2005), 211.

11 John J. Pilch and Bruce J. Malina, "Introduction," *HBSV* xix. See also Berger and Luckmann, *Social Construction of Reality*, 93–94 (under "legitimation"); Margaret L. Anderson and Howard F. Taylor, *Sociology: The Essentials*, 7th ed. (Belmont, CA: Wadsworth Cengage, 2013), 33.

4   CHAPTER 1

To take up stance, then, is not simply to express one's attitudes about entities or propositions within a shared social system; rather, it is to construct community around shared values.[12]

It is this social-constitutive function that enables writers like Paul to construct and to attempt to naturalize axiological models (i.e., social models
determinative of what is normal and deviant, beneficial and harmful, praiseworthy and blameworthy, and so on) by which they believe their putative readers ought to conduct themselves as members "in good standing" of a particular
group or community.[13] To examine these evaluative meanings, a model of
appraisal will be used. The term "appraisal" here refers inclusively to all the
evaluative resources of language that a person may use to adopt particular
stances or value positions and to negotiate these stances with potential and/
or actual respondents.[14] These stances are revealed along three social-semiotic
axes; hence, the model is tri-axial. The basic model is briefly sketched here; a
much more detailed description appears in chapter 2.

The first axis has to do with the attitude of the language user. Focus here
is upon features traditionally discussed under the heading of "affect," namely
how language users overtly encode their own positive or negative feelings,
emotions, and attitudes about an entity or proposition.[15] Appraisal Theory
not only accounts for explicit realizations of attitude (emotions, judgments,
and appreciations) but also considers how writers may attempt more indirectly to evoke or provoke certain attitudinal evaluations to persuade others
to adopt a stance that aligns with their own.[16] Thus, the use of attitude in text
has the rhetorical effect of potentially creating in the assumed readers the

---

12   See Jay L. Lemke, "Interpersonal Meaning in Discourse: Value Orientations," in *Advances
      in Systemic Linguistics: Recent Theory and Practice*, ed. Martin Davies and Louise Ravelli,
      Open Linguistics Series (London: Pinter, 1992), 86.
13   See White, "Evaluative Semantics," 38. *Axiology* is "the study of things with regard to
      their value dimension" (see Robert C. Neville, *Reconstruction of Thinking*, Axiology of
      Thinking 1 [New York: SUNY, 1981], 12). The main interest in this study is in how discourse
      is used to create and maintain axiological communities (i.e., communities of shared val-
      ues) or, in the language of social-scientific criticism, how discourse is used for mapping
      one's symbolic universe in terms of time, space, things, actions (including thinking and
      behaving), and people (see Jerome H. Neyrey, *Paul in Other Words: A Cultural Reading of
      His Letters* [Louisville: Westminster John Knox, 1990], 21–101).
14   Peter R. R. White, "Appraisal: An Overview," http://www.grammatics.com/appraisal/
      appraisalguide/framed/frame.htm.
15   See Elinor Ochs and Bambi Schieffelin, "Language Has a Heart," *Text* 9 (1989): 7–25.
16   Martin and White, *Language of Evaluation*, 2.

same emotional responses the writer feels toward certain phenomena. This is referred to as "attitudinal positioning."[17]

The second axis with which Appraisal Theory is concerned has traditionally been dealt with under such headings as "modality," "epistemic modality," and "evidentiality."[18] Appraisal Theory extends the traditional approach by attending not only to writer certainty, commitment, and knowledge but also to the question of how the writer engages and positions their voice vis-à-vis other voices and value positions sourced in the text.[19] Meanings along this axis allow language users "to present themselves as recognizing, answering, ignoring, challenging, rejecting, fending off, anticipating or accommodating actual or potential interlocutors and the value positions they represent."[20] The rhetorical effects of these kinds of meanings are referred to as "dialogic" and "intertextual positioning."[21]

The third axis accounts for what has traditionally been covered under the headings of "intensification," "vague language," and "hedging."[22] Along this axis lie the values that allow language users to grade or scale other meanings with regard to two dimensions. The first dimension provides the ability to upscale or downscale other meanings according to intensity or amount.[23] The domain of this cline includes categories of inherently scalar assessments in terms of positivity, negativity, size, extent, and so on (e.g., compare "expensive"

---

17   White, "Appraisal: An Overview."

18   See John Lyons, *Semantics*, 2 vols. (Cambridge: Cambridge University Press, 1977), 2:787–849; Frank R. Palmer, *Mood and Modality*, 2nd ed., CTL (Cambridge: Cambridge University Press, 2001); Wallace L. Chafe, "Evidentiality in English Conversation and Academic Writing," in *Evidentiality: The Linguistic Coding of Epistemology*, ed. W. L. Chafe and J. Nichols, Advances in Discourse Processes 20 (Norwood, NJ: Ablex, 1986), 261–72.

19   Martin and White, *Language of Evaluation*, 2. See also Peter R. R. White, "Beyond Modality and Hedging," *Text* 23 (2003): 259–84; Peter R. R. White, "Dialogue and Inter-Subjectivity: Reinterpreting the Semantics of Modality and Hedging," in *Dialogue Analysis VII: Working with Dialogue*, ed. Malcolm Coulthard, Janet Cotterill, and Frances Rock (Tübingen: Max Niemeyer, 2000), 67–80; Michael Stubbs, *Text and Corpus Analysis: Computer-Assisted Studies of Language and Culture* (Cambridge, MA: Blackwell, 1996), 196–229; Fairclough, *Discourse and Social Change*, 158–62.

20   Martin and White, *Language of Evaluation*, 2.

21   Peter R. R. White, "Introductory Tour," http://www.grammatics.com/appraisal/appraisal outline/framed/frame.htm.

22   See William Labov, "Intensity," in *Meaning, Form and Use in Context*, ed. Deborah Schiffrin (Washington, DC: Georgetown University Press, 1984), 43–70; Joanna Channell, *Vague Language* (Oxford: Oxford University Press, 1994), 1–22; George Lakoff, "Hedges: A Study in Meaning Criteria and the Logic of Fuzzy Concepts," *JPL* 2 (1973): 183–228; Ken Hyland, *Hedging in Scientific Research Articles*, Pragmatics and Beyond 54 (Amsterdam: Benjamins, 1998).

23   Martin and White, *Language of Evaluation*, 137.

6   CHAPTER 1

with "*very* expensive"). The second dimension allows language users to grade with regard to prototypicality. The domain of this cline includes culturally-bounded ideational categories or phenomena that are not inherently scalar but may be brought more or less into focus through modification (e.g., compare "love" with "*true* love"). This axis is of key importance for appraisal because it operates across the other two axes so that a language user may foreground or background attitudes or value positions appropriate to the meanings they wish to make.

The basic methodology adopted here is discourse analysis. Although the number of studies laying claim to this designation have increased significantly since Louw introduced the method to New Testament exegesis,[24] its definition, scope, and application vary according to the analyst's research paradigm.[25] When scholars adopt discourse analysis without explicitly identifying the research paradigm from which they commence, the methodology is in danger of appearing ambiguous, if not confusing.[26]

Lemke describes well the perspective and emphasis of discourse analysis that is adopted for the current project:

> Discourse analysis today is trying to formulate the *interactional* semantics of text. We do not use language simply to organize action or to describe (or even create) events and their relations. *Language is also a resource for*

---

24 Johannes P. Louw, "Discourse Analysis and the Greek New Testament," *BT* 24 (1973): 101–18.

25 Elliott, *What Is Social-Scientific Criticism*, 36; Thomas S. Kuhn, *The Structure of Scientific Revolutions*, 3rd ed. (Chicago: University of Chicago Press, 1996), 174–210; Pierre Bourdieu, *Outline of a Theory of Practice*, trans. Richard Nice, Studies in Social and Cultural Anthropology 16 (Cambridge: Cambridge University Press, 1977), 72–95; Bourdieu, *Logic of Practice*, 52–65. On models and methods generally, see John H. Elliott, "Social-Scientific Criticism: More on Methods and Models," *Semeia* 35 (1986): 1–9; Thomas F. Carney, *The Shape of the Past: Models and Antiquity* (Lawrence, KS: Coronado, 1975), 1–43. Of course, research paradigms typically include a number of different research perspectives, each theorizing in ways generally consistent with the traditions and presuppositions of the paradigm, but often putting a unique "spin" on things due to differing emphases and, occasionally, differing opinions regarding the validity or application of certain presuppositions. See Elliott, "More on Methods and Models," 7–8.

26 For an excellent overview of the various schools of discourse analysis, see now Stanley E. Porter, "Discourse Analysis and New Testament Studies: An Introductory Survey," in *Discourse Analysis and Other Topics in Biblical Greek*, ed. Stanley E. Porter and D. A. Carson, JSNTSup 113 (Sheffield: Sheffield Academic, 1995), 14–35 and Stanley E. Porter and Andrew W. Pitts, "New Testament Greek Language and Linguistics in Recent Research," *CBR* 6 (2008): 235–41. See also Cynthia Long Westfall, *A Discourse Analysis of the Letter to the Hebrews*, LNTS 297, SNTG 11 (London: T & T Clark, 2005), 23–27.

the creation and maintenance of social relations and value systems. Every discourse voice, embodied in text, constructs a stance toward itself and other discourse voices. It *evaluates*, explicitly or implicitly, what it has to say and the relation of what it has to say to what *others* do say or may say. Its evaluative orientation includes but is not limited to, certitude of truth value. It can define any value orientation toward what it says and/ or toward what others say: appropriateness, usefulness, morality, pleasurability; all the forms of "rightness" and "goodness."[27]

A host of questions present themselves to the discourse analyst pursuing this course of analysis:[28]
– How do texts embody systems of social values?
– What are the linguistic resources for constructing a value orientation toward one's own and others' texts?
– How are these resources deployed against the background of value positions voiced within and beyond the boundaries of a community?
– How can one best characterize the interactional, orientational, axiological formations of a text and, more generally, how it globally patterns its selections of grammatical resources in these ways?

These questions demand an analytical methodology that is backed by a linguistic theory that strongly ties together language and context and that emphasizes the use of language for social purposes. Thus, the current project openly aligns itself with the research tradition of Systemic-Functional Linguistics (SFL) as pioneered and championed by M. A. K. Halliday.[29] Further, the model of discourse analysis (i.e., appraisal analysis) offered in this project is based in large part upon the analytical approach developed by J. R. Martin and his colleagues,[30] as well as the models developed by Porter and O'Donnell, Reed, and Westfall (for New Testament Greek)—all of which are consonant in essence with the SFL paradigm.[31]

---

27 Jay L. Lemke, "Semantics and Social Values," *Word* 40 (1989): 39. See also Fairclough, *Discourse and Social Change*, 62–100.

28 These questions are from Lemke, "Semantics and Social Values," 39.

29 See esp. Halliday, *Social Semiotic*, 108–26.

30 See James R. Martin, *English Text: System and Structure* (Amsterdam: John Benjamins, 1992); James R. Martin and David Rose, *Working with Discourse: Meaning Beyond the Clause*, 2nd ed. (London: Continuum, 2007). These, of course, are adapted for Hellenistic Greek.

31 Stanley E. Porter and Matthew Brook O'Donnell, *Discourse Analysis* (unpublished manuscript); Jeffrey T. Reed, *A Discourse Analysis of Philippians: Method and Rhetoric in the Debate over Literary Integrity*, JSNTSup 136 (Sheffield: Sheffield Academic, 1997); Westfall, *Hebrews*. Also significant is the model developed for the OpenText.org project

What Rudolf Bultmann articulated more than five decades ago, which has since become axiomatic in biblical studies, applies to the present exegetical endeavor: exegesis without presuppositions is not possible.[32] Following the general practice of the social sciences, the broader realm in which sociolinguistics has its home, the major tenets and presuppositions of the model and its key terminology will be clarified in the following section.

2 Theory: Key Tenets and Presuppositions

2.1 *Language as Social Semiotic*

First and foremost, the present study adopts the fundamental tenet that lies at the heart of the SFL paradigm and from which its other presuppositions emerge: language[33] is a *social semiotic*.[34] This tenet embodies the conceptual framework SFL utilizes to interpret language. The term *social* signifies a point of view on language that stands in opposition to that of language as knowledge or competence.[35] These two rather different styles of theorizing about language are described by Halliday in terms of "nativist" versus "environmentalist":

> Broadly speaking, the nativist model reflects the philosophical-logical strand in the history of thinking about language, with its sharp distinction between the ideal and the real (which Chomsky calls "competence" and "performance") and its view of language as *rules*—essentially rules of syntax. The environmentalist represents the ethnographic tradition, which rejects the distinction of ideal and real, defines what is grammatical as,

---

(see O'Donnell, et. al., "Clause Level Annotation Specification"; Porter and Pitts, "New Testament Greek Language and Linguistics," 234–35).

32 Rudolf Bultmann, "Is Exegesis Without Presuppositions Possible?" in *New Testament & Mythology and Other Basic Writings*, ed. and trans. Schubert M. Ogden (Philadelphia: Fortress, 1984), 145–53. Although Bultmann was speaking specifically about *theological* presuppositions, the axiom holds true for all presuppositions. See Elliott, *What Is Social-Scientific Criticism*, 36.

33 Here and throughout "language" refers to "natural, human, adult, verbal language— natural as opposed to designed semiotics like mathematics and computer languages; adult (i.e., post-infancy) as opposed to infant protolanguages; verbal as opposed to music, dance and other languages of art" (M. A. K. Halliday and Christian M. I. M. Matthiessen, *An Introduction to Functional Grammar*, 3rd ed. [London: Arnold, 2004], 20 [hereafter *IFG3*]).

34 See Halliday, *Social Semiotic*, 1–35; M. A. K. Halliday, "Context of Situation," in *Language, Context, and Text: Aspects of Language in a Social Semiotic Perspective*, 2nd ed. (Oxford: Oxford University Press, 1989), 3–5.

35 Halliday, *Social Semiotic*, 10–12.

THE INTERPERSONAL METAFUNCTION AND DISCOURSE ANALYSIS   9

by and large, what is acceptable, and sees language as *resource*—resource for meaning, with meaning defined in terms of function.[36]

Halliday illustrates this distinction by contrasting two opposing lines of argument with regard to language development. From the nativist perspective, humans have a specific language-learning faculty distinct from other learning faculties that provides "a readymade and rather detailed blueprint of the structure of language."[37] Thus, language learning becomes a matter of a person fitting into a framework that they already possess the patterns of language use manifested as utterances that they hear or read.[38] The environmentalist view rejects this notion and argues that language learning depends upon the same faculties involved in all aspects of learning.[39] These mental faculties, working together, enable a person to process and correlate abstract relations between various semiotic systems and the contexts in which those systems are typically instantiated.[40] In terms of language, one becomes "fluent," not necessarily by learning rules of syntax, but by learning to correlate given contexts of situation with uses of language that are appropriate to those contexts—or, as Halliday puts it, learning how language is functionally related to observable situations in the context of its use.[41]

The term *semiotic* takes on a special nuance in SFL. As Halliday points out, the term derives from the ancient Greek terms σημεῖον (sign) and σημαινομένων (signified) that were used by the Stoics in the 3rd–2nd centuries BCE as they developed a theory of the sign.[42] In the 20th century, Saussure defined

---

36   Halliday, *Social Semiotic*, 17 (italics his); Halliday, "Language as Code and Language as Behaviour: A Systemic-Functional Interpretation of the Nature and Ontogenesis of Dialogue," in *The Semiotics of Culture and Language, Volume 1, Language as Social Semiotic*, ed. Robin P. Fawcett, M. A. K. Halliday, Sydney M. Lamb, and Adam Makkai, Open Linguistics Series (London: Frances Pinter, 1984), 3–35. On Chomsky's distinction between "competence" and "performance," see Noam Chomsky, *Language and the Mind*, 3rd ed. (Cambridge: Cambridge University Press, 2006), 102–4. See also James D. Dvorak, "'Evidence that Commands a Verdict': Determining the Semantics of Imperatives in the New Testament," *BAGL* 7 (2018): 201–23, esp. 204–12.

37   Halliday, *Social Semiotic*, 16–17. See Chomsky's "language capacity" (*Language and the Mind*, 24).

38   Halliday, *Social Semiotic*, 17.

39   Halliday, *Social Semiotic*, 17.

40   Halliday, *Social Semiotic*, 17.

41   Halliday, *Social Semiotic*, 18.

42   Halliday, "Context of Situation," 3. While semiotics generally refers to the study of signs, there are two views of semiotics, which overlap at occasional points, that impact studies in linguistics. The most direct impact is the view of Saussure, who describes semiotics (or "semiology" as he called it) from a social perspective. A less direct impact comes

the linguistic sign as the "combination of a concept and a sound pattern."[43] By extension, he perceived language as "a system of signs expressing ideas."[44] However, in spite of Saussure's view of language as a set of relationships that form a system,[45] Halliday considers his view to be inadequate due to its atomistic view of the linguistic sign. "The sign," says Halliday, "has tended to be seen as an isolate, as a thing in itself, which exists first of all in and of itself before it comes to be related to other signs."[46] Over against Saussure's view, Halliday prefers a broader definition of semiotics, one that refers not to the study of signs but to the study of sign *systems*—"as the study of meaning in its most general sense."[47] He explains further:

> ... we cannot operate with the concept of a sign as an entity. We have to think rather of systems of meaning, systems that may be considered as operating through some external form of output that we call a sign, but that are in themselves not sets of individual things, but rather networks of relationships. It is in that sense that I would use the term "semiotic" to define the perspective in which we want to look at language: language as one among a number of systems of meanings that, taken all together, constitute human culture.[48]

From this perspective, language is not simply a system of isolated signs, but a stratified semiotic system (see below); signs are the "output" of that system or, as will become clearer below, they are the expression of meaning in linguistic form (i.e., text). Language is modeled, then, as a vast resource comprised of networks of systems that offer *meaning potential*—what a person *can mean* or, functionally speaking, what a person can *do* or *accomplish* with language[49]

---

from Peirce, whose view of semiotics is logical-philosophical rather than ethnographic and social. On the former, see Ferdinand de Saussure, *Course in General Linguistics*, Open Court Classics (Chicago: Open Court, 1986), 15–17; on the latter, see Charles S. Peirce, "What is a Sign?" in *The Essential Peirce: Selected Philosophical Writings*, 2 vols. (Bloomington, IN: Indiana University Press, 1963), 2:4–10. See Lyons, *Semantics*, 1:99–109.

43 Saussure, *Course*, 67.

44 Saussure, *Course*, 15.

45 See Saussure, *Course*, 14–15.

46 Halliday, "Context of Situation," 3.

47 Halliday, "Context of Situation," 4. See also M. A. K. Halliday, "Introduction: On the 'Architecture' of Human Language," in *On Language and Linguistics*, CWMAKH 3 (London: Continuum, 2003), 2.

48 Halliday, "Context of Situation," 4. See also the important critique of Saussure in V. N. Vološinov, *Marxism and the Philosophy of Language*, trans. by Ladislav Matejka and I. R. Titunik, Studies in Language 1 (New York: Seminar Press, 1973), 58–63.

49 See Halliday, *Explorations in the Functions of Language*, Explorations in Language Study (London: Arnold, 1973), 51–54. Halliday, *Social Semiotic*, 21: "Language is ... the encoding of

within the bounds of her or his context of culture as well as situational constraints.[50] Signification occurs (i.e., meaning is made and expressed linguistically) when a person selects options from among these linguistic networks and encodes them in grammar, syntax, and lexis.[51]

Eggins suggests that four theoretical claims about language emerge from the social semiotic view: (1) language is functional; (2) the primary function of language is to make meanings; (3) the meanings made with language are influenced or constrained by the social, cultural, and situational contexts in which they are exchanged;[52] (4) the process of using language is a semiotic process; that is, language users make meaning by selecting certain options from the language system.[53] Summarizing these points, she describes the SFL perspective on language as a *functional-semantic* perspective that asks two functional-semantic questions:[54]

1. How do people use language (or, semantically, how many different sorts of meanings do people make with language)?
2. How is language structured for use (or, semantically, how is language organized to make meanings)?

These are the basic questions of SFL-based discourse analysis. Martin and Rose suggest that answering these questions requires understanding two further dimensions of discourse:[55]

– relevant levels of language and context (stratification): as lexicogrammar, discourse, and social context

---

a 'behavior potential' into a 'meaning potential'; that is, as a means of expressing what the human organism 'can do', in interaction with other human organisms, by turning it into what he 'can mean.'" Halliday, *Social Semiotic*, 122: "The *text* is the linguistic form of social interaction." See also James D. Dvorak, "To Incline Another's Heart: The Role of Attitude in Reader Positioning," in *The Language and Literature of the New Testament: Essays in Honor of Stanley E. Porter's 60th Birthday*, edited by Lois K. Fuller Dow, Craig A. Evans, and Andrew W. Pitts, BibInt 150 (Leiden: Brill, 2016), 599–624.

50 See Halliday, "Language in a Social Perspective," in *Language and Society*, CWMAKH 10 (London: Continuum, 2007), 46–47.

51 See Halliday, "Architecture," 7–8.

52 See Stanley E. Porter, "Dialect and Register in the Greek of the New Testament," in *Rethinking Contexts, Rereading Texts: Contributions from the Social Sciences to Biblical Interpretation*, JSOTSup 299 (Sheffield: Sheffield Academic, 2000), 197–200; Bruce J. Malina, "Reading Theory Perspective: Reading Luke-Acts," in *The Social World of Luke-Acts: Models for Interpretation* (Peabody: Hendrickson, 1991), 5–8.

53 Suzanne Eggins, *An Introduction to Functional Linguistics*, 2nd ed. (London: Continuum, 2004), 3.

54 Eggins, *Introduction*, 3.

55 Martin and Rose, *Working with Discourse*, 4.

– three general functions of language in social contexts (metafunction): to enact relationships, to represent experience, and to organize discourse into meaningful text

The next two sections provide accounts of these two dimensions.

2.2 *Stratification*

The functional-semantic questions noted above draw the discourse analyst into that area of analysis where grammar and lexis interface with social activity, so that she or he must do the work of grammarians on the one hand and the work of social theorists on the other.[56] Martin and Rose suggest this is due at least in part to the purview of the analyst.

> Grammarians are particularly interested in types of clauses and their elements. But texts are usually bigger than single clauses, so a discourse analyst has more to worry about than a grammarian (expanded horizons). By the same token, cultures manifest themselves through a myriad of texts, and social theorists are more interested in how social contexts are related to one another than in how they are internally organized as texts (global horizons). Discourse analysis employs the tools of grammarians to identify the roles of wordings in passages of text, and employs the tools of social theorists to explain why they make the meanings they do.[57]

The point here is that although social activity, discourse (i.e., text), and grammar are different phenomena they are interrelated. This is the SFL concept of stratification in which each of the phenomena is related by means of *realization*. Realization entails *metaredundancy*: the notion of patterns at one level "redounding" with patterns at the next level and so on, so that patterns of social activity are realized ("manifested/symbolized/encoded/expressed") as patterns of discourse which are in turn realized as patterns of grammar and lexis (Figure 1).[58] Viewed from the other way around, one may say that patterns of grammar express patterns of discourse which express patterns of social activity (Figure 1).[59]

---

56   Martin and Rose, *Working with Discourse*, 4.

57   Martin and Rose, *Working with Discourse*, 4.

58   Image based on James R. Martin and David Rose, *Genre Relations: Mapping Culture*, Equinox Textbooks and Surveys in Linguistics (London: Equinox, 2008), 10. See Lemke, *Textual Politics*, 166–74; James R. Martin, "Cohesion and Texture," in *The Handbook of Discourse Analysis* (Malden, MA: Blackwell, 2003), 45.

59   See Louis Hjelmslev, *Prolegomena to a Theory of Language* (Madison, WI: University of Wisconsin Press, 1963), 114–25; Martin, *English Text*, 493.

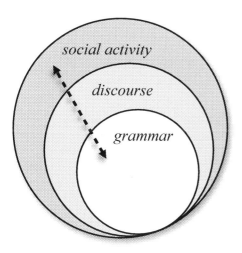

FIGURE 1
Stratification of social activity, discourse, and grammar

A closer look reveals that both context and language exhibit more detailed stratification. With regard to context, one may argue that language users' cultures are realized in each situation in which they interact, and that each situation is realized as unfolding instances of language.[60] Further, language is a stratified semiotic system in which discourse semantics (meanings) are realized as lexicogrammar which are realized as phonology (spoken text) or graphology (written text).[61] Similar to the visualization of social activity, discourse, and grammar in Figure 1, all of these patterns of realization may be illustrated as a series of nested co-tangential circles (Figure 2).

Stratification provides a helpful model for approaching the relationship between context and language. It also offers a means for understanding the purview of SFL-based discourse analysis, demonstrating that the analyst is compelled to think about both linguistic and contextual domains. The ensuing discussion takes a closer look at the point where language and context intersect.

2.3   *Metafunction, Register, and Genre*

The prior discussion of language as social semiotic highlighted SFL's keen interest in what language users can *do* with language by *making, expressing, and exchanging meanings* with it. Equally important, as the notion of stratification emphasizes, is the point that making meanings with language does not occur outside of a context. Language use is constrained by social context because social context constrains social activity, both linguistic and non-linguistic. Two

---

60   See Martin and Rose, *Genre Relations*, 10.
61   See Martin and White, *Language of Evaluation*, 29.

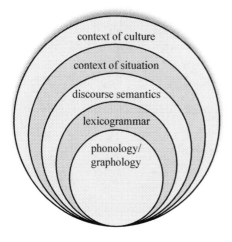

FIGURE 2
Stratification of context and language

questions arise from these points: (1) What kinds of meanings can be made with language (i.e., what are its functions) in social context? and (2) How do these meanings interface with context of situation? SFL answers these questions with the concepts of *metafunction*, *register*, and *genre*.

2.3.1   Metafunction

SFL theory posits that people use language to accomplish three general social functions: (1) to enact social relationships; (2) to represent human experience; and (3) to organize these enactments and reflections as meaningful text.[62] These are known in SFL as the *metafunctions*[63] of language in social activity: the interpersonal metafunction, the ideational metafunction, and the textual metafunction respectively.[64] The linguistic stratum of discourse semantics is organized around these three metafunctions.

The *interpersonal metafunction*, sometimes called the orientational metafunction,[65] is that use of language for organizing and enacting social

---

62   Halliday, "Functions of Language," in *Language, Context, and Text: Aspects of Language in a Social-Semiotic Perspective* (Oxford: Oxford University Press, 1989), 18–23; Martin and Rose, *Working with Discourse*, 7.
63   "Why this rather unwieldy term 'metafunction'? We could have called them simply 'functions'; however, there is a long tradition of talking about the functions of language in contexts where 'function' simply means purpose or way of using language, and has no significance for the analysis of language itself. But the systemic analysis shows that functionality is intrinsic to language: it is as it is because of the functions in which it has evolved in the human species. The term 'metafunction' was adopted to suggest that function was an integral component within the overall theory" (Halliday and Matthiessen, *IFG3*, 30–31).
64   Halliday and Matthiessen, *IFG3*, 29–30; Martin and Rose, *Working with Discourse*, 7.
65   See Lemke, *Textual Politics*, 41.

relationships and interactions among the participants of a given communicative context. These relationships and interactions are enacted with language by means of making statements, asking questions, and giving commands; by evaluating what one thinks or how one feels about people, things, or events; and by indicating one's relative commitment to any given proposal or proposition.[66] Whereas ideational meaning (see below) tends to be privileged in biblical studies (and discourse analysis generally),[67] the current project focuses upon the instrumental impact of making and exchanging interpersonal meaning. Attention is given to how such things as inscribed and implied attitudes (i.e., emotions, judgments, appreciations), various engagement strategies writers employ to enact social relations, and the locutions used for increasing or decreasing emphasis and sharpening or blurring boundaries are put to use by the writers of the New Testament, specifically the Apostle Paul, for the purpose of (re-)orienting or (re-)positioning the readers of the documents to live by a certain set of core values.

The *ideational metafunction*, sometimes referred to as experiential or (re)presentational,[68] describes the linguistic resources that may be drawn upon to portray experience or reality in terms of processes that unfold through time, the participants involved in the processes, and often, though not always, circumstances attendant to the processes.[69] In other words, ideational meaning maps "what's going on, including who's doing what to whom, where, when, why and how and the logical relation of one going-on to another."[70] Although interpersonal meaning is the dominant concern in this work, ideational meaning plays a very important role because the ways in which a language user portrays reality often act as tokens of interpersonal meaning that may invoke or provoke evaluation by the putative reader(s).[71]

The *textual* metafunction organizes interpersonal and ideational meanings into a flow of information that exhibits cohesion and coheres with its context of situation.[72] Although Pike is usually credited as the first linguist to

---

66 See Suzanne Eggins and James R. Martin, "Genres and Registers of Discourse," in *Discourse as Structure and Process*, Discourse Studies 1 (London: Sage, 1997), 238–39.

67 See Lemke, "Interpersonal Meaning in Discourse," 86.

68 See Thompson, *Introducing Functional Grammar*, 2nd ed. (London: Arnold, 2004), 30, 86; Lemke, *Textual Politics*, 41.

69 Halliday and Matthiessen, *IFG3*, 170.

70 Martin and White, *Language of Evaluation*, 7.

71 See White, "Evaluative Semantics," 39–40 and the model presented in the following chapter.

72 See Eggins and Martin, "Genres and Registers," 239; James D. Dvorak, "Thematization, Topic, and Information Flow," *JLIABG* 1 (2008): 17–37; James D. Dvorak and Ryder Dale

acknowledge different kinds of text structuring principles,[73] Halliday and his followers take the further step of associating the various structures of information flow with the kinds of meanings made with language.[74] Martin characterizes ideational meaning as exhibiting *particulate structure* as a way of describing its segmental structure.[75] The particles making up these segments may be organized "orbitally" into configurations consisting of a nucleus (a Process and Medium), margin (Agent), and periphery (circumstances) (experiential meaning);[76] or they may be organized serially into chains of logically related interdependent segments, usually clauses (logical meaning).[77] For example, Table 1 contains a clause from Mark 1:8[78] annotated to illustrate its particulate structure in terms of its experiential meaning.

TABLE 1   Particulate structure (experiential meaning)

Margin (Agent)	Nucleus (Process and Medium)	Periphery (circumstance role)
αὐτός	βαπτίσει ὑμᾶς	ἐν πνεύματι ἁγίῳ
He	*will baptize you*	*in/with the Holy Spirit*

Walton, "Clause as Message: Theme, Topic, and Information Flow in Mark 2:1–12 and Jude," *BAGL* 3 (2014): 31–85.

73   K. L. Pike, *Linguistic Concepts: An Introduction to Tagmemics* (Lincoln, NE: University of Nebraska Press, 1982), 12–13. See Martin and White, *Language of Evaluation*, 17–18.

74   See M. A. K. Halliday, "Modes of Meaning and Modes of Expression: Types of Grammatical Structure and Their Determination by Different Semantic Functions," in *On Grammar*, CWMAKH 1 (London: Continuum, 2002), 202–15; Martin, *English Text*, 10–13; Martin and White, *Language of Evaluation*, 17–19; Lemke, "Interpersonal Meaning in Discourse," 93–94.

75   James R. Martin, "Text and Clause: Fractal Resonance," *Text* 15 (1995): 13.

76   The terms *Process, Medium, Agent*, and *circumstance role* are terms associated with experiential structure in SFL where a quantum of change (i.e., a *figure*) is involved, whether the change is self-engendered or case by an external Actor (see Thompson, *Introducing Functional Grammar*, 137). From an experiential perspective, the Process is the core element in the clause that construes happening, doing, sensing, saying, being, or having; the Medium is the participant through which the Process is actualized; an Agent is a participant that acts as the external cause of a Process. See Christian M. I. M. Matthiessen, Kazuhiro Teruya, and Marvin Lam, *Key Terms in Systemic Functional Linguistics*, Key Terms Series (London: Continuum, 2010), 137 (on Medium) and 164 (on Process).

77   James R. Martin, "Factoring Out Exchange: Types of Structure," in *Dialogue Analysis VII: Working with Dialogue* (Tübingen: Max Niemeyer Verlag, 2000), 19; Martin and White, *Language of Evaluation*, 18–19.

78   Throughout this study, all translations are the author's unless otherwise noted.

THE INTERPERSONAL METAFUNCTION AND DISCOURSE ANALYSIS 17

Next, Martin characterizes textual meaning as exhibiting *periodic structure* which organizes meaning into "waves of information,"[79] establishing "peaks of prominence"[80] at the levels of clause, clause complex, and paragraph.[81] At the clause rank in Greek, this information is organized in terms of position. First position, or *Prime*, is used to highlight who or what the clause is focused upon, while the remainder of the clause, the *Subsequent*, develops or provides additional information about the Prime.[82] Table 2 illustrates Prime and Subsequent analysis for a series of clauses from 1 Cor 3:18.[83]

Information at the level of clause complex is organized around *process chains*.[84] A process chain is a string of one or more verbal groups that have the same Actor.[85] The *Theme* of a clause complex is who or what the complex of

TABLE 2   Prime and Subsequent analysis of clauses from 1 Cor 3:18

Clause	Prime	Subsequent
3_65	μηδείς	ἑαυτὸν ἐξαπατάτω
	no one	*is to deceive him-/herself*
3_66	τις	δοκεῖ σοφὸς εἶναι ἐν ὑμῖν ἐν τῷ αἰῶνι τούτω
	anyone	*who thinks [themselves] to be wise in this age*
3_68	μωρὸς	γενέσθω
	foolish	*one is to become*
3_69	γένηται	σοφός
	to become	*wise*

---

79   Martin and White, *Language of Evaluation*, 19. See Martin, "Text and Clause," 26–31; Martin, "Factoring Out Exchange," 20.

80   Martin, "Text and Clause," 26. On prominence, see Stanley E. Porter, "Prominence: A Theoretical Overview," in *The Linguist as Pedagogue,* NTM 11 (Sheffield: Sheffield Academic, 2009), 45–74; see also Porter and O'Donnell, *Discourse Analysis*, 119–60 (page numbers refer to pre-publication copy).

81   For fuller treatment, see Dvorak, "Thematization," 19–24; Dvorak and Walton, "Clause as Message," 33–34; Porter and O'Donnell, *Discourse Analysis*, 85–118.

82   Dvorak, "Thematization," 20; Dvorak and Walton, "Clause as Message," 42–45; Porter and O'Donnell, *Discourse Analysis*, 91.

83   Note that conjunctions do not factor into Prime and Subsequent analysis. Note, too, that clause numbering follows the OpenText.org model.

84   Dvorak, "Thematization," 21–23; Dvorak and Walton, "Clause as Message," 45–51; Porter and O'Donnell, *Discourse Analysis*, 94–105.

85   Dvorak, "Thematization," 22; Dvorak and Walton, "Clause as Message," 46; Porter and O'Donnell, *Discourse Analysis*, 98–99.

clauses is about, that is, who or what is the primary Actor in a process chain. When a new Actor is explicitly identified in a Primary clause, that Actor is thematic until another new Actor begins a new process chain. The *Rheme* consists of all the additional process information for the current Actor.[86] Together Theme and Rheme demarcate clause complexes into identifiable thematic units. For example, Mark 1:4–6 consists of three thematic units: ἐγένετο Ἰωάννης ὁ βαπτίζων ... κηρύσσων (John the Baptizer came ... preaching) (Theme₁); ἐξεπορεύετο ... πᾶσα ἡ Ἰουδαία χώρα καὶ οἱ Ἱεροσολυμῖται πάντες ... ἐβαπτίζοντο ... ἐξομολογούμενοι (the entire Judean countryside and all the Jerusalemites ... were being baptized ... confessing) (Theme₂); ἦν ὁ Ἰωάννης ἐνδεδυμένος ... ἐσθίων (John was wearing ... eating) (Theme₃). "John the Baptizer" is Theme of the first unit; "the entire Judean region and all the Jerusalemites" is Theme of the second unit; and "John" (contextually, John the Baptizer) is Theme of the third unit. Information about the goings-on or experiences of the Themes in each unit is given in the Rhemes of each unit.

At the level of paragraph,[87] information is organized into what Porter and O'Donnell refer to as *semantic environments*, which they call *Topics*.[88] All of the discursive information that appears between shifts in Topic—that is, information that supports the current Topic—constitutes what they call *Comment*.[89] Shifts in Topic may be signaled in a number of different ways, and, in fact, it is not uncommon for several types of signals to be used at once to create a disruption in cohesion.[90] These disruptions may be created by dropping the use of a certain lexical item (or lexical items that share a semantic domain) and introducing new ones; changes in verbal features such as aspect, mood,

---

86   Dvorak, "Thematization," 22; Dvorak and Walton, "Clause as Message," 46; Porter and O'Donnell, *Discourse Analysis*, 98.

87   The notion of paragraph is fraught with challenges; see Stanley E. Porter, "Pericope Markers and the Paragraph: Textual and Linguistic Considerations," in *The Impact of Unit Delimitation on Exegesis* (Leiden: Brill, 2008), 176–80; Sean A. Adams, "A Linguistic Approach for Detecting Paragraph Divisions in Narrative Greek Discourse: With Application to Mark 14–16" (paper presented at the Annual Meeting of the Society for Textual Studies, New York, NY, 03 March 2007), 21–22; Malcolm Coulthard, *An Introduction to Discourse Analysis*, 2nd ed., Applied Linguistics and Language Study (London: Longman, 1985), 121; Gillian Brown and George Yule, *Discourse Analysis*, CTL (Cambridge: Cambridge University Press, 1983), 95–100; Porter and O'Donnell, *Discourse Analysis*, 106–9. For the notion adopted here, see Porter, "Pericope Markers," 180–82. See also Dvorak, "Thematization," 23–24.

88   Porter and O'Donnell, *Discourse Analysis*, 106. See Dvorak, "Thematization," 24; Dvorak and Walton, "Clause as Message," 51–52.

89   Porter and O'Donnell, *Discourse Analysis*, 106; See Dvorak, "Thematization," 24; Dvorak and Walton, "Clause as Message," 52.

90   See Westfall, *Hebrews*, 36–55; Dvorak, "Thematization," 24; Dvorak and Walton, "Clause as Message," 52–53.

voice, person; person or other kinds of reference; or the use of certain conjunction or other kinds of deictic markers.[91] Discourse boundaries may also be identified or confirmed by Prime and Subsequent and Theme and Rheme analysis. For example, in an analysis of 1 John 2:28–3:17, Dvorak shows how a chain of Themes in Prime position, the most heavily marked thematic option, plays a major role in demarcating a specific semantic environment and formulating the Topic of the section: "People demonstrate by their righteous or sinful deeds whether or not they are children of God, and this is most especially demonstrated by whether or not they love other people by 'laying their lives down' for them in the form of meeting their physical needs."[92]

Finally, Martin characterizes interpersonal meaning as *prosodic structure*.[93] The analogy is taken from phonological studies, where *prosody* describes how tone unfolds in a continuous movement of rising and falling throughout a tone group.[94] Halliday extends the term *prosody* to grammar and semantics to describe the organizational structure of interpersonal meaning:

> The interpersonal component of meaning is the speaker's ongoing intrusion into the speech situation. It is his perspective on the exchange, his assigning and acting out of speech roles. Interpersonal meanings cannot be easily expressed as configurations of discrete elements [as with ideational meanings] ... The essence of the meaning potential of this part of the semantic system is that most of the options are associated with the action of meaning as a whole ... this interpersonal meaning ... is strung throughout the clause as a continuous motif or colouring ... the effect is cumulative ... we shall refer to this type of realisation as "prosodic," since the meaning is distributed like a prosody through a continuous stretch of discourse.[95]

The series of scripture quotations that have been strung together at Rom 3:10–18[96] provides an excellent example of prosodic organization, specifically with regard to attitudinal appraisal:

---

91   See Porter, "Pericope Markers," 180–82; Dvorak, "Thematization," 24.

92   Dvorak, "Thematization," 28–29.

93   Martin, "Text and Clause," 10–12; Martin, "Factoring Out Exchange," 20.

94   Martin, "Text and Clause," 10. See also Matthiessen, Teruya, and Lam, *Key Terms*, 166.

95   Halliday, "Modes of Meaning," 206.

96   Leander Keck argues that Paul is not likely the original compiler of this montage of scriptures. See his "The Function of Romans 3:10–18—Observations and Suggestions," in *God's Christ and His People: Studies in Honor of Nils Alstrup Dahl*, ed. Jacob Jervell and Wayne A. Meeks (Oslo: Universitetsforlaget, 1977), 142–47.

καθὼς γέγραπται ὅτι οὐκ ἔστιν δίκαιος οὐδὲ εἷς, οὐκ ἔστιν ὁ συνίων, οὐκ ἔστιν ὁ ἐκζητῶν τὸν θεόν. πάντες ἐξέκλιναν ἅμα ἠχρεώθησαν· οὐκ ἔστιν ὁ ποιῶν χρηστότητα, [οὐκ ἔστιν] ἕως ἑνός. τάφος ἀνεῳγμένος ὁ λάρυγξ αὐτῶν, ταῖς γλώσσαις αὐτῶν ἐδολιοῦσαν, ἰὸς ἀσπίδων ὑπὸ τὰ χείλη αὐτῶν· ὧν τὸ στόμα ἀρᾶς καὶ πικρίας γέμει, ὀξεῖς οἱ πόδες αὐτῶν ἐκχέαι αἷμα, σύντριμμα καὶ ταλαιπωρία ἐν ταῖς ὁδοῖς αὐτῶν, καὶ ὁδὸν εἰρήνης οὐκ ἔγνωσαν· οὐκ ἔστιν φόβος θεοῦ ἀπέναντι τῶν ὀφθαλμῶν αὐτῶν.

As it is written, "There is *not* a righteous person, *not* even one. There is *not* an understanding person, there is *not* a seeker of God. All *turned away* and at the same time *became corrupt*. There is *not* anyone who does kindness, there is *not* even one. Their throat is *an open grave*; their tongues *deceive*; the *poison of vipers* is under their lips; their mouths contain *a curse and bitterness*; their feet are *swift to shed blood*; *ruin and misery* are in their paths, and they do *not* know the way of peace. There is *not* any fear of God before their eyes."

The negative attitude beginning with οὐκ is carried along through this complex of clauses by additional instances of negation as well as terms and metaphors that carry negative connotations in the culture. The entire clause complex is thereby flooded with negativity, giving a very clear indication of Paul's stance with regard to all humanity who are not in Christ.

2.3.2 Register

Systemic perspectives on context link back to and derive from the work of Malinowski, who argued that to determine the meanings of texts, one must interpret them in light of their context of situation and context of culture.[97] Several decades later, Firth developed Malinowski's ideas into a model for analyzing context.[98] This framework consisted of the following:[99]

– *the participants in the situation*: what Firth referred to as persons and personalities, corresponding more or less to what sociologists would regard as statuses and roles of the participants

---

97   Bronislaw Malinowski, "The Problem of Meaning in Primitive Languages," in *The Meaning of Meaning*, 8th ed. (New York: Harcourt, Brace and World, 1923). See also Halliday, "Context of Situation," 5–8.

98   See John R. Firth, "Personality and Language in Society," in *Papers in Linguistics 1934–1951* (London: Oxford University Press, 1957). See also, R. H. Robins, "The Contributions of John Rupert Firth to Linguistics in the First Fifty Years of *Lingua*," *Lingua* 100 (1997): 205–22.

99   This summary of the framework is from Halliday, "Context of Situation," 8; see also Martin, *English Text*, 497; Eggins, *Introduction*, 89.

THE INTERPERSONAL METAFUNCTION AND DISCOURSE ANALYSIS   21

- *the action of the participants*: what they are doing, including both their verbal action and their non-verbal action
- *other relevant features of the situation*: the surrounding objects and events, in so far as they have some bearing on what is going on
- *the effects of the verbal action*: what changes were brought about by what the participants in the situation had to say

Influenced by the work of both of these men, Halliday, too, models context in relation to language. His model describes context in three distinct dimensions, which he calls field, tenor, and mode:[100]

- *Field* refers to what is happening, to the nature of the social action that is taking place: what it is that the participants are engaged in, in which language figures as some essential component
- *Tenor* refers to who is taking part, to the nature of the participants, their statuses and roles: what kinds of role relationship obtain, including permanent and temporary relationships of one kind or another, both the types of speech roles they are taking on in the dialogue and the whole cluster of socially significant relationships in which they are involved
- *Mode* refers to what part language is playing, what it is that the participants are expecting language to do for them in the situation: the symbolic organization of the text, the status it has, and its function in the context

In order to explain how these three situational variables influence language use and get encoded in instances of text, Halliday developed the semantic notion of *register*. He defines register as a

> configuration of meanings that are typically associated with a particular situational configuration of field, mode, and tenor. But since it is a configuration of meanings, a register must also, of course, include the expressions, the lexico-grammatical and phonological features, that typically accompany or realise these meanings.[101]

In terms of stratification, he conceives register as functioning at the level of semantics and, thus, part of the linguistic system itself, as he noted in an interview with Thibault:

---

100   Halliday, "Context of Situation," 12. See also Halliday, "Categories of the Theory of Grammar," in *On Grammar*, CWMAKH 1 (London: Continuum, 2002), 39, where he includes context as a level of language concerned with the relationship between form and context. See Martin and Rose, *Genre Relations*, 11.

101   M. A. K. Halliday, "Register Variation," in *Language, Context, and Text: Aspects of Language in a Social-Semiotic Perspective*, 2nd ed. (Oxford: Oxford University Press, 1989), 38–39. See also Halliday, *Social Semiotic*, 110–13.

> I would see the notion of register as being at the semantic level, not above it. Shifting in register means re-ordering the probabilities at the semantic level ... whereas the categories of field, mode and tenor belong one level up. These are the features of context of situation; and this is an interface. But the register itself I would see as being linguistic; it is a setting of probabilities in the semantics.[102]

Thus, for Halliday, register is a kind of *interface* between the features of context of situation (field, tenor, and mode) and the linguistic metafunctions (ideational, interpersonal, and textual). Conceptually, Halliday's view derives primarily from the perspective of language in which he projects his intrinsic theory of language function onto context as an extrinsic theory of language use: ideational/experiential meaning projects onto context to give field; interpersonal meaning projects onto context to give tenor; textual meaning projects onto context to give mode.[103]

Recent advances in SFL theory have sought to balance this with a complementary view of context from the perspective of culture, where culture is understood to be a series of social activities or processes.[104] Influenced by Mikhail Bakhtin, these scholars have suggested that context be viewed as a system of social processes.[105] In terms surprisingly similar to Halliday's, Bakhtin writes:

> All the diverse areas of human activity involve the use of language. Quite understandably, the nature and forms of this use are just as diverse as are the areas of human activity.... Language is realized in the form of individual concrete utterances (oral and written) by participants in the various

---

102 Paul J. Thibault, "An Interview with Michael Halliday," in *Language Topics: Essays in Honour of Michael Halliday* (Amsterdam: Benjamins, 1987), 610.

103 See Halliday, *Explorations*, 100–1; Halliday, *Social Semiotic*, 110–11; also Martin, *English Text*, 494.

104 Generally speaking, "culture" refers to "all behavior and related products that human beings, as members of human societies, acquire by means of symbolic interaction; the universal, distinctive characteristic that sets human social life apart from all other forms of life" (Elliott, *What Is Social-Scientific Criticism*, 128; see A. L. Kroeber and Clyde Kluckhohn, *Culture: A Critical Review of Concepts and Definitions* [Cambridge: Peabody Museum, 1952], 181; Bruce J. Malina, *New Testament World: Insights from Cultural Anthropology*, 3rd ed. [Louisville: Westminster John Knox, 2001], 11). The basic model for understanding culture in this project is eclectic, drawing upon structural functionalist, conflict, and symbolic models (see Elliott, "More on Methods and Models," 1–9; James D. Dvorak, "John H. Elliott's Social-Scientific Criticism," *TJ* 28 [2007]: 260–62; and Malina, *New Testament World*, 19–24 for basic descriptions of these models).

105 See Martin, *English Text*, 494–95; Eggins, *Introduction*, 90–112; Martin and Rose, *Genre Relations*, 9–20; Martin and Rose, *Working with Discourse*, 296–309.

areas of human activity. These utterances reflect the specific conditions and goals of each such area not only through their content (thematic) and linguistic style, that is, the selection of the lexical, phraseological, and grammatical resources of the language, but above all through their compositional structure. All three of these aspects—thematic content, style, and compositional structure—are inseparably linked to the *whole* of the utterance and are equally determined by the specific nature of the particular sphere of communication. Each separate utterance is individual, of course, but each sphere in which language is used develops its own *relatively stable types* of these utterances. These we may call *speech genres*.[106]

More will be said about his notion of speech genres below, but what SFL scholars pick up from Bakhtin is the point that all utterances are shaped by the nature of the particular context of situation, including both the conditions of the situation (i.e., what Halliday would call field, tenor, and mode) but also the social goal or "rhetorical purpose" of the one producing the utterance. This suggests field, tenor, mode, and genre (see section below on genre) are not merely part of an interface between context and language, but are semiotic resources in their own right.

TABLE 3   Halliday's and Martin's views of register compared

Halliday	Martin
Context of Situation:	*Register (as connotative semiotic)*:
– field	– field
– tenor	– tenor
– mode	– mode
Redounding with (i.e., construing and construed by)	
language:	*language*:
– semantics (register as meanings at risk)	– discourse semantics
– lexicogrammar	– lexicogrammar
– phonology/graphology	– phonology/graphology

---

106   Mikhail M. Bakhtin, "The Problem of Speech Genres," in *Speech Genres & Other Late Essays* (Austin: University of Texas Press, 1981), 60 (italics his). See also Martin, *English Text*, 494; Lemke, *Textual Politics*, 22–25.

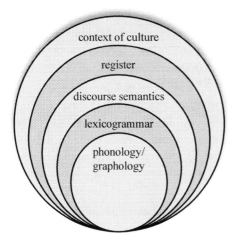

FIGURE 3
Stratification including register

On this basis, Martin modifies Halliday's theory essentially by extracting the contextual variables field, tenor, and mode out of the linguistic system and moving them one level up (see Table 3 above, which compares Halliday's and Martin's views).[107] Martin reserves the term "register" for this stratum and "discourse semantics" for the stratum containing the ideational, interpersonal, and textual linguistic functions (see Figure 3).[108] In Hjelmslevian fashion, Martin stratifies Halliday's "context of situation" so that register becomes the content plane for which discourse semantics is the expression plane. In this model, register remains organized around the contextual variables of field, tenor, and mode,[109] and it still redounds with discourse semantics through the process of realization in a way very similar to what Halliday describes: patterns of field are realized as patterns of ideational meanings; patterns of tenor are realized as patterns of interpersonal meanings; and patterns of mode are realized as patterns of textual meanings.

One important advantage of Martin's revision is that it allows for more delicate characterizations field, tenor, and mode. Field, as a constituent contextual variable in register, has been more technically defined as consisting of "sequences of activities that are oriented to some global institutional purpose, whether this is a local domestic institution such as family or community, or a broader societal institution such as bureaucracy."[110] That is, "it is the contextual

---

107 Martin, *English Text*, 502.
108 Martin, *English Text*, 497–502. See also Eggins and Martin, "Genres and Registers of Discourse," 230–56; Martin and Rose, *Genre Relations*, 11. Compare the figure to Halliday and Matthiessen, *IFG3*, 25.
109 Martin, *English Text*, 502.
110 Martin, *English Text*, 536; Martin and Rose, *Genre Relations*, 13–14.

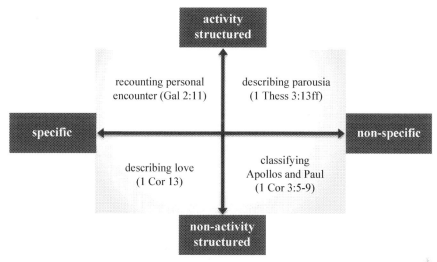

FIGURE 4   Dimensions of variation in field

projection of experiential meaning...."[111] Each activity sequence involves people, things, processes, places, and qualities which may be organized into taxonomies which distinguish one field from another.[112] Discourse patterns of texts vary according to the degree to which they are organized as activity sequences (activity structured to non-activity structured) and whether they are about specific people, things, or about general classes of phenomena (specific to general).[113] This may be illustrated as in Figure 4.

Tenor is concerned with the semiotics of social relations among interlocutors and consists of the dimensions of status (the relative position of interlocutors in a culture's social hierarchy) and solidarity (the degree of institutional involvement between interlocutors).[114] These variables are complementary

---

111 Martin, *English Text*, 536.
112 Martin and Rose, *Genre Relations*, 14. For example, the people, places, and processes involved in status degradation will differ with those involved in other kinds of status transformations (see Bruce J. Malina and Jerome H. Neyrey, "Conflict in Luke–Acts: Labelling and Deviance Theory," in *The Social World of Luke-Acts: Models for Interpretation* [Peabody: Hendrickson, 1991], 97–122; Mark McVann, "Rituals of Status Transformation in Luke-Acts: The Case of Jesus the Prophet," in *The Social World of Luke-Acts: Models for Interpretation* [Peabody: Hendrickson, 1991], 333–60).
113 Martin and Rose, *Genre Relations*, 14.
114 Martin, *English Text*, 523–26; Martin and Rose, *Genre Relations*, 12. See also Cate Poynton, "Address and the Semiotics of Social Relations" (PhD diss., University of Sydney, 1990), 26–49 and 50–101; Andrew Goatly, *Critical Reading and Writing* (New York: Routledge, 2000), 85–86; Roger Brown and Albert Gilman, "The Pronouns of Power and Solidarity,"

and both obtain in all social interactions.[115] Status (or *power*)[116] can be equal or unequal, and if unequal, it is concerned with who dominates and who defers.[117] Solidarity (or *contact*)[118] attends to social distance, which can be close or distant depending upon the amount and kinds of contact people have with one another and the "emotional charge" of these relations.[119] Just as patterns of field may vary in a given text, so also patterns of tenor may vary. For example, at one moment, an author may use an imperative to enact a more unequal and distant relationship,[120] opting at another moment for a modal formulation that realizes a closer, more equal relationship. These dimensions are illustrated in Figure 5.

Mode deals with the channeling of communication, and thus with the texture of information flow as one moves from one mode of communication to another (e.g., speech to writing).[121] The first dimension of mode is the amount of work that language is doing in relation to what is going on.[122] In some contexts language may have a rather small role to play, especially if other modes (e.g., images, music) are more heavily mediating what is going on. In other contexts, language plays a much greater role in mediating activity, sometimes to the point where it nearly completely constitutes field. Thus, this dimension may be characterized as a cline between accompanying field (i.e., language as action) on the one hand and constituting field (i.e., language as reflection)

---

in *Sociolinguistics: The Essential Readings* (Malden, MA: Blackwell, 2003), 158–63. Bruce J. Malina (*Christian Origins and Cultural Anthropology: Practical Models for Biblical Interpretation* [Atlanta: John Knox, 1986], 70) describes solidarity as one of a number of social games in which members of a group establish a sense of belonging; further, solidarity "implies a shared set of values, beliefs, language, feelings, and ideals...."

115 Martin and Rose, *Genre Relations*, 12.
116 Poynton, *Language and Gender*, 76. The term *power* in Martin's scheme is usually reserved for more general relations beyond the scope of a register. Ruqaiya Hasan ("Text in the Systemic-Functional Model," in *Current Trends in Textlinguistics* [Berlin: Walter de Gruyter, 1977], 232–33) appears to use the term "social role" for what is referred to here as status. See also Douglas Biber, "An Analytical Framework for Register Studies," in *Sociolinguistic Perspectives on Register*, Oxford Studies in Sociolinguistics (Oxford: Oxford University Press, 1994), 42.
117 Martin and Rose, *Genre Relations*, 12.
118 Poynton, *Language and Gender*, 77. Hasan ("Text in the Systemic-Functional Model," 231–32) uses the term "social distance" to refer to what is referred to here as solidarity. See also Biber, "Analytical Framework," 42.
119 Martin and Rose, *Genre Relations*, 12. See Hasan, "Text in the Systemic-Functional Model," 231.
120 Note that imperatives (commands) do not realize distance in every context (see Goatly, *Critical Reading*, 88).
121 Martin and Rose, *Genre Relations*, 14.
122 Martin and Rose, *Genre Relations*, 15.

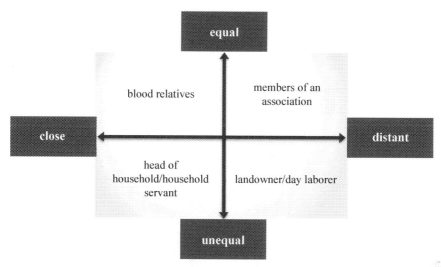

FIGURE 5   Dimensions of variation in tenor

on the other.[123] The second, complementary dimension of mode is characterized as a monologue-through-dialogue cline, the key material factors being whether or not the interlocutors can hear and see one another (aural and visual feedback) and the imminence of a response (immediate or delayed).[124] These variables are illustrated in Figure 6.

Mark 6:1–6a may be used to illustrate how field, tenor, and mode variables are encoded in text.

> Καὶ ἐξῆλθεν ἐκεῖθεν καὶ ἔρχεται εἰς τὴν πατρίδα αὐτοῦ, καὶ ἀκολουθοῦσιν αὐτῷ οἱ μαθηταὶ αὐτοῦ· καὶ γενομένου σαββάτου ἤρξατο διδάσκειν ἐν τῇ συναγωγῇ, καὶ πολλοὶ ἀκούοντες ἐξεπλήσσοντο λέγοντες· πόθεν τούτῳ ταῦτα, καὶ τίς ἡ σοφία ἡ δοθεῖσα τούτῳ, καὶ αἱ δυνάμεις τοιαῦται διὰ τῶν χειρῶν αὐτοῦ γινόμεναι; οὐχ οὗτός ἐστιν ὁ τέκτων, ὁ υἱὸς τῆς Μαρίας καὶ ἀδελφὸς Ἰακώβου καὶ Ἰωσῆτος καὶ Ἰούδα καὶ Σίμωνος; καὶ οὐκ εἰσὶν αἱ ἀδελφαὶ αὐτοῦ ὧδε πρὸς ἡμᾶς; καὶ ἐσκανδαλίζοντο ἐν αὐτῷ. καὶ ἔλεγεν αὐτοῖς ὁ Ἰησοῦς ὅτι οὐκ ἔστιν προφήτης ἄτιμος εἰ μὴ ἐν τῇ πατρίδι αὐτοῦ καὶ ἐν τοῖς συγγενεῦσιν αὐτοῦ καὶ ἐν τῇ οἰκίᾳ αὐτοῦ· καὶ οὐκ ἐδύνατο ἐκεῖ ποιῆσαι οὐδεμίαν δύναμιν, εἰ μὴ ὀλίγοις ἀρρώστοις ἐπιθεὶς τὰς χεῖρας ἐθεράπευσεν· καὶ ἐθαύμαζεν διὰ τὴν ἀπιστίαν αὐτῶν.

---

123   Martin and Rose, *Genre Relations*, 15. See Martin, *English Text*, 516–23.
124   Martin and Rose, *Genre Relations*, 15. See Martin, *English Text*, 510–16.

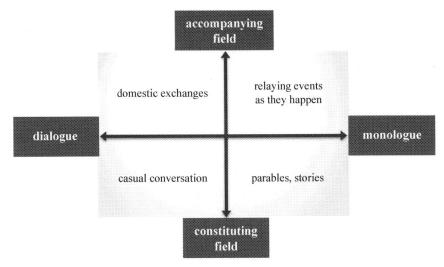

FIGURE 6   Dimensions of variation in mode

And he left there and came to his hometown, and his disciples followed him. And when the Sabbath came, he began to teach in the synagogue, and after hearing him many were shocked and said, "Where are these things from, and what of this wisdom that has been given to him, and what about these miracles being done through his hands? Is this not the builder,[125] the son of Mary and the brother of James, Joses, Judas, and Simon? And are not his sisters here with us?" And they were scandalized[126] by him. And Jesus said to them, "A prophet is not without honor except in his hometown, among his kinfolk, and in his house(hold)." And he was not able to do any miracle there except having laid his hands upon a few sick people he healed them. And he was appalled[127] by their unbelief.

In terms of field, this text is activity sequenced recounting the reaction of the people from Jesus' hometown following his teaching in the synagogue. Despite the fact that the action of the disciples is explicitly mentioned, the activities of this episode center primarily on those of the two main participants, namely

---

[125] See L&N 1:520; Mark Goodacre, "Was Jesus a Carpenter?" *NT Pod*, 1 November 2009, http://podacre.blogspot.com/2009/11/nt-pod-18-was-jesus-carpenter.html.

[126] I.e., "offended" (L&N 1:308–9).

[127] See Stanley E. Porter, "Θαυμάζω in Mark 6:6 and Luke 11:38: A Note on Monosemy," *BAGL* 2 (2013): 75–79.

THE INTERPERSONAL METAFUNCTION AND DISCOURSE ANALYSIS   29

Jesus and the synagogue attendees.[128] The most significant actions in the story are (1) that Jesus taught in the synagogue on the Sabbath and (2) that the hearers were (a) appalled/astounded/confused by the fact that Jesus taught and (b) that they were scandalized by Jesus (more on this below). With regard to the participants it is interesting that there is no full presenting reference for Jesus until v. 4; prior to that point, he is referred to either by verbal person (third person singular), the intensive pronoun (various forms of αὐτός), or a demonstrative pronoun (οὗτος, τούτῳ). The synagogue attendees who respond to Jesus' teaching are presented as πολλοί (many); they are also referred to by means of verbal person (third person plural). In spite of this, the text falls on the more specific end of the specific to non-specific cline because it narrates an incident in which a specific group ("many") and a specific person ("he"/Jesus) interacted with one another.

Interpersonal meaning is foregrounded in this text, which may not be that surprising given that the central issue has to do with how the synagogue attendees and Jesus respond and relate to one another. After the orientation phase of the episode, which follows the typical Markan pattern of establishing a spatial and temporal frame for each episode he records,[129] Jesus is portrayed as taking up the role of prophet/teacher. *What* Jesus taught is of little concern for the narrator; rather, *that* Jesus taught with apparent wisdom and the confirmation of miracles is more to the point of the story: the honor status of the role Jesus took up—not to mention the mastery with which he enacted the role (see Mark 1:21–22)—is not concordant with the honor status into which he was born.[130] Those who heard Jesus teach are, therefore, *astounded* or *confused* if not altogether *shocked* or *appalled* (ἐξεπλήσσοντο). They recall the honor ascribed to him at birth and resort to a segmented genealogy to confirm his place (*Is this not the builder, the son of Mary and brother of James, Joses, Judas, and Simon? And are not his sisters here with us?*).[131] The central issue in this text is one related to tenor: Jesus adopted a role of greater status which

---

128   The disciples are relatively insignificant participants in this text; they are mentioned only once and the only action they perform is to follow Jesus to his hometown.

129   See Stanley E. Porter, "Register in the Greek of the New Testament: Application with Reference to Mark's Gospel," in *Rethinking Contexts, Rereading Texts: Contributions from the Social Sciences to Biblical Interpretation*, JSOTSup 299 (Sheffield: Sheffield Academic, 2000), 217–18. The events of this episode are placed in Jesus' πατρίς (hometown) and, more narrowly, the synagogue; the temporal sphere, indicated by the genitive absolute (γενομένου σαββάτου), is *when the Sabbath came*.

130   See David A. deSilva, *Honor, Patronage, Kinship & Purity* (Downers Grove: InterVarsity, 2000), 162.

131   See deSilva, *Honor, Patronage, Kinship & Purity*, 162.

resulted in the loss of solidarity with the "many" who heard him teach (*they were scandalized/offended by him*).

Finally, with reference to mode, the episode is narrated to the reader through written text and is thus monologue (i.e., the text neither constitutes nor is part of spoken conversation). In fact, two key evaluations in this text—that the hearers were scandalized by Jesus and that Jesus was amazed by the people's unbelief—are the comments of the narrator that are attributed to the characters. Within the story one encounters what might be considered dialogue between the two main participants, but it is unclear whether those who heard Jesus teach actually spoke directly to him or simply spoke among themselves. Based on the fact that Jesus' riposte was directed "to them," one may infer that the speech of the "many" was likely uttered in his hearing. Overall, the language does all the work in this story; no other media or other semiotic system (e.g., images) are employed to convey the story.

2.3.3 Genre

Whereas register explains variation in the use of language on the basis of variation in the variables of context of situation, genre explains variation in register.[132] The term genre likely brings to mind the notion familiarized by literary and film studies where it refers to types of productions such as short stories, poems, novels, action films, dramas, or films noir;[133] however, SFL-based discourse analysis defines the term functionally as a staged, goal-oriented, purposeful social activity in which speakers or writers engage as members of their culture.[134] Less technically, "genres are how things get done, when language is used to accomplish them."[135] Defined this way, it becomes clear that "there are as many genres as there are types of social activity recognized in a given

---

132 See esp. Martin, *English Text*, 546–73. See also Lemke, "Interpersonal Meaning in Discourse," 89–93.

133 Eggins and Martin, "Genres and Registers," 235. See esp. Bakhtin, "Problem of Speech Genres," 60.

134 Martin, "Language, Register, and Genre," 25. See Lemke, "Interpersonal Meaning in Discourse," 90; Eggins, *Introduction*, 55; Eggins and Martin, "Genres and Registers," 236; Martin and Rose, *Genre Relations*, 6; Caroline Coffin, Jim Donohue, and Sarah North, *Exploring English Grammar: From Formal to Functional* (New York: Routledge, 2009), 242–81. Genres are "social because we participate in genres with other people; goal oriented because we use genres to get things done and feel a sense of frustration when we don't resolve our telos; staged because it usually takes us a few steps to reach our goals" (Martin and White, *Language of Evaluation*, 32–33).

135 James R. Martin, "Process and Text: Two Aspects of Semiosis," in *Systemic Perspectives on Discourse*, vol. 1 of *Selected Papers from the 9th Annual International Systemic Workshop*, ed. J. D. Benson and W. S. Greaves (Norwood, NJ: Ablex, 1985), 248.

culture."[136] These would include literary genres (e.g., short stories, autobiographies), popular fictional and non-fictional genres (e.g., instruction manuals, recipes), and educational genres (e.g., lectures, textbooks), as well as an extensive range of "everyday" genres like buying and selling, making appointments, exchanging opinions, arguing, lecturing, preaching.[137]

Prior to Martin's theory of stratified context, genre ("rhetorical purpose") in SFL theory was treated inconsistently, often being subsumed under one register variable or another. For example, Halliday treated genre as part of mode.[138] Hasan identifies genre with the obligatory elements in text structure that are derived from the contextual dimension of field, while the tenor and mode variables control variation in the text structure.[139] However, Martin argues convincingly that each genre involves particular configurations of *all three* register variables rather than being subsumed under any one variable.[140] For example, genres such as reports, recounts, and narratives could be about almost any person or thing (field); their producers could be close, distant, equal, or unequal (tenor); and they could be written or spoken (mode)—in other words, genre and register could vary independently.[141]

Nevertheless, people in a given culture tend to develop patterned ways of achieving the objectives of the social processes they want or need to accomplish in a given situation. These cultural patterns are what constrain all social activities, linguistic and non-linguistic, in a given culture. Eggins, relying on Berger and Luckmann, rightly notes that in order to simplify life humans routinize the way they perform certain social activities in certain situations.[142] Berger and Luckmann call this "habitualization":

> Any action that is repeated frequently becomes cast into a pattern, which can then be reproduced with an economy of effort and which, *ipso facto*, is apprehended by its performer *as* that pattern. Habitualization further implies that the action in question may be performed again in the future in the same manner and with the same economical effort.[143]

---

136 Eggins, *Introduction*, 56.

137 See Eggins, *Introduction*, 56.

138 Halliday, *Social Semiotic*, 145.

139 Ruqaiya Hasan, "The Structure of a Text," in *Language, Context, and Text: Aspects of Language in a Social-Semiotic Perspective*, 2nd ed. (Oxford: Oxford University Press, 1989), 52–69 (esp. 62). See also Hasan, "Text in Systemic-Functional Model," 228–46.

140 See Martin, *English Text*, 505; Eggins, *Introduction*, 56–58.

141 Martin and Rose, *Genre Relations*, 16.

142 Eggins, *Introduction*, 56.

143 Berger and Luckmann, *Social Construction of Reality*, 53. The idea here is similar to Leander E. Keck's definition of *ethos*: "practices and habits, assumptions, problems,

32   CHAPTER 1

This same principle applies to social activities accomplished through language. Bakhtin understood this and pointed out that in certain cultural "spheres" language use becomes habitualized into relatively stable, culturally constrained, predictable types of utterances he calls speech or language genres.[144]

> We learn to cast our speech in generic forms and, when hearing others' speech, we guess its genre from the very first words; we predict a certain length (that is, the approximate length of the speech whole) and a certain compositional structure; we foresee the end; that is, from the very beginning we have a sense of the speech whole, which is only later differentiated during the speech process.[145]

Further, as Eggins points out, Bakhtin claims that language genres are not only "economical" (in Berger and Luckmann's terms), but *essential*: "If speech genres did not exist and we had not mastered them, if we had to originate them during the speech process and construct each utterance at will for the first time, speech communication would be almost impossible."[146] Echoing Bakhtin, Martin and Rose suggest that

> as children, we learn to recognize and distinguish the typical genres of our culture, by attending to consistent patterns of meaning as we interact with others in various situations. Since patterns of meaning are relatively consistent for each genre, we can learn to predict how each situation is likely to unfold, and learn how to interact in it.[147]

Thus, "a genre comes about as particular values for field, tenor, and mode regularly co-occur and eventually become stabilized in the culture as 'typical' situations."[148] Because these patterns of activity interact with register but are constrained by culture, Martin models genre at the level of context of culture

---

values and hopes of a community's style" ("On the Ethos of Early Christians," *JAAR* 42 [1974], 440).

144 Bakhtin, "Problem of Speech Genres," 60. See Eggins, *Introduction*, 57.

145 Bakhtin, "Problem of Speech Genres," 79 quoted in Eggins, *Introduction*, 57.

146 Bakhtin, "Problem of Speech Genres," 79.

147 Martin and Rose, *Working with Discourse*, 8. See also Martin and Rose, *Genre Relations*, 18.

148 Eggins, *Introduction*, 58. See also Bakhtin, "Problem of Speech Genres," 60–102.

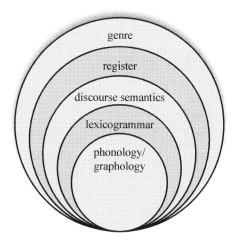

FIGURE 7
Stratification including genre

(Figure 7), "where it could function as a pattern of field, tenor, and mode patterns," though it is not itself organized around field, tenor, and mode.[149]

Martin's model offers at least three significant advantages for discourse analysis.[150] First, "establishing genre as a level of semiosis which is not itself metafunctionally organised means that texts can be classified in ways which cut across metafunctional components in language."[151] For example, a text categorized as narrative genre—which has as its general purpose the working out of a complication typically through a series of four (sometimes recurring) stages (i.e., orientation, complication, evaluation, resolution)[152]—cannot be satisfactorily tied to any one kind of meaning (ideational, interpersonal, textual) because the realization of each of its stages cuts across metafunctions.

Second, "setting up genre as a pattern of register patterns makes it possible to account for the fact that in a given culture, not all combinations of field, mode

---

149 Martin and Rose, *Genre Relations*, 16. Hasan models the relationship between register and generic structure on the "axial" relationship between system and structure (see Ruqaiya Hasan, "The Identity of the Text," in *Language, Context, and Text: Aspects of Language in a Social-Semiotic Perspective*, 2nd ed. [Oxford: Oxford University Press, 1989], 97–116; Ruqaiya Hasan, "The Place of Context in a Systemic Functional Model," in *Continuum Companion to Systemic Functional Linguistics* [London: Continuum, 2009], 166–89). See also Porter, "Register in the Greek of the New Testament," 216, who says, "The question of genre is a question that is best discussed in terms of the context of culture, since it concerns formalized literary patterning particular and peculiar to a specific linguistic community."
150 Martin suggests five advantages (Martin, *English Text*, 505–7).
151 Martin, *English Text*, 505.
152 Martin and Rose, *Genre Relations*, 67–74.

34   CHAPTER 1

and tenor variables occur."[153] For example, in Acts 19 Luke describes Paul's trip
into Ephesus where he found a group of believers who had received John's baptism. When Paul asked if they had received the Holy Spirit, they responded by
saying, "No, we have not even heard that there is a Holy Spirit" (NRSV). This is
an instance where a certain aspect of field (i.e., Holy Spirit) had not yet been
introduced to the believers in Ephesus and, therefore, Paul's inquiry made little if any sense to them. Similarly, in Acts 17:18 Paul is labeled a σπερμολόγος
(babbler or perhaps ignorant show-off)[154] who, in the eyes of the locals, was
"advocating foreign gods" because the content of his proclamation—"the good
news about Jesus and the resurrection," a field variable—was unknown to
them. Thus, they had difficulty understanding Paul's preaching.

    Third, "making genre rather than register variables responsible for gener-
ating schematic structure makes it easier to handle changes in experiential,
interpersonal and textual meaning from one stage to another in a text."[155]
There are many text types where these shifts occur. For example, Stowers
notes that canonical 1 Corinthians "mixes admonition with paraenesis and
advice."[156] Galatians, classified as a letter of rebuke by Stowers,[157] contains other
genres within it such as the recount[158] at Gal 1:11–24 and the exemplum[159] at
Gal 2:11–14. Finally, the gospel accounts have long been known for containing a
variety of generic types that have traditionally been referred to as miracle stories, pronouncement stories, parables, and passion narratives among others.[160]
Eggins refers to this phenomenon as "genre hybridity," the mixing and blending
of genres.[161]

---

153   Martin, *English Text*, 506.
154   L&N 1:328 and 1:432.
155   Martin, *English Text*, 506.
156   Stowers, *Letter Writing in Greco-Roman Antiquity*, LEC 5 (Philadelphia: Westminster,
       1986), 128.
157   Stanley K. Stowers, *Letter Writing*, 134.
158   Martin and Rose (*Genre Relations*, 51) define a recount as a kind of story that has minimal
       disruption and lacks a distinct evaluation stage; these function in a wide variety of social
       contexts to share experiences and attitudes of all kinds.
159   Martin and Rose define an exemplum as a kind of story that provides a judgment of peo-
       ple's character or behavior (*Genre Relations*, 51).
160   See David E. Aune, *The New Testament in Its Literary Environment*, LEC 8 (Philadelphia:
       Westminster, 1987), 50–54; Martin Dibelius, *From Tradition to Gospel* 2nd ed. (London:
       Ivor Nicholson and Watson, 1934); Rudolf Bultmann, *History of the Synoptic Tradition*
       (Oxford: Basil Blackwell, 1968).
161   Eggins, *Introduction*, 81.

2.4 *Ideology*

It was noted above in the introduction that this study is acutely concerned with analyzing the linguistic means involved in ideological positioning or repositioning. Because, as Lemke points out, the term *ideology* is a "protean notion" that can mean what one wishes it to mean, clear definition of its use in the current project is crucial.[162] The general definition of ideology adopted here is provided by Elliott:

> An integrated system of beliefs, perspectives, assumptions, and values, not necessarily true or false, that reflect the perceived needs and interests of a group or class at a particular time in history; that contain the chief criteria for interpreting social reality; and that serve to define, explain, and legitimate collective wants and needs, interests, values, norms, and organizational goals in a continuous interaction with the material forces of history. When ideological formulations refer to God or the gods, divine representatives or agents, sacred tradition, or any instances of power and authority as ultimate or highest sources, warrants norms, and sanctions of behavior, ideology merges with theology and theological constructs are used for ideological ends.[163]

Martin's treatment of ideology is consonant with this definition. He views ideology as sets of "relations that permeate every level of semiosis"[164] and therefore occupies the highest level of contextual semiosis in a culture. He reasons as follows:

> Introducing genre as a level of contextual semiosis with responsibility for integrating the diversity projected from the functional organisation of language onto register, makes it important to introduce diversity of a different kind, at a deeper level in order to keep the model from becoming

---

162 Lemke, *Textual Politics*, 2.

163 Elliott, *What Is Social-Scientific Criticism*, 130 (see also 51–53 for more on the relationship between text and ideology). Fairclough (*Discourse and Social Change*, 87) defines ideology as the "significations/constructions of reality (the physical world, social relations, social identities), which are built into various dimensions of the forms/meanings of discursive practices, and which contribute to the production, reproduction or transformation of relations of domination." See also Lemke (*Textual Politics*, 2): "The central insight which the concept of ideology tries to sum up is simply this: there are some very common meanings we have learned to make, and take for granted as common sense, but which support the power of one social group to dominate another." See Dale B. Martin, *The Corinthian Body* (New Haven: Yale University Press, 1995), xiv–xv.

164 See Martin and Rose, *Genre Relations*, 19.

36   CHAPTER 1

too monolithic and rigidly deterministic. This is necessary because a culture's meaning potential is distributed unevenly across social groups and so constantly changing. Tension among the discourses of these groups means that to achieve metastability, the system must evolve. It is to account for this dialectic of difference, systemic inertia and evolution that a fourth communicative plane, ideology, is proposed.[165]

Two perspectives on ideology emerge from this reasoning. First is the *synoptic view* in which ideology is seen as "the system of coding orientations constituting a culture."[166] This is the perspective Bernstein took when he suggested that coding orientations varied according to contextually specific semantic orientations or *codes* associated with differences in generation, gender, ethnicity, and class.[167] According to Martin, the system of coding orientation positions language users in such a way that genres, registers, and the linguistic system are made "selectively available."[168] This is the case because a language user's social location causes them to construe context in different ways.[169] Social status (or power) may thus be interpreted in terms of the range of linguistic options that are available, the extent to which these options may be used for control, submission, or negotiation, and the degree to which these options may be used to change the context that makes them available.[170] Because discursive social power is unevenly distributed along these continua, there will always be "semiotic tension" in the community.[171]

Given this natural, constant "semiotic tension" within the community, texts are always "multi-voiced" or, in Bakhtin's terms, *heteroglossic* and *dialogic*.[172] Heteroglossia refers to the polyphony of social "voices" forming the backdrop

---

165   Martin, *English Text*, 507 and 573–55.
166   Martin, *English Text*, 507.
167   See Basil Bernstein, *Class, Codes, and Control*, 2 vols. (London: Routledge, 1971–1973).
168   Martin, *English Text*, 507.
169   See Martin, *English Text*, 577; Lemke, "Interpersonal Meaning in Discourse," 83. Halliday (Thibault, "Interview with Michael Halliday," 620) says that code "bifurcates" register so that language users from different classes, generations, ethnicities, genders—and I would add cultures—construe context in different ways. This accounts for, at least in part, the possibility of multiple readings (i.e., interpretations) of a single text.
170   Martin, *English Text*, 507. See Malina, *Christian Origins*, 82: "Power is the capacity to produce conformity" (see also pp. 80–82 on influence, the capacity to persuade).
171   Martin, *English Text*, 581.
172   Martin, *English Text*, 581; Bakhtin, "Discourse in the Novel," in *The Dialogic Imagination: Four Essays* (Austin: University of Texas Press, 1981), 291–2. See also Lemke, *Textual Politics*, 22–25; Susanne Gillmayr-Bucher, "Intertextuality: Between Literary Theory and Text Analysis," in *The Intertextuality of the Epistles: Explorations of Theory and Practice*, NTM 16 (Sheffield: Sheffield Phoenix, 2006), 13–14.

THE INTERPERSONAL METAFUNCTION AND DISCOURSE ANALYSIS   37

against which and in the context of which new texts are produced.[173] Texts are "dialogic" in that when they are produced they always reveal the influence of, refer to, or in some way account for these heteroglossic voices.[174] As Bakhtin put it, "Every utterance must be regarded primarily as a *response* to preceding utterances of the given sphere.... Each utterance refutes, affirms, supplements, and relies on the others, presupposes them to be known, and somehow takes them into account."[175]

This leads to the second perspective on ideology, what Martin calls the *dynamic view*, which attends to the ways in which semiotic resources such as genre, register, and the linguistic system are marshaled to effect or to resist social change.[176] Much if not most of the time this semiotic tension or dissonance is rarely heard because "certain habitual configurations of meaning dominate others and the disharmony goes unnoticed."[177] Occasionally, however, some issue arises which brings the uneven distribution of discursive power into focus with the result that the tension "explodes" and members of a community interact (sometimes violently)—some with a view to maintaining the current distribution of power, others with a view to reallocation.[178]

What is significant about all of this for the present work is the point that all texts are *stanced* in some way; that is, "their content and intended effect have been shaped by the socially rooted self-interests of their producers."[179] This perspective stands in contrast to the traditional truth-functional approaches which are concerned with the language user's commitment to the truth-value,

---

173   Bakhtin, "Discourse in the Novel," 281.

174   Martin and White, *Language of Evaluation*, 92. See esp. Bakhtin, "Problem of Speech Genres," 87–96. Also, White, "Dialogue and Inter-Subjectivity," 67–80; Michael Holquist, *Dialogism: Bakhtin and His World*, 2nd ed. (New York: Routledge, 2002), 40–66; Lemke, "Interpersonal Meaning in Discourse," 84–85; Gillmayr-Bucher, "Intertextuality," 13.

175   Bakhtin, "Problem of Speech Genres," 91. See also Vološinov, *Marxism and the Philosophy of Language*, 94–95.

176   Martin, *English Text*, 507–8. See also Fairclough, *Discourse and Social Change*, 86–91.

177   Martin, *English Text*, 582.

178   Martin, *English Text*, 582.

179   Elliott, *What Is Social-Scientific Criticism*, 51. See also Michael Stubbs, "'A Matter of Prolonged Field Work': Notes Towards a Modal Grammar of English," *Applied Linguistics* 7 (1987): 1. Bakhtin, "Problem of Speech Genres," 84: "There can be no such thing as an absolutely neutral utterance." One must be careful here, however, not to overemphasize the notion of *self*-interest. The ancient circum-Mediterranean world was not individualistic but collectivistic; thus, individual values were generally shaped by group values. See Bruce J. Malina, "Collectivism in Mediterranean Culture," in *Understanding the Social World of the New Testament*, ed. Dietmar Neufeld and Richard E. DeMaris (London: Routledge, 2010), 17–28.

38   CHAPTER 1

factuality, and/or epistemic reliability of their utterances.[180] The meanings at issue from the traditional perspective turn on whether language users "present themselves as able or unable, or as willing or unwilling to commit to the truth of what they assert" and, further, the implication that "the overriding purpose of communication is for the speaker to offer 'truth' or certain knowledge and that these modal, evidential or hedging values are introduced only in communicatively non-optimal circumstances."[181] The perspective adopted in this study, however, understands the linguistic resources at issue as those which may be called upon to negotiate intersubjective stance and ultimately interpersonal meaning, rather than viewing them in terms of truth value and epistemology.[182] These negotiations occur between the text producer(s) and any other heteroglossic "voice(s)."

As part of these negotiations, the author's textual voice attempts either to expand or to contract the semiotic "space" between their own ideologically-based value position(s) and those of others that are referenced in text.[183] By doing so, the writer takes up a certain stance or *subject position* (i.e., creates a textual axiology) and *naturalizes* a certain *reading position*.[184] For example, at

---

180   For example, Lyons contrasts the "subjectivity" of modal meaning with the "objectivity" of bare assertions, characterizing the former as "non-factive" and the latter as "factive." He adds that factive utterances are "straightforward statements of fact [which] may be described as epistemically non-modal" because "the speaker is committing himself to the truth of what he asserts" (Lyons, *Semantics*, 2:797). See also Lakoff, "Hedges," 458–508; White, "Beyond Modality and Hedging," 260–62; White, "Dialogue and Inter-Subjectivity," 67–79.

181   White, "Beyond Modality and Hedging," 69.

182   White, "Beyond Modality and Hedging," 71.

183   The question regarding the status of bare or categorical assertions within a framework emphasizing heteroglossia, dialogism, and intersubjective positioning may be raised here. Bare or categorical assertions have often been characterized as, in Lyons's terms, "objective" or "factual"—in essence intersubjectively neutral. If this is not the case, how does one make sense of categorical assertions such as πᾶς ὁ μισῶν τὸν ἀδελφὸν αὐτοῦ ἀνθρωποκτόνος ἐστίν (Anyone who hates his brother or sister is a murderer; 1 John 3:15) from a dialogic perspective? The answer to this question becomes clear when the heteroglossic backdrop of text is considered. Even in cases where a writer produces monoglossic ("single-voiced") and apparently "undialogized" assertions such as these, they still account for the heteroglossic polyphony of alternative viewpoints that constitute in part the context of the text (see Martin and White, *Language of Evaluation*, 99). Bare assertions allow the writer to contract completely the dialogue in the text so that what is asserted is presented as the *only* viable voice, opinion, or stance.

184   See Goatly, *Critical Reading and Writing*, 147–60; James R. Martin, "Reading Positions/ Positioning Readers," *Prospect* 10 (1995): 27–37. This is similar to Althusser's notion that ideology "interpellates concrete individuals as subjects"; in a manner of speaking, it "hails"

1 Thess 4:1–8 Paul encourages the readers to excel at living to please God. As the identifying clause τοῦτο γάρ ἐστιν θέλημα τοῦ θεοῦ (For this is God's will/desire) indicates,[185] God's desire—and, thus, what is pleasing to God—is for the Thessalonians to live lives that exemplify holiness.[186] What is meant by "holiness" is not left up to the reader to infer; rather, Paul describes what he means through a series of epexegetic infinitives that rely heavily upon appraisal to create and naturalize a certain axiological stance.[187] First, ἀπέχεσθαι ὑμᾶς ἀπὸ τῆς πορνείας (your separation from sexual immorality) implicitly appraises πορνεία negatively as something that holy, God-pleasing people must avoid. Second, εἰδέναι ἕκαστον ὑμῶν τὸ ἑαυτοῦ σκεῦος κτᾶσθαι ἐν ἁγιασμῷ καὶ τιμῇ (knowing how to control one's one sex organ[188] with holiness and honor) implicitly appraises sexual promiscuity negatively by portraying sex drive as something that holy, God-pleasing people keep under control. Finally, τὸ μὴ ὑπερβαίνειν καὶ πλεονεκτεῖν ἐν τῷ πράγματι τὸν ἀδελφὸν αὐτοῦ (not doing wrong and taking advantage of his brother or sister with regard to sexual activity) further appraises sexual promiscuity negatively as something that could result in jeopardizing the fictive-familial relationship believers share in Christ.[189] Additionally, by commenting that ἔκδικος κύριος περὶ πάντων τούτων (the Lord is an avenger in all these things [NRSV]), that οὐ ... ἐκάλεσεν ἡμᾶς ὁ θεὸς ἐπὶ ἀκαθαρσίᾳ ἀλλ' ἐν

---

them and prompts them to accept or reject certain value positions (Louis Althusser, "Ideology and Ideological State Apparatuses (Notes Toward an Investigation)," in *Essays on Ideology* [New York: Verso, 1984], 44–51).

185   An identifying clause is a type of relational clause; its function is to identify one entity in terms of another. See Halliday and Matthiessen, *IFG3*, 227–39; Thompson, *Introducing Functional Grammar*, 96–100.

186   Taking up Mary Douglas's model of purity presented in her *Purity and Danger: An Analysis of the Concept of Pollution and Taboo*, Routledge Classics (New York: Routledge, 2002), social-scientific critics offer a simple yet profound understanding of holiness in Paul: holiness (purity, cleanness, etc.) has to do with order; when people, things, etc. occupy the physical and/or social space for which they were created, they exhibit holiness. See Malina, *New Testament World*, 161–96; Neyrey, *Paul*, 22–31.

187   On the epexegetic function of infinitives, see Stanley E. Porter, *Idioms of the Greek New Testament*, 2nd ed. BLG 2 (London: Sheffield Academic, 1999), 198–99; Richard A. Young, *Intermediate New Testament Greek* (Nashville: Broadman and Holman, 1994), 175.

188   It is likely that σκεῦος is a euphemism for "genitals" here. See Charles A. Wanamaker, *Epistles to the Thessalonians*, NIGTC (Grand Rapids: Eerdmans, 1990), 152–3; Jay E. Smith, "1 Thessalonians 4:4: Breaking the Impasse," *BBR* 11 (2001): 65–105; Robert W. Yarbrough, "Sexual Gratification in 1 These 4.1–8," *TJ* 20 (1999): 215–32; Bruce J. Malina and John J. Pilch, *Social-Science Commentary on the Letters of Paul* (Minneapolis: Fortress, 2006), 47. For an alternative interpretation, see Abraham J. Malherbe, *The Letters to the Thessalonians*, AB 32B (New York: Doubleday, 2000), 226–28, who interprets σκεῦος as "wife."

189   See Yarbrough, "Sexual Gratification," 225–27.

ἁγιασμῷ (God did not call us to impurity but in holiness [NRSV]), and that ὁ ἀθετῶν οὐκ ἄνθρωπον ἀθετεῖ ἀλλὰ τὸν θεόν (whoever rejects this teaching does not reject human [authority] but rejects God), Paul imbues his interpretation of "God-pleasing living" with divine approval. All of this factors significantly in creating a subject position and naturalizing a reading that accepts his view as "good," "right," and/or "proper." Of course, the readers of the letter could reject the axiological stance Paul has created (resistant reading) or tactically suspend a decision about it or ignore it altogether (tactical reading), but it is impossible to know for certain without more data how the intended readers received the text. Thus, sights are set on the linguistic means by which Paul creates stance and the meaning(s) he intends to communicate.

2.5 Text

A number of times in the preceding discussion, reference was made to *text*. Before closing this chapter, a clear definition of this term that takes into account the previous discussion must be provided. In line with SFL tradition, "text" in this study is understood *semantically* as a unit of social meaning realized as stretches of spoken or written language.[190] Put another way, text is the simultaneous expression of ideational, interpersonal, and textual meaning as written or spoken grammar and lexis. Following Fairclough, it is assumed here that text not only reflects or represents social structure and activity, but it is also "a mode of action, one form in which people may act upon the world and especially upon each other."[191] Returning to a point made at the outset of this chapter, text in sociological terms is the primary instrument of socialization and resocialization. A key property of text that distinguishes it from non-text is *texture*. Texture is created when language users connect parts of text together (*cohesion*) and connect texts to their situational and cultural contexts (*coherence*).[192] When instances of language do not exhibit texture, readers and/or hearers cannot readily grasp meaning.

---

190 See Halliday and Hasan, *Cohesion in English*, English Language Series 9 (London: Longman, 1976), 2; Martin, *English Text*, 381–82; Eggins, *Introduction*, 24.

191 Fairclough, *Discourse and Social Change*, 63; Norman Fairclough, *Analysing Discourse: Textual Analysis for Social Research* (London: Routledge, 2003), 26–28. See Halliday, *Social Semiotic*, 122: "The *text* is the linguistic form of social interaction." See also Goatly, *Critical Reading and Writing*, 147 on "subject positions."

192 See Halliday and Hasan, *Cohesion*, 1–2; Eggins, *Introduction*, 23–24. Fairclough (*Analysing Discourse*, 27) refers to this process as *texturing*.

2.5.1 Cohesion

Cohesion is a *textual* phenomenon; it refers to how a text "hangs together" by means of various cohesive resources.[193] Halliday and Hasan explain it as follows:

> Cohesion occurs where the INTERPRETATION of some element in the discourse is dependent on that of another. The one PRESUPPOSES the other, in the sense that it cannot be effectively decoded except by recourse to it. When this happens, a relation of cohesion is set up, and the two elements, the presupposing and the presupposed, are thereby at least potentially integrated into a text.[194]

There are a number of linguistic resources that make texts hang together. One of these resources is *reference*. Reference refers to the way a writer or speaker introduces and subsequently tracks participants (i.e., people, places, and things) in a text.[195] For example, reference chains such as person deixis indicate who are the major human participants in a text, as well as their relative importance for the text's meaning—they help answer the question, *"Who is this text about?"*[196]

Another cohesive resource is *lexical cohesion*. This resource refers to how a writer uses lexical items (e.g., nouns, verbs, adjectives, adverbs) and event sequences (i.e., chains of clauses and sentences) to relate the text to a certain subject or topic (i.e., field).[197] Lexical cohesion often occurs through *taxonomic relations* such as *classification* (co-hyponymy, class/sub-class, contrast, similarity [synonymy, repetition]) or *composition* (meronymy, co-meronymy).[198] Texts also exhibit lexical relations through *expectancy relations* (relationships between nominal elements and verbal elements [e.g., γεωργός/καθαίρει (vinedresser/he prunes; John 15:1–2)]).[199] These kinds of cohesion help answer the question, *"What is this text about?"*[200]

---

193   Thompson, *Introducing Functional Grammar*, 179.

194   Halliday and Hasan, *Cohesion*, 4 (words in all caps indicate systemic selection).

195   See Jeffrey T. Reed, "The Cohesiveness of Discourse: Towards a Model of Linguistic Criteria for Analyzing New Testament Discourse," in *Discourse Analysis and the New Testament*, JSNTSup 170 (Sheffield: Sheffield Academic, 1999), 36–38; Eggins, *Introduction*, 33–42; Martin and Rose, *Working with Discourse*, 155–85.

196   Eggins, *Introduction*, 38.

197   Eggins, *Introduction*, 42.

198   See Eggins, *Introduction*, 42–43.

199   Eggins, *Introduction*, 43–44.

200   See Reed, "Cohesiveness of Discourse," 42–43; Westfall, *Hebrews*, 30–31, 39–55. Martin and Rose (*Working with Discourse*, 73–114) treat lexical cohesion under the rubric of Ideation.

A third cohesive resource is *conjunction*. This resource refers to how writers create and express logical relations between parts of text.[201] Conjunction is an important resource that helps "to create that semantic unity that characterizes unproblematic text,"[202] by helping the reader see how the propositions and proposals of a text are linked together.[203] These kinds of cohesion help answer the question, "*How do the meanings of this text fit together to create a 'composite' textual meaning?*"

2.5.2 Coherence

Coherence has to do with the way text is connected to context. Whereas cohesion is a *textual* phenomenon, coherence is, as Thompson notes, a *mental* phenomenon that takes place in the minds of the writer and readers as they formulate connections between the text itself and the situational and cultural contexts in which it was produced.[204] Because there are two levels of context (register [situation] and genre [culture]), coherence may be discussed in terms of *registerial coherence* and *generic coherence*.[205]

A text exhibits registerial coherence when one can identify the situation in which all the clauses of the text could occur.[206] More technically, a text has registerial coherence when one can correlate the ideational meanings of a text with a particular field, the interpersonal meanings of a text with a particular tenor, and the textual meanings of a text with a particular mode. This is often a challenging exercise for interpreters of biblical texts. Ascertaining what these texts originally meant or could have been taken to mean in their original contexts requires knowledge of both the situation that prompted them as well as the social and cultural milieu in which they were produced.[207] Historical and sociocultural distance, incomplete or lacking evidence, and the unilateral perspective of extant texts all present formidable challenges.[208] These gaps in the evidence, for whatever reason they may exist, force interpreters to reconstruct

---

201 Eggins, *Introduction*, 47. Martin and Rose (*Working with Discourse*, 115–54) treat conjunction on its own.

202 Eggins, *Introduction*, 47.

203 Because of this, as will be shown in the next chapter under engagement, conjunction figures prominently in writers' engagement strategies.

204 Thompson, *Introducing Functional Grammar*, 179.

205 These apposite terms are from Eggins, *Introduction*, 29.

206 Eggins, *Introduction*, 29.

207 Elliott, *What Is Social-Scientific Criticism*, 50.

208 These are fundamental issues in hermeneutical/exegetical discussions. See, e.g., Stanley E. Porter and Kent D. Clarke, "What is Exegesis," in *Handbook to the Exegesis of the New Testament* (Leiden: Brill, 2002), 11–13; John H. Hayes and Carl R. Holladay, *Biblical Exegesis*, 3rd ed. (Louisville: Westminster John Knox, 2007), 5–12; William W. Klein,

abductively[209] a context of situation that could have plausibly precipitated the textual evidence. This reconstructed context is then used to reinterpret the text itself. It is out of the interplay between the textual data and further analysis of the interpreter that one hopes to gain greater insight into both the context of situation and the content of the letter.[210] Nevertheless, the results of this necessarily circular process can only be taken as provisional and subject to change. "What is to be avoided is simply reading pre-conceived ideas into the data, and finding 'confirmation' of one's hypotheses in them."[211]

A text exhibits generic coherence when one can "identify a unified purpose motivating the language (for example, it tells a story or accomplishes a transaction), usually expressed through a predictable generic or schematic structure."[212] For example, Stowers classifies Philemon as a letter of mediation or recommendation.[213] This social action may be identified as a genre because of the "typical" components or "habitualized" uses of language used to accomplish the task of recommending someone or mediating some sort of relationship on their behalf. Stowers, drawing upon Chan-Hie Kim, suggests that recommendations included (but were not limited to) the following components: identifying the one who was being recommended; providing some background or reason as to why the person was being recommended and should be received by the addressee; and the recommendation proper, which in the ancient world was often cast in terms of the recommender offering "gratitude" in exchange for granting "favor" upon the one being recommended.[214] Even among fairly straightforward genres such as recommendations, some amount of genre hybridity

---

Craig L. Blomberg, and Robert L. Hubbard, Jr., *Introduction to Biblical Interpretation* (Dallas: Word, 1993), 12–16.

209 I.e., "a process of logic of the discovery procedure of working from evidence to hypothesis, involving a back-and-forth movement of suggestion checking" (Linda Woodson, *Handbook of Modern Rhetorical Terms* [Urbana, IL: National Council of Teachers of English, 1979], 1 [quoted in Elliott, *What Is Social-Scientific Criticism*, 48]) from the available textual evidence to the most plausible description of the context that produced it. This is also called "retroduction." See Charles S. Peirce, "Letters to Samuel P. Langley, and 'Hume on Miracles and Laws of Nature,'" in *Values in a Universe of Chance* (Garden City, NY: Doubleday, 1958), 320; Elliott, *What Is Social-Scientific Criticism*, 48–49; Dvorak, "Social-Scientific Criticism," 262–63.

210 Stanley E. Porter, "Exegesis of the Pauline Letters, Including the Deutero-Pauline Letters" in *A Handbook to the Exegesis of the New Testament* (Leiden Brill, 2002), 515. See John M. G. Barclay, "Mirror-Reading a Polemical Letter: Galatians as a Test Case," *JSNT* 31 (1987): 77.

211 Porter, "Exegesis of the Pauline Letters," 515.

212 Eggins, *Introduction*, 29.

213 Stowers, *Letter Writing*, 155.

214 Stowers, *Letter Writing*, 153–54.

exists. For example, Demetrius notes that commendations may include "mixing in praise" for the one being commended; praise is, itself, a genre, but it is not the primary, overarching purpose in a letter of recommendation.[215]

3 Conclusion

The goal of this chapter has been to lay the theoretical foundation upon which a model of discourse analysis may be constructed. The key element of this foundation is the systemic-functional notion of language as social semiotic, that people put language to use for purposes of social interaction. Meanings made with language cannot be viewed as only reflecting or representing social structure and activity, though this is certainly one function of language; rather, meanings made with language are intended to be exchanged with others as a means of acting upon them to achieve some social goal. This point of view is well summarized by the following words of Malina, which serve as a fitting conclusion to this chapter:

> Language here takes on the nuance of a verb, "to language." To language is to mean; to language is what a speaker/writer and/or hearer/reader can do. To language is a social activity, a form of social interaction much like buying and selling, marrying and bearing children, or ruling and being ruled. To language is to interact socially according to cultural rules and meanings.[216]

215   Stowers, *Letter Writing*, 154 (see also pp. 77–90).
216   Malina, *Christian Origins*, 9.

CHAPTER 2

"What's Your Take?" A Model for the Analysis of Intersubjective Stance in Written Discourse

1   Introduction

As noted in the previous chapter, in order to determine the values with which Paul wanted his readers to align themselves, as well as those values he wanted them to eschew, it is necessary to adopt a methodology that is capable of analyzing and describing the sociolinguistic features that are realized in text as the semantics of persuasion or convincing get encoded. This kind of analysis has typically fallen under the purview of rhetorical criticism.[1] The main problem with traditional or classical rhetorical criticism, in both the Betz and Kennedy schools,[2] is that it paints with too coarse a brush. The major concerns of traditional rhetorical methodology is to determine the species of a text or its parts (i.e., deliberative, epideictic, judicial), to analyze the steps in the process of composing the text (i.e., invention, arrangement, style, memory, and delivery), and to identify the use of rhetorical devices (e.g., rhetorical questions) in text.[3] Although there are a number of valuable theoretical principles undergirding this approach (e.g., its view of texts as forms of *activity* that have an *effect* on their readers),[4] it falls short primarily because it is based on the ancient rhetorical handbooks and not on linguistic theory. Even the "new rhetoric" of

---

1 See Wilhelm Wuellner, "Where is Rhetorical Criticism Taking Us?" *CBQ* 49 (1987): 448–63, esp. 450–54; and his "Rhetorical Criticism in Biblical Studies," *Jian Dao* 4 (1995): 73–96. See also Dennis L. Stamps, "Rhetorical Criticism of the New Testament," in *Approaches to New Testament Study*, ed. Stanley E. Porter and David Tombs, JSNTSup 120 (Sheffield: Sheffield Academic Press, 1995), 129–69.
2 See Hans Dieter Betz, "The Problem of Rhetoric and Theology According to the Apostle Paul," in *L'apôtre Paul: Personalité, Style et Conception du Ministère*, ed. A. Vanhoye, BETL 17 (Leuven: Leuven University Press, 1986), 16–48; George Kennedy, *New Testament Interpretation through Rhetorical Criticism*, Studies in Religion (Chapel Hill: University of North Carolina Press, 1984).
3 See Patricia K. Tull, "Rhetorical Criticism and Intertextuality," in *To Each Its Own Meaning: An Introduction to Biblical Criticisms and Their Application*, rev. ed. (Louisville: Westminster John Knox, 1999), 156–57.
4 Wuellner, "Where is Rhetorical Criticism Taking Us?" 453.

© JAMES D. DVORAK, 2021 | DOI:10.1163/9789004453814_003

Perelman and Olbrechts-Tyteca,[5] which moves away from ancient rhetorical theory to offer a theory of argumentation, fails to address aptly how people use language to realize the semantics of persuasion and/or convincing.[6] Although both classical and new rhetorical models may help interpreters determine *that* a text is intended to be persuasive or convincing, because these models are not grounded in linguistic theory they lack the heuristic capacity to explain *why* and/or *how* a text may be persuasive or convincing. For this reason, models based on classical and new theories of rhetoric are set aside in favor of a theory that is firmly grounded in the SFL paradigm known as Appraisal Theory.[7]

Appraisal Theory is concerned with the linguistic resources that people use to take up positive or negative stances as they negotiate points of view and value positions with others sharing their social system. These linguistic resources are presented in this chapter as a semiotic system (Figure 8)[8]— more precisely, a system consisting of a number of subsystems—from which language users make selections in order to exchange with others the meanings they wish to make. Each axis of this system corresponds to a particular subsystem (i.e., ATTITUDE, ENGAGEMENT, GRADUATION);[9] these subsystems are discussed in further detail in the following sections. The APPRAISAL system and its subsystems constitute the model to be used to analyze the intersubjective stance of the apostle Paul in 1 Cor 1–4 in the chapters to follow.

---

5   Chaim Perelman and Lucie Olbrechts-Tyteca, *The New Rhetoric: A Treatise on Argumentation*, trans. and ed. John Wilkinson and Purcell Weaver (Notre Dame: University of Notre Dame Press, 1969).

6   See the literature review in the appendix to this study where a number of works utilizing models from classical rhetoric and new rhetoric are critiqued. See also James D. Dvorak, "'Prodding with Prosody': Persuasion and Social Influence through the Lens of Appraisal Theory," *BAGL* 4 (2015): 85–120.

7   "Appraisal Theory" is a misnomer because, technically, it is not a theory; rather, it is a description of the linguistic resources that are available for expressing evaluations, for dialoguing with other value positions, and, generally speaking, taking up ideological stance. Systemic-Functional Linguistics is the theory upon which this description is grounded. Nevertheless, because the name is now established in the literature, this study will continue to use "Appraisal Theory." See James R. Martin, "The Discourse Semantics of Attitudinal Relations: Continuing the Study of Lexis," *Russian Journal of Linguistics* (2017): 22–47.

8   See Martin and White, *Language of Evaluation*, 34–38. This is not a complete network; it is intended as an initial overview only.

9   Throughout this work, names of systems and subsystems appear in SMALL CAPS. Terms within a system use lowercase letters.

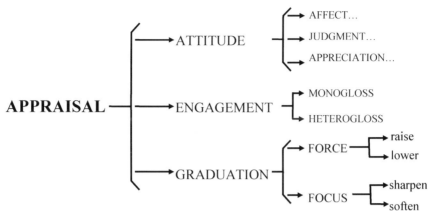

FIGURE 8   A basic overview of the APPRAISAL network

2   Modeling APPRAISAL

2.1   *The System of ATTITUDE*

The first subsystem of APPRAISAL is ATTITUDE. Broadly speaking, ATTITUDE consists of the resources for construing feelings in text. These feelings constitute the semantic regions that are traditionally covered under the headings of emotion, ethics, and aesthetics.[10] Because it is rooted in SFL, Appraisal Theory classifies these kinds of attitudes in terms of systems of opposition.[11] Thus, ATTITUDE is subdivided into three further semiotic subsystems:[12]

- AFFECT (emotion) includes the resources by which a writer encodes their emotional disposition with regard to people, things, processes, or states of affair
- JUDGMENT (ethics) includes the resources by which a writer makes assessments of human behavior, often making reference to behavioral rules or norms
- APPRECIATION (aesthetics) includes the resources by which a writer makes assessments of form, appearance, composition, impact, significance, and value of human and natural artifacts, as well as individuals or groups of people (excluding human behavior) by reference to aesthetics or other systems of social value[13]

---

10   Martin and White, *Language of Evaluation*, 42.
11   Martin and White, *Language of Evaluation*, 46.
12   Martin and White, *Language of Evaluation*, 42–45.
13   The reason for including APPRECIATION in the model may not be readily transparent. If one understands, as Malina (*Christian Origins*, 50) points out, that aesthetic achievements are often used as "weapons of justification and legitimation" for various ideologies

48 CHAPTER 2

2.1.1 Common Realization Schemes

Since the resources for making attitudinal meanings are modeled as discourse semantic systems, their realizations tend to diversify across a range of lexico-grammatical structures as qualities, processes, comments, and metaphors.[14] The following list illustrates the kinds of lexicogrammatical realizations of ATTITUDE that are fairly typical in the Greek of the New Testament (this list is not intended to be exhaustive):[15]

- attitudinal lexis: Ἦν δὲ θυμομαχῶν Τυρίοις καὶ Σιδωνίοις (But [Herod] was *angry* with [the people of] Tyre and Sidon [Acts 12:20])
- modification of participants (e.g., attribution, predication) by means of adjectival elements (including adjectival participles and attributive uses of the Genitive case)[16]
  - *attribution*: σὺ εἶ ὁ υἱός μου ὁ *ἀγαπητός* (You are my *beloved* son [Luke 3:22]), positive affect as attributed quality
  - *predication*: εἷς ἐστιν ὁ *ἀγαθός* (One is *good* [Matt 19:17]), a positive judgment as predicated quality
- modification of processes by means of circumstantial elements (including adverbs, adverbial participles, and prepositional phrases)
  - *adverbial participles of manner*: καὶ εὑρὼν ἐπιτίθησιν ἐπὶ τοὺς ὤμους αὐτοῦ *χαίρων* (And having found [the lost sheep] he places it upon his shoulders *rejoicing* [Luke 15:5])
  - *prepositional phrases*: Καὶ αὐτοὶ προσκυνήσαντες αὐτὸν ὑπέστρεψαν εἰς Ἰερουσαλὴμ *μετὰ χαρᾶς μεγάλης* (And after worshiping him they returned to Jerusalem *with great joy*[17] [Luke 24:52])
- behavioral and mental processes that express attitude[18]
  - *behavioral*: ἐδάκρυσεν ὁ Ἰησοῦς (Jesus *wept* [John 11:35])
  - *mental*: Μάρθα Μάρθα, *μεριμνᾷς* καὶ *θορυβάζῃ* περὶ πολλα (Martha, Martha, you *worry* and *are troubled* about many things [Luke 10:41])

---

    and value positions, then evaluations of those aesthetic achievements are very important indicators of stance.

14   Martin and White, *Language of Evaluation*, 45; White, "Beyond Modality and Hedging," 260.

15   See Martin and White, *Language of Evaluation*, 45–46; White, "Appraisal: An Overview."

16   On the attributive genitive, see esp. Stanley E. Porter, "The Adjectival Attributive Genitive in the NT: A Grammatical Study," *TJ* 4 (1983): 3–17.

17   Or, "exceedingly joyfully."

18   Behavioral processes relate to specifically human physiological processes (i.e., behavioral surges) such as *laugh* (γελάω), *weep/cry* (κλαίω), *sigh* (στενάζω). Mental processes include perception (processes of seeing, hearing, etc.), cognition (processes of deciding, knowing, understanding), and most significant for attitudinal analysis, emotion (processes of feeling) and desideration (processes of wanting). Examples of the latter variety include *love* (ἀγαπάω), *hate* (μισέω), *long for* (ἐπιθυμέω), *hope* (ἐλπίζω).

"WHAT'S YOUR TAKE?" 49

- *grammatical metaphor (nominalized realizations of qualities and processes)*:[19] Ἡ ἀγάπη μακροθυμεῖ, χρηστεύεται ἡ ἀγάπη (*Love* is patient, *love* is kind [1 Cor 13:4]), where the affective process ἀγαπάω (*loving*) is nominalized and, thus, may be modified by predication
- Πᾶσαν χαρὰν ἡγήσασθε (Consider it all *joy* [Jas 1:2]), a nominalized quality modified by attribution
- *lexical metaphor*:[20] καὶ ἡγοῦμαι *σκύβαλα*, ἵνα Χριστὸν κερδήσω (I consider [all things that might have brought me gain] as *excrement*[21] so that I might gain Christ [Phil 3:8]), a negative appreciation via metaphor

2.1.2   The Rhetorical Effects of ATTITUDE

One obvious reason that writers make selections from ATTITUDE is to indicate the kinds of emotional responses either they themselves or others experience with regard to various phenomena. However, Appraisal Theory suggests the rhetorical or instrumental[22] effects of these selections may create solidarity and/or align readers' stances with regard to certain phenomena.[23] The rhetorical effects produced by instances of ATTITUDE in text vary slightly depending on whether the source of the evaluation is the writer (i.e., authorial or "first person" evaluation) or some other participant (i.e., non-authorial or "second" or "third person" evaluation).[24] For example, consider the following text excerpts:

---

19   In addition to M. A. K. Halliday, *An Introduction to Functional Grammar*, 2nd ed. (London: Edward Arnold, 1994), 626–58 (hereafter *IFG2*) and Martin, *English Text*, 406–17, see esp. L. J. Ravelli, "Grammatical Metaphor: An Initial Analysis," in *Pragmatics, Discourse and Text: Some Systemically-Inspired Approaches*, ed. E. H. Steiner and Robert Veltman (London: Pinter, 1988), 133–47.

20   See esp. Anne-Marie Simon-Vandenbergen, "Lexical Metaphor and Interpersonal Meaning," in *Grammatical Metaphor: Views from Systemic Functional Linguistics*, ed. Anne-Marie Simon-Vandenbergen, Miriam Taverniers, and Louise Ravelli (Amsterdam: John Benjamins, 2003), 223–55; Susan Hood and J. R. Martin, "Invoking Attitude: The Play of Graduation in Appraising Discourse," in *Continuing Discourse on Language: A Functional Perspective*, ed. Ruqaiya Hasan, Christian Matthiessen, and Jonathan Webster (London: Equinox, 2007), 2:745–46; and Esther G. Cen, "The Metaphor of Leaven in 1 Corinthians 5," *Dialogismos* 3 (2019): 1–26.

21   Friedrich Lang, "σκύβαλον," *TDNT* 7:445–47; J. I. Packer, "σκύβαλον," *NIDNTT* 1:480; Moisés Silva, *Philippians*, BECNT (Grand Rapids: Baker, 1992), 180; Peter T. O'Brien, *Epistle to the Philippians*, NIGTC (Grand Rapids: Eerdmans, 1991), 390; Gerald F. Hawthorne, *Philippians*, rev. and ed. R. P. Martin, WBC 43 (Nashville: Thomas Nelson, 2004), 192; Ceslas Spicq, "σκύβαλον," *TLNT* 3:265: "to convey the crudity of the Greek … : 'It's all crap'" (*c'est de la crotte*).

22   Ann M. Gill and Karen Whedbee, "Rhetoric," in *Discourse as Structure and Process*, ed. Teun A. van Dijk, Discourse Studies 1 (London: Sage, 1997), 157.

23   Martin and White, *Language of Evaluation*, 2.

24   See White ("Appraisal: An Overview"), who discusses authorial and non-authorial evaluation as part of AFFECT; however, as is shown here, any attitudinal evaluation (AFFECT, JUDGMENT, APPRECIATION) may be authorial or non-authorial.

Νῦν χαίρω ἐν τοῖς παθήμασιν ὑπὲρ ὑμῶν (Now, I rejoice in the sufferings on your behalf [Col 1:24])

μισεῖς τὰ ἔργα τῶν Νικολαϊτῶν ἃ κἀγὼ μισῶ (You hate the deeds of the Nicolaitans, which I also hate [Rev 2:6])

εἶπέν τις ἐξ αὐτῶν ἴδιος αὐτῶν προφήτης· Κρῆτες ἀεὶ ψεῦσται, κακὰ θηρία, γαστέρες ἀργαί. ἡ μαρτυρία αὕτη ἐστὶν ἀληθής (One from among their own prophets said, "Cretans are always liars, evil beasts, lazy gluttons." This testimony is true [Titus 1:12–13a])

Οὐαὶ ὑμῖν, ὁδηγοὶ τυφλοὶ ... μωροὶ καὶ τυφλοί (Woe to you, blind guides ... foolish and blind ones [Matt 23:16, 17a])

The first excerpt (Col 1:24) is an example of authorial evaluation where, by a selection from the system of AFFECT (i.e., χαίρω), Paul indicates that the phenomenon of his suffering on behalf of the readers triggers within him feelings of joy, which are manifested in the act of rejoicing.[25] Paul assumes responsibility for expressing his feelings of joy;[26] not surprisingly, then, the textual realization of first-person affective evaluation is the first-person singular verb χαίρω (I rejoice).[27] First-person attitudinal evaluations like this are the most subjective of attitudinal realizations. By their use, writers directly inscribe, and thus foreground, their subjective presence in the communicative process. Rhetorically, this functions as an invitation for the readers to share the same emotional response thereby attempting to establish an interpersonal rapport and bond with the readers to the extent that the readers will agree with or at least understand and perhaps sympathize with the writer.[28] If the readers accept the invitation by means of compliant reading (or even tactical reading), then some level of solidarity between the writer and reader will have been achieved.[29]

The second excerpt (Rev 2:6) provides an example of non-authorial, second-person positive judgment followed upon immediately by an authorial,

---

25   Joy in the face of suffering is a common Pauline theme (see J. D. G. Dunn, *The Epistles to the Colossians and to Philemon*, NIGTC [Grand Rapids: Eerdmans, 1996], 114).

26   See Peter T. O'Brien, *Colossians, Philemon*, WBC 44 (Waco: Word, 1982), 75.

27   This is not the only way to realize authorial, first-person attitude. They can also be realized through the use of personal pronouns.

28   See esp. White, "Appraisal: An Overview."

29   On compliant, tactical, and resistant reading, see Martin and White, *Language of Evaluation*, 206–7; Martin, "Reading Positions/Positioning Readers," 27–37.

"WHAT'S YOUR TAKE?"   51

first-person negative judgment. In this text there is a twist of irony in the evaluation in that a term that typically carries negative emotive connotations (μισέω, *I hate*) is used in the realization of *positive* judgment. At Rev 2:4 Jesus (in John's vision) has negatively judged the church at Ephesus for having abandoned their first love (ἀγάπην σου τὴν πρώτην ἀφῆκες). Here, however, he returns to a positive judgment by noting their hate for the deeds of the Nicolaitans, which is only positive because he, too, hates their deeds (first-person negative judgment).[30] Thus, after having reprimanded them, Jesus capitalizes on the rhetorical effects of positively judging their behavior in order to rebuild some level of solidarity with the church at Ephesus.

The third excerpt (Titus 1:12) is a clear example of third-person evaluation. In this excerpt, Paul cites[31] a Cretan prophet as a means of providing a negative evaluation—more specifically, a negative judgment—of Cretan people,[32] especially "those of the circumcision group" (see Titus 1:10). On the heels of this evaluation is one of Paul's own (*this testimony is true*) with which he positively appreciates the prophet's negative judgment, thereby taking up the prophet's stance in support of his own value position. These evaluations, both positive and negative, help Paul achieve two goals in this portion of the letter to Titus. First, he is able to communicate to Titus that troublesome characters such as are described in 1:10–11 are to be expected in Crete, as one of the Cretans has "admitted."[33] Second, because troublesome characters are to be expected, it is

---

30   In this instance, the line between APPRECIATION and JUDGMENT is unclear. I have interpreted this text as an instance of JUDGMENT because it appears that what is negatively judged here is the *behavior* of the Nicolaitans (i.e., that they do certain deeds) and not necessarily some "product" or "result" of their actions or even the deeds themselves. However, this is *not* clear in the text and is open to an alternative interpretation.

31   See below on the use of attribution as part of the system of ENGAGEMENT.

32   See the discussion in Martin Dibelius and Hans Conzelmann, *The Pastoral Epistles*, Hermeneia (Philadelphia: Fortress, 1972), 136–37; J. N. D. Kelly, *The Pastoral Epistles*, BNTC XIV (Peabody: Hendrickson, 1960), 235–36; Thomas D. Lea and Hayne P. Griffin, Jr., *1, 2 Timothy, Titus*, NAC 34 (Nashville: Broadman, 1992), 289–90.

33   George W. Knight, III, (*The Pastoral Epistles*, NIGTC [Grand Rapids: Eerdmans, 1992], 299) says that Paul is not necessarily making an "ethnic slur" here; rather, he is "accurately observing, as the Cretans themselves and others did, how the sin that affects the whole human race comes to particular expression in this group" (see also William D. Mounce, *Pastoral Epistles*, WBC 46 [Nashville: Thomas Nelson, 2000], 397–99). Thiselton argues that "the writer of Titus 1:12, 13 is well aware that placing the proposition 'Cretans are always liars' in the mouth of a Cretan transforms the status of the proposition into one which does *not assert a contingent state of affairs about Cretans*. It functions, in effect, as *meta-language*, asserting a proposition which *prima facie* entails its own denial by *logical necessity*. The additional comment 'This testimony is true' is not a sign that the writer (or editor) is oblivious to the nature of the paradox; it is more likely to have been intended as a light touch underlining the absurdity of a regress *ad infinitum*" (Anthony C. Thiselton,

all the more necessary for Titus to "silence" (see 1:11) and "rebuke" them "so that they might become sound in the faith" (1:13)—that is, that they might accept the same value position that Paul himself (and presumably Titus) maintains.[34]

The last excerpt from Matt 23:16 and 17a presents an interesting interpretive challenge. At one level, the text may be interpreted as first-person evaluation of JUDGMENT. It is clear from context that it is Jesus who negatively judges the Pharisees for their actions (or lack thereof) and assumes responsibility for those judgments. However, this excerpt appears as part of a larger narrative text. Certainly, as Labov and Waletsky have pointed out, evaluations occurring in narratives function to make the story relevant for its readers by constantly warding off the question "So what?"[35] This means, however, that the writer of the narrative text assumes at least some responsibility for the judgments included in the story. By doing so, perhaps with his own judgments in mind, the *author* may be making an evaluation *through* the text by means of evaluation *in* the text.[36] Thus, responsibility for the judgments in the excerpted example that are portrayed as having been uttered by Jesus are at the very least *shared* by both the writer of the gospel account and Jesus. In this case, at the discourse level of the narrative the judgments may be interpreted as third-person evaluations, whereby the author makes an evaluation through the voice of another.

"The Logical Role of the Liar Paradox in Titus 1:12, 13: A Dissent from the Commentaries in Light of Philosophical and Logical Analysis," *BibInt* 2 [1994]: 207). He argues that for the writer to assert "this testimony is true" with regard to the proposition of a self-confessed habitual liar logically cannot have any truth value ("Logical Role of the Liar," 208). However, it seems most likely that Paul quotes a stereotype that is based on geography. Such stereotyping was common in the circum-Mediterranean world (see Bruce J. Malina and Jerome H. Neyrey, *Portraits of Paul: An Archaeology of Ancient Personality* [Louisville: Westminster John Knox, 1996], 192).

34   It is likely that Paul means something like "that they might have a correct understanding of the teachings they have received." See Knight, *Pastoral Epistles*, 300; also Mounce, *Pastoral Epistles*, 400.

35   The other function is referential, that is narratives provide information to an audience. See William Labov and Joshua Waletsky, "Narrative Analysis: Oral Versions of Personal Experience," in *Essays on the Verbal and Visual Arts*, ed. J. Helm (Seattle, WA: American Ethnological Society, 1967), 33; Martin Cortazzi and Lixian Jin, "Evaluating Evaluation in Narrative," in *Evaluation in Text: Authorial Stance and the Construction of Discourse*, ed. Susan Hunston and Geoff Thompson (Oxford: Oxford University Press, 1999), 105. See also Eggins, *Introduction*, 70–72.

36   See Cortazzi and Jin, "Evaluating Evaluation in Narrative," 116–18. See also Jacob L. Mey, "Literary Pragmatics," in *The Handbook of Discourse Analysis*, ed. Deborah Schiffrin, Deborah Tannen, and Heidi E. Hamilton (Maldon, MA: Blackwell, 2003), 787–97; Grant R. Osborne, *The Hermeneutical Spiral*, rev. ed. (Downers Grove, IL: InterVarsity, 2006), 204–6; W. Randolph Tate, "Point of View," in *Interpreting the Bible*, 268–69.

"WHAT'S YOUR TAKE?" 53

2.1.3   AFFECT

In Appraisal Theory, AFFECT is categorized typologically based on six criteria or variables.[37] The first of these considers whether the feelings are construed as positive (feelings that are enjoyable to experience such as *happy*) or negative (feelings best to be avoided such as *sad*) within a text's context of culture.[38]

- positive AFFECT: *χάρητε* ἐν ἐκείνῃ τῇ ἡμέρᾳ καὶ *σκιρτήσατε* (*Rejoice* in that day and *be extremely joyful*[39] [Luke 6:23])
- negative AFFECT: Δεῦτε πρός με πάντες οἱ *κοπιῶντες* καὶ *πεφορτισμένοι* (Come to me all who are *weary* and *heavy-laden* [Matt 11:28])

The second criterion has to do with whether the feelings are realized as a surge of emotion "involving some paralinguistic or extralinguistic manifestation" or as a "more internally experienced ... emotive state or ongoing mental process."[40] Lexicogrammatically, this distinction is maintained in the difference between behavioral processes and mental processes.

- behavioral response: ἀμὴν ἀμὴν λέγω ὑμῖν ὅτι *κλαύσετε* καὶ *θρηνήσετε* ὑμεῖς (Truly truly I say to you that you *will weep* and you *will wail*[41] [John 16:20])
- mental process: τὸν δὲ φόβον αὐτῶν μὴ *φοβηθῆτε* μηδὲ *ταραχθῆτε* (You ought not *fear* them or *be afraid* [1 Pet 3:14])

The third criterion opposes directed and undirected feelings. Directed feelings are those that are directed toward or reacting to some specific (typically conscious) external agent. Undirected feelings are those that are construed as general ongoing moods or emotional states.[42] Directed feelings are realized grammatically as affective mental processes, whereas undirected feelings are

---

37   See Martin and White, *Language of Evaluation*, 46–52. See also Martin and Rose, *Working with Discourse*, 64–67; J. R. Martin, "Beyond Exchange: Appraisal Systems in English," in *Evaluation in Text: Authorial Stance and the Construction of Discourse*, ed. Susan Hunston and Geoff Thompson (Oxford: Oxford University Press, 1999), 149–52.

38   Appraisal Theory is not concerned with the value that a particular psychological framework might place on one or another emotion (e.g., "It's probably productive that you're feeling sad because it is a sign that ...") (Martin and White, *Language of Evaluation*, 46). See also Martin and Rose, *Working with Discourse*, 64.

39   On σκιρτάω, see L&N 1:303–4.

40   Martin and White, *Language of Evaluation*, 47.

41   θρηνήσετε is often glossed "mourn" or "lament" in English versions (e.g., NIV, NRSV, NASV), but in Jesus' cultural context, the term likely referred to auditory wailing, which would be classified as an emotional surge. See J. H. Bernard, *A Critical and Exegetical Commentary on the Gospel According to John*, 2 vols., ICC (Edinburgh: T & T Clark, 1999), 2:514; D. A. Carson, *The Gospel According to John*, PNTC (Grand Rapids: Baker, 1993), 543–44.

42   Martin and White (*Language of Evaluation*, 47) suggest that the latter feelings are the kind for which one might ask "Why are you feeling that way?" and receive the answer, "I'm not sure."

54   CHAPTER 2

typically realized in terms of relational states.[43] Passive mental processes of
the "please" type fall between these poles, especially where the triggering phenomenon is implicit (e.g., *He is pleased*).[44]

- directed: διὸ *προσώχθισα* τῇ γενεᾷ ταύτῃ (Therefore, I was *angry* at that generation [Heb 3:10])
- directed or undirected: *εὐδόκησεν* ὁ πατὴρ ὑμῶν δοῦναι ὑμῖν τὴν βασιλείαν
  (Your father *was pleased* to give the kingdom to you [Luke 12:32])
- undirected: ἐγὼ γὰρ ἔμαθον ἐν οἷς εἰμι *αὐτάρκης* εἶναι (I have learned to be
  content in whatever circumstances [Phil 4:11])

Criterion four accounts for how the feelings are graded along a cline from
lower intensity to higher intensity. The values low, median, and high are not
to be taken as discrete values; rather, they represent points along an evenly
scaled cline. This criterion exemplifies how the system of GRADUATION (discussed below) cuts across ATTITUDE. The following sample realizations are
tentatively placed[45] along a cline based on senses given in the Louw and Nida
lexicon (see domain 88)[46] for the *underscored* lexical items:

- low intensity: *ὀργὴ*[47] γὰρ ἀνδρὸς δικαιοσύνην θεοῦ οὐ κατεργάζεται (For human
  anger does not produce the justice of God [Jas 1:20])[48]
- medium intensity: καὶ ἐπλήσθησαν πάντες *θυμοῦ*[49] ἐν τῇ συναγωγῇ (And all
  that were in the synagogue were filled with *fury* [Luke 4:28])

---

43   Martin and White, *Language of Evaluation*, 47; Martin and Rose, *Working with
      Discourse*, 65.
44   Martin and White, *Language of Evaluation*, 47.
45   Tentativeness here is due to the understanding that other contextual factors—e.g., the
      addition of an intensifier such as λιάν (very/exceedingly)—may change the level of
      graduation.
46   L&N 1:742–77.
47   L&N 1:761: "a relative state of anger—'anger, fury.'"
48   On glossing δικαιοσύνην as *justice* rather than *righteousness*, see Brown ("δικαιοσύνη," *NIDNTT*
      3:369–70): "The situation [of James] is one in which the rich could be indifferent to the
      starving and the ill-clad, content with their own spirituality (Jas 2:14–18; 3:13 ff.; see 5:1 ff.),
      and in which church members saw no inconsistency between their spirituality and gossip
      and slander (Jas 3:1 ff., 11 ff.)"—i.e., basic injustice, reminiscent of that described in Isaiah
      (e.g., Isa 33:14–16; 56:1). See the discussion in John N. Oswalt, *Isaiah*, NIVAC (Grand Rapids:
      Zondervan, 2003), 51–55; John N. Oswalt, *Isaiah 1–39*, NICOT (Grand Rapids: Eerdmans,
      1986), 110. However, see also David P. Nystrom, *James*, NIVAC (Grand Rapids: Zondervan,
      1997), 91–92 and Douglas J. Moo, *The Letter of James*, PNTC (Grand Rapids: Eerdmans,
      2000), 84.
49   L&N 1:762: "a state of intense anger, with the implication of passionate outbursts—'anger,
      fury, wrath, rage.'"

"WHAT'S YOUR TAKE?" 55

– high intensity: αὐτοὶ δὲ ἐπλήσθησαν ἀνοίας[50] (But they were filled with extreme *rage* [Luke 6:11])

The fifth criterion in the typology considers whether the feelings are based on *intention* with regard to some *potential* stimulus or trigger, as opposed to *reaction* to some *actual* trigger.[51] The difference between the third and fifth criteria is slight: whereas the third variable simply classifies on the basis of whether the emotion is a surge of behavior or a mental state, the fifth variable classifies on the basis of whether or not the emotion is a reaction to a realis stimulus (e.g., *The boy hated being sick*, where "being sick" is a realis state of affairs that triggered hate) or an irrealis stimulus (e.g., *The young mother shuddered at the thought of her child being kidnapped*, where the child being kidnapped is an irrealis state of affairs that nevertheless caused an emotive response).

– irrealis trigger: φοβούμενοί τε μή που κατὰ τραχεῖς τόπους ἐκπέσωμεν (*Fearing* that we might be run aground somewhere on the rocks [Acts 27:29])
– realis trigger: μισεῖς τὰ ἔργα τῶν Νικολαϊτῶν (You *hate* the deeds of the Nicolaitans [Rev 2:6])

The final criterion in the typology of AFFECT divides emotions into three principal categories based on (un)happiness, (in)security, and (dis)satisfaction.[52] The set of meanings categorized as (un)happiness includes "moods of feeling happy or sad, and the possibility of directing these feelings at a Trigger by liking or disliking it" (Table 4).[53]

The set of meanings grouped under (in)security are concerned with eco- and psycho-social feelings of well-being such as fear, anxiety, confidence, and trust with regard to a person's world and any others with whom they share it (Table 5).[54] Feelings in this category are tuned to protection from the outside world or competing groups and/or individuals.[55]

(Dis)satisfaction has to do with feelings of achievement and frustration with regard to social activities in which people are actively or passively involved

---

50 L&N 1:762: "a state of such extreme anger as to suggest an incapacity to use one's mind— 'extreme fury, great rage.'"

51 Martin and White, *Language of Evaluation*, 48.

52 Martin and White, *Language of Evaluation*, 49–52; Martin and Rose, *Working with Discourse*, 66–67.

53 See Martin and White, *Language of Evaluation*, 49.

54 Martin and White, *Language of Evaluation*, 49.

55 See the similar suggestion made by Martin and White (*Language of Evaluation*, 49) that "in stereotypically gendered communities the feelings [in this category] are associated with 'mothering' in the home—tuned to protection from the world outside (or not)."

CHAPTER 2

TABLE 4   AFFECT—(un)happiness

(Un)happiness	Behavioral response	Disposition
Unhappiness		
misery (mood "in me")	κλαίω (weep)	λύπη (sad)
	θρηνέω (wail)	ἀγωνία (sorrowful)
antipathy (mood directed "at you")	δέρω (beat)	μισέω (hate)
	βρύχω τοὺς ὀδόντας (gnash teeth)	βδελύσσομαι (detest)
Happiness		
cheer (mood "in me")	γελάω (laugh)[a]	εὐδοκέω (be pleased)
	χαίρω (rejoice)	μακαρισμός (happy)
affection (mood directed "at you")	φιλέω (kiss)	ἀγαπάω (love)
	ἐναγκαλίζομαι (embrace)	πλατύνω τὴν καρδίαν (*show affection*)[b]

a   Of course, not all laughter indicates cheer; in fact, this same lexical item may be used in contexts where laughing is used to ridicule or shame another (see L&N 1:304).
b   Lit. "to broaden one's heart"—an idiom meaning to show compassion. See 2 Cor 6:11 (see L&N 1:295).

TABLE 5   AFFECT—(in)security

(In)security	Behavioral response	Disposition
Insecurity		
disquiet	τρέμω (tremble)	μεριμνάω (be anxious)
	οὐαί (woe!)[a]	συνέχομαι (be distressed)
surprise	ἔα (ah!)[b]	θαυμάζω (be surprised)
	οὐά (Aha!)[c]	θροέομαι (be startled)

a   An interjection expressing displeasure.
b   An exclamatory particle (often left untranslated) that indicates surprise. See L&N 1:763.
c   An interjection expressing surprise or astonishment.

"WHAT'S YOUR TAKE?"

TABLE 5   AFFECT—(in)security (*cont.*)

(In)security	Behavioral response	Disposition
Security		
confidence	παρρησιάζομαι (speak boldly)[d] ἡ καρδία ἔστιν μετά (confide)[e]	πείθω τὴν καρδίαν (be confident) ἀσθένεια (timid)[f]
trust	παρατίθεμαι (entrust) τὴν μέριμναν ἐπιρίπτω ἐπί (cast cares upon)[g]	πιστεύω (believe) ὑποτάσσω (submit)

d H. C. Hahn, "παρρησία" *NIDNTT* 2:734–37. See also J. Paul Sampley, "Paul and Frank Speech," in *Paul in the Greco-Roman World: A Handbook*, ed. J. P. Sampley (Harrisburg, PA: Trinity Press International, 2003), 293–318.
e An idiom (lit. "the heart is with") that in certain contexts means "confide" (see Judg 16:15 LXX).
f See 1 Cor 2:3; L&N 1:318.
g See L&N 1:316.

(Table 6).[56] According to Martin and White, directed emotions in this category key on how active a role one is playing in the activity triggering the emotional reaction.[57] For example, as a participant in some activity one's (dis)satisfaction depends upon a number of factors, including especially whether or not their goal is being accomplished or frustrated (see e.g., Col 1:24). Similarly, (dis)satisfaction as a spectator also depends upon a number of factors, such as whether or not one is pleased by the motives and actions of others doing the action (see e.g., Acts 20:37–38).

The purpose of this section has been to demonstrate in a very general manner the ways in which human emotions get encoded in text and the kinds of meanings they may exhibit. Several things must be mentioned as it is brought to a close. First, the sample lexical items provided in the tables in this section are simply intended to provide very basic illustrations of the range of meanings involved with the encoding of emotions. Second, the choice of one lexical item over another in this realm always involves grading the depth of feeling[58]—something not clearly exemplified in the illustrations. The issue of graduation

56   Martin and White, *Language of Evaluation*, 50.
57   Martin and White, *Language of Evaluation*, 50.
58   Martin and White, *Language of Evaluation*, 50.

58   CHAPTER 2

TABLE 6   AFFECT—(dis)satisfaction

(Dis)satisfaction	Behavioral response	Disposition
Dissatisfaction		
ennui	καταφέρομαι ὕπνῳ (become sleepy)[a] ἀχανής (yawn)[b]	κάμνω τῇ ψυχῇ (be weary)[c] ἀθυμέω (be discouraged)
displeasure	ἐμβριμάομαι (scold) προσαπειλέομαι (threaten)	ὀργίζομαι (be angry) προσοχθίζω (be irritated)
Satisfaction		
interest	στηρίζω τὸ πρόσωπον (decide firmly)[d] ἐπέχω (pay attention)	φρονέω (keep thinking about)[e] καταχράομαι (be fully involved)[f]
pleasure	ἀποδίδωμι (give a reward)[g] δεξιὰς διδόναι (to shake hands)[h]	χορτάζω (be satisfied) κορέννυμι (be content)

a   See Acts 20:9; L&N 1:259.
b   See Wis 19:17.
c   See L&N 1:320.
d   See L&N 1:360.
e   See L&N 1:352.
f   See 1 Cor 7:31 (NIV: "engrossed"); L&N 1:505.
g   See L&N 1:491; Matt 6:6.
h   An idiom referring to making an agreement, often involving the actual shaking of hands. See L&N 1:451.

will be covered in more detail below. Finally, it bears repeating that the lexical illustrations provided in this section were given without any detailed context. Thus, one should not view the lexical items as if they are "locked in" to the categories in which they appear. For example, καταφέρομαι ὕπνῳ (become sleepy) likely does not *always* indicate boredom. Eutychus (Acts 20:9) may have become sleepy because he had worked a full day of hard labor and not because he was disinterested in Paul's teaching (although apparently Paul did talk for a long time [διαλεγομένου τοῦ Παύλου ἐπὶ πλεῖον]). Context is vital for interpreting these kinds of locutions.

"WHAT'S YOUR TAKE?" 59

2.1.4   JUDGMENT

As mentioned above, JUDGMENT is that region of meaning where attitudes with regard to others' or one's own behavior or character are construed.[59] Generally speaking, selections from JUDGMENT are of two main types, those oriented toward social esteem and those oriented toward social sanction.[60]

> Judgments of esteem have to do with 'normality' (how unusual some-one is), 'capacity' (how capable they are), and 'tenacity' (how resolute they are); judgments of sanction have to do with 'veracity' (how truthful someone is) and 'propriety' (how ethical someone is).[61]

Realizations of JUDGMENT follow the basic patterns of ATTITUDE as noted above. For example, judgments may be inscribed via participant modification by attribution (e.g., ὁ δίκαιος κριτής [the *righteous* judge (2 Tim 4:8)]) or predication (e.g., ἔτι γὰρ σαρκικοί ἐστε [for you are still *fleshly* (1 Cor 3:3)]); or by means of certain behavioral processes (e.g., οὐκ ἠδυνήθησαν εἰσελθεῖν δι' ἀπιστίαν [they *were* not *able* to enter because of their unbelief (Heb 3:19)]). Table 7 provides a number of examples of lexical realizations of judgments of esteem; Table 8 provides examples of judgments of sanction (neither list is intended to be exhaustive). Similar to AFFECT, judgments of esteem and sanction may be either positive (behaviors and traits that are admired or praised) or negative (behaviors and traits that are criticized or condemned) depending upon contextual circumstances and the value position(s) of the appraiser or the appraiser's group.[62] Additionally, accounting for context is vital when interpreting instances of JUDGMENT. There are instances in which a lexical item that at face value denotes negative JUDGMENT functions in its context to

---

59   An example of self-directed judgment may be found at 1 Tim 1:15, 16. Another possible example is Rom 7:14–25, but see Porter, *Idioms*, 76 for reasons why this text may not be as clear an example as one might think.

60   Martin and White, *Language of Evaluation*, 52; Martin and Rose, *Working with Discourse*, 67–68; Martin, "Beyond Exchange," 155–57.

61   Martin and White, *Language of Evaluation*, 52.

62   See, e.g., Acts 5:28, where the Sanhedrin (through the mouth of the high priest) criticized Peter and John for not complying with the "strict orders" they had previously issued in which they proscribed preaching and teaching about Jesus—a negative JUDGMENT of sanction with regard to propriety. However, 5:29–32, 41–42 indicate that Peter and John considered the sanction to be a positive JUDGMENT of esteem regarding their tenacity. See Ben Witherington, III, *The Acts of the Apostles: A Socio-Rhetorical Commentary* (Grand Rapids: Eerdmans, 1998), 231–32; Dennis Gaertner, *Acts*, CPNIVC (Joplin, MO: College Press, 1993), 112–16.

60   CHAPTER 2

TABLE 7   JUDGMENT—social esteem

Social esteem	Positive (admire)	Negative (criticize)
Normality (*how special?*)	δοξάζω (pass., glorified, honored) μακάριος (blessed, honored)[a]	ἀνάθεμα (cursed) ἀνάξιος (unworthy)
Capacity (*how capable?*)	δύνατος (able) τέλειος (mature)	ἀδύνατος (incapable) νήπιος (immature)
Tenacity (*how dependable?*)	πιστός (faithful, trustworthy) μακροθυμέω (exhibit patience)	ἄπιστος (unfaithful, untrustworthy) σκληροτράχηλοι (stubborn)

a K. C. Hanson ("How Honorable! How Shameful! A Cultural Analysis of Matthew's *Makarisms* and Reproaches," *Semeia* 68 [1994]: 81–111) argues convincingly that μακάριος is not an expression of a positive human emotion (AFFECT), but instead shares the same semantic domain as τιμάω / τιμή.

TABLE 8   JUDGMENT—social sanction

Social sanction	Positive (praise)	Negative (condemn)
Veracity (*how honest?*)	ἀληθής (truthful) ἀψευδής (truthful)	ὑποκριτής (hypocrite, pretender) ψεύστης (liar)
Propriety (*how ethical?*)	ἀρετή (goodness, moral) ἀνεπίλημπτος (above reproach)	δόλιος (deceitful) πλεονέκτης (greedy)

inscribe positive JUDGMENT and *vice versa*. For example, the adjective πιστός may serve as a *judgment* of esteem in some contexts, as in 1 Cor 1:9, where God is said to be trustworthy—a character judgment based on God's prior activity and a certain ideological/theological interpretation of God.[63] However, in

---

63   See C. K. Barrett, *The First Epistle to the Corinthians*, HNTC (New York: Harper and Row, 1968), 40; Richard E. Oster, Jr., *1 Corinthians*, CPNIVC (Joplin, MO: College Press, 1995), 48–49.

"WHAT'S YOUR TAKE?"

61

other contexts the same adjective may inscribe an APPRECIATION (see below), as in 1 Tim 1:15, where a bit of discourse (a "saying" or "message" [λόγος]) is *appreciated* for its trustworthiness.[64]

Finally, it is significant to note that although judgments are, indeed, subjective, they are less explicitly subjective than the emotional states construed by AFFECT. This is seen in the fact that AFFECT construes evaluations as some kind of emotional response or state of some human individual or group, but JUDGMENT construes evaluations as though they are qualities of the phenomenon being evaluated.[65] Note for example the difference in the evaluations realized in the following clause: ἱλαρὸν γὰρ δότην ἀγαπᾷ ὁ θεός (God *loves* a *cheerful* giver [2 Cor 9:7]).[66] The affective value of "loving" in this clause is attributed to God; it is God's subjective attitude toward the giver. By contrast, the affective value of "cheerfulness" is attributed to the giver as if cheerfulness is a property of the giver being appraised. Cheerfulness in this text is neither presented as an explicit subjective attitude of God, nor as an explicit subjective attitude of the giver. Instead, it is an inexplicit appraisal made by the writer and is, therefore, less "personal" and subjective.

2.1.5   APPRECIATION

APPRECIATION is concerned with what has traditionally been considered a subcategory of aesthetics.[67] Positive and negative assessments of objects, artifacts, processes, states of affair, ideas, relationships, and the like are categorized as selections from APPRECIATION. Human participants may also be appreciated (as opposed to judged), but only in instances where the evaluation does not focus upon rightness (morality) or wrongness (immorality) of their behavior.[68] For example, ἐξετάσατε τίς ἐν αὐτῇ ἄξιός ἐστιν (Search for someone who is *worthy* [Matt 10:11]) is an appreciation of a person (albeit indefinite) that is not directly tied to behavior.[69] However, ὃς οὐ λαμβάνει τὸν σταυρὸν αὐτοῦ καὶ ἀκολουθεῖ ὀπίσω μου, οὐκ ἔστιν μου ἄξιος (Whoever does not take up their

---

64   See Dibelius and Conzelmann, *Pastoral Epistles*, 28–29; Mounce, *Pastoral Epistles*, 56–57; Jerome D. Quinn and William C. Wacker, *The First and Second Letters to Timothy*, ECC (Grand Rapids: Eerdmans, 2000), 132–33.

65   White, "Appraisal: An Overview."

66   Ἱλαρόν may be glossed *generous* or *liberal* (see Victor Paul Furnish, *II Corinthians*, AB 32A [Garden City, NY: Doubleday, 1984], 447; but, see Ralph P. Martin, *2 Corinthians*, WBC 40 [Waco: Word, 1986], 290).

67   White, "Appraisal: An Overview."

68   White, "Appraisal: An Overview."

69   It should be noted that worthiness in the ancient circum-Mediterranean world is directly related to honor, and honor may be *achieved* on the basis of behavior (it may also be *ascribed* on the basis of birth) (see now deSilva, *Honor, Patronage, Kinship & Purity*, 28–29; Jerome H. Neyrey, *Honor and Shame in the Gospel of Matthew* [Louisville: Westminster

62   CHAPTER 2

TABLE 9   Examples of APPRECIATION

	Positive	Negative
Reaction	προσφιλής (lovely)	ῥυπαρός (filthy)
	ἀστεῖος (beautiful)	ἀσχήμων (ugly)
Composition	ὀρθός (straight)	σκολιός (crooked)
	ἄδολος (pure)	βαρύς (difficult)
Value	ἄξιος (worthy)	ἀνάξιος (unworthy)
	χρήσιμος (useful)	ἀχρεῖος (useless)

cross and follow me is not *worthy* of me [Matt 10:38]) is a judgment based on behavior.[70]

APPRECIATION is divided into three broad categories: (1) *reaction* is concerned with the impact of an object, entity, or text/process on our attention and its attitudinal impact; (2) *composition* is concerned with perceptions of order and/or balance and detail in an object, entity, or text/process; and (3) *valuation* is concerned with considered opinions regarding the social significance of an object, entity, or text/process.[71] For illustrative purposes, a number of lexical realizations of APPRECIATION are presented in Table 9. As with JUDGMENT, APPRECIATION is oriented more toward the appraised than toward a subjective appraiser; values of appraisal are presented as properties of that which is appraised rather than to some human subject who gives the appraisal.[72] For this reason, appreciations are relatively less explicitly subjective than affective evaluations.

2.1.6   Inscribed versus Evoked and Provoked ATTITUDE

Before concluding this discussion of ATTITUDE, an additional and somewhat complicating issue must be discussed. To this point the model for ATTITUDE

John Knox, 1998], 15–27). That said, in the case of Matt 10:11, there is no explicit mention of behavior with regard to the one to be deemed *worthy* (i.e., honorable).

70   Jesus' teaching in this context (see Matt 10:34–38) is concerned primarily with loyalty/allegiance (see Richard T. France, *The Gospel of Matthew*, NICNT [Grand Rapids: Eerdmans, 2007] 406–11; on loyalty/allegiance, see Bruce J. Malina, "Faith/Faithfulness," *HBSV*, 61–63).

71   Martin and White, *Language of Evaluation*, 56; Martin, "Beyond Exchange," 159–60; Monika Bednarek, *Emotion Talk across Corpora* (New York: Palgrave, 2008), 15.

72   White, "Appraisal: An Overview."

"WHAT'S YOUR TAKE?" 63

has only accounted for attitudinal evaluations that are directly inscribed in text either through the use of attitudinal lexis or various grammatical structures. However, attitudinal evaluations may be construed in seemingly incongruous ways.[73] Of interest here is the ability of a writer to *evoke* or *provoke* attitudinal response(s) in the reader—at least *potentially*[74]—by employing "attitudinal tokens" rather than directly inscribing attitude via the kinds of locutions discussed above.[75] According to White, attitudinal tokens are "formulations where there is no single item which, of itself and independently of its current co-text, carries a specific positive or negative value. Rather the positive/negative viewpoint is activated via various mechanisms of association and implication."[76] Evocation can occur when experiential ("informational") material is selected and brought to focus in a context where it may trigger an attitudinal reaction by way of inference; provocation can occur by means of locutions that are evaluative, but not of an explicitly positive or negative type.[77] The difference between evoked and provoked attitudinal evaluations is sometimes difficult to perceive.

Two texts are presented here as examples of evocation and provocation. First, as an example of a text that likely *evokes* an evaluation, one may consider Acts 13:1–3:

Ἦσαν δὲ ἐν Ἀντιοχείᾳ κατὰ τὴν οὖσαν ἐκκλησίαν προφῆται καὶ διδάσκαλοι ὅ τε Βαρναβᾶς καὶ Συμεὼν ὁ καλούμενος Νίγερ καὶ Λούκιος ὁ Κυρηναῖος, Μαναήν τε Ἡρῴδου τοῦ τετραάρχου σύντροφος καὶ Σαῦλος. Λειτουργούντων δὲ αὐτῶν τῷ κυρίῳ καὶ νηστευόντων εἶπεν τὸ πνεῦμα τὸ ἅγιον· ἀφορίσατε δή μοι τὸν Βαρναβᾶν καὶ Σαῦλον εἰς τὸ ἔργον ὃ προσκέκλημαι αὐτούς. τότε νηστεύσαντες καὶ προσευξάμενοι καὶ ἐπιθέντες τὰς χεῖρας αὐτοῖς ἀπέλυσαν.

---

73 This is similar to instances where assertions (Indicative Mood) are interpreted as directives (Imperative Mood). E.g., Jesus' statement from the cross, "I am thirsty" (John 19:28–29), appears to have been interpreted as "I want a drink," "Give me a drink," or "May I have a drink?" See Dvorak, "Evidence that Commands a Verdict," 201–23.

74 This, of course, depends upon a number of factors including genre, register, deixis, reference, and, not least, the ability of the reader both to "pick up" on what is being meant and to choose a reading position (compliant, tactical, or resistant). See George Yule, *The Study of Language*, 2nd ed. (Cambridge: Cambridge University Press, 1999), 127–38; Martin, "Reading Positions/Positioning Readers," 31–33; Martin and White, *Language of Evaluation*, 62–63.

75 See White, "Evaluative Semantics," 39–40; Martin, "Reading Positions/Positioning Readers," 31–33.

76 White, "Evaluative Semantics," 39.

77 White, "Evaluative Semantics," 40.

64 CHAPTER 2

> Now in Antioch, in the church that was there, there were prophets and teachers: Barnabas; Simeon, the one called Niger; Lucias the Cyrene; Manean, who had been raised with Herod the Tetrarch; and Saul. While they were worshiping the Lord and fasting, the Holy Spirit said, "Appoint for me, then, Barnabas and Saul to the work to which I have called them." Then, after fasting and praying and laying their hands on them, they sent them.

There are no instances of *directly inscribed* selections from AFFECT, JUDGMENT, or APPRECIATION in this text. It is a text in which ideational meaning is foregrounded; it is focused on providing information. Yet the information in this text is designed to evoke an attitude, likely positive, in the reader. Consider the following representations in the text:

- Not only does the text emphasize that the church in Antioch had prophets and teachers, but it goes on to list a number of them by name, and one may presume from this level of specificity that those listed were respected at least by those in Antioch, if not also by Luke's addressees
- The text represents these prophets and teachers (or perhaps a broader group) as being involved in activities appropriate to their role, namely worshiping the Lord and fasting
- The Holy Spirit is represented as speaking (presumably) to these prophets and teachers, a "fact" that may indicate the writer's positive evaluation of the Antioch assembly
- The prophets and teachers (1) appear to recognize that it was, indeed, the Holy Spirit that spoke, thus they (2) obeyed the command they were given—"facts" that further represent the prophets and teachers as being involved in activities appropriate to their role

Although this text foregrounds ideational meaning, it is likely to evoke positive attitudinal evaluations of the participants in the text and their behavior. Additionally, this sets the reader up for what comes in subsequent text, in particular that in spite of the challenges and difficulties that Barnabas and Saul would face on their "mission" as well as the concomitant pain and suffering their message would cause those who would believe it, the two men, their teaching, and their deeds are ultimately presented as praiseworthy because of the (potentially) attitudinally positive connection to obedience to the Spirit's command.[78]

---

78 While one might argue that the attitudinal reading naturalized by this text is positive, it is, of course, possible that readers (both then and now) may, given their own value positions (e.g., perhaps a disbelief that the Holy Spirit spoke), have a negative reaction to the text.

"WHAT'S YOUR TAKE?"

An example of a text that is likely to *provoke* an attitudinal evaluation, one may consider Matt 2:16:

> Τότε Ἡρῴδης ἰδὼν ὅτι ἐνεπαίχθη ὑπὸ τῶν μάγων ἐθυμώθη λίαν, καὶ ἀποστείλας ἀνεῖλεν πάντας τοὺς παῖδας τοὺς ἐν Βηθλέεμ καὶ ἐν πᾶσιν τοῖς ὁρίοις αὐτῆς ἀπὸ διετοῦς καὶ κατωτέρω ...

> Then Herod, perceiving that he had been deceived by the Magoi, became extremely angry, so having commissioned (emissaries) he killed all the children who were in Bethlehem and its vicinity who were two years old and younger ...

Here again is a text that foregrounds ideational meaning, but there are a few distinctive features that may cause it not simply to evoke, but to *provoke* an attitudinal response, and that response will likely be a negative judgment of Herod. Here are several features one must account for:

- Although Herod is not the only participant in these two clauses (others are the *magoi*, the children, and possibly, though not explicitly, emissaries sent out by Herod), he is foregrounded[79] over the others because (1) things are done/happen to him (e.g., he is deceived [ἐνεπαίχθη]; he becomes angry [ἐθυμώθη]) and (2) he is the only participant represented as Actor of a material process (ἀνεῖλεν)
- The attitudinal process "becoming angry" realizes negative AFFECT: unhappiness, the negative prosody of which "radiates" both prospectively and retrospectively to give this text a negative tone/mood[80]
- The material process "killing" is a surge of behavior manifesting negative AFFECT: unhappiness, the trigger of which is said to be Herod's perception that the *magoi* had deceived him

---

79 Although the *magoi* are represented as the Agents who deceived Herod, the passive structure puts them in a less focal position. On this, see Porter, *Idioms*, 64; Trew, "Theory and Ideology at Work," in *Language and Control*, ed. Roger Fowler, Bob Hodge, Gunther, Kress, and Tony Trew (London: Routledge & Kegan Paul, 1979), 98. See also M. A. K. Halliday, "Language Structure and Language Function," in *On Grammar*, CWMAKH 1 (London: Continuum, 2002), 173–95.

80 On the prosodic nature of evaluation, see Halliday, "Modes of Meaning," 206; Martin, *English Text*, 10–13; James R. Martin, "Analysing Genre: Functional Parameters," in *Genre and Institutions: Social Processes in the Workplace and School*, ed. F. Christie and J. R. Martin (London: Cassell, 1997), 16–17; Martin and White, *Language of Evaluation*, 17–23; Martin and Rose, *Working with Discourse*, 59–63. On the radiating prosody of evaluation, see Susan Hood, "The Persuasive Power of Prosodies: Radiating Values in Academic Writing," *JEAP* 5 (2006): 37–49 and Dvorak, "Prodding with Prosody," 85–120.

- Herod's anger is accentuated in at least two ways: (1) by using an intensifier (λίαν) to amplify (the representation of) the force of Herod's anger (see below on GRADUATION), and (2) by describing the scope of Herod's killing as including all children[81] two years old and younger living in Bethlehem and vicinity

Each of these features contributes to the sense that Herod's actions in this instance were capricious, emotionally driven, and unjustified. Thus, the reading position naturalized by this text is one of negative judgment and, in fact, this text is more likely to provoke a negative attitude toward Herod and his behavior.[82] The quotation of Jer 31:15 immediately following this text (Matt 2:18) supplies further negative appraisal of Herod's action (albeit from a third party's voice and not directly that of the narrator) and continues the negative prosody.

The distinction between directly inscribed and indirectly evoked/provoked attitudes can present interpreters with a significant challenge. In texts where the writer chooses to inscribe emotions, judgments, and appreciations, the reading position of the text is more clearly naturalized, and generally speaking it would take an intentional act of resistant reading not to comply with the naturalized reading. However, in cases like those exemplified above, interpreters must heighten their awareness as they search for clues as to how the writer wants the reader to interpret the text. A further challenge arises due to the historical and cultural distance and situational differences that stand between the ancient readers of the New Testament documents and contemporary interpreters. Lacking full knowledge of the cultural and contextual situations lying behind these texts opens the door for reading meaning into a text and misinterpretation. These challenges, however, do not negate the importance of asking of a text the kinds of pragmatic questions exemplified in the present model.

---

81   TNIV/NIV and NLT gloss παῖδας as *boys*. Although the term is masculine gender, there is no one-to-one equivalence between the grammatical gender of a term and natural gender (male/female); in fact, this lexeme (παῖς) could be used of either girls or boys (see L&N 1:110). It is likely that the TNIV/NIV and NLT assume the reference is to males because (a) Herod's purpose is to eliminate a "king" and (b) the underlying analogy with Pharoah suggests males are targeted (see France, *Matthew*, 82 n. 2; Robert H. Gundry, *Matthew: A Commentary on His Handbook for a Mixed Church under Persecution*, 2nd ed. [Grand Rapids: Eerdmans, 1994], 34–35). That said, it is certainly possible (if not probable) that in his anger Herod ordered *all* children, both males and females under the age of two, to be killed. Moreover, would Herod's lackeys have even taken the time to check the sex of each child before dispatching her/him?

82   That Herod and his behavior could trigger negative judgment would not be out of the question given what is known about his character. See Richard T. France, "Herod and the Children of Bethlehem," *NovT* 21 (1979): 114–16.

"WHAT'S YOUR TAKE?" 67

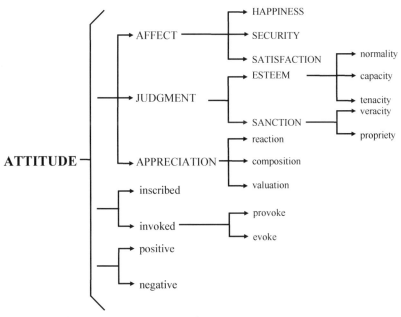

FIGURE 9   The ATTITUDE system network

2.1.7   Summary of ATTITUDE

ATTITUDE and its subsystems provide the framework in the APPRAISAL system for mapping feelings as they are construed in text. The kinds of feelings accounted for include those of emotion (AFFECT), those concerning morality (JUDGMENT), and those concerning aesthetics (APPRECIATION). Figure 9 provides a visual overview of the system of ATTITUDE.

2.2   *The System of ENGAGEMENT*

In this section, attention is turned to the second major portion of the Appraisal model, namely the system of ENGAGEMENT. As described in the previous chapter, the framework of engagement resources presented here presumes that all texts—even those that are monoglossic or "single-voiced," such as law codes—are produced and interpreted against the heteroglossic backdrop of other "voices" on the same theme, "a background made up of contradictory opinions, points of view and value judgments … pregnant with responses and objections."[83] Language users may respond to these alternative voices in one of two ways. First, they may produce monoglossic texts. Quite often monoglossic

---

83   Bakhtin, "Discourse in the Novel," 281. See Martin and White, *Language of Evaluation*, 92–95. Lemke, *Textual Politics*, 22–25.

texts give the impression that no alternative proposition(s)—no alternative voices or opinions—exist with respect to the issue taken up by the language user. For example, the proposition πᾶς ὁ μισῶν τὸν ἀδελφὸν αὐτοῦ ἀνθρωποκτόνος ἐστίν (everyone who hates his/her brother or sister is a murderer [1 John 3:15]) is a categorical assertion that presents a proposition as a given, as presupposed or taken for granted.[84] Locutions such as these neither recognize nor engage with any other voice or opinion regarding the proposition(s) being advanced.[85] However, there are instances in which a proposition is monoglossically declared, but that is not taken for granted; rather, it is asserted as a point to be discussed or debated.[86] For example, at 1 Cor 3:19 Paul categorically asserts ἡ γὰρ σοφία τοῦ κόσμου τούτου μωρία παρὰ τῷ θεῷ ἐστιν (for the wisdom of this world is foolishness to God). That Paul goes on to support this proposition with back-to-back Scripture quotations construes it as "very much at issue and the focus of a debate."[87] It construes a readership that does not necessarily share Paul's point of view and, thus, needs to be convinced of it.

Second, language users may engage in dialogue with these other "voices," presenting themselves as in varying degrees standing with them or against them, as neutral, or as not yet having taken a stance toward them.[88] The framework of ENGAGEMENT, which has heterogloss as its entry condition, systemically organizes the linguistic features used to achieve such positioning (see Figure 10). These resources are divided into two broad functional categories according to whether they are "dialogically contractive" or "dialogically expansive," a distinction that "turns on the degree to which an utterance ... actively makes allowances for alternative positions and voices (dialogic expansion), or, alternatively, acts to challenge, fend off or restrict the scope of such (dialogic contraction)."[89] It is extremely important to bear in mind that the framework presented here is oriented toward contextual meanings and rhetorical effects that get expressed variously through both grammar and lexis. Consequently,

> it brings together a lexically and grammatically diverse selection of locutions on the basis that they all operate to locate the writer/speaker with respect to the value positions being referenced in the text and with

---

84   Note the subsequent clause that builds on this proposition: "and *you know* that every murderer does not have eternal life abiding in them."

85   See Martin and White, *Language of Evaluation*, 99.

86   See Martin and White, *Language of Evaluation*, 101.

87   Martin and White, *Language of Evaluation*, 102.

88   Martin and White, *Language of Evaluation*, 93.

89   Martin and White, *Language of Evaluation*, 102.

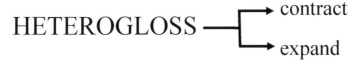

FIGURE 10   A basic overview of HETEROGLOSS

respect to, in Bakhtin's terms, the backdrop of alternative opinions, points of view and value judgments against which all texts operate.[90]

2.2.1   Dialogic Contraction

In overtly heteroglossic contexts, language users may contract dialogic space (i.e., restrict alternative "voices") in two basic ways: either through proclamation or through disclamation. Proclamation contracts dialogue by construing the authorial voice as setting itself against, suppressing, or ruling out any alternative positions offered by other voices.[91] Disclamation on the other hand restricts other voices by construing the authorial voice as disagreeing with, denying, or rejecting outright any alternative voices that may be represented in a text.[92] Proclamation and disclamation each have a variety of means by which they may be realized, each of which will be discussed briefly here.

2.2.1.1   *PROCLAIM: CONCUR*

Concurrence involves formulations that overtly signal that a writer stands in agreement with or has the same knowledge as some projected dialogic partner, typically the putative addressee.[93] These formulations are realized by locutions such as conjunctive adverbs, emphatic particles and/or conjuncts, and certain kinds of rhetorical or "leading" questions.[94] Rhetorically, concurrence contracts dialogue by representing certain shared values or beliefs as widely accepted in their communicative context and, thus, rendering moot any

---

90   Martin and White, *Language of Evaluation*, 94.
91   Martin and White, *Language of Evaluation*, 117; White, "Appraisal: An Overview."
92   Martin and White, *Language of Evaluation*, 117; White, "Appraisal: An Overview."
93   Martin and White, *Language of Evaluation*, 122.
94   Martin and White, *Language of Evaluation*, 123; Goatly, *Critical Reading and Writing*, 89. Wilhelm Wuellner, in addressing the function of rhetorical questions in 1 Cor, suggested that a time would come when "socio-linguistics and language as social semiotic"—from which extends the model offered here—would affect the scope of rhetorical criticism. See his "Paul as Pastor: The Function of Rhetorical Questions in First Corinthians," in *L'Apôtre Paul: Personnalité, Style, et Conception du Ministère*, ed. A. Vanhoye, BETL 73 (Leuven: University Press, 1986), 49–77, here 51. Also, see below under "Consideration" regarding "expository" or open-ended questions.

alternative value positions or beliefs in the ongoing colloquy.[95] Heb 3:15–16 provides an interesting example:

ἐν τῷ λέγεσθαι· σήμερον ἐὰν τῆς φωνῆς αὐτοῦ ἀκούσητε, μὴ σκληρύνητε τὰς καρδίας ὑμῶν ὡς ἐν τῷ παραπικρασμῷ. τίνες γὰρ ἀκούσαντες παρεπίκραναν; ἀλλ' οὐ πάντες οἱ ἐξελθόντες ἐξ Αἰγύπτου διὰ Μωϋσέως;

As was just quoted, "Today if you would hear his voice, do not harden your hearts as in the rebellion." For who rebelled even though they heard? Was it not, *indeed*, all those who came out of Egypt through Moses?

In the co-text just prior to this excerpt, the writer quotes a passage of Scripture (Ps 95:7–11) that poetically recounts an event from the history of a people group to which, in all likelihood, both the writer and readers belonged. This has the effect of creating a communicative context in which the writer and readers share the same knowledge. Thus, in the text excerpt cited here, which restates the portion of the citation from which the writer wishes to make a point,[96] the writer employs a so-called rhetorical question[97] that, because the answer is so "obvious,"[98] construes the addresser and addressees as being completely in alignment. Moreover, the question itself uses the conjunction ἀλλά, not in its more typical role as a contrastive conjunction, but as an emphatic particle (*indeed*)—another realization of concurrence.[99]

2.2.1.2   *PROCLAIM: ENDORSE*

Endorsement refers to formulations by which an author construes some externally sourced proposition as "correct, valid, undeniable, or otherwise

---

95   Martin and White, *Language of Evaluation*, 124.

96   See William L. Lane, *Hebrews 1–8*, WBC 47A (Waco: Word, 1991; repr., Nashville: Thomas Nelson, 2003), 88.

97   See Martin and White, *Language of Evaluation*, 123, where these kinds of questions are referred to as "leading questions." See also their remarks regarding "expository" or open ended questions [*Language of Evaluation*, 110]).

98   Here, because of the negative particle οὐ, a positive answer is expected. See Porter, *Idioms*, 278–79. See also James D. Dvorak, "Ask and Ye Shall Position the Readers': James's Use of Questions to (Re-)Align His Readers," in *The Epistle of James: Linguistic Exegesis of an Early Christian Letter*, LENT 1 (Hamilton, ON: McMaster Divinity College Press; Eugene: Pickwick, 2019), 196–245, esp. 211–19.

99   On the use of ἀλλά as an emphatic particle, see Porter, *Idioms*, 205–6; Daniel B. Wallace, *Greek Grammar beyond the Basics* (Grand Rapids: Zondervan, 1996), 673. See also BDF, 232–33.

"WHAT'S YOUR TAKE?" 71

maximally warrantable,"[100] as well as authoritative and relevant to the context of situation. By construing externally-sourced texts as insuperable, writers are able to contract dialogic space and functionally disallow alternative voices. One way endorsement is realized in the New Testament is through quotation.[101] The source of the quotation, which may or may not be explicitly stated, may be a person, deity, or some other text. Occasionally, greater weight is added to the endorsement through either positive judgment of the source (if personal) for making the proposition or through positive appreciation of the quotation itself. Lexicogrammatically, endorsement entails the use of verbal or mental processes (or their nominalized forms) attributed to an external source. If the source or the quotation itself is positively evaluated, then the locutions of positive judgment or positive appreciation as described above will occur as part of the instance.

By way of example, Mark 7:6–7 records Jesus' rejoinder to an accusation made by the Pharisees that his disciples were sinners (which is tantamount to an attack on his own honor),[102] because they had deviated from the tradition

---

100 Martin and White, *Language of Evaluation*, 126. Compare endorsement, which is dialogically *contractive*, with attribution (below), which is dialogically *expansive*.

101 On issues surrounding Scripture quotation in the New Testament, see Stanley E. Porter, "The Use of the Old Testament in the New Testament: Brief Comment on Method and Terminology," in *Early Christian Interpretation of the Scriptures of Israel: Investigations and Proposals*, ed. Craig A. Evans and James A. Sanders, JSNTSup 148, SSEJC 5 (Sheffield: Sheffield Academic Press, 1997), 79–96; Stanley E. Porter, "Further Comments on the Use of the Old Testament in the New Testament," in *The Intertextuality of the Epistles: Explorations of Theory and Practice*, ed. Thomas L. Brodie, Dennis R. MacDonald, and Stanley E. Porter, NTM 16 (Sheffield: Sheffield Phoenix, 2006), 98–113; Christopher D. Stanley, "The Rhetoric of Quotations: An Essay on Method," in *Early Christian Interpretation of the Scriptures of Israel: Investigations and Proposals*, ed. Craig A. Evans and James A. Sanders, JSNTSup 148, SSEJC 5 (Sheffield: Sheffield Academic Press, 1997), 44–58; Christopher D. Stanley, "Paul's 'Use' of Scripture: Why the Audience Matters," in *As It Is Written: Studying Paul's Use of Scripture*, ed. Stanley E. Porter and Christopher D. Stanley (Atlanta: SBL, 2008), 125–55; Christopher D. Stanley, "'Pearls Before Swine': Did Paul's Audiences Understand His Biblical Quotations?" *NovT* 41 (1999): 124–44; Dennis L. Stamps, "The Use of the Old Testament in the New Testament as a Rhetorical Device: A Methodological Proposal," in *Hearing the Old Testament in the New Testament*, ed. Stanley E. Porter (Grand Rapids: Eerdmans, 2006), 9–37.

102 The question asked by the Pharisees (v. 5) must not be read as a simple request for information. It is, rather, an "ambiguous affront" (an insult put forward "accidentally on purpose" [Malina, *New Testament World*, 40]) aimed at Jesus, though it appears in the form of a question about the behavior of Jesus' disciples (διὰ τί οὐ περιπατοῦσιν οἱ μαθηταί σου κατὰ τὴν παράδοσιν τῶν πρεσβυτέρων, ἀλλὰ κοιναῖς χερσὶν ἐσθίουσιν τὸν ἄρτον;). See also Dvorak, "Ask and Ye Shall Position the Readers," 214–19.

CHAPTER 2

of the elders by not washing their hands prior to eating.[103] A significant point of the riposte includes a strong endorsement through a quotation:

καλῶς ἐπροφήτευσεν Ἡσαΐας περὶ ὑμῶν τῶν ὑποκριτῶν, ὡς γέγραπται ὅτι οὗτος ὁ λαὸς τοῖς χείλεσίν με τιμᾷ, ἡ δὲ καρδία αὐτῶν πόρρω ἀπέχει ἀπ᾽ ἐμοῦ· μάτην δὲ σέβονταί με διδάσκοντες διδασκαλίας ἐντάλματα ἀνθρώπων.

Isaiah *rightly prophesied* about you hypocrites, *as it is written,* "This people honors me with their lips, but their hearts are far from me; they worship me in vain by teaching human precepts as doctrine."

In this instance, Isaiah, a prophet of great significance and figure of authority, is explicitly identified as the source of the quotation.[104] The endorsement of the quoted text is given prominence in many ways. The quotation is construed as something more than a simple saying; it is called prophecy, which implies that although the text was produced at a prior time in a different context, it was in some way uttered to describe the Pharisees whom Jesus was addressing. Further, Isaiah was judged positively for having made the prophecy (καλῶς ἐπροφήτευσεν). Still further, the words of the prophecy were significant enough to be codified in the sacred Scriptures (ὡς γέγραπται). The rhetorical effect of this endorsement is to enervate not only the attack on Jesus' honor but, more importantly, of the value position(s) upon which the attack was based.

2.2.1.3 *PROCLAIM: PRONOUNCE*

In Appraisal Theory, pronouncements are formulations that involve "authorial emphases or explicit interventions or interpretations."[105] These emphases and interventions imply some level of resistance or contrary pressure (e.g., doubt or challenge) against which the writer asserts their own voice.[106] By using pronouncements, a writer "raises their voice," so to speak, in order to be heard above the other voices constituting the heteroglossic background of the

---

103   See Ralph P. Martin, *Mark: Evangelist & Theologian* (Exeter: Paternoster, 1972), 219–20; Christopher M. Tuckett, "Mark," in *The Gospels,* ed. John Muddiman and John Barton, OBC (Oxford: Oxford University Press, 2001), 102–3; Richard T. France, *The Gospel of Mark,* NIGTC (Grand Rapids: Eerdmans, 2002), 276–79; Richard T. France, *Jesus and the Old Testament* (Vancouver: Regent College Publishing, 1998), 68–69; Jerome H. Neyrey, "The Idea of Purity in Mark's Gospel," *Semeia* 35 (1986): 91–128.

104   On the importance of Isaiah in Mark's gospel, see Joel Marcus, *Mark 1–8,* AB 27 (New York: Doubleday, 1999), 139–40; Joel Marcus, "Mark and Isaiah," in *Fortunate the Eyes that See,* ed. Astrid B. Beck (Grand Rapids: Eerdmans, 1995), 449–66.

105   Martin and White, *Language of Evaluation,* 127.

106   Martin and White, *Language of Evaluation,* 128.

"WHAT'S YOUR TAKE?" 73

utterance. The rhetorical impact of pronouncements varies depending upon whom they confront. If the pronouncement confronts the addressee, solidarity is threatened since the writer overtly presents himself as opposed to the value position of the addressee.[107] When this occurs, it is not uncommon for the writer to employ some further dialogic strategy in order to save face and maintain solidarity. Alternatively, when a writer confronts a third party on behalf of the addressees, writer-reader solidarity is built and/or strengthened.[108]

A clear example of pronouncement occurs at Gal 5:2–3 where Paul writes:

> Ἴδε ἐγὼ Παῦλος λέγω ὑμῖν ὅτι ἐὰν περιτέμνησθε, Χριστὸς ὑμᾶς οὐδὲν ὠφελήσει. μαρτύρομαι δὲ πάλιν παντὶ ἀνθρώπῳ περιτεμνομένῳ ὅτι ὀφειλέτης ἐστὶν ὅλον τὸν νόμον ποιῆσαι.

> *Behold, I Paul tell you*: if you are circumcised, Christ will be of no benefit to you. But *I insist*[109] again to every person who receives circumcision that he is obliged to obey the whole law.

Authorial interpolation is manifestly evident in these clauses via the locutions "Behold, I Paul tell you" and "I insist." That these pronouncements occur virtually back-to-back adds to their force (see below on GRADUATION). The first pronouncement is clearly directed toward the readers as indicated by the explicit second person personal pronouns (ὑμῖν and ὑμᾶς) in both the protasis and apodosis of the conditional construction, as well as the second person personal ending of περιτέμνησθε in the protasis. Focus shifts in the second pronouncement from second person ("you") to third person ("every person"), which has the potential effect of lessening the threat to solidarity. At this point, discussion turns from dialogic contraction by way of proclamation to dialogic contraction by way of disclamation.

2.2.1.4 *DISCLAIM: DENY*
Disclamations are formulations whereby a language user invokes other utterances or alternative positions only to explicitly reject, replace, or show them to be unsustainable.[110] As might be expected, key clues for interpreting disclamation include negative polarity and/or the use of negatively charged lexis. As

---

107 Martin and White, *Language of Evaluation*, 130.
108 Martin and White, *Language of Evaluation*, 130.
109 On this meaning for μαρτύρομαι, see L&N 1:391; *ANLEX*, s.v. μαρτύρομαι; Eph 4:17; 1 Thess 2:12; Richard N. Longenecker, *Galatians*, WBC 41 (Waco: Word, 1990), 226.
110 Martin and White, *Language of Evaluation*, 118.

74 CHAPTER 2

with proclamation, disclamation may be realized by means of multiple locutions, one of which is denial.

First John 2:27 provides a straightforward example of denial: οὐ χρείαν ἔχετε ἵνα τις διδάσκῃ ὑμᾶς (You *do not have* any need that anyone should teach you). The writer of 1 John perceived that the readers were in danger of being deceived (see 2:26) into thinking they were in need of additional teaching.[111] The writer invokes the point of view that the readers *do* need someone to instruct them, but then utilizes negative polarity to deny it.

A second example of denial is from Acts 23:9: οὐδὲν κακὸν εὑρίσκομεν ἐν τῷ ἀνθρώπῳ τούτῳ (We find nothing wrong with this person). Here, too, negative polarity is called upon to formulate the denial. The co-text spells out the context of situation: Paul is given a hearing before the Sanhedrin (requested by the Roman commander [Acts 22:30]) regarding the teaching that had previously incited a mob in Jerusalem (Acts 21:27–36). Realizing the council was made up of both Sadducees and Pharisees, Paul claimed that he was under investigation because of his belief and hope in the resurrection (Acts 23:6). This incited an argument among the council members.[112] The Pharisees, who believed in resurrection of the dead, uttered the denial that they could find nothing wrong with Paul that warranted any discipline—a denial of the alternative view presumably held by the Sadducees, who did not believe in resurrection of the dead, that discipline, perhaps even corporal punishment, of Paul was warranted.

2.2.1.5 *DISCLAIM: COUNTER*

As noted, disclamations are formulations in which alternative voices or views are invoked in order to be rejected or replaced. The most congruent realizations in which propositions are replaced or supplanted are concession/counter formulations. Rhetorically, counters are similar to denials in that "they project on to the addressee particular beliefs or expectations or ... particular axiological paradigms"[113] by supplanting and replacing one proposition

---

111   See Colin G. Kruse, *The Letters of John*, PNTC (Grand Rapids: Eerdmans, 2000), 97–109; Raymond E. Brown, *The Epistles of John*, AB 30 (New York: Doubleday, 1982), 359.

112   See Witherington, *Acts*, 690–91. Luke Timothy Johnson (*The Acts of the Apostles*, SP 5 [Collegeville, MN: Liturgical Press, 1992], 400): "At one level, Luke portrays this as a clever rhetorical ploy; Paul sees a way of dividing the assembly and thus extricating himself. But it is also a way of exposing to the reader for the first time the most fundamental issue dividing Paul from his opponents, and Messianists from all non-Messianist Jews: the resurrection of Jesus as the realization of the hope of Israel."

113   Martin and White, *Language of Evaluation*, 121.

"WHAT'S YOUR TAKE?" 75

with another proposition that would not have been expected in its place.[114] Lexicogrammatical cues for recognizing these kinds of locutions include the concessive use of participles and certain kinds of conjunctions/particles such as εἰ or εἰ καί.[115]

Romans 1:22 provides an initial illustration: φάσκοντες εἶναι σοφοὶ ἐμωράνθησαν (*Although claiming* to be the wise ones, they are foolish). Here, the concessive participle introduces the proposed claim that "they" regard themselves as being wise. This view is promptly supplanted and replaced by Paul's counter proposition that, in fact, "they are foolish."[116] A second example may be found at 2 Cor 12:11: οὐδὲν γὰρ ὑστέρησα τῶν ὑπερλίαν ἀποστόλων *εἰ καί* οὐδέν εἰμι (For in no way am I inferior to the 'super-apostles,' *even though* I am nothing). In this example, Paul concedes that he is "nothing"—a notion that perhaps he held of himself or that he perceived his readers held about him[117]—but he counters or supplants this point with the proposition that he was not in any way inferior to any of the other apostles, "super apostles" though they may be.

2.2.2 Dialogic Expansion

Standing opposed to dialogic contraction is dialogic *expansion*. As described above, locutions in this functional category actively make allowances for alternative value positions and voices. The model presented here describes two fundamental means by which dialogic space may be expanded: Consideration and Attribution.

2.2.2.1 CONSIDER

Consideration is concerned with those locutions that indicate that a writer has created greater or lesser degrees of "dialogic space" for alternative "voices" or value positions (when propositions are offered) or alternative action (when proposals are offered), thus considering or entertaining those alternatives.[118]

---

114 See Martin and White, *Language of Evaluation*, 120.

115 For an overview of the concessive use of participles, see Porter, *Idioms*, 191 and Young, *Intermediate New Testament Greek*, 185.

116 The theme of reversal, an important theme in 1 Cor 1–4, is evident here. See James D. G. Dunn, *Romans 1–8*, WBC 38A (Dallas: Word, 1988), 60–61; Douglas J. Moo, *The Epistle to the Romans*, NICNT (Grand Rapids: Eerdmans, 1996), 108.

117 Martin, *2 Corinthians*, 427: "The irony of calling himself 'nothing' is noteworthy. Paul is 'nothing' because he admits his weaknesses and confesses that everything he has is from God. But if Paul were pressed he would admit that to say he is nothing is equivalent to saying that in Christ's power he is everything and more. He is more than the opponents that slur him and not any less than the super-apostles." See also Furnish, *II Corinthians*, 555.

118 Martin and White, *Language of Evaluation*, 104.

This is realized in a number of different ways, including expository or open questions,[119] verbal Mood, modal adjuncts, modal attributes, circumstances of the "in my view" type, evidence/appearance-based postulations of the "it seems, it appears, apparently" type, and certain mental verb/attribute projections.[120]

The last of these (i.e., realizations via mental verb/attribute projections) needs further explanation as well as illustration. First, the term "mental verb" (or mental process) needs definition. These are processes of the "I think" or "I suppose" type (e.g., νομίζω, δοκέω, ἡγέομαι, θαυμάζω). According to Halliday and Matthiessen, these processes function as interpersonal modality metaphors that extend the domain of modality to include explicit indications of subjective and objective evaluation rather than simply providing ideational or informational content for the communicative context.[121] The rhetorical effect of interpersonal metaphors of this kind is to "upgrade" the assessment from group rank so that it extends across the entire clause (or clause nexus if the projection includes a content clause).[122] Second, in Greek these projections tend to appear in one of two basic constructions, either as a single clause or across a primary-secondary clause nexus if the mental projection includes a content clause. When the projection occurs in a single clause, the Complement

---

119 I.e., questions that do not assume a specific response (see Porter, *Idioms*, 276–77; Martin and White, *Language of Evaluation*, 105; Goatly, *Critical Reading and Writing*, 89; Dvorak, "Ask and Ye Shall Position the Readers," 211–12). These kinds of questions serve to raise the possibility that some proposition holds or to bring it into play in the communicative context (e.g., Ὦ ἀνόητοι Γαλάται, τίς ὑμᾶς ἐβάσκανεν; [Gal 3:1], which raises the possibility that the Galatians had, indeed, succumbed to the evil eye [see John H. Elliott, "Paul, Galatians, and the Evil Eye," *CurTM* 17 (1990): 262–73; J. Stafford Wright, "μαγεία," *NIDNTT* 2:359; Jerome H. Neyrey, "Bewitched in Galatia: Paul and Cultural Anthropology," *CBQ* 50 (1988): 72–100; Susan Eastman, "The Evil Eye and the Curse of the Law: Galatians 3.1 Revisited," *JSNT* 83 (2001): 69–87]).

120 See Martin and White, *Language of Evaluation*, 104–45. It is important to make clear that, following Stubbs (*Text and Corpus Analysis*, 196–229) and Martin and White (*Language of Evaluation*, 95), the term "modality" throughout this study is extended far beyond modal verbs (which Hellenistic Greek did not have [Stanley E. Porter, *Verbal Aspect in the Greek of the New Testament, with Reference to Tense and Mood*, SBG 1 (New York: Peter Lang, 1993), 165]) to include *all wordings and formulations by which writers modulate their attachment to or detachment from any given proposition*. This neither stands in conflict with nor is intended to supplant descriptions of verbal Mood that foreground ideational meaning (e.g., Porter, *Verbal Aspect*, 163–77); rather, it intentionally adds an interpersonal perspective (viz., that of evaluation) that has, perhaps, been lacking. See also Fairclough, *Discourse and Social Change*, 158–62.

121 Halliday and Matthiessen, *IFG3*, 626. See Martin and White, *Language of Evaluation*, 21–23, 105.

122 Halliday and Matthiessen, *IFG3*, 626.

"WHAT'S YOUR TAKE?" 77

to the first-person mental process may be an evaluative attribute, an embedded infinitival clause, or both. This clause may or may not be followed up by a secondary clause that provides the cause, ground, or reason for the writer's evaluation.

An example of the single-clause construction appears at Phil 2:25: Ἀναγκαῖον δὲ ἡγησάμην Ἐπαφρόδιτον ... πέμψαι πρὸς ὑμᾶς (I think [it is] necessary to send Epaphroditus to you).[123] In this instance, Paul evaluates as *necessary* the sending of Epaphroditus to Philippi; his subjective assessment, realized as a mental process/attribute projection ἀναγκαῖον δὲ ἡγησάμην, modalizes the embedded clause that functions as an element of the Complement.[124] This clause is followed upon by a causal clause (2:26) that provides the reason for sending him ἐπειδὴ ἐπιποθῶν ἦν πάντας ὑμᾶς καὶ ἀδημονῶν, διότι ἠκούσατε ὅτι ἠσθένησεν [because he has been longing for all of you and is distressed because you heard he was sick]).[125]

At Luke 7:43 one finds an example where a primary and secondary clause nexus is utilized. After having been anointed with perfume by a "sinful woman" and subsequently needing to respond to the thoughts of the Pharisee Simon, Jesus told a parable of a moneylender who forgave the debts of two debtors, one of whom owed a great deal more money than the other (7:40–41).[126] Upon concluding the story, Jesus asked the Pharisee which (former) debtor would love the creditor more (7:42), to which the Pharisee responded ὑπολαμβάνω ὅτι ᾧ τὸ πλεῖον ἐχαρίσατο (I assume the one who had much forgiven more) (7:43). Here the mental process ὑπολαμβάνω (I assume),[127] another explicitly subjective modality metaphor, modalizes the entire content clause ὅτι ᾧ τὸ πλεῖον ἐχαρίσατο (the one who had much forgiven).

2.2.2.2   *ATTRIBUTE*

Whereas realizations of CONSIDER present the writer as the source of an evaluation or proposition/proposal, ATTRIBUTE attends to those formulations whereby a writer separates his or her own voice from a proposition by

---

123   The clause structure, following OpenText.org is: ||^C ⋯ ἀναγκαῖον |^{cj} δὲ |^P ἡγησάμην |⋯ ^{C} [[^{C} Ἐπαφρόδιτον τὸν ἀδελφὸν καὶ συνεργὸν καὶ συστρατιώτην μου |^P πέμψαι |^A πρὸς ὑμᾶς]] ||

124   Grammatically, ἀναγκαῖον and the secondary embedded clause stand in apposition in which the embedded clause further defines the head term ἀναγκαῖον. See OpenText.org word group annotation for this clause (http://www.opentext.org/texts/NT/Phil/view/wordgroup-ch2.vo.html#Phil.w832).

125   See O'Brien, *Philippians*, 333.

126   See now Joel B. Green, *The Gospel of Luke*, NICNT (Grand Rapids: Eerdmans, 1997), 305–15; Darrell L. Bock, *Luke 1:1–9:50*, BECNT (Grand Rapids: Baker, 1994), 689–709.

127   L&N 1:369; *ANLEX*, s.v. ὑπολαμβάνω. See Bock, *Luke 1:1–9:50*, 700–1.

78   CHAPTER 2

attributing it to some external source.[128] This is typically achieved through the grammar of reported speech: framing of propositions via verbal processes (e.g., Titus 1:12: εἶπέν τις ἐξ αὐτῶν ἴδιος αὐτῶν προφήτης [Some prophet from among their own *said* ...]), references to mental processes of others, whether explicitly specified or not (e.g., John 11:13: ἐκεῖνοι δὲ *ἔδοξαν* ὅτι περὶ τῆς κοιμήσεως τοῦ ὕπνου λέγει [But they *thought* that he was talking about ordinary sleep]), or nominalizations of these processes.[129]

There are two subcategories within attribution: ACKNOWLEDGE and DISTANCE. As these two categories indicate, a writer may dissociate their own voice from a proposition for positive or negative purposes. A writer may wish to let another voice they deem to be more authoritative than their own "speak for itself," as in, for example, Scripture quotations/citations.[130] At other times, a writer may wish to bring a proposition into play, but do so in a way that does not necessarily indicate their approval of the value position it represents.[131] This is the basic difference between the subcategories acknowledge and distance.

According to Martin and White, ACKNOWLEDGE attends to "those locutions where there is no overt indication, at least via the choice of framer, as to where the authorial voice stands with respect to the proposition,"[132] and DISTANCE "involves formulations in which, via the semantics of the framer employed, there is an explicit distancing of the authorial voice from the attributed material."[133] Thus, the distinction appears to depend upon the type of framer (i.e., reporting verb) employed by the writer (e.g., *they said* as opposed to *they claimed*).[134] However, this distinction turns more on context and co-text than on the framer itself. While this appears to be the case for English, it is

---

128   Martin and White, *Language of Evaluation*, 111.

129   Geoff Thompson and Ye Yiyun ("Evaluation in the Reporting Verbs Used in Academic Papers," *Applied Linguistics* 12 [1991]: 369) note that reporting opens an "evaluative space" for writer comment. See also Maggie Charles, "Construction of Stance in Reporting Clauses: A Cross-Disciplinary Study of Theses," *Applied Linguistics* 27 (2006): 493.

130   See Stanley, "Rhetoric of Quotations," 56.

131   See Stanley, "Rhetoric of Quotations," 55. See also James R. Martin, "Negotiating Difference: Ideology and Reconciliation," in *Communicating Ideologies*, ed. Martin Pütz, JoAnne Jeff van Aertselaer, and Teun A. van Dijk, DASK 53 (Frankfurt: Peter Lang, 2004), 87–92 on "scribing" as a means of introducing voices into a text. One valuable point he makes is that "quoting constructs the projected voice as more 'authentic' than reporting, since it fashions what is projected as an exact wording; reporting on the other hand simply takes responsibility for the gist of the meaning, not the wording per se—and in this sense it subsumes the voice of the other to some degree" (87).

132   Martin and White, *Language of Evaluation*, 112.

133   Martin and White, *Language of Evaluation*, 113.

134   Martin and White, *Language of Evaluation*, 112–13.

"WHAT'S YOUR TAKE?"   79

undoubtedly true of Greek where, for example, a verb such as λέγεις (he says) may indicate either ACKNOWLEDGE or DISTANCE depending upon the context.[135]

With this caveat in place, examples of both ACKNOWLEDGE and DISTANCE can be identified in the New Testament when context and co-text are taken into account. For example, an instance of ACKNOWLEDGE may be found at 1 Thess 3:6: Ἄρτι δὲ ἐλθόντος Τιμοθέου πρὸς ἡμᾶς ἀφ᾽ ὑμῶν καὶ *εὐαγγελισαμένου ἡμῖν* τὴν πίστιν καὶ τὴν ἀγάπην ὑμῶν (But Timothy has now come to us from you and told us the good news about your faith and love). This text, as with other acknowledgements, is obviously dialogic in that it associates the proposition being advanced (i.e., the Thessalonians are faithful and loving) with an external voice (in this case, that of Timothy), thus "signaling that it is individual and contingent and therefore but one of a range of possible dialogic options."[136] The co-text additionally indicates that the author, Paul, aligns himself with this "external" point of view. This is signaled by means of the positive connotation of the participle εὐαγγελισαμένου (bringing the good news), as well as the fact that the positive attributes πίστιν (faith) and ἀγάπην (love) are ascribed to the readers by a trustworthy companion of Paul.[137]

> Distancing formulations are dialogistically expansive on the same basis as acknowledgements. They explicitly ground the proposition in an individualised, contingent subjectivity, that of some external source. They go somewhat further than acknowledgements in that, in presenting the authorial voice as explicitly declining to take responsibility for the proposition, they maximise the space for dialogistic alternatives.[138]

---

135 With regard to English, Martin and White (*Language of Evaluation*, 113), citing Caldas-Coulthard, argue that the verb "claim" (or its nominalized form "the claim") has a distancing effect by which the author "detaches him/herself from responsibility from what is being reported" (Carmen R. Caldas-Coulthard, "On Reporting Reporting: The Representation of Speech in Factual and Factional Narratives," in *Advances in Written Text Analysis*, ed. Malcolm Coulthard [London: Routledge, 1994], 295). They emphasize, however, that not all uses of "claim" function in this way, varying systematically "under the influence of different co-textual conditions, and across registers, genres and discourse domains" (*Language of Evaluation*, 103). The same holds true for λέγω. E.g., Jas 2:14: Τί τὸ ὄφελος, ἀδελφοί μου, ἐὰν πίστιν *λέγῃ* τις ἔχειν, ἔργα δὲ μὴ ἔχῃ; (What good is it, my brothers and sisters, if someone *claims* to have faith but does not have deeds?), where context allows the English gloss "claims" (see also 2:18). See Moo, *James*, 122.

136 Martin and White, *Language of Evaluation*, 113.

137 See Gene L. Green, *The Letters to the Thessalonians*, PNTC (Grand Rapids: Eerdmans, 2002), 166–68; Wanamaker, *Thessalonians*, 133–34.

138 Martin and White, *Language of Evaluation*, 114.

80   CHAPTER 2

An example of DISTANCE occurs at Acts 11:12: εἶπεν δὲ τό πνεῦμά μοι συνελθεῖν αὐτοῖς μηδὲν διακρίναντα (*The Spirit told me* to go with them and not to make a distinction between them and us [NRSV]). Peter (likely subconsciously) employs distancing attribution as part of his self-defense strategy[139] in regards to his actions in relation to Cornelius and his household. Although he accepted responsibility for teaching Cornelius and his household (v. 15), by saying the Spirit told him to go, he attributes to the Spirit the motivation for his going with the three men from Caesarea to the household of Cornelius. Thus, although he does not deny going to and eating with uncircumcised people, he distances himself from the potentially damaging effects of such a proposition.

2.2.3   Confluence of Expansion and Contraction

There are formulations in which both dialogic expansion and contraction occur and play off one another. Conditional constructions are an example of this. These constructions posit a relationship between some hypothesis and its consequent,[140] and in many cases (if not most) an author's stance and his view of the readers' (or an opponent's) stance are articulated very clearly. Although all classes of conditions may be used for intersubjective positioning, the two most common are first and third class conditions. Ideationally speaking, first class conditions make an assertion for the sake of argument;[141] third class conditions project some hypothetical action or event for consideration.[142] However, the following examples will be considered from an interpersonal perspective:

---

139   That Peter was, indeed, defending himself becomes clear when one understands that 11:2–3 was an accusation of deviance: "Why did you go to uncircumcised men and eat with them?" (v. 3) (see Bruce J. Malina and John J. Pilch, *Social-Science Commentary on the Book of Acts* [Minneapolis: Fortress, 2008], 81; on labeling and deviance theory, see Malina and Neyrey, "Conflict in Luke-Acts," 97–110).

140   Porter, *Idioms*, 255.

141   Rarely, if ever, should first class conditions be glossed "since," as though the condition is true/reality (contra BDF, 188–89; G. B. Winer, *Treatise on the Grammar of NT Greek*, trans. W. F. Moulton [Edinburgh: T & T Clark, 1882], 364). In fact, it may be even too much to say that the first class condition means the condition is *assumed true* for sake of argument (Wallace, *Beyond the Basics*, 690), since the protasis of a condition is "non-factive," committing the language user to neither the truth nor the falsity of the condition (see Lyons, *Semantics*, 2:796; Porter, *Verbal Aspect*, 294). To borrow a criticism from Porter, these interpretations fail to consider the role of verbal attitude (or overinterpret it), in particular the mood of assertion realized by Indicative Mood (*Verbal Aspect*, 292).

142   See Porter, *Idioms*, 254–67 (esp. 262) and Porter, *Verbal Aspect*, 291–320 for discussions of each class of condition.

"WHAT'S YOUR TAKE?" 81

Εἰ ἀπεθάνετε σὺν Χριστῷ ἀπὸ τῶν στοιχείων τοῦ κόσμου, τί ὡς ζῶντες ἐν κόσμῳ δογματίζεσθε;

If you have died with Christ from the basic principles of the world, then why as though living in the world do you submit to those dogmas? (Col 2:20) (a first class condition in conjunction with a rhetorical question)

Μὴ ἀγαπᾶτε τὸν κόσμον μηδὲ τὰ ἐν τῷ κόσμῳ. ἐάν τις ἀγαπᾷ τὸν κόσμον, οὐκ ἔστιν ἡ ἀγάπη τοῦ πατρὸς ἐν αὐτῷ

Do not love the world or the things in the world. If anyone loves the world, the love of the Father is not in that person (1 John 2:15) (a third class condition following a prohibition)

In the first example, the protasis of the first class condition entertains—a means of dialogic expansion—the assertion that the readers had "died with Christ"; however, the rhetorical question in the apodosis indirectly proclaims—a means of dialogic contraction—that the readers are not living in a way that is consonant with having died with Christ, which introduces a point of view that questions whether the readers really had died with him. This is followed up in Col 3:1 with another first class conditional construction (Εἰ οὖν συνηγέρθητε τῷ Χριστῷ, τὰ ἄνω ζητεῖτε), with which Paul overtly begins his attempt to (re-)align his readers to the type of behavior that is valued by the in-group of Jesus followers, which is confirmed by the sudden increase in imperatives in 3:1–4:5.[143]

The second example demonstrates how a third class conditional construction, along with a prohibition,[144] may be used to create distance between two opposing value positions. The prohibition itself, because of its negative polarity (*do **not***) already introduces the writer's negative view with regard to, in this case, *loving the things of the world*.[145] The third class condition (marked by ἐάν + verb in Subjunctive Mood in the protasis [ἐάν τις ἀγαπᾷ τὸν κόσμον]) makes his stance even more emphatic through the hypothetical proclamation that if anyone should happen to love the world,[146] then the love of the Father is not

---

143   See the discussion in Murray J. Harris, *Colossians and Philemon*, EGGNT (Nashville: Broadman & Holman, 2010), 119–71.

144   See now Porter, *Verbal Aspect*, 335–61.

145   The affective process of loving has to do with attachment and loyalty; to love a person or deity is to be bonded to that person or deity, to the exclusion of others (Malina, "Love," *HBSV* 106–9; see also Malina, "Faith/Faithfulness," *HBSV* 61–63).

146   The gloss *should happen to love* reflects hypothetical nature of the condition created by the Subjunctive Mood/projective attitude (ἀγαπᾷ). Subjunctive Mood / projective attitude

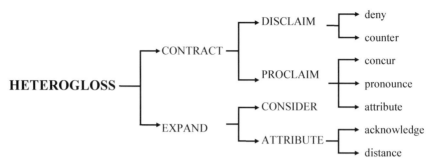

FIGURE 11 The ENGAGEMENT network

in that person (note the shift to Indicative Mood/assertive attitude in the apodosis). This is a clear example of dialogic restriction; no alternative viewpoints are allowed with regard to "loving the world." This type of construction not only depicts the writer as distancing himself from the point of view that finds it possible and/or acceptable to love both the things of the world and God, it effectively disallows the latter point of view from the colloquy.

2.2.4   Summary and Conclusion

The framework described in this section is intended to model the key dialogic effects of the linguistic resources of intersubjective positioning. As mentioned previously, the orientation of the framework defined here is towards meanings in context and their rhetorical effects, rather than towards grammatical forms. Its main purpose is to show how these meanings function to locate the writer with respect to, in Bakhtin's terms, the backdrop of alternative value positions against which all texts operate.[147] The systemic resources, diagrammed in Figure 11, include disclamation, proclamation, consideration, and attribution.

2.3   *The System of* GRADUATION

The third area of the model of appraisal is GRADUATION, which describes the linguistic features employed for up-scaling or down-scaling.[148] These features are interpreted as interpersonal because they "deal with subjective assessments of meaning by degree rather than the categorical distinctions [associated] with the ideational metafunction."[149] It was noted in the introduction

---

        expands dialogic space as it allows alternative voices or actions to enter into consideration. Of course, this opening is severely contracted if not closed completely in the apodosis.

147 Martin and White, *Language of Evaluation*, 94.

148 Martin and White, *Language of Evaluation*, 135; Martin and Rose, *Working with Discourse*, 42–48.

149 Hood and Martin, "Invoking Attitude," 743.

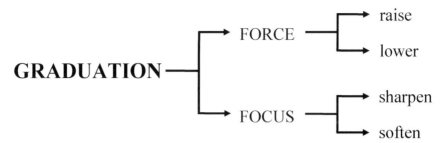

FIGURE 12 Preliminary network of GRADUATION

to this chapter that GRADUATION was a key system in the model because it functions across both the ATTITUDE and ENGAGEMENT domains. It functions across ATTITUDE because a defining property of all three of its subdomains—AFFECT, JUDGMENT, and APPRECIATION—is their gradability; that is, each of these subsystems exhibits greater or lesser degrees of positivity or negativity.[150] Although the meanings that are scaled vary depending upon which of its subsystems is described, gradability is also a general feature of ENGAGEMENT whereby a writer's intensity or degree of investment in a clause may be scaled up or toned down.[151]

GRADUATION is a delicate system, consisting of two subsystems of scalability (see Figure 12). When a language user up-scales or down-scales according to intensity or amount (e.g., ἐθυμώθη λίαν [*very* angry (Matt 2:16)]), they are making selections in terms of FORCE.[152] When they grade according to prototypicality (i.e., according to the precision with which category boundaries are drawn as in τὸ τῆς ἀληθοῦς παροιμίας [the *true* proverb (2 Pet 2:22)]), they are making selections with regard to FOCUS.[153] As these rather straightforward examples illustrate, instances of graduation are typically realized by means of adjectives and adverbs, though other means such as comparative metaphors (e.g., συγκακοπάθησον ὡς καλὸς στρατιώτης [share in suffering *like a good soldier* (2 Tim 2:3)]) may be used.

Rhetorically, selections from GRADUATION play a significant role in writer–reader relationships. When a writer chooses to sharpen focus "the effect is to indicate maximal investment … in the value position (either positive or negative) being advanced and hence to strongly align the reader into the value

---

150 Martin and White, *Language of Evaluation*, 135.
151 Martin and White, *Language of Evaluation*, 135–36.
152 Martin and White, *Language of Evaluation*, 140.
153 Martin and White, *Language of Evaluation*, 137.

position being advanced" (e.g., ἡ *τελεία* ἀγάπη ἔξω βάλλει τὸν φόβον [*Perfect* love casts out fear (1 John 4:18)]).[154] In the case of softening focus where the softened term is negative (or negative polarity is involved), the effect is to lessen the writer's investment in the value position and to offer a "conciliatory gesture" in order to maintain solidarity (γίνεσθε δὲ ποιηταὶ λόγου καὶ μὴ *μόνον* ἀκροαταὶ παραλογιζόμενοι ἑαυτούς [Be doers of the word and not *merely* hearers who deceive themselves (Jas 1:22 NRSV)]).[155] However, in instances where the writer wishes to offer a positive evaluation of a value position that might in some way challenge solidarity, the writer may choose to soften focus in order to lower the threat to solidarity.[156]

The rhetorical effect of FORCE is to increase or decrease the "volume" of the attitude as evaluative prosodies wax and wane across a text. With regard to alignment and solidarity, upscaling attitude tends to construe a writer as maximally committed to the value position being advanced and strongly attempting to align the reader to that value position (e.g., *Ἐχάρην λίαν* ὅτι εὕρηκα ἐκ τῶν τέκνων σου περιπατοῦντας ἐν ἀληθείᾳ [I *rejoiced greatly* because I found some of your children living in the truth (2 John 4)]).[157] Downscaling tends to have the opposite effect of construing the writer as being less than fully committed to the value position (e.g., οὐ μόνον Ἐφέσου ἀλλὰ *σχεδὸν* πάσης τῆς Ἀσίας ὁ Παῦλος οὗτος πείσας μετέστησεν ἱκανὸν ὄχλον [not only in Ephesus but in *almost* all of Asia this Paul has persuaded and led away a considerable crowd (Acts 19:26)]).[158]

2.3.1 *FOCUS*

Scaling with regard to prototypicality is most often applied to categories that from an ideational perspective are "clearly bounded, either-or categories which operate in experiential taxonomies where category membership is more or less precisely determined by some combination of sufficient and necessary conditions."[159] For example, the term χήρα (widow) is the taxonomic designation of a culturally bounded kinship category to which belong women whose husbands have died. Yet this relatively precisely defined category may be reconstrued by means of graduation as in 1 Tim 5:3: χήρας τίμα τὰς ὄντως χήρας

---

154 Martin and White, *Language of Evaluation*, 139.
155 Martin and White, *Language of Evaluation*, 139.
156 Martin and White, *Language of Evaluation*, 140.
157 Martin and White, *Language of Evaluation*, 152.
158 Martin and White, *Language of Evaluation*, 153.
159 Martin and White, *Language of Evaluation*, 137. Note that it is possible to scale up or down an attitudinal—and hence inherently scalable—term with regard to prototypicality as in γνησίως ... μεριμνήσει (*genuinely concerned* [Phil 2:20]).

"WHAT'S YOUR TAKE?" 85

(Honor widows who are *real* widows).[160] In these cases, ideational categories (in this instance χήρα) are reconstrued to an interpersonal semantic with the result that membership in the category "is no longer an either-or proposition but a matter of degree."[161] Thus, one may sharpen the specification to indicate greater prototypicality (as in 1 Tim 5:3, 5) or soften the specification to indicate a more marginal membership in a category or blur apparent categorical distinctions (see the use of τι for these kinds of softening as in ἵνα τι μεταδῶ χάρισμα [so that I might share *some type* of gift (Rom 1:11)]).

Instances of FOCUS may be attitudinally invested.[162] On the one hand, sharpened focus may mark positive attitudinal assessment as in the following example: τὸν μόνον *ἀληθινὸν* θεὸν (the only *true* God [John 17:3]). On the other hand, softened focus may flag negative assessment as in the following example: ἰσχύσαμεν *μόλις* (we were *barely* able [Acts 27:16]). Despite these fairly straightforward examples, interpreters must carefully attend to features of context and co-text within which instances of GRADUATION appear in order to be sure FOCUS is properly interpreted. For example, at 2 Cor 11:5 (see also 2 Cor 12:11) in an apparent conflict with competing apostles, Paul refers to these apostles as "super apostles" (τῶν ὑπερλίαν ἀποστόλων).[163] In this epithet, Paul sharpens focus on ἀποστόλων, but the endued attitude is *not* positive as co-textual features indicate. In v. 2 Paul adopts kinship language to assume the role of a father whose responsibility is to protect with zeal the honor (i.e., her virginity/purity) of his daughter—the role in which he places the readers— whom he has betrothed to Christ.[164] Beginning at v. 3, Paul employs locutions that generate a negative prosody that carries throughout the passage: he "fears" (negative emotion) that as the "serpent deceived Eve" (an ideational token of negative judgment likely regarding Eve's capacity [although a negative judgment of the serpent's action is not ruled out]) the betrothed readers might

---

160 Note that ὄντως is functioning as a definer of the second instance of χήρα in this clause, not as an adverb modifying τίμα (see the word group annotation at OpenText.org). Additionally, it should be noted that "real" in this locution is not opposed to "false" or "phony." Rather, as 1 Tim 5:4–5 makes clear "real" stands opposed to "ordinary" or "typical."

161 Martin and White, *Language of Evaluation*, 138.

162 Martin and White, *Language of Evaluation*, 139.

163 See Nicholas H. Taylor, "Apostolic Identity and Conflicts in Corinth and Galatia," in *Paul and His Opponents*, ed. Stanley E. Porter, PAST 2 (Leiden: Brill, 2005; repr., Atlanta, SBL, 2009), 118–22; and his "Conflict as Context for Defining Identity: A Study of Apostleship in the Galatian and Corinthian Letters," *HTS* 59 (2003): 915–45.

164 For an overview of kinship and marriage in the ancient circum-Mediterranean world, see Malina, *New Testament World*, 134–60 and deSilva, *Honor, Patronage, Kinship & Purity*, 157–239.

likewise be "led astray[165] from a sincere and pure devotion to Christ" (an attitudinal token of negative judgment of the readers' capacity). The negative prosody continues through v. 4 in which Paul asserts for the sake of his argument that if false teachers come along, the readers appear to accept their teachings as valid (καλῶς ἀνέχεσθε); another ideational token of negative judgment of the readers' capacity). The negative prosody created by these features indicates that one should interpret Paul's use of "super apostles" as ironic.[166]

2.3.2 FORCE: INTENSIFICATION

In addition to providing features for grading degrees of prototypicality (FOCUS), the system of GRADUATION provides features for scaling of FORCE in terms of intensity and amount. Assessments of intensity, referred to systemically as INTENSIFICATION (a subsystem of FORCE), operate over linguistic phenomena such as *qualities* (e.g., περισσοτέρως ζηλωτὴς [*extremely* zealous (Gal 1:14)]) and *processes* (e.g., πολὺ πλανᾶσθε [you have been deceived *greatly* (Mark 12:27)]).[167] Assessments of amount, referred to systemically as QUANTIFICATION (a subsystem of FORCE alongside INTENSIFICATION), operate over entities rather than qualities and processes; these allow for imprecise measuring of number (e.g., *few* or *many*) and presence or mass of entities (e.g., small, large, near, far). QUANTIFICATION is discussed below.

2.3.2.1 *Modes of INTENSIFICATION: Isolation*

Assessments of intensity divide into two broad lexicogrammatical classes or modes: *isolating* and *infusing*.[168] According to Martin and White, the distinction "turns on whether the up-scaling/down-scaling is realized by an isolated, individual [lexical] item which solely, or at least primarily, performs the function of setting the level of intensity, or whether the sense of up/down-scaling is fused with a meaning which serves some other semantic function."[169] Isolating intensifications may be realized in a number of ways; Table 10 displays these means along with examples from the New Testament.

---

165 Perhaps "would be seduced" (with overtones of sexual seduction) is a better gloss of φθαρῇ (aorist passive subjunctive third person singular of φθείρω) given the metaphor used in this context. See Furnish, *II Corinthians*, 487; L&N 1:770–1; BDAG, s.v. φθείρω; Diogn. 12:8.

166 It is for this reason a number of English versions place the term in "scare quotes." See NAB, TNIV, NET.

167 Martin and White, *Language of Evaluation*, 140; Martin and Rose, *Working with Discourse*, 44.

168 Martin and White, *Language of Evaluation*, 141.

169 Martin and White, *Language of Evaluation*, 141.

"WHAT'S YOUR TAKE?" 87

TABLE 10 Examples of isolating INTENSIFICATION

Realization	Example
Modification of adjective[a]	ὁ δὲ ἀκούσας ταῦτα περίλυπος ἐγενήθη· ἦν γὰρ *πλούσιος σφόδρα* (But having heard these things, he became very sad, for he was *very wealthy* [Luke 18:23])
Modification of adverb[b]	αὐτοὶ *μᾶλλον περισσότερον* ἐκήρυσσον (they proclaimed *more abundantly* [Mark 7:36])
Up/Down-scaling of processes	οἱ δὲ *περισσῶς* ἔκραζον (but they cried out *excessively* [Matt 27:23])
Comparatives and Superlatives[c]	ἐγὼ δὲ *ἥδιστα* δαπανήσω καὶ ἐκδαπανηθήσομαι ὑπὲρ τῶν ψυχῶν ὑμῶν (I will *most gladly* spend and be expended for your souls [2 Cor 12:15])

a This may include modification of adjectival participles.
b Including adverbial participles.
c Comparatives and superlatives are used for localized or relative scaling.

Some isolating intensifications construe the up-scaling to be at the highest possible intensity; this is referred to as *maximization*.[170] Greek has a number of adjectives and adverbs that may function as maximizers. For example:

– ἐστε *μεστοὶ* ὑποκρίσεως καὶ ἀνομίας (You are *completely full* of hypocrisy and lawlessness[171] [Matt 23:28])
– ἐγὼ δὲ λέγω ὑμῖν μὴ ὀμόσαι *ὅλως* (But I tell you do not swear *at all* [Matt 5:34])
– *ὑπερπερισσῶς* ἐξεπλήσσοντο (They were *utterly* shocked/confused [Mark 7:37])
– πιστὸς ὁ λόγος καὶ *πάσης* ἀποδοχῆς ἄξιος (This message is faithful and worthy of *full* acceptance [1 Tim 1:15])
– *πρὸ πάντων* δέ ... μὴ ὀμνύετε (But *above all* ... do not swear [Jas 5:12]).

Included among these maximizers is the highest value of modal assessment: *always* (ἀεί, πάντοτε, ἀδιαλείπτως). "Often this value operates hyperbolically to convey strong writer/speaker investment in the proposition, rather than any 'literal' sense of constancy or uninterrupted repetition."[172] For example, ἡμεῖς εὐχαριστοῦμεν τῷ θεῷ *ἀδιαλείπτως* (we *unceasingly* give thanks to God [1 Thess 2:13]); *πάντοτε* χαίρετε (*always* rejoice [1 Thess 5:16]).

---

170 Martin and White, *Language of Evaluation*, 142.
171 L&N 1:691.
172 Martin and White, *Language of Evaluation*, 142.

It is noteworthy that only a small set of verbal processes appear to be scalable by means of grammatical intensifiers such as σφόδρα (exceedingly) or πολύς (when functioning adverbially, *greatly*).[173] These include processes conveying attitudinal assessments (ἐφοβήθησαν *σφόδρα* [they were *exceedingly* frightened (Matt 17:6)]); processes of transformation (ἐπληθύνετο ὁ ἀριθμὸς τῶν μαθητῶν ... *σφόδρα* [the number of disciples ... multiplied *greatly* (Acts 6:7)]); and processes of conation (ὃς παραγενόμενος συνεβάλετο *πολὺ* τοῖς πεπιστευκόσιν διὰ τῆς χάριτος [who, upon his arrival, *greatly* helped those who had become believers by grace (Acts 18:27)]).[174]

2.3.2.2 *Modes of INTENSIFICATION: Infusion*

As noted above, with infused INTENSIFICATION scaling is conveyed as one aspect of the meaning of a single term.[175] Lexical items often referred to as "attitudinal lexis" fit under this rubric.[176] These attitudinally-charged lexical items convey intensity as they contrast with other semantically related terms, whether they are lexis of qualities, processes, or modality. Table 11 contains examples of attitudinal lexis in use along with tentative clines of GRADUATION from lesser to greater intensity.[177]

TABLE 11   Attitudinal lexis with tentative clines of INTENSIFICATION

Example	Cline (lesser to greater intensity)
ὅτι *πολύσπλαγχνός* ἐστιν ὁ κύριος (The Lord is *very compassionate* [Jas 5:11])	εὔσπλαγχνος (compassionate) / πολύσπλαγχνος (very compassionate)
περίλυπός ἐστιν ἡ ψυχή μου ἕως θανάτου (My soul is *very distressed*, even to death [Matt 26:38])	λύπη (sad) / περίλυπος (very sad) / ἀγωνία (intense sorrow) / τὴν ψυχὴν διέρχεται ῥομφαία (to feel intense sorrow)
καὶ *ἠγαλλίασεν* τὸ πνεῦμά μου ἐπὶ τῷ θεῷ τῷ σωτῆρί μου (And my spirit *is very happy* in God my savior [Luke 1:47])	ἀγαλλιάω (to be very happy) / σκιρτάω (to be extremely happy; elated)
μόλις γὰρ ὑπὲρ δικαίου τις ἀποθανεῖται (For *rarely* will anyone die for a righteous person [Rom 5:7])	μόλις (rarely/scarcely) / πυκνός (often) / πυκνότερον (more often)

---

173   See Martin and White, *Language of Evaluation*, 145.
174   Possibly also verbal processes: ὁ δὲ ἐξελθὼν ἤρξατο κηρύσσειν πολλὰ (he went out and began to proclaim greatly/freely [Mark 1:45]).
175   Martin and White, *Language of Evaluation*, 143.
176   Martin and Rose, *Working with Discourse*, 44.
177   The clines here are tentative; they are based on L&N entries.

"WHAT'S YOUR TAKE?"   89

2.3.2.3   Modes of INTENSIFICATION: Repetition

INTENSIFICATION is also realized via repetition either of the same lexical item or by means of lists of terms that are related semantically (including synonymy, hyponymy, and meronymy).[178] At Rev 4:8, for example, one finds the *trisagion* ("thrice holy") attributed to God: ἅγιος ἅγιος ἅγιος κύριος ὁ θεὸς ὁ παντοκράτωρ (*Holy, holy, holy* is the Lord God Almighty). The triple repetition serves not only to emphasize God's holy character, but also to bring to a climax the introduction of God into the story of the apocalypse.[179]

Virtue and vice lists provide excellent examples of lists of semantically related terms. Meeks has described the significant role these lists played in the development and maintenance of early Christian morals.[180] As he notes, the function of these lists "is not to name *all* of the wicked things one should eschew or *all* of the good traits one ought to cultivate."[181] Rather, they serve the purpose of *emphasizing* the kinds of behavior/character to avoid or to cultivate. For example, at Col 3:12–13 Paul assembles a string of attitudinal lexical items to emphasize the kind of life the readers ought to live: Ἐνδύσασθε ... σπλάγχνα οἰκτιρμοῦ χρηστότητα ταπεινοφροσύνην πραΰτητα μακροθυμίαν, ἀνεχόμενοι ἀλλήλων καὶ χαριζόμενοι ἑαυτοῖς (... clothe yourselves with *compassion, mercy, goodness, humility, gentleness, patience*, as you *bear with* one another and *forgive* each other).

2.3.3   FORCE: QUANTIFICATION

Another means of scaling FORCE is through QUANTIFICATION. QUANTIFICATION involves scaling with respect to amount (i.e., size, weight, strength, number) and extent, where extent covers elements of time and space (i.e., how recent, how near).[182] The meanings of this subsystem are complex because the quantified entity may be concrete (ἰχθύων μεγάλων [large fish (John 21:11)]) or abstract (χαρᾶς μεγάλης [great joy (Luke 24:52)]). Often, as in the latter example, the abstract entities will express attitudinal meanings.[183]

---

178   Martin and White, *Language of Evaluation*, 144. Repetition and other kinds of elaborating relations are nearly always discussed solely in terms of cohesion (see e.g., Halliday and Matthiessen, *IFG3*, 571–78; Reed, "Cohesiveness of Discourse," 41–43) with little or no attention given to its interpersonal impact (see Geoff Thompson and Jianglin Zhou, "Evaluation and Organization in Text: The Structuring Role of Evaluative Disjuncts," in *Evaluation in Text: Authorial Stance and the Construction of Discourse*, ed. Susan Hunston and Geoff Thompson [Oxford: Oxford University Press, 1999], 122–23).

179   See David E. Aune, *Revelation*, WBC 52A (Nashville: Thomas Nelson, 1997), 276–78, 302–3; Craig S. Keener, *Revelation*, NIVAC (Grand Rapids: Zondervan, 2000), 175.

180   Meeks, *Origins of Christian Morality*, 66–71.

181   Meeks, *Origins of Christian Morality*, 68–69 (italics his).

182   Martin and White, *Language of Evaluation*, 149.

183   Martin and White, *Language of Evaluation*, 150.

Quantifications scale via imprecise reckonings of number (e.g., ὀλίγος [few], πολύς [many]), imprecise measures of mass or presence (e.g., μικρός [small], μέγας [large]; ἐλαφρός [light], βαρύς [heavy]), and imprecise measures of temporality or proximity (e.g., καινός [new, recent], ἀρχαῖος [old, ancient]; ἐγγύς [near], μακρός [distant]) or distribution (e.g., βραχύς [short (of time or distance)], ἱκανός χρόνος [long time], ἰδοὺ δέκα καὶ ὀκτὼ ἔτη [eighteen long years]).[184] Like intensifications of FORCE, quantifications may occur via isolation (e.g., ὄχλος πλεῖστος [large crowd]) or infusion (e.g., ἀσωτίας ἀνάχυσιν [a flood of dissipation]), though isolated terms modifying some graduated entity is typical.

2.3.4 Summary and Conclusion

The system of GRADUATION (Figure 13) describes the options a language user has for increasing or decreasing the "volume" of evaluations (FORCE), as well as sharpening or softening the boundaries of a culturally bounded entity (FOCUS). Variations in scaling contribute to the rhetorical effects of evaluations. Upscaling FORCE or sharpening FOCUS tends to indicate that a writer is maximally invested in the value position being offered. Downscaling FORCE or softening FOCUS of a negative category tends to have the opposite effect of construing a writer as having only partial or even waning investment in the value position. Softening positive values, however, has the effect of decreasing the threat to writer-reader solidarity in those instances where the positive value may, at face value, challenge solidarity.

3 Analytical Procedure

The procedure for the analysis of 1 Cor 1–4 will follow the basic structure of the model presented above. Each unit of text will be analyzed for patterns of ATTITUDE followed by an analysis of ENGAGEMENT. It should be noted that because, as noted above, GRADUATION generalizes across both ATTITUDE and ENGAGEMENT, significant instances of GRADUATION are discussed in conjunction with those instances of ATTITUDE or ENGAGEMENT with which they interact rather than in a section of their own. Attitudinal analysis involves an analysis of the lexicogrammar of each clause in search of attitudinal lexis, participant modification via definers, process modification via circumstantial elements, attitude-infused behavioral and mental processes, and

---

184 Martin and White, *Language of Evaluation*, 151. On the last of these examples, see Luke 13:16 NRSV.

"WHAT'S YOUR TAKE?" 91

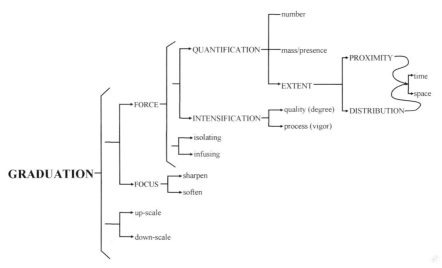

FIGURE 13   The GRADUATION network

grammatical or lexical metaphors that realize values of AFFECT, JUDGMENT, or APPRECIATION. It is determined for each instance whether the feelings are directly inscribed in the text or implied via an ideational token. It is also noted when the attitude is non-authorial (i.e., not the feelings of Paul) and how this impacts the interpersonal meaning of the text.

The analysis and classification of AFFECT applies the six criteria presented above: (1) Are the feelings construed as positive or negative? (2) Are the feelings expressed as a behavioral response or experienced as an internal emotive state? (3) Are the feelings directed toward an external agent or an ongoing emotive state? (4) How intense are the feelings? (5) Are the feelings an intentional response (rather than a reaction) to a real or potential Trigger? (6) Do the feelings reflect (un)happiness, (in)security, or (dis)satisfaction? Instances of AFFECT are annotated beginning with plus (+) or minus (−) symbols to indicate whether or not the feeling is positive or negative. This is followed by the name of the subsystem, AFFECT, and the type of feeling that is realized, separated by a colon. So, for example, + AFFECT: happiness indicates a positive feeling/emotion of happiness.

Selections from ATTITUDE directed toward one's own or others' behavior or character are classified as JUDGMENT. A key analytical difference between AFFECT and JUDGMENT lies in the fact that instances of JUDGMENT are oriented more toward the appraised than the appraiser; that is, values of JUDGMENT, whether inscribed or implied, are portrayed as properties of the one(s) being judged. These values along with their positivity or negativity are used to determine whether the judgment assesses social sanction (i.e., praise-worthiness or blameworthiness) or social esteem (i.e., admiration or criticism). For example, πιστός in πιστὸς ὁ θεός (God is faithful [1 Cor 1:9]) realizes a positive JUDGMENT with regard to God's tenacity and so is a judgment of esteem. Similar to the way AFFECT is annotated, instances of JUDGMENT are annotated with a plus or minus sign to indicate positive or negative feeling followed by the subsystem name, JUDGMENT, and its type separated by a colon. Thus, 1 Cor 1:9 would be annotated + JUDGMENT: tenacity.

Whereas with JUDGMENT feelings are directed toward peoples' behavior, with APPRECIATION feelings are directed toward objects, processes, states of affair, and such (e.g., θρησκεία καθαρὰ καὶ ἀμίαντος [religion that is pure and undefiled] [Jas 1:27]). Human participants are often the objects of appreciation (e.g., 1 Cor 1:26–31), but only where "rightness" and "wrongness" of behavior are not at issue. Instances related to affection as in ἀρεστόν ἐστιν (it is desirable/pleasing) are classified as APPRECIATION: reaction; those focused on perception (one's view of order, including social order) as in τροχιὰς ὀρθάς (straight paths) are classified as APPRECIATION: composition; and those that signify measured opinions as in ἄξια τῆς μετανοίας ἔργα (deeds worthy of repentance) are classified as APPRECIATION: valuation. As with AFFECT and JUDGMENT, appreciations can be positive or negative and are annotated accordingly with plus or minus symbols.

In those instances where an attitude is implied rather than directly inscribed in text, they are identified as tokens. The term *token* is used throughout this study in the sense that something serves as a sign of something else; more specifically, it refers to ideational meanings that indirectly or implicitly evoke or provoke interpersonal meanings even though no explicitly attitudinal evaluative terminology is used. In this study, such tokens are marked by a lower case "t" preceding the annotation for ATTITUDE. For example, "t, + JUDGMENT: tenacity" indicates a "token of positive JUDGMENT of tenacity."

The analysis of ENGAGEMENT aims at characterizing Paul's rhetorical strategies according to whether or not he construes his utterances[185] as heteroglossic (i.e., recognizing other voices value positions) or monoglossic (i.e., not recognizing other voices or value positions). The formulations of dialogic contraction (PROCLAIM, DISCLAIM) and expansion (CONSIDER, ATTRIBUTE) laid out above are used (1) to determine if Paul's utterance is, indeed, heteroglossic[186]

---

185   Often the boundaries of an utterance match those of the clause, but occasionally the scope of an utterance extends to the clause complex (e.g., a cause-consequence nexus).

186   If PROCLAIM, DISCLAIM, CONSIDERATION, or ATTRIBUTION appear, then the text is heteroglossic; otherwise, it is monoglossic.

and (2) to classify more delicately how Paul contracts or expands dialogue with the other voices or value positions that are construed. In cases where none of the formulations of dialogic expansion or contraction occur, the utterance is tagged monoglossic. It is then determined from context—what Martin and White refer to as the "disposition of the text"[187]—whether the monoglossic utterance presents a "given" (i.e., a proposition that is taken for granted as non-contentious) or if it is a point that is up for further discussion or debate. The various instances of ENGAGEMENT are annotated by giving the expansive or contractive type name and a subtype name if one is necessary. For example, the annotation ATTRIBUTE: acknowledge would indicate an instance where Paul has expanded the dialogic nature of the text by bringing in some external voice (ATTRIBUTION) and aligns himself with it (ACKNOWLEDGEMENT).

The discussion of each unit of text concludes with a brief summary of how the patterns of ATTITUDE and ENGAGEMENT interact to construe Paul's stance toward the topic at hand and how they contribute to Paul's goal of (re-)aligning the readers to an ideology that is both founded upon and demonstrated through the cross. It must be noted that although every instance of ATTITUDE and ENGAGEMENT contributes to the achievement of this interpersonal goal, reporting on every single instance is prohibited by boundaries of space. Therefore, the analyses offered in the following chapters describe those instances and patterns of ATTITUDE and ENGAGEMENT that bear most significantly on Paul's goal of resocializing the intended audience.

Finally, a note must be made regarding the divisions of 1 Cor 1–4 for analysis. The basic division in the subsequent chapters generally follow the paragraph divisions found in the Nestle-Aland 28th edition Greek New Testament. However, these divisions were tested, first, against criteria developed by epistolary theorists[188] to establish major sections (e.g., greeting, thanksgiving, body) and, second, against criteria established by Porter, Porter and O'Donnell, Reed, and Westfall to establish smaller units.[189]

---

187   Martin and White, *Language of Evaluation*, 101.
188   Primarily John L. White, *Light from Ancient Letters*, FF (Philadelphia: Fortress, 1986).
189   See Porter, "Pericope Markers"; Porter and O'Donnell, *Discourse Analysis*; Reed, *Philippians*; and Westfall, *Hebrews*.

CHAPTER 3

"Tell Us How You Really Feel, Paul!" (Part 1)

An Appraisal Analysis of 1 Cor 1:1–2:16

1 Introduction

Attention is now turned to the analysis of 1 Cor 1–4. The goal of this analysis is to explore how Paul, through localized instances of APPRAISAL, takes up stances relative to the entities, propositions, or proposals[1] referenced in the text. As established in chapter 1, these stances are not to be thought of as mere expressions of Paul's attitudes as though their purpose is simply to inform the readers about Paul's feelings and opinions; rather, they should be seen as instrumental in reader alignment. From a social semiotic point of view, the adoption and inscription of stance is the most significant means of constructing an axiological framework for a community. Thus, through the taking up of stances Paul construes and constructs the system of values by which members of the ἐκκλησία in Corinth ought to evaluate what, for the community, is normal and deviant, beneficial and harmful, praiseworthy and blameworthy, and so on. The present study sets out to describe how Paul achieves this social task linguistically.

2 To Corinth with Love: The Letter Opening and Thanksgiving (1 Cor 1:1–9)

2.1 *The Letter Opening (1 Cor 1:1–3)*
Letter openings or greetings serve several related purposes. First, they introduce the main participants to be involved in the communicative event and their basic discursive roles such as sender(s), co-sender(s), and intended recipient(s).[2] Second, greetings serve the philophronetic purpose of generating friendly contact between the recipients primarily by extending greetings

---

1 In SFL, the term *proposition* refers to the semantic function of a clause in the exchange of information (i.e., statements, questions); *proposal* refers to the semantic function of a clause in the exchange of goods and services (i.e., offers, demands/commands). See Halliday and Matthiessen, *IFG3*, 110–11.

2 Peter T. O'Brien, "Letters, Letter Forms," *DPL*, 551.

© JAMES D. DVORAK, 2021 | DOI:10.1163/9789004453814_004

from sender to recipient.[3] Finally, and most important for the current study, greetings serve the interpersonal purpose of initially positioning the communicative participants mainly through the enactment of roles.[4] As will be shown, in the letters of Paul, elaborations on the writer and reader roles meet all these purposes, but especially the last one. Selections from both ATTITUDE and ENGAGEMENT are made to enact and support status relations in the text between the writer and putative addressees. That will be the case with the opening of canonical 1 Corinthians in which Paul creates an attitudinal disposition naturalizing his role as an apostle and the readers' role as the church which God had called him to plant and to maintain.

2.1.1   Attitudinal Analysis

In the prescript, Paul defines himself as an ἀπόστολος (apostle). Although this term bore significant, positive semiotic weight among the early Christians, for whom it named a specially commissioned emissary or envoy,[5] it appears that not everyone at Corinth was willing to acknowledge Paul in this role (cf. 1 Cor 9:1–2).[6] This may have been what motivated Paul to further elaborate ἀπόστολος with the adjective κλητός (κλητὸς ἀπόστολος [a called apostle]). Syntactically, κλητὸς ἀπόστολος (adjective^substantive)[7] is ambiguous: it could be interpreted either as an attributive structure (4th position) or as a predicate structure. The former would be glossed *a called apostle* and the latter something like *an apostle who is called*. The former attributes the feature of "called-ness" to *apostle*; the latter ascribes "called-ness" to *apostle* or asserts that *apostle* is *called*. The former reading is preferred here, but interpersonally either reading

---

3   Dennis L. Stamps, "A Literary-Rhetorical Reading of the Opening and Closing of 1 Corinthians" (PhD diss., University of Durham, 1994), 236–37.

4   See Philip L. Tite, "How to Begin and Why?" in *Paul and the Ancient Letter Form*, ed. Stanley E. Porter and Sean A. Adams, PAST 6 (Leiden: Brill, 2010), 59. Tite comes at the text from a rhetorical-critical perspective, though he draws on positioning theory (see Luk van Langenhove and Rom Harré, "Introducing Positioning Theory," in *Positioning Theory*, ed. Luk van Langenhove and Rom Harré [Oxford: Blackwell, 1999], 14–31). See also Stamps, "Literary-Rhetorical Reading," 253; Philip L. Tite, "The Compositional Function of the Petrine Prescript: A Look at 1 Pet 1:1–3," *JETS* 39 (1996): 47–56.

5   See Müller, "ἀποστέλλω," *NIDNTT* 1:128–34; Meeks, *First Urban Christians*, 131–12; Stamps, "Literary-Rhetorical Reading," 258.

6   Gordon D. Fee (*The First Epistle to the Corinthians*, NICNT [Grand Rapids: Eerdmans, 1987], 6, 28) maintains that the Corinthians stood at odds with Paul and called into question his apostleship. However, see Scott J. Hafemann, "Corinthians, Letters to the," *DPL*, 174; Oster, *1 Corinthians*, 19–21; Jerry L. Sumney, "Studying Paul's Opponents: Advances and Challenges," in *Paul and His Opponents*, ed. Stanley E. Porter, PAST 2 (Leiden: Brill, 2005; repr., Atlanta: SBL, 2009), 13–14; Taylor, "Apostolic Identity," 115.

7   The caret (^) means "followed by."

96   CHAPTER 3

would function to position the readers to appraise Paul positively. Co-text suggests the definer is attitudinally invested. In terms of graduation, it may be interpreted as sharpening the focus of ἀπόστολος in terms of prototypicality (GRADUATION: FOCUS): Paul portrays himself as no "ordinary" apostle, but as a *called* apostle. Working together with the qualifier Χριστοῦ Ἰησοῦ and the prepositional phrase διὰ θελήματος θεοῦ (through the will of God),[8] κλητός depicts Paul's apostolic role as divinely ordained.[9] Moreover, the prepositional phrase infuses the "called-ness" of Paul's apostleship with divine intention or purpose. This both naturalizes and warrants a positive appraisal of Paul both *as* an apostle of Christ Jesus and *because* he is an apostle of Christ Jesus (t, + JUDGMENT: ESTEEM: normality).[10] This has significant interpersonal ramifications with regard to attitudinal positioning. Because of the way it is portrayed, any negative evaluation of Paul as an apostle would be tantamount to resisting or rejecting God's will.

After introducing the co-sender of the letter, Sosthenes[11]—who is also appraised positively as *brother* (ἀδελφός) (t, + JUDGMENT: ESTEEM: normality)—Paul names the readers-in-the-text collectively as an ἐκκλησία τοῦ θεοῦ.[12] With this epithet, Paul construes the readers as having lower status

---

8   The prepositional group plays off the implied passive sense of κλητός (see C. F. D. Moule, *An Idiom Book of New Testament Greek*, 2nd ed. [Cambridge: Cambridge University Press, 1959], 95–96) to indicate the divine agency of the call. See A. T. Robertson and Alfred Plummer (*A Critical and Exegetical Commentary on the First Epistle to the Corinthians*, ICC [Edinburgh: T & T Clark, 1999], 1 [hereafter *I Corinthians*]) who translate: "Paul, a *divinely chosen* Apostle...." See also Frederic L. Godet, *Commentary on First Corinthians*, trans. A. Cusin (Edinburgh: T & T Clark, 1889; repr., Grand Rapids: Kregel, 1977), 37–38; David E. Garland, *1 Corinthians*, BECNT (Grand Rapids: Baker, 2003), 25.

9   See Tucker, *You Belong to Christ*, 32; Fee, *First Epistle*, 28–29. In Paul's writings, κλητός (as well as καλέω and κλῆσις) is nearly always used to refer to divine stationing (see Lothar Coenen, "καλέω," *NIDNTT* 1:275; Jost Eckert, "καλέω," *EDNT* 2:242). Exceptions to this are Rom 9:7, 25, 26 (all quotations from the LXX) (but see Moo, *Romans*, 530 n 126); 1 Cor 10:27; 15:9.

10   By way of reminder, a lowercase "t" preceding the annotation signals that the instance is an attitudinal *token* (i.e., the attitude is implied, not directly inscribed).

11   On co-senders, see Sean A. Adams, "Paul's Letter Opening and Greek Epistolography," in *Paul and the Ancient Letter Form*, ed. Stanley E. Porter and Sean A. Adams, PAST 6 (Leiden: Brill, 2010), 40–44. On Sosthenes, see Anthony C. Thiselton, *The First Epistle to the Corinthians*, NIGTC (Grand Rapids: Eerdmans, 2000), 69 (hereafter *First Corinthians*). On the significance of the term ἀδελφός and ἀδελφή (see 7:15; 9:5) relative to the social institution of kinship and the cultural value of family-centeredness, see Mark McVann, "Family-Centeredness," *HBSV* 64–67; Joseph H. Hellerman, *The Ancient Church as Family* (Minneapolis: Augsburg Fortress, 2001), 27–58, 59–91; deSilva, *Honor, Patronage, Kinship & Purity*, 157–97, 199–239.

12   On ἐκκλησία in Paul, see Meeks, *First Urban Christians*, 107–10.

than he. This enacts a discursive relationship in which "Paul-in-the-text," as the apostle "over them," may demand and expect respect from the readers-in-the-text.[13] Paul qualifies ἐκκλησία with τοῦ θεοῦ (of God). Although many scholars interpret this qualifier as a (subtle) strike against some number of arrogant patrons in the assembly (t, – JUDGMENT: SANCTION: propriety),[14] given the philophronetic nature of the letter opening, it is highly unlikely such a negative appraisal is intended at this point in the letter.[15] More likely the qualifier simply distinguishes the readers' group from every other ἐκκλησία (e.g., workers guild, court) in Corinth. They are special because they belong to God (t, + JUDGMENT: ESTEEM: normality).[16]

Paul further defines the ἐκκλησία with ἡγιασμένοις ἐν Χριστῷ Ἰησου (sanctified in Christ Jesus) and κλητοῖς ἁγίοις (called holy ones/saints).[17] Experientially,

---

13   As Paul sees it, a local church falls under the authority of the apostle(s) who was called by God (or Christ Jesus) to represent him and to proclaim his message to that church (see Meeks, *First Urban Christians*, 131–13). Paul was that apostle to the Corinthian church, since it was he who first took the gospel to them and established the group there (see Acts 18; 1 Cor 3:6, 10; 4:15). For this reason he may demand their respect and expect obedience (see Jerome H. Neyrey, "Group Orientation," *HBSV* 82).

14   For the basic contours of this position, consult the following sources: Gerd Theissen, "Social Stratification in the Corinthian Community: A Contribution to the Sociology of Early Hellenistic Christianity," in *The Social Setting of Pauline Christianity*, ed. and trans. John H. Schütz (Philadelphia: Fortress, 1982), 69–119, 121–43; Meeks, *First Urban Christians*, 51–73; Abraham J. Malherbe, *Social Aspects of Early Christianity*, 2nd ed. (Eugene, OR: Wipf & Stock, 2003), 29–59; David A. deSilva, "'Let the One Who Claims Honor Establish That Claim in the Lord': Honor Discourse in the Corinthian Correspondence," *BTB* 28 (1998): 62–63; Stephen M. Pogoloff, *Logos and Sophia: The Rhetorical Situation of 1 Corinthians*, SBLDS 134 (Atlanta: Scholars Press, 1992), 113; Martin, *Corinthian Body*, 47–52; Robert S. Dutch, *The Educated Elite in 1 Corinthians: Education and Community Conflict in Graeco-Roman Context*, JSNTSup 271 (London: T & T Clark, 2005), 215–98); Edwin A. Judge "The Social Pattern of the Christian Groups in the First Century," in *Social Distinctives of the Christians in the First Century: Pivotal Essays by E. A. Judge*, ed. David M. Scholer (Peabody: Hendrickson, 2008), 43; Thiselton, *First Corinthians*, 73; John K. Chow, *Patronage and Power: A Study of Social Networks in Corinth*, JSNTSup 75 (Sheffield: Sheffield Academic Press, 1992), 113–90; Ben Witherington, III, *Conflict & Community in Corinth: A Socio-Rhetorical Commentary* (Grand Rapids: Eerdmans, 1998), 19–35.

15   See Stamps, "Literary-Rhetorical Reading," 252–53.

16   See Chrysostom, *Hom. 1 Cor.* 1:1. See Thiselton, *First Corinthians*, 73; Garland, *1 Corinthians*, 27; Raymond F. Collins, *First Corinthians*, SP 7 (Collegeville, MN: Liturgical Press, 1999), 45; Robert S. Nash, *1 Corinthians*, SHBC (Macon, GA: Smyth & Helwys, 2009), 60.

17   See the OpenText.org word group annotation (http://www.opentext.org/texts/NT/1Cor/view/wordgroup-ch1.v0.html#1Cor.w14). See also Robertson and Plummer, *I Corinthians*, 2; Margaret M. Mitchell, *Paul and the Rhetoric of Reconciliation: An Exegetical Investigation of the Language and Composition of 1 Corinthians* (Tübingen: Mohr Siebeck, 1991), 193 n 35; Garland, *1 Corinthians*, 27; Thiselton, *First Corinthians*, 76–77; Joseph A. Fitzmyer, *First Corinthians*, AB 32 (New Haven: Yale University Press, 2008), 126.

the cognate terms ἡγιασμένοις and ἁγίοις signify the readers' *condition* as believers in Jesus and members of the ἐκκλησία rather than the process of the formation of their moral character.[18] The adjectival participle ἡγιασμέ-νοις prominently depicts[19] the readers as dedicated to God[20] because of what God has done *through Christ Jesus*.[21] For Paul to call the readers *sanctified* is to admire them for the special status they have before God through Christ Jesus (t, +JUDGMENT: ESTEEM: normality). The term ἅγιος "marks the fundamental identity of the Christian assembly."[22] As used here, the term is not an ethical expression *per se* but a means of positively identifying believers with an assem-bly belonging to God and bound together by the Holy Spirit.[23] The definer κλη-τοῖς has the effect of imbuing the readers' holy/dedicated status with a sense of divine calling and purpose.[24] Like *sanctified, holy ones/saints* depicts a special status and betokens positive evaluation (t, +JUDGMENT: ESTEEM: normality). Additionally, the use of the cognate terms (ἡγιασμένοις and ἅγιος) has an effect

---

18   Contra Witherington (*Conflict & Community*, 80) who asserts that "the stress here is probably on behavior." On holiness and sanctification as condition or process, see Stanley E. Porter, "Holiness, Sanctification," *DPL*, 397–402. See also Thiselton, *First Corinthians*, 76.

19   The participle, a perfect tense-form, grammaticalizes stative aspect and, thus, conveys "being dedicated," from Paul's point of view, as a state of affairs or condition (see Porter, *Verbal Aspect*, 256–59). Additionally, the perfect tense-form is the most prominent of the tense-forms (see Porter, *Verbal Aspect*, 245–51).

20   See Fitzmyer (*First Corinthians*, 126) who rightly recognizes that ἡγιασμένοις κτλ. speaks to the "dedicated status" of the Corinthian believers. See also L&N 1:538.

21   It is possible that ἐν Χριστῷ is locative, indicating the sphere in which they as sanctified ones now belong (*in Christ*). More likely, however, following the passive participle the phrase is instrumental meaning "by what God has accomplished through Christ Jesus" (Fee, *First Epistle*, 32 n 20) or "by Christ Jesus." First Corinthians 6:9–11 may provide insight into what Paul may have had in mind here. At 6:9–10, one finds a vice list that charac-terizes various kinds of wrongdoers (ἄδικοι) who will not inherit the kingdom of God (vv. 9–11)—the kinds of people, Paul says, the readers once were (καὶ ταῦτά τινες ἦτε; v. 11a). He then reminds them of their conversion with three successive contrastive clauses: ἀλλ' ἀπελούσασθε, ἀλλ' ἡγιάσθητε, ἀλλ' ἐδικαιώθητε ... (but you were washed, [but] you were sanctified, [but] you were justified ...). See Fee, *First Epistle*, 32; Meeks, *Origins of Christian Morality*, 33–36 (esp. 34).

22   Garland, *1 Corinthians*, 27. See Horst Seebass, "ἅγιος," *NIDNTT* 2:229. Hans Conzelmann, *1 Corinthians: A Commentary on the First Epistle to the Corinthians*, ed. George W. MacRae, trans. James W. Dunkly, Hermeneia (Philadelphia: Fortress, 1975), 22–23: "Holiness is not a quality of the individual, but a communal state in which we are placed by baptism."

23   See Seebass, *NIDNTT* 2:229.

24   In fact, Seebass (*NIDNTT* 2:229) says that *holy ones/saints* (ἅγιοι) is "parallel" to concepts like "called," "elect," and "faithful." See Fee, *First Epistle*, 33.

"TELL US HOW YOU REALLY FEEL, PAUL!" (PART 1)   99

similar to repetition[25] in that together they increase the force or intensity of Paul's evaluation of the readers (GRADUATION: FORCE: intensification).

The greeting section closes with the greeting proper (v. 3): χάρις ὑμῖν καὶ εἰρήνη ἀπὸ θεοῦ πατρὸς ἡμῶν καὶ κυρίου Ἰησοῦ Χριστοῦ (Grace to you and peace from God our father and from the Lord Jesus Christ).[26] Interpersonally, this "wish-prayer"[27] enhances solidarity between Paul and the readers. Wishing or praying χάρις and εἰρήνη upon the addressees demonstrates the affection Paul feels toward them (t, + AFFECT: happiness), which are likely intended to evoke reciprocal feelings toward Paul.

2.1.2   Engagement Analysis

The letter opening (vv. 1–3) is entirely monoglossic, which is not surprising since its basic interpersonal function is to identify the communicants and to establish the basic discursive roles of each (i.e., the apparent author/writer, co-sender, and recipients); the elaborations of the greeting[28] function discursively to position those participants.[29] That is, the expanded greeting enacts in the text the fundamental social relationship that will condition and constrain the interaction between Paul and the readers throughout the remainder of the letter, namely that Paul is the apostle (ἀπόστολος) to the assembly (ἐκκλησία) in Corinth of which the ostensible addressees are members.[30] By enacting this relationship, Paul takes up a position of status/power in the

---

25   On the interpersonal effects of repetition and synonymy in discourse, see Deborah Tannen, *Talking Voices*, Studies in Interactional Sociolinguistics, 2nd ed. (Cambridge: Cambridge University Press, 2007), 48–101 (fosters interaction); Poynton, *Language and Gender*, 80 (amplification); Martin and White, *Language of Evaluation*, 144–45 (GRADUATION: FORCE: intensification).

26   On the greeting proper, see Adams, "Paul's Letter Opening," 45–55; Thiselton, *First Corinthians*, 81–82; Fee, *First Epistle*, 34–35; Stanley E. Porter, "Peace, Reconciliation," *DPL* 699.

27   Thiselton, *First Corinthians*, 81; Gordon P. Wiles, *Paul's Intercessory Prayers: The Significance of the Intercessory Prayer Passages in the Letters of St. Paul*, SNTSMS 24 (Cambridge: Cambridge University Press, 1974), 140–41 (Wiles calls it a "blessing"). See also Fitzmyer, *1 Corinthians*, 128; Garland, *1 Corinthians*, 29–30.

28   On the basic formula, see Francis X. J. Exler, *The Form of the Ancient Greek Letter of the Epistolary Papyri (3rd c. B.C.–3rd c. A.D.): A Study in Greek Epistology* (Chicago: Ares, 1976), 13–68; Adams, "Paul's Letter Opening," 39, 45–48. On Paul's expansion of the greeting, see Stamps, "Literary-Rhetorical Reading," 188–251; Hafemann, "Corinthians," 164; O'Brien, "Letters," 551; White, *Light*, 198–200.

29   See Tite, "How to Begin," 59.

30   Of course, writers enact discursive relations throughout an entire text, not just in the address; thus, Wire is correct to say, "From the first word ... to the last lines of the fourth chapter ... Paul is presenting himself to [the Corinthians]" (Antoinette Clark Wire, *The Corinthian Women Prophets* [Eugene, OR: Wipf & Stock, 2003], 39). That said, many relationships and roles that are enacted in text lose salience or even terminate as the text

100   CHAPTER 3

relationship, which is required if he is to gain a hearing among the readers, especially because his purpose is to reorient their thinking and behavior.[31] To this end he employs the grammar of definition and naming,[32] which tend to "monologize" text by presenting propositions without reference to any dialogic alternatives.[33] Propositions are presented as "the way it is" and in cases where the disposition of the text is not argumentative (as in letter greetings like the one here) may be "taken-for-granted."[34] This, in terms of dialogic positioning,

---

continues to unfold, but the relationship enacted in the prescript tends to remain intact until the discourse itself ends.

31   This is especially crucial for exposition/argumentation in moral discourse (see Perelman and Olbrechts-Tyteca, *New Rhetoric*, 16; Wire, *Corinthian Women Prophets*, 9–11). Undoubtedly, this will raise the oft-discussed question regarding (the rhetoric of) power that occupies a central place in much of the recent literature on the nature of Paul's apostleship. On this topic consult the following works, which are by no means univocal: Michel Foucault, "The Subject and Power," in *Michel Foucault: Beyond Structuralism and Hermeneutics*, ed. H. Dreyfus and P. Rabinow (Chicago: University of Chicago Press, 1982), 208–26; Joyce E. Bellous, "Foucault, Michel," in *Dictionary of Biblical Criticism and Interpretation*, ed. Stanley E. Porter (New York: Routledge, 2007), 120–21; Castelli, *Imitating Paul*, 21–58; Charles A. Wanamaker, "A Rhetoric of Power: Ideology and 1 Corinthians 1–4," in *Paul and the Corinthians: Studies on a Community in Conflict: Essays in Honour of Margaret Thrall*, ed. Trevor J. Burke and J. Keith Elliott (Leiden: Brill, 2003), 115–37; Francis H. Agnew, "The Origin of the NT Apostle-Concept: A Review of the Research," *JBL* (1986): 75–96; Karl H. Rengstorf, "ἀπόστολος," *TDNT* 407–45; John Andrew Kirk, "Apostleship Since Rengstorf: Toward a Synthesis," *NTS* 21 (1975): 249–64; Müller, *NIDNTT* 128–35; Rudolf Schnackenburg, "Apostles Before and During Paul's Time," in *Apostolic History and the Gospel*, ed. W. Ward Gasque and Ralph P. Martin (Grand Rapids: Eerdmans, 1970), 287–303; John H. Schütz, *Paul and the Anatomy of Apostolic Authority*, NTL (Louisville: Westminster John Knox, 2007), 22–34; Thiselton, *First Corinthians*, 64–68 and 666–73; Ernest Best, "Paul's Apostolic Authority—?," *JSNT* 27 (1986): 11; Garland, *1 Corinthians*, 24–25; Bruce W. Winter, *Philo and Paul among the Sophists*, SNTSMS 96 (Cambridge: Cambridge University Press, 1997); Taylor, "Apostolic Identity," 99; Meeks, *First Urban Christians*, 131; John J. Pilch, "Power," *HBSV* 137–39; Bruce J. Malina, "Authoritarianism," *HBSV* 9–14; John J. Pilch, "Domination Orientation," *HBSV* 42–43.

32   On naming, see Poynton, *Language and Gender*, 12–14; Fairclough, *Analysing Discourse*, 88–89.

33   See Martin and White, *Language of Evaluation*, 99; Sook Hee Lee, "An Integrative Framework for the Analyses of Argumentative/Persuasive Essays from an Interpersonal Perspective," *Text & Talk* 28 (2008): 245–47; Gary S. Morson and Caryl Emerson, *Mikhail Bakhtin: Creation of a Prosaics* (Stanford, CA: Stanford University Press, 1990), 56–59.

34   See Martin and White, *Language of Evaluation*, 98–102; Anne-Marie Simon-Vanderbergen, Peter R. R. White, and Karin Aijmer, "Presupposition and 'Taking-for-Granted' in Mass Communicated Political Argument," in *Political Discourse in the Media*, ed. Anita Fetzer and Gerda Eva Lauerbach (Amsterdam: John Benjamins, 2007), 31–74; Susan Hunston, "Evaluation and the Planes of Discourse," in *Evaluation in Text: Authorial Stance and Construction of Discourse*, ed. Susan Hunston and Geoff Thompson (Oxford: Oxford University Press, 1999), 176–207, esp. 184–86.

is a very powerful means of reader positioning, of naturalizing a reading position and/or building solidarity.[35]

2.1.3 Summary

From an interpersonal perspective, the address and greeting is an indispensable act of discursive positioning. The language Paul puts to work in the address is clearly philophronetic and serves the purpose of building solidarity with the readers. It is here that Paul enacts the apostle-church relationship, in which he takes up the position of status/power necessary for making claims on the lives of the readers. The grammar of definition and naming dominates the entire unit (vv. 1–3) resulting in monoglossic text; Paul simply portrays himself, the readers, and their relationship as "the way it is." This naturalizes a reading position in which the readers acknowledge that Paul, indeed, has the status to give them moral guidance, and that they should accept the guidance he gives. As a means of building solidarity, Paul employs positive appraisal, construing the readers as *dedicated to God* and as *called saints*. He also extends a greeting to them in the form of a wish-prayer in which he prays grace and peace to be upon them. This generates a positive prosody that will continue to reverberate into the next unit of text.

2.2 *Thanksgiving (1 Cor 1:4–9)*

The thanksgiving period is even more forwardly philophronetic than the letter greeting. Its main purpose is to build solidarity between the writer and readers. The attitudinal evaluations made in this section generate a positive disposition toward the readers and increase the probability that the readers will think positively of Paul as well. Interestingly, the positive evaluations of the readers are indirect, implied in ideational tokens that describe what God has done for them. Thus, for example, when Paul says the readers have been made rich, the passive voice suggests the readers are rich not by any machination of their own, but by the work of God, which is a positive appreciation of the readers that gets mediated through thanksgiving to God. Like the letter opening, much of the thanksgiving period is monoglossic in that Paul speaks categorically without acknowledging alternative voices or points of view that may exist (except for the single use of the future form in v. 8).

---

35   See Goatly, *Critical Reading and Writing*, 90 on assertiveness.

102   CHAPTER 3

2.2.1   Attitudinal Analysis

With the principal verb of the thanksgiving section, εὐχαριστῶ (I thank), Paul directly inscribes[36] his feelings of gratitude[37] (+ AFFECT: satisfaction) for the readers (περὶ ὑμῶν [for you]).[38] By revealing his emotions he seeks to establish solidarity with the readers such that they will understand why he feels the way he does, find it to be valid and significant, and join him in feeling the same way about whatever triggered the emotion.[39] Significantly, neither the readers nor their accomplishments triggered Paul's gratitude; rather, the trigger is clearly what God had accomplished for the readers. Several textual features make this both obvious and emphatic. First, Paul directs his feelings of gratitude towards God (εὐχαριστῶ τῷ θεῷ) rather than towards the readers. Second, Paul states clearly that he gives thanks based on[40] *the benefaction*[41] *of God that has been given to [the readers] through Christ Jesus* (εὐχαριστῶ ... ἐπὶ τῇ χάριτι τοῦ θεοῦ τῇ δοθείσῃ ὑμῖν ἐν Χριστῷ Ἰησοῦ). Third, the prevalent use of passive voice throughout the thanksgiving,[42] especially in the clause stating the reason for his emotional reaction (v. 5: ὅτι ... ἐπλουτίσθητε ... [because ... you have been made rich ...]), shifts both the responsibility of the depicted actions and any praiseworthiness attached to them away from the readers and to the Agent, God. Additionally, there are only two active verbs in the thanksgiving unit, namely εὐχαριστῶ (v. 4) of which Paul is the subject/Actor, and the future form βεβαιώσει (v. 8) of which God is the subject/Actor. The readers (plural "you")

---

36   That the verb is first person singular indicates Paul takes responsibility for the attitudinal assessment that it inscribes. Incidentally, this is also the first finite verb in 1 Cor.

37   See L&N 1:428–29.

38   Note that all further instances of ATTITUDE in the thanksgiving period are realized indirectly, betokened by ideational figures.

39   See White, "Appraisal: An Introduction."

40   The preposition ἐπί is governed by the dative case of its head term (τῇ χάριτι) and, therefore, portrays *the benefaction of God* as the basis of thanksgiving. See Young, *Intermediate New Testament Greek*, 97; Moule, *Idiom Book*, 50; Nigel Turner, *Syntax*, vol. 3 of *A Grammar of New Testament Greek*, by James Hope Moulton, 4 vols. (Edinburgh: T & T Clark, 1908–1976), 271.

41   On rendering χάρις as *benefaction*, see Zeba A. Crook, "Grace as Benefaction in Galatians 2:9, 1 Corinthians 3:10, and Romans 12:3; 15:15," in *The Social Sciences and Biblical Translation*, ed. Dietmar Neufeld, SBLSS 41 (Atlanta: SBL, 2008), 25–38.

42   See δοθείσῃ (v. 4); ἐπλουτίσθητε (v. 5); ἐβεβαιώθη (v. 6); ὑστερεῖσθαι (v. 7); ἐκλήθητε (v. 9). Passivization casts the readers in the role of the Affected/Patient in processes rather than Agents. From a textual perspective, the dominance of passive voice in this unit creates cohesion and therefore aids in identifying the boundaries of the unit (see Westfall, *Hebrews*, 44–45).

"TELL US HOW YOU REALLY FEEL, PAUL!" (PART 1)   103

are never portrayed as subjects/Actors in the thanksgiving unit.[43] Paul clearly takes up the point of view that God is the faithful patron who gives favor (grace, benefaction) to those who have believed the testimony about Jesus Christ (cf. v. 6).[44] The positive value orientation is stated straightforwardly in the summary at v. 9, which rounds out the thanksgiving period:[45] πιστὸς ὁ θεός (God is faithful). This admiration of God's character (+ JUDGMENT: ESTEEM: tenacity) is based on the beneficence he has demonstrated in the lives of the readers as just described in vv. 4–8.[46] The positive attitudinal evaluations expressed by the principal verb εὐχαριστῶ, the closing summary statement, and the beneficent actions of God described between them are all intended to reorient the readers to the same value position held by Paul.

The readers are also evaluated in the thanksgiving section but only indirectly through ideational tokens. Paul speaks of them as having been given God's grace (v. 4), as having been made rich (v. 5), as having the testimony about Christ confirmed among them (v. 6), as not lacking any gift (v. 7), as people who can expect to be confirmed blameless on the day of judgment (v. 8),[47] and as having been called into the fellowship of Jesus Christ (v. 9). All of these evaluations together rather forcefully betoken Paul's positive stance toward the readers and continue the positive prosody begun in the letter opening: they are certainly blessed people (t, + JUDGMENT: ESTEEM: normality). Packing these six depictions one right after another in the rather limited space of the thanksgiving has an effect similar to repetition, thereby increasing the force of Paul's value position (GRADUATION: FORCE: intensification). That Paul holds this view indicates that it is neither wrong nor bad for the readers to view themselves as special, but this view, like Paul's view of himself (cf. 3:5;

---

43   On passivization, see Fairclough, *Analysing Discourse*, 145; Trew, "Theory and Ideology at Work," 98–99; Goatly, *Critical Reading and Writing*, 75–76.

44   See Jerome H. Neyrey, "God, Benefactor and Patron: The Major Cultural Model for Interpreting the Deity in Greco-Roman Antiquity," *JSNT* 27 (2005): 465–92; John H. Elliott, "Patronage and Clientism in Early Christian Society," *FFF* 3 (1987): 39–48; Crook, "Grace as Benefaction," 25–38; Bruce J. Malina, "Patronage," *HBSV* 131–34; Malina, "Grace/Favor" *HBSV* 77.

45   See Jack T. Sanders, "The Transition from Opening Epistolary Thanksgiving to the Body in Letters of the Pauline Corpus," *JBL* (1962): 359.

46   See Barrett, *First Epistle*, 40; Oster, *1 Corinthians*, 48–49.

47   On the significance of this point from an apocalyptic worldview, see David E. Aune, Timothy J. Geddert, and Craig A. Evans, "Apocalypticism," *DNTB*, 45–48 (esp. 52–57 on Paul and apocalypticism); David E. Aune, "Apocalypticism," *DPL*, 25–35. See also Meeks, *Origins of Christian Morality*, 174–88, who discusses the effects of apocalypticism on Christian morality and group loyalty.

104 CHAPTER 3

4:1), must be tempered by the fact that they are special only because God has chosen to make them so (cf. 1:26–31).

2.2.2 Engagement Analysis

The verb εὐχαριστῶ (*I thank*) marks the opening of the thanksgiving period,[48] which is mostly monoglossic. This is realized primarily by Paul's selection of assertive attitude (Indicative Mood) for the finite verbs in four of the seven clauses comprising the unit:[49] εὐχαριστῶ in the principal clause at v. 4; ἐπλουτίσθητε in the causal clause at v. 5; ἐβεβαιώθη in the comparative clause at v. 6; and ἐκλήθητε in the relative clause at v. 9. However, in the fifth clause in the unit (v. 8), the authorial voice briefly becomes dialogic with the future form βεβαιώσει.[50] The modalized locution [*I expect*

---

48 See Paul Schubert, *Form and Function of the Pauline Thanksgivings*, BZNW 20 (Berlin: Töpelmann, 1939), 10–39 (esp. 30–31 on 1 Cor 1:4–9) and Peter T. O'Brien, *Introductory Thanksgivings in the Letters of Paul*, NovTSup 49 (Leiden: Brill, 1977), 107–37. See also David W. Pao, "Constraints of an Epistolary Form: Pauline Introductory Thanksgivings and Paul's Theology of Thanksgiving," in *Paul and the Ancient Letter Form*, ed. Stanley E. Porter and Sean A. Adams, PAST 6 (Leiden: Brill, 2010), 101–27; Peter Arzt-Grabner, "Paul's Letter Thanksgiving," in *Paul and the Ancient Letter Form*, ed. Stanley E. Porter and Sean A. Adams, PAST 6 (Leiden: Brill, 2010), 129–58; Jeffrey T. Reed, "Are Paul's Thanksgivings 'Epistolary'?" *JSNT* 61 (1996): 87–99; Raymond F. Collins, "A Significant Decade: The Trajectory of the Hellenistic Epistolary Thanksgiving," in *Paul and the Ancient Letter Form*, ed. Stanley E. Porter and Sean A. Adams, PAST 6 (Leiden: Brill, 2010), 159–84; Peter T. O'Brien, "Thanksgiving in Pauline Theology," in *Pauline Studies: Essays Presented to Professor F. F. Bruce on his 70th Birthday*, ed. Donald A. Hagner and Murray J. Harris (Exeter: Paternoster, 1980), 50–66.

49 Note that embedded clauses were not counted as clauses since they have been shifted down the rank scale to function as word groups.

50 The future form in Greek is challenging to interpret because, as Porter has shown (*Verbal Aspect*, 404–16), it is both aspectually and modally vague: it is "similar both to the aspects and to the attitudes, but fully neither ..." (414). It "offers no clear aspectual choice in establishing an author's conception of the constituency of a process" (410) and it illustrates affinities with both the Indicative and non-Indicative Moods (412–13). Like the Subjunctive Mood from which it developed (Porter, *Verbal Aspect*, 177, 412) the future form projects a process that is capable of realization, awaits realization, or may even now be realized (e.g., commands using the volitive future project an action that may, in fact, already be realized by those receiving the command) (see Jan Gonda, *The Character of the Indo-European Moods with Special Regard to Greek and Sanskrit* [Wiesbaden: Otto Harrassowitz, 1956], 69–70; Porter, *Verbal Aspect*, 172). In addition to this, the future form projects the language user's subjective assessment regarding either (a) the probability that the action will occur (if a proposition) or (b) the inclination of the Agent to perform the action (if a proposal)—as informed by the context and co-text in which it is used, of course. In other words, the future form in context conveys both the projection of a verbal event and the language user's subjective modal assessment relative the verbal event. Locutions such as these are considered interpersonal modality metaphors because the

that][51] *God*[52] *will confirm you* (v. 8) construes a heteroglossic backdrop for the text, at least for that brief textual moment, by overtly grounding the proposition in Paul's subjective perspective on God's action.[53] He stops short of making a categorical statement and signals his recognition that, at least potentially, someone in the current communicative context may not share the same point of view. In so doing, he creates dialogic space for those alternative voices (CONSIDER). Two questions arise here: (1) to what extent does Paul entertain alternative voices on this point? (2) on what point(s) might these entertained voices take issue with Paul? These questions are concerned respectively with (1) the value (high, median, low) attached to Paul's modal assessment and (2) determining whether the locution is a modalization or a modulation.

Co-text gives a strong indication as to the modal value of [*I expect that*] *God will confirm you.* The instance occurs in a textual environment where dialogue is for the most part contracted (if not monoglossic) due to the fact that a number of things are depicted as taken for granted or assumed to be the case. First, it is asserted as a given that the readers *have been made rich* in both *speech* and

---

mental clause *I expect* that serves as the projecting part of the clause nexus—even if only implied—is a metaphorical realization of modality (either of probability or of inclination). They modalize the proposition or modulate the proposal in the projected clause (see Martin and White, *Language of Evaluation*, 22–23; Halliday and Matthiessen, *IFG3*, 614). This appears to be what Porter has in mind when he says the future form grammaticalizes a language user's "marked and emphatic expectation toward a process" (Porter, *Verbal Aspect*, 414) and would explain his suggestion to gloss future forms into English using a mental projection/attribute structure (e.g., "I expect that ..." or "The speaker expects that ...") (Porter, *Verbal Aspect*, 415; see Halliday and Matthiessen, *IFG3*, 448–53 on reporting/projecting ideas).

51   *I expect that* is placed in brackets to indicate that it is implied by the future form and not literally inscribed in the text.

52   Whether the relative pronoun ὅς refers to God or to Christ is difficult to decide. Based on the portrayal of reality that God is the one who made the readers "rich" (albeit through Christ) and on an apocalyptic worldview (note *the revelation of our Lord Jesus Christ* [v. 7] and *on the day of our Lord Jesus Christ* [v. 8]) it is maintained that God is the one who will confirm the readers on the day of judgment. O'Brien (*Introductory Thanksgivings*, 127–28), Fee (*First Epistle*, 44), Fitzmyer (*First Corinthians*, 133), and Conzelmann (*1 Corinthians*, 28) are among those who read God as referent of ὅς, while Heinrich A. Meyer (*Critical and Exegetical Handbook to the Epistles to the Corinthians*, trans. D. Douglas Bannerman [New York: Funk & Wagnalls, 1884], 15), Joseph B. Lightfoot (*Notes on the Epistles of St. Paul* [London: Macmillan, 1890; repr., Grand Rapids: Zondervan, 1974], 149), and Barrett (*First Epistle*, 39) are among those who read Christ as its referent. Thiselton (*First Corinthians*, 101) shares Schrage's view that an unequivocal decision may be impossible (see Wolfgang Schrage, *Der erste Brief an die Korinther*, 4 vols., EKKNT 7 [Düsseldorf: Benziger Verlag, 1991–1999], 1:121).

53   Martin and White, *Language of Evaluation*, 105.

knowledge (v. 5).[54] Second, it is asserted as a given that God's enrichment of the readers has resulted in the fact that they *do not lack in any gift* (v. 7). It is on the basis of these givens that Paul anchors his expectation that God *will confirm* the readers on *the day of our Lord Jesus Christ* (v. 8). Additionally, immediately following Paul's modal assessment come two further givens, namely that *God is faithful* and that through him the readers were *called into the fellowship of his son Jesus Christ*. All of this monogloss emphasizes what God has done for the readers and, thus, naturalizes high modal value. This effectively minimizes, though does not completely restrict, the dialogic space created by his assessment. In other words, although the locution is dialogically expansive, the dialogic space for alternative points of view is limited by the monoglossic co-text.

The question of whether Paul's assessment is a modalization or modulation is more challenging to answer. If a modalization, Paul's assessment is about the probability or likelihood ("may be") that God *will confirm* the readers; if a modulation, the assessment is about the relative inclination or intention ("wants to") of God to confirm them. As already noted, the thanksgiving unit emphasizes God's gracious acts for the readers, mainly that he has gifted them ἐν παντὶ λόγῳ καὶ πάσῃ γνώσει (in all speech and all knowledge).[55] In light of this, it is possible Paul's train of thought is something like, "Given all that God has done for you, *I expect that he certainly will confirm* you as blameless...." If this is the case, then the future form realizes a modalization. On the other hand, the line of thinking may be something like, "Given all that God has done for you to this point, *I expect that he fully intends to confirm* you as blameless...." If this is the case, the future form realizes a modulation. What makes the latter position slightly more favorable is that Paul has asserted as givens a number of

---

54   This is likely a reference to miraculous linguistic abilities and rhetorical competency, including such things as proclamation/preaching, prophecy, glossolalia, and even confession of faith (see, e.g., 1 Cor 12:3–11; 14:1–25). See Pogoloff, *Logos and Sophia*, 110; Andrew D. Clarke, *Secular and Christian Leadership at Corinth: A Socio-Historical and Exegetical Study of 1 Corinthians 1–6* (Leiden: Brill, 1993), 36–39; Brian K. Peterson, *Eloquence and the Proclamation of the Gospel at Corinth*, SBLDS 163 (Atlanta: Scholars Press, 1998), 59; A. Duane Litfin, *St. Paul's Theology of Proclamation: 1 Corinthians 1–4 and Greco-Roman Rhetoric*, SNTSMS 83 (Cambridge: Cambridge University Press, 1994), 14; Martin, *Corinthian Body*, 47–55; Witherington, *Conflict & Community*, 87; Thiselton, *First Corinthians*, 91–92; Garland, *1 Corinthians*, 33. For an alternative view, see R. Dean Anderson, *Ancient Rhetorical Theory and Paul*, rev. ed., CBET 18 (Leuven: Peeters, 1999), 265–76.

55   Fee cogently suggests that λόγος and γνῶσις were likely the Corinthians' terms and referred to spiritual gifts they had received at their conversion. He goes on to suggest that these were two gifts that caused the Corinthian addressees to become "a bit too *self*-confident" (Fee, *First Epistle*, 39–40).

intentional acts of God toward the implied readers: God has given them grace/ benefaction; God has made them rich; and God has confirmed the testimony about Christ among them. The logic appears to be that if God has intentionally acted toward them in these ways, then it is to be expected, at least from Paul's point of view, that God intends to confirm them as blameless on the day of judgment. In spite of this brief dialogic moment, the thanksgiving is primarily monoglossic. By depicting himself and the readers as operating with the same knowledge, beliefs, and values, Paul constructs a strong sense of solidarity with the readers, a solidarity that he will rely upon and put at risk in his attempt to reorient the readers in the body of the letter.[56]

2.2.3 Summary

The readers are portrayed especially positively in the thanksgiving period. Through a number of betokened instances of positive attitude, this section picks up and contributes to the positive prosody begun in the greeting section. Paul directs gratitude to God for the readers and considers them special because God has treated them with beneficence, making them rich in everything in Christ Jesus (v. 5) so that they do not lack in any spiritual gift (v. 7). The primary social goal of these betokened appraisals along with the highly monoglossic nature of the utterances is to build solidarity between Paul and the readers, which, as noted above, he will put at risk not only throughout 1 Cor 1–4 but the entire letter.

3 Is Christ Divided? The Problem of Coteries in Corinth (1 Cor 1:10–4:21) (Part I)

Prior to this point, Paul's main effort has been to enact the apostle-church relationship between himself and the readers and to establish solidarity with them by evaluating them positively. As a result, he did not overtly lay any demands upon the readers. Beginning with this unit and continuing throughout the letter, Paul clearly draws on his status and begins making overt claims on their lives, consequently putting at risk the solidarity he assumes to have established with the readers. He demands certain beliefs and behaviors from the readers while proscribing others (e.g., 1:10); he clearly portrays God's wisdom and actions as superior to the *wisdom of this age* (σοφία τοῦ αἰῶνος τούτου) and the

---

56   See White, "Beyond Modality and Hedging," 264–65.

actions of the *rulers*[57] *of this age* (ἀρχόντων τοῦ αἰῶνος τούτου) (e.g., 1:18–25; 2:7); he depicts humility as superior to self-aggrandizement (e.g., 1:26–31; 3:5–8; 4:6); and he directly challenges the readers' honor by questioning whether they really were πνευματικοί (i.e., that they had received and live by the Spirit from God) or if they were merely ψυχικοί (i.e., that they had not received the Spirit from God and live by the standards of the world) (e.g., 2:10–16, esp. vv. 15–16). In the language of Critical Discourse Analysis, these discursive actions and the various positive and negative appraisals associated with them are Paul's way of defining and privileging a theocentric manner of living that is mediated through Χριστὸν ἐσταυρωμένον (the crucified Messiah) (cf. 1 Cor 1:23; 2:2).

3.1 Σχίσματα *and* Ἔριδες: *Symptoms of a Deeper Problem (1 Cor 1:10–17)*

The primary function of this unit is to introduce and to begin to deal with the problem that apparently exists among the addressees, and that problem may be described with a single word: discord.[58] Because the section treats a "problem," one can expect attitudinal appraisals to be mostly negative as they reflect Paul's dissatisfaction and disappointment with the readers' behavior. In terms of ENGAGEMENT, Paul will choose strategies (e.g., PROCLAIM: CONCUR) that position the readers to agree with Paul that their current behavior is inappropriate. These strategies contract dialogue with the potential to squelch other possible points of view.

3.1.1 Attitudinal Analysis

It had been reported to Paul by *those from Chloe* that the ἐκκλησία in Corinth was plagued by σχίσματα (divisions) (v. 10) and ἔριδες (conflicts) (v. 11). It almost goes without saying that the term σχίσματα bears a negative connotation and its use indicates Paul's negative stance toward disunity. In fact, Mitchell is surely correct to say that Paul viewed disunity as a "serious social threat to the life of the church community."[59] He considers it *wrong* behavior (t, – JUDGMENT: SANCTION: propriety). From Paul's primarily Jewish worldview, discordant, argumentative behavior (i.e., ἔρις) would have been

---

57 I.e., "respected people." *Respect* is "the attitude one must have and the behavior one is expected to follow relative to those who control one's existence" (Malina, *New Testament World*, 30).

58 See Margaret M. Mitchell, "The Corinthian Correspondences and the Birth of Pauline Hermeneutics," in *Paul and the Corinthians: Studies on A Community in Conflict, Essays in Honour of Margaret Thrall*, ed. Trevor J. Burke and J. Keith Elliott, NovTSup 109 (Leiden: Brill, 2003), 25–26.

59 Mitchell, *Rhetoric of Reconciliation*, 72. See also L. L. Welborn, *Politics and Rhetoric in the Corinthian Epistles* (Macon, GA: Mercer University Press, 1997), 3.

"TELL US HOW YOU REALLY FEEL, PAUL!" (PART 1)   109

viewed as out of line because it stood opposed to the value of wholeness; any such behavior, then, Paul would have considered unholy and shameful (t, – JUDGMENT: SANCTION: propriety).[60] Thus, he urges them to unity which implies that he sees unity as good and proper behavior for those who claim to have faith in Christ (t, + JUDGMENT: SANCTION: propriety).

Although Paul does not explicitly announce that he believed the report from Chloe's people, co-text makes it likely that he did. The first indication of this lies in the selection of ἐδηλώθη (it has been made evident) as the reporting verb rather than ἐρρέθη (it was said).[61] Δηλόω carries the sense of making something plain or evident and here implies that Paul considered what was pointed out to him to be convincing (t, + APPRECIATION: reaction),[62] as his compulsion to respond with a letter confirms. Second, and perhaps more telling, is the way Paul quite strikingly portrays the readers as perpetrators of discord, which he does through the use of reported speech.[63] The so-called "slogans" in v. 12, *I belong to Paul ... Apollos ... Cephas ... Christ*, are probably not quotations of the *actual* talk of the Corinthians.[64] More likely Paul produced[65]

---

60   See Neyrey, "Wholeness" *HBSV* 175–78.

61   Thiselton (quoting Thomas C. Edwards, *A Commentary on the First Epistle to the Corinthians*, 2nd ed. [London: Continuum, 2004], 18) rightly says ἐδηλώθη ... μοι is "stronger than 'it was told [to] me'" (Thiselton, *First Corinthians*, 120).

62   See L&N 1:340. See Robertson and Plummer, *I Corinthians*, 10: "The verb implies that [Paul] was unable to doubt the unwelcome statement." See Martin and White, *Language of Evaluation*, 126.

63   On the nature of reported speech and the challenge of interpreting it, see Tannen, *Talking Voices*, 102–32; Stanley, "Rhetoric of Quotations," 44–58; Stanley, "Paul's 'Use' of Scripture," 125–55; Stamps, "Use of the Old Testament," 9–37.

64   E.g., Mitchell suggests that Paul employs προσωποποιΐα (impersonation or speech-in-character; see Stanley K. Stowers, "Romans 7.7–25 as Speech-in-Character (προσωποποιΐα)," in *Paul in His Hellenistic Context*, ed. Troels Engbert-Pederson [Minneapolis: Fortress, 1995], 180–91; Stanley K. Stowers, *A Rereading of Romans: Justice, Jews, and Gentiles* [New Haven: Yale University Press, 1994], 16–21; Aune, *Literary Environment*, 31). For alternative readings, see L. L. Welborn, "On the Discord in Corinth: 1 Corinthians 1–4 and Ancient Politics," *JBL* 106 (1987): 85–111; Welborn, *Politics and Rhetoric*, 1–42; Bruce W. Winter, *After Paul Left Corinth: The Influence of Secular Ethics and Social Change* (Grand Rapids: Eerdmans, 2001), 31–43 (esp. 41).

65   Textual evidence for this includes the clause λέγω δὲ τοῦτο, which introduces Paul's commentary on the report (Mitchell, *Rhetoric of Reconciliation*, 86; see Elisabeth Schüssler Fiorenza, "Rhetorical Situation and Historical Reconstruction in 1 Corinthians," *NTS* 33 [1987]: 396). Also, the phrase ἕκαστος ὑμῶν λέγει (each/every one of you says) introduces "choral dialogue," i.e., speech that is attributed to more than one speaker as if they all spoke in unison as a chorus (Tannen, *Talking Voices*, 114–15). Tucker (*You Belong to Christ*, 160–61) opposes the view of Betz and Mitchell (see *ABD* 1:1141) that the clause is ironic, claiming "there is nothing in the context of 1:10–17 that indicates that this is an ironic statement, and furthermore it would limit the persuasive impact of 3:23 if Paul was

110   CHAPTER 3

these sayings as a means of framing, foregrounding, and vividly illustrating[66] the disputatious behavior of the readers, as well as signaling that a critique is forthcoming.[67] The sayings obviously play off of the exhortation τὸ αὐτὸ λέγητε πάντες (all of you say the same [v. 10]), but here Paul vividly depicts and emphasizes that *each one* (ἕκαστος) of the readers as *not* saying the same.[68] For Paul to depict the Corinthians' (verbal) behavior as that of *each individual* in a sociocultural context—and even the sub-cultural context of the ἐκκλησία—that tends toward strong group and prefers collectivism over individualism would likely have evoked a negative feeling about their behavior.[69] The Corinthians are not *bound together in the same mind and in the same purpose,* for the inability to *say the same* betrays a fundamental lack of concord in thought and purpose. They lack wholeness and, thus, holiness.[70] In Paul's estimation, the Corinthians were not living up to their status as sanctified and called saints

---

not convinced that the Corinthians' identity had its basis in their belonging to Christ." However, Tucker's denial of irony on the basis of context (co-text) is questionable. First, structurally, all four sayings are a cohesive unit: they are all part of the same structure of reported speech and, with the exception of the particles μέν and δέ, they all have the same formula (see OpenText.org). Second, as pointed out above, the point of the sayings is to depict behavior (i.e., clique formation [see Malina and Pilch, *Letters of Paul,* 63, 342–43]) that is diametrically opposed to the exhortation to "say the same" (v. 10). This suffuses negativity over all four sayings so that all of them function ironically. The sayings are Paul's way to parody the readers' behavior so as to challenge their honor. See Thiselton, *First Corinthians,* 133; Richard B. Hays, *First Corinthians,* Interpretation (Louisville: Westminster John Knox, 2007), 23.

66   Reported dialogue heightens vividness and creates involvement and/or interaction and thereby creates prominence at that textual moment (see Tannen, *Talking Voices,* 25–47; Robert E. Longacre, *The Grammar of Discourse,* 2nd ed., Topics in Language and Linguistics [New York: Plenum, 1996], 40–43 [esp. 42]).

67   This is certainly not to deny that the sayings *represent* the kind of behavior in which the readers were purported to be engaged, but they are very likely "exaggerated caricatures" of that behavior (Mitchell, *Rhetoric of Reconciliation,* 86).

68   From an ideational and textual perspective, this word group (ἕκαστος [head term] ὑμῶν [qualifier]) functions as Subject in the causal clause and is in Prime position; thus, it is both marked and prominent (see above on the textual metafunction). Note, too, the contrast in GRADUATION: FORCE: QUANTIFICATION realized by πάντες and ἕκαστος.

69   On group and grid theory, see Mary Douglas, *Natural Symbols,* Routledge Classics (New York: Routledge, 2003), 57–71. For modification and application of group and grid theory for use in New Testament studies, see Malina, *Christian Origin,* 37–44. On collectivism and individualism in the first century circum-Mediterranean world, see Bruce J. Malina, "Collectivism in Mediterranean Culture," 17–28.

70   On the relationship between the values of wholeness and holiness, see Neyrey, "Wholeness" *HBSV* 175. Paul operates by the same "common sense" principle as Jesus, who taught that one could know good and bad "trees" by the fruit they bear (Matt 7:15–20; Luke 6:43–45). In other words, actions speak louder than words.

"TELL US HOW YOU REALLY FEEL, PAUL!" (PART 1)   111

(1:2); thus, the sayings realize negative judgments of the readers' behavior (t, – JUDGMENT: SANCTION: propriety).

At v. 13, Paul asks three questions (see engagement analysis below for more details), the implied answers to which realize indirectly further negative judgment of the readers' discordant behavior. The first question, *Has Christ been divided?*, appears to launch a *reductio ad absurdum* argument. The sense of the verb is something like *apportioned out* or *separate into component parts*,[71] which, following the "slogan" *I belong to Christ*, gives the question the sense, "Can Christ be made into a 'party' or faction along the same lines as the others?"[72] Although it is an open question, the proposition it insinuates would (or *should*) be considered completely absurd by believers in Christ, so in a sense a negative answer is expected, at least on the basis of logic.[73] This implies further that the readers should see their own factionalism as absurd, especially since they claim to be members of the one body of Christ (cf. 1 Cor 12).[74] Yet, they apparently continue to be divided, and Paul here implies that they are in the wrong (t, – JUDGMENT: SANCTION: propriety).

The last of the three questions introduces the topic of baptism, which dominates the remainder of the unit.[75] Knowing Paul's high regard for baptism[76] and the fact that the rite was part of his ministry when he founded

---

71 See Fee, *First Epistle*, 60; Thiselton, *First Corinthians*, 136–37.

72 See Fee, *First Epistle*, 60. Alternatively, Lightfoot (*Notes*, 154; followed by Garland, *1 Corinthians*, 51) interprets the question as expressing a rhetorical entailment of v. 12 in which case the answer to the question would be "Yes." If correct, then Paul is issuing an accusation rather than a corrective warning (see Thiselton, *First Corinthians*, 137). Porter (*Idioms*, 277) notes μεμέρισται ὁ Χριστός may be a statement rather than a question serving as an ironic negative commentary on the discord among the believers at Corinth, but see Lightfoot, *Notes*, 154.

73 Note that the second question, which does expect a negative answer (μή), continues the argument from absurdity.

74 See Conzelmann, *1 Corinthians*, 35.

75 Words on the βαπτ– root spike in 1:13–17, appearing six times in three different forms.

76 For the early Christian groups, baptism was the decisive point of entry into the church, functioning as a sort of "threshold" between the in-group and the out-group as well as a point of status transformation (see Rom 6:4, 8; 1 Cor 12:12–13; Gal 3:28; Col 2:11–12; 3:10; Eph 2:5). On baptism, consult the following: Meeks, *First Urban Christians*, 153–55; Neyrey, *Paul*, 87–88; Everett Ferguson, *Baptism in the Early Church: History, Theology, and Liturgy in the First Five Centuries* (Grand Rapids: Eerdmans, 2009), 99–198; George R. Beasley-Murray, *Baptism in the New Testament* (Grand Rapids: Eerdmans, 1962), 127–216; I. H. Marshall, "The Meaning of the Verb Baptize," in *Dimensions of Baptism: Biblical and Theological Studies*, ed. Stanley E. Porter and Anthony R. Cross, JSNTSup 234 (London: Sheffield Academic Press, 2002), 8–24; Anthony R. Cross, "Baptism among Baptists," in *Baptism: Historical, Theological, and Pastoral Perspectives*, ed. Gordon L. Heath and James D. Dvorak, MTSS 4 (Eugene, OR: Pickwick, 2011), 143–54; Curt Niccum, "Baptism and the Restoration

112   CHAPTER 3

the church at Corinth (see Acts 18:8), the assertion of thankfulness (εὐχαριστῶ
τῷ θεῷ ὅτι οὐδένα ὑμῶν ἐβάπτισα) for baptizing none of the addressees (except
Crispus, Gaius, and the household of Stephanas [v. 14b, 16]) must be interpreted as ironic if not sarcastic (t, − AFFECT: dissatisfaction), running counter
to reader expectations. After all, how could Paul as one having a high view
of baptism feel gratitude (+ AFFECT: satisfaction)—directed toward God, no
less[77]—for not having baptized more of the readers into Christ? The answer to
this becomes clear in v. 15: ἵνα μή τις εἴπῃ ὅτι εἰς τὸ ἐμὸν ὄνομα ἐβαπτίσθητε (lest
someone[78] could claim that you were baptized in my name). This negative
purpose statement betokens Paul's negative evaluation of the idea that anyone would say they were baptized in his (or anyone else's) name (t, − AFFECT:
disinclination).[79] In this the irony of the text becomes clear: Paul is thankful
not for the fact that he baptized so few[80] but for how this reality "works in his

---

Movement," in *Baptism: Historical, Theological, and Pastoral Perspectives*, 181–91. Meeks
(*Origins of Christian Morality*, 92), drawing upon Nils Dahl's "Anamnesis," notes that allu-
sions to baptism typically appear in the Pauline corpus in hortatory contexts in which
Paul is trying to correct some sort of misunderstanding (see Nils A. Dahl, "Anamnesis:
Memory and Commemoration in Early Christianity," in *Jesus in the Memory of the Early
Church* [Minneapolis: Augsburg, 1976], 11–29). This is the case here, though the rite is
introduced to discourage negative behavior rather than encourage positive behavior.

77   A handful of important manuscripts (e.g., ℵ* B) omit τῷ θεῷ but others (e.g., ℵ²
C D F G L P) include it. Eckhard J. Schnabel (*Der erste Brief des Paulus an die Korinther*,
Historisch Theologische Auslegung [Wuppertal: R. Brockhaus, 2006], 85) points out,
however, "Paulus hat nach εὐχαριστῶ gewöhnlich das Dativobjekt τῷ θεῷ" (see 1:4; 14:18;
Rom 1:8; 7:25; Phil 1:3; Col 1:3; 1 Thess 1:2; 2:13; Phlm 4); thus, it is read here (however, see
Bruce M. Metzger, *A Textual Commentary on the Greek New Testament*, 2nd ed. [New
York: UBS, 1994], 479; Thiselton, *First Corinthians*, 140). Its inclusion intensifies the cogni-
tive dissonance generated by Paul's seeming gratitude for not having baptized many of
the readers.

78   Most commentators probably rightly assume τις (someone, anyone) refers to a person
among the readers (e.g., Fee assumes the referent of τις is someone among "those baptized by [Paul]" [*First Epistle*, 61]). The thinking appears to be that ὑμῶν (of/among you) is
implied on the basis on its use in the prior verse. However, without the explicit restriction
of the genitive qualifier ὑμῶν, it is possible the text reflects Paul's fear (t, − AFFECT: insecurity) that someone from *outside* the group, upon hearing the talk or seeing the behavior of
the readers, might possibly claim Paul had baptized the readers in his name—a point that
would certainly fit the dyadic, group-oriented context of culture (see Jerome H. Neyrey,
HBSV "Dyadism," 46–49; Malina, *New Testament World*, 60–67). Perhaps this view lies
behind later variations in which ἐβάπτισα (I baptized) rather than ἐβαπτίσθητε (you were
baptized) is read, though this reading could just as well reflect the view of an insider or
member of the group.

79   One may also presume from this statement that Paul would negatively appraise anyone
actually being baptized in his name (not just claiming to be).

80   Conzelmann, *1 Corinthians*, 36: "εὐχαριστῶ, 'I am thankful,' is used as a rhetorical phrase:
'Thank God!' (see 14:18)."

favor," so to speak, to minimize the possibility that someone could claim to be baptized in his name as though the baptizand was becoming his disciple rather than a disciple of the Lord.[81]

3.1.2 Engagement Analysis

Paul's fatherly exhortation[82] to unity (v. 10) was prompted by what he had heard from *those from Chloe* (τῶν Χλόης) (v. 11) (HETEROGLOSS: EXPAND: ATTRIBUTE).[83] He opens the letter body by demanding[84] that the readers-in-the-text be unified (v. 10). However, rather than using an imperative, the most straightforward linguistic means of directing behavior, Paul opts for a less direct, though equally directive, petition formula: παρακαλῶ ... ὑμᾶς (I urge you).[85] This is an interpersonal modality metaphor[86] in which the more

---

81 Fee, *First Epistle*, 61, 63; Beasley-Murray, *Baptism*, 179. See Tucker, *You Belong to Christ*, 163.

82 The grammar of v. 10 provides some insight into how Paul construed his relationship to the readers at this textual moment. On the one hand, he continues to construe unequal status between himself and the readers-in-the-text, in which he holds greater status. This indicates that Paul wants and likely expects the readers to respect him as their apostle, their leader. This is balanced, on the other hand, by the use of the modal formulation rather than an imperative (see Fairclough, *Discourse and Social Change*, 203–5) and by addressing the implied readers as ἀδελφοί (*brothers and sisters*) (t, + APPRECIATION: valuation), each of which operates to narrow the social distance between the communicants thereby construing greater solidarity between them (see Meeks, *First Urban Christians*, 87–89; Tucker, *You Belong to Christ*, 154–55). Given Paul's view of the church as an "extended family" (i.e., fictive kin group) (see Hellerman, *Ancient Church as Family*, 92–126), it is likely that he understood the apostle-church relationship as something of a father-child(ren) relationship (see Meeks, *First Urban Christians*, 131; Martin, *Corinthian Body*, 58–9; Witherington, *Conflict & Community*, 95). This is confirmed at 1 Cor 4:14–15 where he explicitly invokes the father-child(ren) relationship to assure the readers that his intent was not to shame them (ἐντρέπω), but to instruct/correct them (νουθετέω) them as a father instructs/corrects his children.

83 Though a number of scholars have proffered guesses on the matter, knowing the exact identity of Chloe or those who reported to Paul is unnecessary. It is more important to understand the discursive and social function of the attribution. Yet, for various speculations, see Thiselton, *First Corinthians*, 121; Fee, *First Epistle*, 54; Fitzmyer, *First Corinthians*, 141–42; Conzelmann, *1 Corinthians*, 32; Garland, *1 Corinthians*, 43–44; Witherington, *Conflict & Community*, 99; Wire, *Corinthian Women Prophets*, 41.

84 "Demand" (as opposed to offer) refers to a basic speech role (see Halliday and Matthiessen, *IFG3*, 107–8).

85 See Terence Y. Mullins, "Petition as a Literary Form," *NovT* 5 (1962): 46–54; Carl J. Bjerkelund, *Parakalō: Form, Function, und Sinn der parakalō-Sätze in den paulinischen Briefen*, Biblioteca Theologica Norvegica 1 (Oslo: Universitetsforlaget, 1967), 141; John L. White, "Introductory Formulae in the Body of the Pauline Letter," *JBL* 90 (1971): 91–97; Sanders, "Transition," 348–62; Aune, *Literary Environment*, 188–89.

86 See Halliday and Matthiessen, *IFG3*, 626–35; Eggins, *Introduction*, 174; J. R. Martin, "Interpersonal Meaning, Persuasion and Public Discourse," *Australian Journal of Linguistics* 15 (1995): 36–37; Martin, *English Text*, 412–5; Martin and White, *Language of Evaluation*, 22.

114 CHAPTER 3

congruent command τὸ αὐτὸ λέγετε (say the same, i.e., be united)[87] gets realized instead as a hypotactic clause nexus as if it were a projection sequence:[88]

Projecting clause: παρακαλῶ δὲ ὑμᾶς ...
Now I urge you ...

Projected clause: ἵνα τὸ αὐτὸ λέγητε πάντες
that you all should say the same[89]

Using a modality metaphor rather than an imperative makes a significant difference in dialogic nature of the text. Imperatives are monoglossic and dialogically inert; discursively, they neither reference nor allow for any alternative action. If Paul had selected the imperative τὸ αὐτὸ λέγετε (say the same), the only "choice" depicted discursively for the readers would have been

---

87   As Lightfoot has noted (*Notes*, 151), *say the same* is a classical expression "used of political communities which are free from factions, or of different states which entertain friendly relations with each other." See also Robertson and Plummer, *1 Corinthians*, 10; Conzelmann, *1 Corinthians*, 32; Mitchell, *Rhetoric of Reconciliation*, 68.

88   The projecting clause modalizes the demand/proposal realized in the projected clause, yet—here is the grammatical metaphorical part—it gets "upgraded" from group rank to clause rank and thereby gains the status of a proposition in its own right (i.e., *I urge you ...*). See Halliday and Matthiessen, *IFG3*, 626–27; Eggins, *Introduction*, 174–75.

89   The conjunction ἵνα initiates a content clause that spells out what is projected by the mental process παρακαλῶ. The relationship between the projected clause (ἵνα τὸ αὐτὸ λέγητε πάντες [that you all would say the same]) and the paratactic clause immediately following it (καὶ μὴ ᾖ ἐν ὑμῖν σχίσματα [and divisions would not exist among you]) needs some clarification. Fee interprets καί as opening an "explicative" or epexegetic clause and thus glosses it *that is* rather than *and* (Fee, *First Epistle*, 53; see BAGD [also BDAG] s.v. καί; see also Wallace, *Beyond the Basics*, 673 under "explanatory conjunctions"; Turner, *Syntax*, 335). In this view, the clause functions as a paratactic elaboration or restatement, albeit negative (μή), of the projected proposal (on elaboration, see Jeffrey T. Reed, "Discourse Analysis," in *A Handbook to the Exegesis of the New Testament*, ed. Stanley E. Porter [Leiden: Brill, 2002], 206; Halliday and Matthiessen, *IFG3*, 396–405; Martin, *English Text*, 310–14; Thompson, *Introducing*, 204–5; Eggins, *Introduction*, 47). However, the change of both polarity (positive to negative) and subject (*you* [pl] to *schismata*) in the paratactic clause suggests that it *extends* rather than elaborates the proposal (on extension, see Reed, "Discourse Analysis," 206–7; Halliday and Matthiessen, *IFG3*, 405–10; Martin, *English Text*, 314–16; Thompson, *Introducing*, 206–7; Eggins, *Introduction*, 47–48). As Halliday and Matthiessen say, "In extension, one clause extends the meaning of another by *adding something new to it*" (*IFG3*, 405 [italics added]). In this instance, then, Paul adds to the initial demand (i.e., you all should be united) the further demand that *schismata* ought not exist among the readers.

"TELL US HOW YOU REALLY FEEL, PAUL!" (PART 1)

compliance.[90] The modality metaphor, however, construes a heteroglossic backdrop for the text and is dialogically expansive (HETEROGLOSS: EXPAND: CONSIDER). Besides being attitudinally charged,[91] παρακαλῶ (*I urge/exhort*) explicitly grounds the demand in Paul's assessment (viz. high modulation) of obligation[92] thereby allowing dialogic space to remain open in the communicative context for the possibility of resistance.[93] Of course, this dialogic space is constrained by the "authorizing prepositional phrase"[94] διὰ τοῦ ὀνόματος τοῦ κυρίου ἡμῶν Ἰησοῦ Χριστου (through the name of our Lord Jesus Christ). This word group suffuses Paul's exhortation with the authority of the one who called him to be an apostle to the ἐκκλησία τοῦ θεοῦ at Corinth.[95] A reading position is naturalized in which resistance to Paul's exhortation would be tantamount to resistance of the Lord Jesus Christ. Therefore, although the text is dialogically expansive, the dialogic space is constrained by the effects of the prepositional group.

Commentators sometimes refer to the questions at v. 13 as "rhetorical,"[96] but this is technically incorrect for two of the questions. As the text stands,[97] both the first and the third questions are open, expository questions; the second question is a closed, leading ("rhetorical") question. Expository questions are heteroglossic and dialogically expansive because they do not include a negator (οὐ or μή) to signal the expectation of an affirmative or negative response.

---

90   Of course, an actual reader may choose to resist the demand realized by the imperative, but the point here has to do with *discursive* positioning and naturalizing reading positions.

91   Tucker's claim that the primary function of παρακαλῶ is that of a "discourse marker" is shortsighted if not linguistically suspect (see *You Belong to Christ*, 154). The verb represents a mental process that betokens an attitude of desideration (t, + AFFECT: inclination [desire]) with respect to the fulfilling the demand.

92   See Martin and White, *Language of Evaluation*, 111.

93   Locutions concerned with obligation and permission construe dialogic relationships of control and compliance/resistance rather than the offering of alternative propositions or points of view (see Martin and White, *Language of Evaluation*, 110–11). Thus, alternative *actions*, viz. compliance and resistance, are spoken of here rather than alternative voices or value positions.

94   Fee, *First Epistle*, 52.

95   Drawing on Austin's Speech Act Theory, Thiselton refers to this as an "illocutionary authorization" (see Thiselton, *First Corinthians*, 115; A. C. Thiselton, "The Supposed Power of Words in Biblical Writings," *JTS* 25 [1974]: 293–96; see also John L. Austin, *How to Do Things With Words*, 2nd ed. [Cambridge: Harvard University Press, 1975]; John R. Searle, *Speech Acts: An Essay in the Philosophy of Language* [Cambridge: Cambridge University Press, 1969]). Thiselton likens locutions such as these to prophets who speak in or through the name of (i.e., "for") Yahweh.

96   See, e.g., Hays, *First Corinthians*, 23; Witherington, *Conflict & Community*, 103.

97   𝔓[46], an important Pauline textual witness, may read μή prior to μεμέρισται at the beginning of v. 13, but the editors of NA[28] have tagged it *ut videtur*.

Such questions are left open for the interrogated to provide their subjective response, which is why they are dialogically expansive. The second question, on the other hand, does include a negator (μή) and is, thus, a leading question that expects a particular response.[98]

Undoubtedly, Paul asked all three of these questions with the intent of aligning the Corinthian readers with his point of view.[99] With the initial question, Paul introduces a topic for the readers to entertain (CONSIDER), namely that the Messiah is divided or apportioned out (μεμέρισται ὁ Χριστός).[100] Regardless of whether or not Paul presumes an affirming or contradicting response on the part of the addressees, the expository question performs the function of making salient the notion of division among believers.[101] The second question, because it is a leading question, contracts the dialogue and even begins to suggest to the readers an appropriate answer. The question is *Paul was not crucified on your behalf, was he?* (μὴ Παῦλος ἐσταυρώθη ὑπὲρ ὑμῶν), where the negator μή creates the expectation of a negative response, "No, Paul was not crucified on our behalf." The strategy here is to create an agreement between Paul and the addressees (PROCLAIM: CONCUR) such that the proposition "Paul was not crucified on your behalf" is presented as so commonsensical that any other point of view ought to be considered deviant (– APPRECIATION: valuation) and therefore excluded. Paul then returns to an expository question, *Or were you baptized in the name of Paul?* (ἢ εἰς τὸ ὄνομα Παύλου ἐβαπτίσθητε), again expanding dialogue but now making salient the memory of their baptism in the name of the Messiah Jesus. The negative prosody generated by μή in the second question bleeds over into the third, tilting the expected response toward the negative, "No, we were not baptized in the name of Paul," but, again, the lexicogrammar of the question itself does not presume this concurrence. Nevertheless, all three questions taken together operate to naturalize the point

---

98   See Porter, *Idioms*, 277–78; Dvorak, "Ask and Ye Shall Position the Readers," 211–13.

99   See Goatly, *Critical Reading and Writing*, 89, who rightly discusses questions (including "expository" and "rhetorical") under the rubric of "regulating behavior." See also Wuellner, "Paul as Pastor," 63–67. Benjamin Fiore ("'Covert Allusion' in 1 Corinthians 1–4," *CBQ* 47 [1985]: 85–102 esp. 88) considers the questions (the first two, at least) to be "*logoi eschēmatismenoi*"—"covert allusions," primarily in the forms of hyperbole, contrast, irony, and metaphor (including simile and allegory)—employed for the purpose of "awakening the audience's attention to the fact that things are not what they seem to be" (89).

100   On μεμέρισται as "divided" or "apportioned out," see comments in Thiselton, *First Corinthians*, 136–37; Lightfoot, *Notes*, 154–55.

101   It is possible that Paul already presumed an affirmative answer to his question, taking their inability to "say the same" (compare vv. 10 and 12) as evidence of such a response (see discussion in Lightfoot, *Notes*, 154). That, however, cannot be gleaned solely from lexicogrammar.

"TELL US HOW YOU REALLY FEEL, PAUL!" (PART 1)

of view that, if one is a true follower of Jesus, it would—that is, *should*—be thought quite foolish, inappropriate, and wrong to claim that the Christ has been divided up, that Paul (or anyone else) was crucified for humanity, or that a person would be baptized into the name of anyone besides Jesus.

Paul is so put off by the idea that someone might claim to be baptized in his name that he thanks God that he baptized *none* of the readers, a very strong, almost monoglossic denial (DISCLAIM: DENY). However, Paul immediately counters his own assertion (DISCLAIM: COUNTER) by naming exceptions (εἰ μὴ), namely Crispus, Gaius (v. 14), and the household of Stephanas (v. 16). It seems unlikely that Paul would have forgotten that he baptized Stephanas and his household; after all, at 1 Cor 16:15 he refers to Stephanas as "the firstfruits of Achaia." More likely this is a deliberate part of his interpersonal strategy. As Hays insightfully notes, "The 'afterthought' of verse 16 functions rhetorically to emphasize the relative triviality of the issue of who baptizes whom.... Perhaps the Corinthians were splitting up into house-church communities that placed undue emphasis on who had performed the baptisms; on the other hand, perhaps all this is merely an elaborate rhetorical flourish on Paul's part, a *reductio ad absurdum* of the Corinthians' tendency to magnify the messengers and miss the message."[102]

3.1.3 Summary

First Corinthians 1:10–17 is crucial for the argument inscribed in chapters 1–4 and perhaps even for the entire letter. Here the root problem at Corinth is exposed: a fundamental lack of wholeness in the group. The patterns of attitude and engagement reveal the fundamental axiological position with which Paul hopes to align the readers. The negative judgments directed toward the manifestations of σχίσματα and ἔριδες exhibited by the readers generates a negative prosody that functions to dissuade the readers from participating in such divisive activities as breaking into factions around those in the church considered to have status. Instead, the readers are strongly urged to *say the same* and *be of the same mind and purpose*. These kinds of behaviors are, from Paul's perspective, the right way to behave as members of the community of God.

3.2 The Great Reversal 1: The "Foolishness" of the Cross Supplants the "Wisdom" of the World (1 Cor 1:18–25)

In this section, one finds the bedrock precept upon which rests the remaining points of the argument Paul offers through 1 Cor 4: God has rejected the dominant ideology of the world and the evaluative superstructure built upon

---

102 Hays, *First Corinthians*, 23–24; see Garland, *1 Corinthians*, 54–55.

118 CHAPTER 3

it, supplanting it with his own system of values.[103] Paul draws upon the thematic formations and evaluative stances of Jewish apocalypticism to argue that through the crucified Messiah God has nullified the wisdom of the world, draining it of its power and significance.[104] As regards the resocialization of the readers, Paul wishes to convey that continuing to live by an ideology that God has destroyed will only result in being destroyed along with it.

3.2.1 Attitudinal Analysis

As deSilva notes, "Part of Paul's re-socialization of the believers involves drawing the sharp contrast between the 'wisdom of the world' and the 'wisdom of God'...."[105] Thus, Paul seeks to set side-by-side for comparison two divergent points of view on the cross, and appraisal plays a major role in accomplishing this. He construes two social groups[106] which he names with terms laden with evaluation. The first category Paul calls *those who are perishing* (τοῖς ἀπολλυμένοις). To this group is attributed the negative appraisal of the message of the cross—that is, the idea of a crucified Messiah (cf. v. 23)—that is realized by the adjective μωρία (foolishness) (– APPRECIATION: valuation). He names the second category *those who are being saved* (τοῖς σῳζομένοις), and to this group he attributes the positive appraisal of the message of the cross that is realized by the adjective δύναμις (power) (t, + APPRECIATION: valuation), which is further qualified by θεοῦ (of God).[107] It is not uncommon for interpreters to discuss the evaluations attributed to these groups; however, the evaluations of Paul implicit in the names he gives to each of the groups is often neglected if not completely left unexplored. The epithet *those who are perishing* (ἀπολλυμένοις) does more than refer to a group of people who do not appreciate Paul's (or anyone else's) preaching about the cross. The name and corresponding social category represents a way of being, thinking, doing, viewing, and evaluating the world (i.e., an ideology) that according to Paul has been emptied of its power and significance because God has rejected it.[108] On the opposite end of the spectrum, *those who are being saved* (σῳζομένοις) represents an ideology

---

103 See Martin, *Corinthian Body*, 59–61.
104 deSilva, "Honor Discourse," 64: "The crucified Messiah, the central feature of Paul's gospel, reveals the upside-down nature of the world's way of thinking and evaluating."
105 deSilva, "Honor Discourse," 64.
106 See Tucker, *You Belong to Christ*, 166–68.
107 See Schütz, *Anatomy of Apostolic Authority*, 192; Thiselton, *First Corinthians*, 158–59.
108 Note that κενόω (v. 17), δύναμις (v. 18), ἀθετέω (v. 20) are all classified by Louw and Nida in domain 76 (Power, Force). I would also add ἀπόλλυμι (vv. 18, 19) and μωραίνω (v. 20) to this semantic complex given that Paul, by collocating the terms, effectively adds these terms to the semantic chain he has strung together (see Cynthia Long Westfall, "Blessed Be the Ties that Bind: Semantic Domains and Cohesive Chains in Hebrews 1.1–2.4 and

"TELL US HOW YOU REALLY FEEL, PAUL!" (PART 1)   119

not based on the dominant standards of the world or the power structures of the elite.[109] Rather, it represents an ideology—a *theology*—from which stem the norms and values demonstrated in the "foolishness" of a crucified Messiah. The negative (i.e., *perishing*) and positive (i.e., *being saved*) names that Paul assigns to each of these opposing ideologies reveal his posture toward each: the dominant ideology of the world and its system of values holds no value for Paul because of its impotence (– APPRECIATION: valuation), but the ideology/theology revealed through the "foolishness" of a crucified Messiah is highly valued as profoundly meaningful (+ APPRECIATION: valuation).[110]

Despite the fact that these appraisals are realized indirectly, they play a crucial role in achieving Paul's social goal of aligning the assumed readers to this God-oriented worldview and its values. By negatively evaluating worldly wisdom and thereby taking up a stance against it, Paul intends to evoke among the assumed readers feelings that would deter them from thinking and behaving in ways associated with such a group (AFFECT: disinclination). Alternatively, the positive evaluation implied in *those ... being saved* is meant to evoke feelings of inclination, even desideration, that would persuade them to take up the type

---

12.5–8," *JGRChJ* 6 [2009]: 199–216). Note, too, that καταργέω—classified by Louw and Nida as belonging to domain 76 (Power, Force) (L&N 1:683)—also appears at 2:6.

109   See 1 Cor 2:6: Σοφίαν δὲ λαλοῦμεν ἐν τοῖς τελείοις, σοφίαν δὲ οὐ τοῦ αἰῶνος τούτου οὐδὲ τῶν ἀρχόντων τοῦ αἰῶνος τούτου τῶν καταργουμένων (But we speak wisdom among the mature, but not the wisdom of this age nor of the rulers of this age who are coming to an end). See Thiselton, *First Corinthians*, 166, who argues σοφίαν τοῦ κόσμου should be interpreted as "present world order," but doesn't go into detail as to what this means. Garland (*1 Corinthians*, 66–67) takes the phrase as referring not so much to "a system of thought so much as 'a style of life'" or "'attitude' characterized by hubris." This makes sense in context, but it does not seem to account for the fact that the Corinthians were using the wisdom of the world as a standard by which to evaluate others. Thus, throughout this study, *wisdom of the world/of this age* is understood as an ideology, a set of values, attitudes, and beliefs by which people in a shared context evaluate one another.

110   See Martin, *Corinthian Body*, 59–60. The theme of reversal is apparent in these representations (see deSilva, "Honor Discourse," 64–65). Fee (*First Epistle*, 69–70) keenly remarks, "[T]he crucifixion and resurrection of Jesus for Paul marked the 'turning of the ages,' whereby God decisively judged and condemned the present age and is in process of bringing it to an end. Those who still belong to it, therefore, are in process of 'perishing' with it," for "[i]n the cross, the promised 'great reversal' has been played out before human eyes in its ultimate way." Hays (*First Corinthians*, 30) states more succinctly, "The fundamental theological point is that if the cross itself is God's saving event, all human standards of evaluation are overturned." "Reversal" language reveals Paul's Jewish apocalyptic worldview (see Martin, *Corinthian Body*, 60–61; Meeks, *Origins of Christian Morality*, 117–18; Hays, *First Corinthians*, 28). For a basic overview of apocalypticism and apocalyptic worldview, see Aune, "Apocalypticism," 25–35; Aune, Geddert, and Evans, "Apocalypticism," 45–58.

of thinking and behavior that would be considered appropriate for this group (AFFECT: inclination). In this way, as Tucker argues, Paul seeks to "change the social identity of his hearers from an identity primarily shaped by the world's view of wisdom to one shaped by the gospel accurately applied in the life of the community"[111]—that is, "to *realign* the Corinthians' social categorization in hopes of adjusting current levels of intergroup discrimination."[112]

Thus, Appraisal makes it quite clear that Paul privileges the view that the cross symbolizes the *power of God*. The Scripture quotation in v. 19 provides divine justification for his appraisal. Using a Scripture quotation for this purpose has at least the potential for making a deeply profound impact on the assumed readers. Assuming they revere the God of Israel, the use of a text in which God is the presumed speaker would implicitly give Paul's appraisal a sense of divine endorsement.[113] Even if the actual audience, being primarily Gentiles, would not have connected the broader context of Isaiah 29 to the immediate context of situation,[114] as fluent users of Greek, they likely would have picked up on Paul's use of the related terms ἀπολλυμένοις (v. 18) and ἀπολῶ // ἀθετήσω and the negativity of each. This is the connection Paul wanted them to make. He wanted to connect God's judgment of the σόφοι and συνητοί[115] with his own negative appraisal of the same social group(s) and the system of values they represent in order to reconstrue the σόφοι and συνητοί of the world as powerless (– APPRECIATION: valuation).[116] God's actions of destroying and rejecting the wisdom and intelligence of the wise and intelligent carry with them extremely negative social connotations. As members of an honor/shame culture, the readers would likely have considered these actions something akin to public shaming in which the one(s) being shamed[117] undergoes a status transformation from "normal" (i.e.,

---

111 Tucker, *You Belong to Christ*, 167. See Henri Tajfel, "Social Categorization, Social Identity, and Social Comparison," in *Differentiation between Social Groups: Studies in Social Psychology of Intergroup Relations*, ed. Henri Tajfel, European Monographs in Social Psychology 14 (London: Academic Press, 1978), 61–76; Richard Jenkins, "Categorization: Identity, Social Process, and Epistemology," *Current Sociology* 48 (2000): 7–25.

112 Tucker, *You Belong to Christ*, 168 (italics added).

113 Christopher D. Stanley, *Arguing with Scripture* The Rhetoric of Quotations in the Letters of Paul (New York: T & T Clark, 2004), 83.

114 See Stanley, *Arguing with Scripture*, 79–83; Stanley, "Paul's 'Use' of Scripture," 132–46.

115 I.e., people with status and influence in the present age (see Pogoloff, *Logos and Sophia*, 113–18).

116 Paul does not construe this as JUDGMENT. He does not mention any specific behavior or character trait to be judged by God.

117 *Being* shamed is not the same as *having* shame; the latter is positive, but the former is negative. See Bruce J. Malina and Jerome H. Neyrey, "Honor and Shame in Luke-Acts:

abiding by group or societal norms) to "deviant" (i.e., deviating from group or societal norms).[118] The σόφοι and συνητοί are ascribed deviant status and, therefore, ought to be avoided, because they jeopardize the social status of anyone who associates with them.[119] By extension, this indicates God's negative attitude toward the ideology and values by which they live and which they perpetuate (t, – APPRECIATION: valuation). Associating with the σόφοι and συνητοί and adopting the values, attitudes, and beliefs by which they operate will result in being destroyed and rejected along with them.[120]

Similar to the Scripture quotation at v. 19, the function of the cause-consequence structure in v. 21 is to show that not just Paul, but God himself, negatively appraises the wisdom of the world. The proposition of the causal clause in v. 21, *the world does not know God through its wisdom*, betokens this negative appraisal through an emphasis on its ineffectiveness to bring people into relationship with God (t, – APPRECIATION: valuation).[121] This ineffectiveness is portrayed as the underlying reason why God *preferred as better* (εὐδόκησεν)[122] (+ APPRECIATION: valuation) *to save those who believe through the foolishness of the proclamation* (i.e., a crucified Messiah [cf. v. 23]), which implies both God's and Paul's evaluation that it is, indeed, the *power of God* (v. 18). Here then the juxtaposition of positive and negative appreciation is used to invoke the theme of reversal common in apocalyptic thinking: the dominant ideology and values of the world are shown to be impotent (t, – APPRECIATION: valuation), while the supposed "foolishness" of God is shown to be powerful (t, + APPRECIATION: valuation).

Pivotal Values in the Mediterranean World," in *The Social World of Luke–Acts: Models for Interpretation*, ed. Jerome Neyrey (Peabody, MA: Hendrickson, 1991), 44–46.

118   See Malina and Neyrey, "Conflict in Luke-Acts," 99–101.

119   See Malina and Neyrey, "Conflict in Luke-Acts," 100.

120   Construing the σόφοι and συνητοί in this way harnesses the readers' desire for honor (praise) and desire to avoid negative shame (blame) and uses it as a means of resocialization (see deSilva, *Honor, Patronage, Kinship & Purity*, 78).

121   A negative appraisal of the *world* in general (t, – JUDGMENT: ESTEEM: capacity) may also be implied here, but because Paul is in the process of comparing/contrasting more specifically the world's values and God's values, it is more likely he is evaluating the *effectiveness* of the world's system to help people to know God.

122   See L&N 1:362 (see NRSV's *decided* or Barrett's *chose* [*First Epistle*, 50]). A semantic connection on the idea of God's choice/preference exists between this verb and the prepositional group ἐν τῇ σοφίᾳ τοῦ θεοῦ in the previous clause. Barrett (*First Epistle*, 53) seems to capture this connection with the gloss "by God's wise plan." The idea seems to be, as Garland puts it (*1 Corinthians*, 67), "God was wise enough not to let human wisdom be the key to knowing God" (see Robertson and Plummer, *I Corinthians*, 21). For more on this prepositional group, see Thiselton, *First Corinthians*, 167–69; Fitzmyer, *First Corinthians*, 157–58; and Alexander J. M. Wedderburn, "ἐν τῇ σοφίᾳ τοῦ θεοῦ—1 Kor 1:21," *ZNW* 64 (1973): 132–34.

122   CHAPTER 3

The reversal theme iterates through the remainder of the section. First, in
vv. 22–23, Paul says that even though[123] *Jews ask for signs and Greeks seek wisdom*, he responds in accordance with the reversal God has enacted by proclaiming Χριστὸν ἐσταυρωμένον, *Christ crucified*. To some number of Jews and
Gentiles, this message is offensive and/or foolishness (t, – APPRECIATION:
valuation), but others, both Jews and Greeks, accept the *crucified Messiah* as
power and wisdom of God (t, + APPRECIATION: valuation) and thereby experience salvation (v. 24). Finally, the assertion Paul makes to close the section
(v. 25) inscribes the reversal theme in strictly evaluative terms: *for the foolish
thing of God is wiser than human* [*wisdom*] *and the weak thing of God is mightier
than human* [*might*].[124] The comparisons in this instance function to reconstrue the *foolish thing* as positive (+ APPRECIATION: valuation) by virtue of
the fact that it is *wiser than human wisdom* (i.e., the way of the world) and to
reconstrue the *weak thing* as positive (+ APPRECIATION: valuation) by virtue
of the fact that it is *mightier than human might*.

3.2.2   Engagement Analysis

The two clauses opening this section (v. 18) are significant with regard to Paul's
engagement strategy. The first clause construes a heteroglossic backdrop and
introduces into the dialogue the pessimistic view of the cross, namely that
the message of the cross is foolishness, and attributes it to *those who are perishing*. That Paul associates this view with the notion of *perishing* is a strong
clue that Paul wishes to distance himself from this point of view, so in terms
of engagement it may be tagged as an expression of ATTRIBUTE: DISTANCE.
The second clause attributes *to those who are being saved* the positive assessment that the cross is the *power of God*, which may be tagged as ATTRIBUTE:
ACKNOWLEDGE. However, there are occasions in text where the monoglossia of the attitudinal assessment—in the current case, "the message of the
cross is power of God"—overrides the heteroglossia of the attribution.[125] This
appears to be the case here because Paul categorically aligns himself with this
latter position. Three linguistic features signal this. The first is his association
of salvation (*those being saved*) with the message of the cross. Second is the
assessment that the message of the cross is the *power of God*. Third, and most

---

123   It is unclear whether ἐπειδὴ καί (v. 22) should be interpreted as concessive or causal. It is
       read as concessive here.
124   On *foolish thing* and *weak thing*, see Thiselton, *First Corinthians*, 173. It is maintained
       here that the neuter singular article refers to the death of the Messiah on the cross (see
       Johannes Weiss, *Der erste Korintherbrief*, KEK [Göttingen: Vandenhoeck & Ruprecht,
       1910], 10).
125   See Martin and White, *Language of Evaluation*, 115–16.

"TELL US HOW YOU REALLY FEEL, PAUL!" (PART 1) 123

telling, is that he explicitly aligns himself with the voice of positive appraisal by including himself in the category of *those being saved* through the use of the plural first person personal pronoun ἡμῖν (those of *us* who are being saved). As a result, the proposition of the latter clause does more than simply state the opinion of those belonging to the group; it makes a strong bid to align the readers into this point of view.

In the early Christian community, it was a common discursive practice[126] to quote or to allude[127] to the Scriptures for the purpose of reader positioning and alignment, and this is certainly Paul's practice.[128] The quotation at 1 Cor 1:19, the first of six in 1 Cor 1–4 explicitly marked by the formulaic γέγραπται,[129] comes from Isa 29:14 LXX.[130] Rhetorically, Paul uses the quotation to make an argument from authority,[131] which Appraisal Theory interprets as an instance of PROCLAIM: ENDORSE.[132] Paul uses the quotation to exclude any voices

126 See Lemke, *Textual Politics*, 19–36 (esp. 31–36) and Jay L. Lemke, "Discourse, Dynamics, and Social Change," *Cultural Dynamics* 6 (1993): 244–49 on discursive practices among communities.

127 On the challenge of defining these terms, see Porter, "Brief Comment," 79–96; Porter, "Further Comments," 98–113. For definitions of the words as used here, see Stanley E. Porter, "Allusions and Echoes," in *As It Is Written: Studying Paul's Use of Scripture*, ed. Stanley E. Porter and Christopher D. Stanley, SBLSS 50 (Atlanta: SBL, 2008), 29–40.

128 See Meeks, *Origins of Christian Morality*, 88–90. James W. Aageson ("Written Also for Our Sake: Paul's Use of Scripture in the Four Major Epistles, with a Study of 1 Corinthians 10," in *Hearing the Old Testament in the New Testament*, ed. Stanley E. Porter [Grand Rapids: Eerdmans, 2006], 155) is right to say that Paul does not "merely view [Scripture] as an authoritative record to prove his arguments" but as "a source of edification, inspiration, and stimulation, both verbal and conceptual." However "edification," "inspiration," and "stimulation" may be used to persuade, convince, or provide warrantability ("proof") for a proposal or proposition in an argument (see Stanley, "Rhetoric of Quotations," 44–58; Stamps, "Use of the Old Testament," 9–37; Roy E. Ciampa, "Scriptural Language and Ideas," in *It Is Written*, 55–56).

129 The six quotations are found at 1:19, 31; 2:9; 3:19, 20; and 4:6. See Steve Moyise, "Quotations," in *As It Is Written*, 15; Stanley, *Arguing with Scripture*, 78; John P. Heil, *The Rhetorical Role of Scripture in 1 Corinthians*, SBLMS 15 (Atlanta: SBL, 2005), 10.

130 It is typically pointed out that Paul substitutes κρύψω (I will hide), the final word of the LXX rendering of the verse, with ἀθετήσω (I will reject, thwart). For suggestions as to why Paul made this change, see Heil, *Rhetorical Role of Scripture*, 17–18; Thiselton, *First Corinthians*, 160–61; Fee, *First Epistle*, 69 n 11; Fitzmyer, *1 Corinthians*, 155–56. For a brilliant discussion of Paul, his education, and his access to and use of the Bible, see Stanley E. Porter, "Paul and His Bible: His Education and Access to the Scriptures of Israel," in *It Is Written*, 97–124.

131 See Perelman and Olbrechts-Tyteca, *New Rhetoric*, 305–10.

132 See Martin and White, *Language of Evaluation*, 126–27. Scholarly opinion varies with regard to how much context from Isaiah Paul "imports" into the current colloquy and how much Paul presumed the readers knew, if anything, about the context and text of Isaiah (see, e.g., Fee, *First Epistle*, 69–70; Collins, *First Corinthians*, 96; and Thiselton, *First*

124   CHAPTER 3

opposing the claim that those who think the message of the cross is foolish are perishing. The semiotic strength of this endorsement lies in the fact that the quoted text is, presumably, the voice of God himself. This is a powerful strategy for positioning the readers-in-the-text because it construes divine warrantability for Paul's claim (i.e., God and Paul stand in agreement on this point). This implies that to disagree with Paul would be equivalent to disagreeing with God.

The three questions following the quotation (v. 20)—ποῦ σοφός (Where is the wise person?), ποῦ γραμματεύς (Where is the scholar?),[133] and ποῦ συζητητὴς τοῦ αἰῶνος τούτου (Where is the debater of this age?)[134]—are all expository questions intended to guide the readers to the conclusion that not even the esteemed pundits of the world understand what God has accomplished through a crucified Messiah.[135] They are open-ended questions[136] and, thus, dialogistically expansive, construing a heteroglossic backdrop of alternative voices (CONSIDER). Yet, Paul does not wish to leave the readers to answer the question, so he immediately follows these three questions with an additional rhetorical question[137] (οὐχὶ ἐμώρανεν ὁ θεὸς τὴν σοφίαν τοῦ κόσμου [Has not God made foolish the wisdom of the world?]) that implies the answer Paul wants, thereby contracting and allowing into the dialogue only the voice that agrees with his position (PROCLAIM: CONCUR): "Yes, God has made foolish the

---

    Corinthians, 161 who bring the context of Isaiah to bear on the meaning of the quotation in 1 Corinthians). Recently, however, a growing number of scholars have been suggesting it is more important to consider how Paul uses the quotations for his own argumentative purposes (see Stanley, *Arguing with Scripture*, 22–61; Stanley, "Pearls Before Swine," 124–44; Stanley, "Paul's 'Use' of Scripture," 125–55 [though, see Brian J. Abasciano, "Diamonds in the Rough: A Reply to Christopher Stanley Concerning the Reader Competency of Paul's Original Audiences," *NovT* [2007]: 153–83 for an alternative view]; Stamps, "Use of the Old Testament," 23–36).

133 Fee (*First Epistle*, 71) argues γραμματεύς should be glossed *expert in the law* alongside σοφός (wise person) in anticipation of the distinction between Jew and Greek in v. 22. L&N 1:328–29, however, suggest the term could refer not only to an expert in the Law (i.e., Torah) but to a scholar in the Holy Scriptures.

134 The genitive group τοῦ αἰῶνος τούτου (of this age) clearly qualifies συζητητής (debater), but Conzelmann's suggestion that it "applies in content to all three" is legitimate (Conzelmann, *1 Corinthians*, 43; see Fee, *First Epistle*, 71).

135 Hays, *First Corinthians*, 30; Fee, *First Epistle*, 70. This betokens – JUDGMENT: ESTEEM: capacity of these three representative authorities.

136 See Porter, *Idioms*, 276–77; Dvorak, "Ask and Ye Shall Position the Readers," 211–12.

137 Expository or open-ended questions are those that entertain rather than assert a proposition; leading or closed ("rhetorical") questions are those that assert a proposition (see Martin and White, *The Language of Evaluation*, 110 and 123; Goatly, *Critical Reading and Writing*, 89).

"TELL US HOW YOU REALLY FEEL, PAUL!" (PART 1) 125

wisdom of the world."[138] The claim of this proposition is that the expectation generated in the Scripture quotation (v. 19) has been met; God has done what he said he would do. This is precisely why the message of the cross, despite its negative appraisal from the world's point of view, is for Paul and those who believe it the *power of God*. The theme of reversal becomes apparent: it is through this "paradoxical twist of God's grace"[139] that God supplanted the wisdom of the world with his own wisdom.

In vv. 21 and 22, Paul employs the semantics of cause and effect (or cause-consequence) in order to align the readers to his point of view.[140] In v. 21, the causal conjunction ἐπειδή modulates (MODULATION: OBLIGATION)[141] the relation between the event described in the causal clause and the event in the main clause; in other words, that *the world does not know God through its wisdom* is portrayed by Paul as the cause that motivates God's *preference to save those who believe through the foolishness of the proclamation*. Because Paul presents the proposition of the causal clause as a non-negotiable "given" or "fact"[142] upon which he and the readers-in-the-text presumably stand in agreement, it is classified as an instance of PROCLAIM: CONCUR. The consequence to this cause, that *God was pleased to save those who believe through the foolishness of the proclamation*, is stated in the main clause of v. 21. Although this proposition is declared monoglossically, it is still rhetorically heteroglossic because as the consequence or effect of a cause, the proposition takes on the status of "argued for" but not "taken-for-granted" or "given." This assumes heteroglossia in that it responds to the alternative point of view that someone could come to know God or has come to know God through the wisdom of the world.[143]

---

138 Because οὐχί is used in the question, an affirmative answer is expected (see Porter, *Idioms*, 278–79; Dvorak, "Ask and Ye Shall Position the Readers," 212).

139 Hays, *First Corinthians*, 30.

140 The interpersonal impact of the logic of discourse is almost always neglected, especially as it relates to reader positioning. This is largely because interpreters tend to privilege ideational meanings by focusing on the semantics of the logical relations being construed. For example, in Porter's discussion of causal clauses (*Idioms*, 237) he describes their ideational function—"A causal [or inferential] clause establishes a cause and effect relation between events"—but says nothing about their interpersonal function (i.e., signaling expectancy or counterexpectancy as a means of positioning readers). Unfortunately, this is common in the majority of grammars and commentaries.

141 See Martin and Rose, *Working with Discourse*, 128.

142 This is typical of dependent causal clauses (see Halliday and Matthiessen, *IFG3*, 603). Interestingly, embedded in in this instance of PROCLAIM: CONCUR is an instance of DISCLAIM: DENY (οὐκ ἔγνω ὁ κόσμος [the world does *not* know]), which recognizes and then rejects the voice that argues that the world does know God.

143 Additionally, the ironic group τῆς μωρίας τοῦ κηρύγματος indicates Paul's recognition of and opposition to a voice claiming the κήρυγμα is not wise but foolish (see v. 18).

Nevertheless, the clause has a rhetorical effect similar to that of PRONOUNCE (although with less salient subjectivity) in that it contracts dialogic space by insisting upon a certain point of view. That "insistence" makes a strong bid to align the readers to the view that God's preference to save through a crucified Messiah trumps anything the world has to offer.

The strategy changes slightly in vv. 22–23. Rather than opening the clause complex with a causal clause, Paul shifts to concession (ἐπειδὴ καί [even though]). The effect of this concession is dialogically contractive (DISCLAIM: CONCUR); Paul portrays himself as agreeing with the point that *Jews ask for signs* and *Greeks seek wisdom*. However, he counters (δέ) this in the subsequent clause (v. 23) with the assertion *we proclaim a crucified Messiah* (DISCLAIM: COUNTER). This concede + counter pair draws attention to Paul's actions, namely that he proclaims the "foolish" message of a crucified Messiah despite the world's demands for a message that measures up to its standards. It signals that for Paul, the crucified Messiah *is* the sign and *is* the wisdom the world needs, though, as noted in v. 21, they are not able to recognize it since they operate and evaluate by standards that cannot bring them to God. Thus, Paul recognizes that some number of Jews will determine the gospel to be an offense, and some number of Gentiles will determine the gospel to be foolish (v. 23). Yet, as Paul states monoglossically, still others made up of both Jews and Greeks will experience the call of God because they will be able to grasp that a crucified Messiah is the power and wisdom of *God* (v. 24).

In a way, the causal conjunction ὅτι at v. 25 signals that Paul is about to give the reason why the message of the cross causes some to perish and others to be saved. It is because *the foolish thing of God is wiser than human [wisdom] and the weak thing of God mightier than human [might]*. As mentioned above the reversal theme is evident in this assertion, and it is emphatic as a monoglossic assertion since no alternative voices are acknowledged. This bare assertion boldly states the value position to which Paul wants the readers to align.

3.2.3 Summary

In this section, Paul's selections from both attitude and engagement function to set the world's wisdom and God's wisdom side-by-side for comparison. Attitudinally, the world's wisdom is evaluated negatively as powerless (– APPRECIATION: valuation). Because it leads people to assess that the crucified Messiah is foolish, it can only prevent people from knowing God and experiencing salvation (cf. v. 23). However, God's wisdom is evaluated positively as *power* (+ APPRECIATION: valuation). Ironically, God's power was demonstrated through the shameful death of the Messiah on a Roman cross, but this, Paul argues, was what God preferred over against the standards of

"TELL US HOW YOU REALLY FEEL, PAUL!" (PART 1) 127

the world. Through a series of dialogue-contracting strategies, Paul works to align the readers to the conclusion that God, by his choosing, has flipped "the way things work" upside-down. God said he would reject the ways of the world (v. 19) (PROCLAIM: ENDORSE) and he fulfilled that expectation at the cross (v. 21) (MONOGLOSS). Of course this causes some amount of stumbling among those who live by the world's standards (vv. 22–23), but those who are called, those who can see past the world's ideology, recognize that the crucified Messiah is, indeed, the power and wisdom of God at work. This leads to the final statement of the unit in which the theme of reversal is explicit: *the foolish thing of God is wiser than human [wisdom] and the weak thing of God is mightier than human [might]*.

3.3 *The Great Reversal II: The Undeserving Receive What They Do Not Deserve (1 Cor 1:26–31)*

Drawing upon the theme of reversal, Paul has just made the point that the world's wisdom has no power to save because God has emptied it of its power through the "foolishness" of a crucified Messiah. Now wishing to bring the point home to the readers in a profound way, he calls the readers to think of their own station in life.[144] Using the world's standards, he leads the readers through a self-assessment that reveals them to be less than exceptional. Then in a powerful move he depicts God as having chosen intentionally those whom the world despises (which would have included the readers) for the express purpose of shaming those who despise them. The triple repetition of ἐξελέξατο ὁ θεός gives prominence to God's election, which stands as the basis for the directive against boasting.

3.3.1 Attitudinal Analysis

This unit of text is dominated by selections from APPRECIATION. After telling the implied readers to think about their calling (βλέπετε … τὴν κλῆσιν ὑμῶν),[145] Paul uses attitudinal evaluations to guide them directly to what he wants them to consider. Taking up human standards of evaluation (cf. κατὰ σάρκα

---

144 The term κλῆσιν is understood here as primarily a reference to the social status of the readers (see Theissen, "Social Stratification," 70–73; Pogoloff, *Logos and Sophia*, 197–212; Witherington, *Conflict & Community*, 113; deSilva, "Honor Discourse," 65–66). This is not necessarily, as some commentators assume, mutually exclusive with the view that it refers to the circumstances surrounding the readers' coming to faith (see Barrett, *First Epistle*, 57; Fee, *First Epistle*, 79; Thiselton, *First Corinthians*, 180; Garland, *1 Corinthians*, 72–73).

145 See L&N 1:349–50. Attitudinally, imperatives are tokens of the writer's + AFFECT: inclination in terms of desideration; prohibitions are – AFFECT: inclination in terms of desideration.

in v. 26)[146] Paul leads them to three negative assessments: οὐ πολλοὶ σοφοί (not many were wise), οὐ πολλοὶ δυνατοί (not many were influential), οὐ πολλοὶ εὐγενεῖς (not many were of high status).[147] Analysis of these appraisals reveals a number of important features. First, each appraisal is an instance of APPRECIATION (as opposed to JUDGMENT), evaluating as they do the assumed readers' social status (i.e., their social value) rather than their behavior. Second, the adjectives used in each appraisal signify a reasoned opinion and, therefore, may be classified as APPRECIATION: valuation. Third, each evaluation is negative, though this negativity is realized somewhat indirectly (i.e., the implication of *not many were wise/influential/of high status* is that *many were not wise/influential/of high status*). Finally, Paul "piles up" these semantically parallel appraisals in three nearly identical clauses, which, having an effect similar to repetition, intensifies the negative prosody generated by each negative evaluation.[148] All of this negativity functions to evoke among the readers a negative evaluation of themselves when viewing themselves through the lenses of the world. That is, through the linguistics of APPRECIATION, Paul positions the readers-in-the-text to conclude that by the standards of the world there was really nothing all that extraordinary about them.[149]

Having positioned the assumed readers to a negative view of themselves, the stage is now set for Paul to make the point that it is only by God's beneficent choosing that they have become honorable. Paul continues to make selections from APPRECIATION to achieve this purpose, but he no longer depicts himself as the one offering these appraisals; instead, God is the appraiser. Whereas Paul's appraisals were directly inscribed, God's are betokened by his actions. These are described in a series of three cause-condition clause complexes.[150] The complexes are:

[1] ἀλλὰ τὰ μωρὰ τοῦ κόσμου ἐξελέξατο ὁ θεός,
     ἵνα καταισχύνῃ τοὺς σοφούς

[2] καὶ τὰ ἀσθενῆ τοῦ κόσμου ἐξελέξατο ὁ θεός,
     ἵνα καταισχύνῃ τὰ ἰσχυρα

[3] καὶ τὰ ἀγενῆ τοῦ κόσμου καὶ τὰ ἐξουθενημένα ἐξελέξατο ὁ θεός, τὰ μὴ ὄντα,
     ἵνα τὰ ὄντα καταργήσῃ

---

146 See L&N 1:322–23.

147 Wilhelm Wuellner, "The Sociological Implications of 1 Corinthians 1:26–28 Reconsidered," *SE* 4 (1973): 667–69 unconvincingly argues these should be read as questions rather than statements. Even if they were, they would each assume an affirmative answer and the basic rhetorical impact would be the same.

148 I.e., they realize GRADUATION: FORCE: intensification.

149 See Tucker, *You Belong to Christ*, 174.

150 See Halliday and Matthiessen, *IFG3*, 418; Reed, "Discourse Analysis," 206–8.

"TELL US HOW YOU REALLY FEEL, PAUL!" (PART 1)   129

This threefold structure corresponds to Paul's three evaluations in v. 26. Just as those three appraisals realize GRADUATION: FORCE: intensification, so also do these three clause complexes given the structural and lexical repetition. Additionally, because the final complex varies slightly in length, lexical selection, and scope (though it has the same basic structure), it is the most prominent of the three complexes. In each of the main clauses, the desiderative/volitional process ἐξελέξατο (he chose)[151] operates as a token of God's positive appreciation toward the μωρά (foolish), ἀσθενῆ (non-influential), and ἀγενῆ (insignificant) respectively. By choosing those who inhabit these social categories,[152] God bestows honor upon them and thereby demonstrates his attitude toward them, that he values them (t, + APPRECIATION: valuation). However, that he makes this choice for the purpose of (ἵνα) shaming the *wise* and *influential* and rendering powerless the "*somebodies*"[153] signifies his negative opinion of those inhabiting these latter categories and, by extension, the ideology by which they operate (t, – APPRECIATION: valuation).[154] Following the grammatical structure, the appraisals alternate between positive and negative APPRECIATION: valuation. This alternation expresses again the theme of reversal introduced in 1 Cor 1:18–25: those whom the world considers worthless God considers of value and those the world considers of value God considers worthless. The major interpersonal function of this is to move the readers away from the world's "upside-down" way of thinking and evaluating and to bring them into alignment with the "right-side-up" system that God enacted and demonstrated through the crucified Messiah.[155]

---

151   See L&N 1:361–62. This connects back to εὐδόκησεν in v. 21, which shares the same semantic domain (see L&N 1:362).

152   Although each epithet is neuter plural (τὰ μωρά, τὰ ἀσθενῆ, τὰ ἀσθενῆ, τὰ ἐξουθενημένα, and τὰ μὴ ὄντα), they each refer to social categories and, thus, may be thought of personally. See Theissen, "Social Stratification," 70–72; Garland, *1 Corinthians*, 76; Troels Engberg-Pedersen, "The Gospel and Social Practice According to 1 Corinthians," *NTS* 33 (1987): 562; Tucker, *You Belong to Christ*, 173–76.

153   On glossing τὰ ὄντα as "somebodies" (and τὰ μὴ ὄντα as "nobodies"), see Thiselton, *First Corinthians*, 185 (although he uses "somethings" and "nothings").

154   This is represented by the processes καταισχύνῃ (he would shame) and καταργήσῃ (he would destroy). As mentioned previously, being shamed refers to the social process of status degradation in which one's honor is stripped which results in being seen as "less than valuable" by the group (see deSilva, *Honor, Patronage, Kinship & Purity*, 25; Malina and Neyrey, "Honor and Shame in Luke-Acts," 45). The sense of καταργήσῃ is constrained by virtue of its collocation with καταισχύνῃ, so here it signifies taking away the power and influence of the "somebodies."

155   "Upside-down" and "right-side-up" reflect Paul's opinion about the world's value system. As seen before in 1 Corinthians, Paul draws upon the actions of God in support his point of view.

130 CHAPTER 3

At v. 29 there is a marked shift from APPRECIATION to JUDGMENT, which indicates that Paul now wishes to use the reversal theme to appraise a behavior.[156] This clause portrays the reason why God exalted the humble and humbled the exalted: *so that all humanity should not boast in the presence of God* (ὅπως μὴ καυχήσηται πᾶσα σὰρξ ἐνώπιον τοῦ θεοῦ).[157] In light of the actions of God described in vv. 27–28, *should not boast* speaks to the impropriety of making a claim to honor on the basis of one's own achievement or using the benefactions of God for self-aggrandizing purposes (– JUDGMENT: SANCTION: propriety).[158] The clause *the one who boasts is to boast in the Lord* (v. 31), which forms something of an inclusio with v. 29, speaks to the propriety of boasting in the Lord (+ JUDGMENT: SANCTION: propriety), that is, giving due honor to the Lord for his beneficence rather than claiming honor for oneself. Sandwiched between these verses is a poignant explanation as to why it is the Lord and not any human that deserves honor: *it is by him you are in Christ Jesus* (v. 30). The readers, who earlier in this unit were appraised as less than remarkable, are now re-appraised positively but only because they are *in Christ* (t, + APPRECIATION: valuation) and they are so only because God's election of the despised made it possible. Application of the reversal theme is complete: the underserving receive what they do not deserve.

3.3.2 Engagement Analysis

This unit is largely construed as heteroglossic, although the main thread of argument is dialogically contractive due to selections from DISCLAIM. The negative particle οὐ in each of the three paratactic content clauses (ὅτι κτλ.)[159] in v. 26 indicates that each clause realizes DISCLAIM: DENY. In the first clause, Paul rejects the view that *many were wise according to the flesh*; in the second he rejects the view that *many were influential*; and in the third he rejects the view that *many were of high status*. These denials potentially put writer-reader solidarity at risk since they reject positive assessments of the readers' social status. However, ἀλλά is counterexpectant and signals to the readers that Paul is about to offer some kind of alternative proposition. This is indeed the case as Paul pairs[160] each of the denials with a corresponding instance of DISCLAIM:

---

156 Tucker rightly says the ὅπως "encompasses the three previous ἵνα clauses" (*You Belong to Christ*, 175) and, thus, states the greater overall purpose of the three previous cause-condition complexes.

157 deSilva, "Honor Discourse," 67.

158 See deSilva, "Honor Discourse," 67.

159 The ὅτι governs all three clauses, each of which defines the "content" of κλῆσιν.

160 Textually, the connection between each instance of deny and counter is based on the semantics of antonymy: σοφοί : μωρά :: δυνατοί : ἀσθενῆ :: εὐγενεῖς : ἀγενῆ.

"TELL US HOW YOU REALLY FEEL, PAUL!" (PART 1) 131

COUNTER found throughout vv. 27–28. Following denials, counters are frequently aligning rather than disaligning as is the case here; each counter puts forward a positive proposition that supplants each negative proposition in the corresponding denial (Table 12).

Each of the four purpose clauses in this unit are dialogically expansive rather than contractive. This is indicated by the fact that the verbs in the purpose clauses are Subjunctive Mood forms (καταισχύνη [2×], καταργήσῃ, καυχήσηται) grammaticalizing projective attitude. Context suggests the first three (καταισχύνη [2×] and καταργήσῃ) imply MODALIZATION: PROBABILITY (e.g., *God chose ... so that he* would *shame*; *God chose ... so that he* would *reduce to nothing*) and the fourth one (καυχήσηται) implies MODULATION: OBLIGATION (e.g., *God chose* [3×] *... so that all people* should/must *not boast*). Because modality (i.e., both modalization and modulation) "refers to the area of meaning that lies between yes and no—the intermediate area between positive and negative polarity,"[161] alternative voices around these claims are acknowledged and space is opened up for negotiation or dialogue.[162] Thus, in the model of Appraisal, they are categorized as CONSIDER. Paul does not pursue further dialogue or negotiation with those voices at this point in the ongoing colloquy.

There are two instances of MONOGLOSS in this unit. The first is realized via the imperative βλέπετε at the unit's opening (v. 26).[163] As noted above,[164] imperatives are monoglossic in that textually they only allow for compliance in relation to the proposal/demand they present (i.e., the alternative action of non-compliance is not recognized as an option in the text). The second, more significant instance of MONOGLOSS appears in vv. 30–31 where Paul

TABLE 12   Deny/counter pairs in 1 Cor 1:26–28

Deny	Counterexpectancy	Counter
οὐ πολλοὶ σοφοὶ		τὰ μωρὰ τοῦ κόσμου ἐξελέξατο ὁ θεός
οὐ πολλοὶ δυνατοί	ἀλλὰ	καὶ τὰ ἀσθενῆ τοῦ κόσμου ἐξελέξατο ὁ θεός
οὐ πολλοὶ εὐγενεῖς		τὰ ἀγενῆ τοῦ κόσμου καὶ τὰ ἐξουθενημένα ἐξελέξατο ὁ θεός

161 Halliday and Matthiessen, *IFG3*, 618.
162 Martin and Rose, *Working with Discourse*, 54.
163 Incidentally, this is the first imperative form to appear in 1 Corinthians (there are only nine imperative forms in 1 Cor 1–4).
164 See the discussion on 1 Cor 1:10 where Paul opts for a modality metaphor rather than using an imperative to direct the readers behavior.

132   CHAPTER 3

asserts emphatically *by him* (i.e., God) *you are in Christ Jesus, who for us was made wisdom from God and righteousness, holiness, and forgiveness.* Because it appears in an overtly argumentative context, this instance of MONOGLOSS cannot be interpreted as a given upon which both Paul and the readers agree. Nevertheless, Paul capitalizes on the categorical nature of the bare assertion to place special emphasis on a major point in his argument by not overtly referencing or recognizing any alternative positions.

The final clause of the unit, *so that—just as it is written—"The one who boasts is to boast in the Lord,"* creates a peak in the unit. Several features contribute to this. First, the conjunction ἵνα appears to introduce the quotation,[165] which may be classified as anacoluthon.[166] Second, that Paul cites Scripture (Jer 9:22–23 LXX) signals PROCLAIM: ENDORSE which construes a heteroglossic backdrop and dialogic contraction, yet the third person imperative in the citation itself, καυχάσθω, construes MONOGLOSS. Contextually, Paul's point is that all boasting is excluded, except boasting "in the Lord" (cf. Rom 3:27; 1 Cor 10:17). For this reason, the quotation and its categorical, monoglossic imperative are primary and the realization of PROCLAIM: ENDORSE is secondary. On this point about boasting there is no room for discussion: only boasting in the Lord (i.e., giving honor to the Lord) is allowed; all other boasting is excluded.

3.3.3   Summary

Selections from ATTITUDE and ENGAGEMENT in this section continue to construe the theme of reversal. In terms of ATTITUDE, the readers are appraised negatively by the world's standards, but this is reversed by God's action of election, which betokens a positive appraisal of the readers. Moreover, by choosing the *foolish, non-influential,* and *insignificant,* which results in their exaltation, God reverses the fortunes of the "somebodies," supplanting them with the "nobodies." ENGAGEMENT selections aid in applying the reversal theme to behavior. After thrice denying that the readers were in any way special as the world evaluates, Paul uses a countering strategy to supplant those denials with positive evaluations. Most interesting, however, is where Paul slips into monoglossic text at the moment in the colloquy where he wishes to apply the reversal theme to behavior. Immediately after saying *all flesh should/must not boast*—an instance of dialogically-expansive CONSIDER—Paul slips into

---

165   The phrase καθὼς γέγραπται (as it is written) seems to be circumstantial, which is signaled
        in the gloss offered here by separating it with em dashes.
166   See Thiselton, *First Corinthians*, 195. It may also be a case of ellipsis in which the finite
        verb in Subjunctive Mood is omitted (see Lightfoot, *Notes*, 168).

"TELL US HOW YOU REALLY FEEL, PAUL!" (PART 1)   133

monogloss to tell the readers that it is by God that they are in Christ Jesus, thus *the one who boasts is to boast in the Lord.*

3.4   *The Great Reversal III: Power Is Delivered through Weakness (1 Cor 2:1–5)*

Whereas in the previous section Paul used the world's standards to evaluate the readers, in this section he takes them up to evaluate himself and his preaching at the time he first proclaimed the gospel to them. Just as the readers were found wanting by these standards, so too Paul fails to measure up. Yet, in spite of Paul's weaknesses and imperfect speech, God's power was revealed to the Corinthians through the "foolish" message of a crucified Messiah.

3.4.1   Attitudinal Analysis

There are not as many significant selections from ATTITUDE in this unit as there were in the previous one. Nevertheless, the instances that appear are important for Paul's argument. The unit opens with Paul taking up the world's standards to evaluate the *speech* (λόγου)[167] he used when he first proclaimed *the mystery of God* (i.e., the message of a crucified Messiah [cf. v. 2]) to the Corinthians.[168] He admits that by the world's standards his speech was *not in accordance with excellence of speech or wisdom* (v. 1). At v. 4 he adds the further evaluation *my speech and proclamation were not [proclaimed] with persuasive words of wisdom.* Both of these assessments are instances of negative APPRECIATION: reaction. From the world's perspective, then, Paul's use of language was less than remarkable.

In addition to his speech, his demeanor would not have been viewed approvingly. At v. 3 Paul describes the feelings he exhibited when he first preached the gospel in Corinth: *I came to you in weakness and fear and much trembling.* All three of these bespeak feelings of insecurity (– AFFECT: insecurity), and *much trembling* (*much* realizes GRADUATION: FORCE: intensification), a physical surge of behavior, also indicates the intensity of these feelings. Presumably,

---

167   There may be double meaning in these evaluations. On the one hand, it is fairly clear the evaluations pertain to his use of language, perhaps his lack of rhetorical skill. On the other hand, v. 2 suggests some of the negative evaluation may be directed toward the content of his speech, that is, *Jesus Christ and him crucified.* This would be nothing new since the "foolishness" of a crucified Messiah was part of his earlier discussion (see 1 Cor 1:18–25). In the end, however, his point remains the same: by the standards of the world, his *speech* would be assessed as less than appealing (and perhaps less than appropriate), if not less than compelling.

168   Paul will return to the language of "mystery" at 1 Cor 2:7, where it implies something of a negative judgment of those who live by the "spirit of the world" and, therefore, cannot understand it (– JUDGMENT: ESTEEM: capacity).

all of these feelings—and especially physical manifestation of them—would have added to the overall negative assessment of Paul in the eyes of the world (– APPRECIATION: valuation). These were not characteristics that demanded respect and honor; rather, they were traits that would "detract from the standing and dignity of someone in the estimation of other people."[169]

Yet, none of these negatives thwarted the power of God. In fact, although the world might assess Paul's speech/proclamation negatively for its seeming lack of rhetorical power, when viewed from the perspective of God's value system, Paul says it was proclaimed *with a demonstration of the Spirit and power* (t, + APPRECIATION: reaction), so that the readers' faith would not be placed in *human wisdom* (i.e., the ideology of the world) but in *the power of God* (i.e., the crucified Messiah).[170] Thus, once again, the theme of reversal appears: where the world expects powerful messages to be delivered through whom it considers to be powerful people, God chooses to deliver his powerful message through weakness.

3.4.2 Engagement Analysis

This entire unit is construed against a heteroglossic backdrop; that is, at every turn, Paul construes himself as responding to alternative voices and points of view. That said, Paul contracts dialogue at nearly every turn; the only exception to this occurs in the purpose clause at v. 5, where the modality[171] of the process (ᾖ [*would be*]) leaves open space for negotiation (CONSIDER).

The first clause (v. 1) offers an interesting interpretive challenge. On the one hand, the use of οὐ typically signals instances of DISCLAIM: DENY, and if that is the case here, then Paul is rejecting the potential view that he came proclaiming the gospel *in accordance with excellence of speech and wisdom*. On the other hand, there is a strong sense from context that the readers would have inhabited this voice and expressed this very opinion (i.e., that Paul came proclaiming the gospel not in accordance with excellence of speech and wisdom). Thus, it seems more likely that Paul construes himself as agreeing with the readers on this point (especially if he is evaluating himself by worldly standards) in which case this is an instance of PROCLAIM: CONCUR.

---

169   John Calvin, *First Epistle of Paul the Apostle to the Corinthians*, Calvin's New Testament Commentaries 9, trans. J. W. Fraser, ed. D. W. Torrence and T. F. Torrence (Grand Rapids: Eerdmans, 1960), 50.

170   *So that your faith would not be in human wisdom, but in the power of God* bespeaks a negative appraisal of human wisdom (t, – APPRECIATION: valuation).

171   The projective attitude, grammaticalized by the Subjunctive Mood form, implies MODULATION: OBLIGATION (*so that your faith* should *not be in human wisdom*) and thus leaves semiotic space for negotiation.

"TELL US HOW YOU REALLY FEEL, PAUL!" (PART 1)   135

Concurring with the readers on this point requires further explanation, and the conjunction γάρ in the second clause of the unit (v. 2) alerts the readers Paul is about to give it. The explanation comes in two clauses that function as a rhetorical pair, the first clause of which is an instance of DISCLAIM: DENY and the second an instance of DISCLAIM: COUNTER. Together these clauses reject the idea that Paul had any intention of proclaiming anything other than *Jesus Christ and him crucified* to the readers—and this is precisely why he *came not in accordance with excellence of speech or wisdom.* By the standards of the Corinthians' world (which Paul has taken up at this point) the message of a crucified Messiah is foolishness, and coming to the readers with the single-minded intention of proclaiming such foolishness would preclude the use of speech that the world would value as excellent or wise. It is as though Paul says, "Yes, when I came proclaiming the mystery of God to you, my speech did not live up to your standards of excellence and 'wisdom,' but that is because I came solely for the purpose of knowing among you the crucified Messiah— a message you think is foolish."

The next two clauses—*I came in weakness and fear and much trembling* and *my speech and my proclamation were not [proclaimed] with persuasive words of wisdom*—present two more instances of PROCLAIM: CONCUR. These are followed by a counterproposal, as signaled by ἀλλά: *but [my speech and my proclamation were proclaimed] with a demonstration of the Spirit and power.* At this moment in the colloquy, Paul now shifts away from the world's standards of evaluation to those based on God's values, and the reversal theme appears again. Whereas the world appraises speech about the cross (not just rhetorical prowess but content as well) as both repulsive (– APPRECIATION: reaction) and lacking honor (– APPRECIATION: valuation), God (and Paul) appraise it as the power of God (+ APPRECIATION: valuation). For this reason one should not put their faith in human ideology and values, but in the power of God, namely the crucified Messiah (v. 5).

3.4.3   Summary

Attitudinal evaluations and engagement strategies play a major role in construing the reversal theme even in this brief unit of text where instances of each are few. Paul uses selections of negative APPRECIATION to make the point that by the world's standards his speech was less than excellent and "uneducated" (i.e., not wise). Furthermore, his deportment was less than what the world considers dignified and honorable—and Paul does not disagree with these assessments. Yet, many of the readers came to faith in Christ despite Paul's weaknesses. This, to Paul, is a sign that God is neither constrained by nor operates by the world's values; rather, he chooses to demonstrate his power through weakness.

136 CHAPTER 3

3.5 *Wisdom from Above (1 Cor 2:6–16)*

In this unit, Paul argues that his proclamation is, indeed, wisdom, but not wisdom that derives from or is dependent upon this age or its social entrepreneurs (v. 6)—it is God's wisdom (v. 7). Because it is from God, one who is world-oriented is unable to understand it (v. 14); however, the one who has received the Spirit of God is able to discern it (v. 15). Of course, Paul's goal is to do more than simply inform the readers of these value positions; he wants to bring the so-called rulers into alignment with them. Thus, on the one hand he positively appraises the content of his preaching, those who can discern it as God's wisdom, and God himself for revealing his "hidden" wisdom through his Spirit to those who love him. On the other hand, he negatively appraises the world's wisdom, those who perpetuate the world's wisdom, and those who do not accept God's Spirit and, thus, cannot discern God's wisdom. With regard to engagement, Paul noticeably displays a penchant in this unit for deny + counter rhetorical pairs. This is a strong indicator that in this unit he is about the business of reader alignment since these strategies often are used "to project on to the addressee particular beliefs or expectations or ... particular axiological paradigms."[172]

3.5.1 Attitudinal Analysis

The unit opens with Paul's pronouncement (see below under Engagement Analysis) σοφίαν δὲ λαλοῦμεν ἐν τοῖς τελείοις (Now, we speak wisdom among the mature).[173] Because *wisdom* is not modified in any way, it appears at first to be attitudinally neutral or "objective." However, by appraising as τέλειοι (*mature*) those who discern what he speaks as wisdom, which inscribes positive JUDGMENT: ESTEEM: capacity, Paul generates a wave of positive prosody that not only radiates forwards but also backwards to give *wisdom* a positive attitudinal value (+ APPRECIATION: valuation).[174]

In the next phase (v. 6b), Paul employs the engagement strategy of DISCLAIM: DENY (see Engagement Analysis below) in two parts (οὐ ... οὐδέ). First he rejects the notion that the wisdom he preaches derives from or is in any way comparable to the *wisdom of this age*. Implicit in this rejection is Paul's negative appreciation for the world's wisdom; one may assume from prior text that he thinks this so-called wisdom lacks power (t, – APPRECIATION:

---

172   Martin and White, *Language of Evaluation*, 119–20, 121.

173   Of course, the plural forms throughout this section indicate that Paul speaks not just of himself. Likely, they are inclusive of those who constitute the *mature ones*. That said, focus is placed on Paul throughout the interpretation given here, mostly for brevity.

174   See Hood, "Persuasive Power of Prosodies," 46–47.

"TELL US HOW YOU REALLY FEEL, PAUL!" (PART 1)   137

valuation). Paul more explicitly appraises the *rulers of this age* (τῶν ἀρχόντων τοῦ αἰῶνος τούτου). The adjectival participle καταργουμένων defines them as *being reduced to nothing*. This connects back to 1 Cor 1:28, where Paul says God's election of the "nobodies" was done so that the "somebodies" would be reduced to nothing (καταργήσῃ), which implies these *rulers* do not have the ability to discern true wisdom. The rulers of this age, then, stand opposed to the *mature* just introduced thereby drawing attention to the rulers' inability to discern (t, – JUDGMENT: ESTEEM: capacity). These negative appraisals generate a negative attitudinal disposition toward anything associated with *this age* and its social entrepreneurs. It is this that stands in contrast to the positive disposition construed toward the wisdom Paul speaks.

In v. 7. Paul defines the wisdom he speaks as *the secret wisdom of God* (θεοῦ σοφίαν ἐν μυστηρίῳ τὴν ἀποκεκρυμμένην).[175] By this he does not mean it is a wisdom that God keeps only for himself. Rather, it is his way of describing the wisdom as deriving from the very mind of God and, therefore, is special (t, + APPRECIATION: valuation). Additionally, Paul says God determined (προώρισεν) before the ages—*this age* or any prior age—that this secret wisdom would be *for our glory/honor* (v. 7b).

> Just as God *chose* the foolish and weak for salvation and thereby "shamed" the wise and the powerful, who are being brought to nothing (1:26–28), so now Paul repeats that God "destined" his people for glory (not shame), and has done so in contrast to the rulers of this age who are "coming to nothing."[176]

In other words, God determined that his wisdom would result in honor for those who are able to discern it while the *rulers of this age*, because they operate by the wisdom of the world and therefore do not understand God's wisdom (t, – JUDGMENT: ESTEEM: capacity), did what human wisdom demanded— they *crucified the Lord of glory* (t, – JUDGMENT: SANCTION: propriety).[177] This act resulted in their shame, not glory.

---

175   A number of English versions (e.g., NRSV, NET, NIV) read ἐν μυστηρίῳ (in mystery) as modifying or intensifying ἀποκεκρυμμένην: "we speak God's wisdom, *hidden in a mystery*" or "*secret and hidden*." It is maintained here, following OpenText.org, that the prepositional group modifies the predicator λαλοῦμεν (we speak): *we speak God's secret wisdom in a mystery.* See OpenText.org (http://www.opentext.org/texts/NT/1Cor/view/clause-ch2 .vo.html#1Cor.c2_16).

176   Fee, *First Epistle*, 105–6.

177   See Fee, *First Epistle*, 106.

138   CHAPTER 3

Several significant attitudinal evaluations are betokened by the Scripture quotation[178] at v. 9. First, in describing the inability of humans to comprehend *such things* (ἃ), presumably a reference to the wisdom of God that Paul preaches, the Scripture endorses Paul's view that the world's wisdom is powerless (t, – APPRECIATION: valuation) to provide insight into God's *secret wisdom*. This implies, second, that the *rulers of this age* have incorrectly evaluated the content of Paul's preaching as foolishness because they do not have the capacity to understand it (t, – JUDGMENT: ESTEEM: capacity). Finally, that *God has prepared these things for those who love him*[179] bespeaks further positive appraisal of what Paul preaches. As Paul has shown previously (cf. 1:26–28), God's choice infuses that which is chosen with value, and that is also the case with regard to what Paul preaches (i.e., a crucified Messiah through whom salvation is offered) (t, + APPRECIATION: valuation).

In addition to completing the contrast between God's and the world's wisdom, the Scripture quotation (v. 9) provides a transition into the next phase of Paul's argument in this unit (vv. 10–16). Commentators often assert that the main point of this portion of the unit is to argue that God's wisdom can only be ascertained by those who have received the Spirit from him.[180] Although this is not necessarily incorrect, it must be nuanced, for Paul's argument is more specific. In effect he argues, "What we speak is wisdom from God (vv. 6–9), and we know this because God has given us his Spirit to discern it (vv. 10, 12); further, if one is to understand the wisdom that we speak, they, too, must have the Spirit to discern it (vv. 14–15)." Thus, this section of the argument is as much about endorsing Paul and the message he preaches as it is about needing the Spirit to discern it.

At v. 10, Paul makes the pronouncement ἡμῖν δὲ ἀπεκάλυψεν ὁ θεὸς διὰ τοῦ πνεύματος (Now, God has revealed [these things][181] to us through his Spirit). That God reveals his secret wisdom to Paul through the Spirit bespeaks a positive judgment of Paul. Upon first reading, it appears as though the judgment concerns Paul's special relationship with God (t, + JUDGMENT: ESTEEM:

---

178   Determining what Scripture text is quoted here—if it is from Scripture—has befuddled many scholars. See Thiselton, *First Corinthians*, 250–52 and Fee, *First Epistle*, 108–9 for discussion.

179   Note that *those who love him* parallels *mature* in v. 6 creating a "bookend" of sorts.

180   See e.g., Fee, *First Epistle*, 109; Garland, *1 Corinthians*, 98–99.

181   The verb ἀπεκάλυψεν has no object, but one may be inferred from prior co-text. The nearest possible choice is the second ἃ in v. 9, which, itself, refers back to *what things the eye has not seen, the ear has not heard, and has not arisen in the human heart* (even these things ultimately refer to God's "secret" wisdom). Consider, too, the structure of vv. 9c and 10a: *those who love him* (v. 9) seems to be parallel with *us* (v. 10) and *prepared* (v. 9) seems to be parallel with *revealed* (v. 10). See Fee, *First Epistle*, 111 n 54.

"TELL US HOW YOU REALLY FEEL, PAUL!" (PART 1)   139

normality). However, Paul's emphasis on the Spirit's work of searching even
the *deep things of God* (τὰ βάθη τοῦ θεοῦ), as well as the analogy presented in
v. 11, suggests that the appraisal refers to Paul's ability to discern the intentions
of God (t, + JUDGMENT: ESTEEM: capacity). This is confirmed in v. 12 where
Paul says he has received the Spirit of God *so that we would understand the
things God has freely given to us*. Paul's understanding (εἰδῶμεν) of the things of
God, then, comes from insights given to him through the Spirit. Paul returns to
the matter of his own preaching in v. 13, where he explains that because he has
special insight into the *deep things of God*, that which he speaks as he *explains
spiritual things to spiritual people*[182] is *spirit taught* (λαλοῦμεν ... ἐν διδακτοῖς
πνεύματος [λόγοις]). *Spirit taught* betokens Paul's (and by implication God's)
positive appraisal of the content of what he speaks: his message consists of the
genuine wisdom of God because it comes to him through the very Spirit of God
(t, + APPRECIATION: valuation).

Fee rightly observes, "In a sense, the argument to this point has been con-
summated with v. 13,"[183] in that Paul has explained how it is that the message
he speaks really is wisdom, and why those who live by the values of the world
are not able to see it as such. Yet, he wishes to make this point very clearly and
with some emphasis, so he introduces two new participants into the discourse,
the *world-oriented person* (ψυχικὸς δὲ ἄνθρωπος)[184] (v. 14) and the *spiritual person* (ὁ πνευματικός [i.e., the person with the Spirit]) (v. 15), to act as reference
individuals that the readers may use as standards for self-evaluation.[185] In light
of the argument to this point, it is not surprising that the *world-oriented person*
is appraised negatively, clearly indicating that Paul does not want the readers
to imitate this kind of person. Such a person *does not accept the things of the
Spirit of God* (τὰ τοῦ πνεύματος τοῦ θεοῦ), a behavior that betokens Paul's negative appraisal (t, – JUDGMENT: SANCTION: propriety). Paul goes on to explain
that the world-oriented person rejects the things of the Spirit because such a
person appraises these things by the dominant values of the world. For that

---

182   This participial clause is notoriously challenging. On the possible renderings, see Fee,
       First Epistle, 115; Garland, *1 Corinthians*, 99–100; Thiselton, *First Corinthians*, 264–67.

183   Fee, *First Epistle*, 115.

184   Clearly, the ψυχικὸς ἄνθρωπος refers to a person who has not received/accepted the Spirit
       of God; in fact, this term likely describes the kind of person who is completely devoid of
       the Spirit (Garland, *1 Corinthians*, 100; Fitzmyer, *First Corinthians*, 183). The gloss preferred
       here, *world-oriented person*, captures the sense that such a person operates and evaluates
       by the values of the world (compare Thiselton's "person who lives on an entirely human
       level" [*First Corinthians*, 269]).

185   See Wayne A. Meeks, "The Circle of Reference in Pauline Morality," in *Greeks, Romans, and
       Christians: Essays in Honor of Abraham J. Malherbe*, ed. David Balch, Everett Ferguson, and
       Wayne A. Meeks (Minneapolis: Fortress, 1990), 306.

reason the ψυχικὸς ἄνθρωπος is *not able to understand* [*the things of the Spirit*] *because they are spiritually discerned* (t, – JUDGMENT: ESTEEM: capacity).

By contrast, the πνευματικός is held up as a positive reference person. Such a person *examines all the things* [*of the Spirit*], presumably because she or he has received the Spirit (cf. v. 10) and, therefore, has the capacity to examine and understand the things of the Spirit (t, + JUDGMENT: ESTEEM: capacity). Additionally, the person with the Spirit is not judged (i.e., examined, criticized) by anyone. Paul likely makes a play on the word ἀνακρίνω and gives it a negative sense here (*criticized* or *judged*),[186] which is likely a further (implied) negative point with regard to the ψυχικὸς ἄνθρωπος: the person lacking the Spirit cannot discern what God is doing; therefore that person cannot make appropriate judgments on the person with the Spirit (t, – JUDGMENT: ESTEEM: capacity). To judge the πνευματικός as wrong with regard to the message they speak (i.e., that it is foolishness) is tantamount to thinking God is foolish since the message comes from him and is mediated through people who have *the mind of Christ* (v. 16). According to Fee, Paul "probably means the thoughts of Christ as they are revealed by the Spirit."[187]

3.5.2   Engagement Analysis

Many scholars read the conjunction δέ in v. 6 as adversative (i.e., "however," "but," "yet"), so that the assertion in v. 6 is understood as a counter to the point made in 2:1–5 that his preaching was *not* with *persuasive words of wisdom*, but is wisdom *nevertheless*.[188] However, it is unclear how the claim regarding the *content* of what is preached would supplant the point about the *form* of what is preached or why Paul would want to counter the point about form since it is an important point of his own in his argument. More likely, δέ simply marks the transition to the new discourse unit ("now")[189] and, thus, realizes PROCLAIM: PRONOUNCE. The pronouncement construes the readers as to some degree doubting that what Paul preaches really qualifies as wisdom, so Paul "raises his voice" to insist that it does.

Immediately following this pronouncement comes an instance of DISCLAIM: DENY: [*we speak*] *wisdom not of this age and not of the rulers of this age* (v. 6b). Paul here rejects the notion that what he preaches derives from this age and is mediated through the social entrepreneurs of this age. This construes

---

186   See Fee, *First Epistle*, 118.

187   Fee, *First Epistle*, 119. See Malina and Pilch, *Letters of Paul*, 72.

188   See Fee, *First Epistle*, 101 (esp. n 12).

189   The new unit is also marked by the present tense-form (imperfective aspect) λαλῦμεν, the shift from first singular to first plural, and perhaps most telling, the shift from discussing σοφία in terms of *form* to discussing it in terms of *content*.

"TELL US HOW YOU REALLY FEEL, PAUL!" (PART 1)   141

a readership that, according to Paul, wrongly tries to evaluate Paul's preaching
with standards prescribed by the world and its so-called "rulers." Hence, Paul
excludes this point of view from the colloquy via the denials. He then replaces
this point of view with the proposition in the ensuing instance of DISCLAIM:
COUNTER (the two functions form a rhetorical pair), *but we speak God's secret
wisdom in mystery.*[190] The function of this counter is to align the readers with
the view that the wisdom Paul preaches cannot be evaluated by worldly standards because it is *God's secret wisdom* and is spoken *in mystery*. The world's
ideology and value system are simply not capable of discerning God's wisdom
in Paul's message.

The instance of DISCLAIM: DENY in the relative clause at v. 8 targets the
readers' view that the so-called *rulers of this age* know what "real" wisdom is
and on that basis have correctly evaluated Paul's message as foolishness. Paul
outright denies that these social entrepreneurs understand God's wisdom.
In what appears to be an aside, he expands the dialogue for a brief textual
moment (a rare occurrence in this unit) to suggest via a second class (contrary
to fact) conditional structure[191] that if the *rulers of this age* had really understood God's wisdom, they *would not have crucified the Lord of Glory*. However,
they *did*, in fact, crucify the Messiah which implies they *did not* understand
God's wisdom and still do not. For Paul, this logic warrants his denial.

In line with the pattern of engagement realized thus far in the unit, Paul follows the previous denial with an instance of DISCLAIM: COUNTER, signaled by
adversative ἀλλά. With this counter Paul construes an intended audience that
either disagrees with or is simply flummoxed by Paul's denial that the social
entrepreneurs do not understand God's wisdom. Thus, the construed audience
needs further evidence and/or explanation. Paul meets this need with an "allusion" to Scripture:[192] *What things the eye has not seen ... God has prepared [all]
these things for those who love him.* Paul leaves it to the readers to infer from
this "quotation" the reason why the *rulers of this age* are not able to understand God's wisdom. If God has prepared his wisdom *for those who love him*
(an epithet that parallels *mature* in v. 6) then the reason why the *rulers of this*

---

190   The perfect passive participle ἀποκεκρυμμένην defines σοφίαν (see OpenText.org word
       group view [http://www.opentext.org/texts/NT/1Cor/view/wordgroup-ch2.vo.html#1Cor
       .w597]). The prepositional group is an adjunct providing circumstantial information
       related to the predicator. Note, too, the connection to *mystery* back at 2:1.

191   The second class (contrary to fact) condition realizes CONSIDER and expands dialogue
       because the apodosis realizes MODULATION: INCLINATION (*they* would *not have cru-
       cified*), thereby leaving semiotic space for negotiation with regard to Paul's (subjective)
       point of view.

192   This is an instance of PROCLAIM: ENDORSE embedded in the counter.

142   CHAPTER 3

age cannot discern God's wisdom is that they are not *mature* like *those who love him.*

The emphatic use of ἡμῖν (to us)[193] along with emphatic δέ[194] at v. 10 signals an instance of PROCLAIM: PRONOUNCE, which is prominent because it breaks the chain of deny + counter instances that have dominated the unit thus far. With this pronouncement, Paul insists that *God has revealed* what the eye has not seen *to us* (i.e., to him and the mature ones) *through his Spirit*. This pronouncement, as is the case with pronouncements in general, assumes some level of resistance to what it proposes, hence the need for Paul to respond by insisting upon it. Contextually, it is quite possible the readers could object, "How could you or anyone know and proclaim the 'secret' wisdom of the divine—something that no human has ever known or thought of before?"[195] To this possible protest and others like it Paul responds by insisting that God has revealed it to him through his Spirit.

This pronouncement needs further explanation, which, as γάρ (*for*) indicates,[196] Paul begins to offer in latter half of v. 10 with another instance of PROCLAIM: PRONOUNCE.[197] Paul asserts, even *insists*, that the Spirit searches *even the deep things of God*. *Deep things of God* (τὰ βάθη τοῦ θεοῦ) may better be glossed *deep secrets of God* in this context, especially in light of the prior reference to God's *secret* (or *hidden*) *wisdom* that God *foreordained* (v. 7) and *prepared* (v. 9) for those who love him. In any case, the reference here is to God's inner thoughts as the ensuing analogy confirms. In terms of the dialogue, the pronouncement thwarts the view that humans, through their own wisdom,

---

193   The pronoun appears in Prime position in the clause which makes it the focal point of the clause (see Dvorak, "Thematization," 19–20).

194   Δέ is read here rather than γάρ (see Bruce M. Metzger, *A Textual Commentary on the Greek of the New Testament*, 2nd ed. [Stuttgart: United Bible Societies, 1994], 481; Thiselton, *First Corinthians*, 254–55; Fee, *First Epistle*, 109 [Fee argues unconvincingly for γάρ]). It is possible δέ is adversative, signaling another instance of DISCLAIM: COUNTER, but only if the point is to say "the so-called 'rulers of this age' are not among those who love God (a.k.a., the 'mature'), but we are." But this seems unlikely since Paul now wishes to move on to how he and those who are mature are able to discern God's wisdom and the "rulers of this age" are not. As a means of launching the dialogue in that direction, he uses emphatic δέ and pushes ὑμῖν to Prime position: *Indeed, to us God has revealed....*

195   See Garland, *1 Corinthians*, 98.

196   See Stephanie L. Black, *Sentence Conjunctions in the Gospel of Matthew:* καί, δέ, τότε, γάρ, οὖν, *and Asyndeton in Narrative Discourse*, JSNTSup 216 (Sheffield: Sheffield Academic Press, 2002), 280; Steven E. Runge, *Discourse Grammar of the Greek New Testament*, LBRS (Peabody: Hendrickson, 2010), 51–54.

197   This utterance construes a heteroglossic background by its insistence that the Spirit of God searches *even the deep things of God*.

"TELL US HOW YOU REALLY FEEL, PAUL!" (PART 1)   143

can directly search out God's thoughts and intentions unaided; the Spirit of God must serve as a mediator.[198]

Paul uses an analogy to position the readers to accept this point. The opening portion of the analogy is presented in the form of a leading ("rhetorical") question: *For who among humans knows the [deep] things of a human if not the human spirit that is in them?* The negative particle μή in the negative condition (εἰ μὴ) indicates the question expects a negative answer ("No one besides the human spirit knows the [deep] things of a human"). This realizes an instance of PROCLAIM: CONCUR in which Paul portrays himself and the implied readers as so thoroughly in alignment that the proposition may be taken for granted. This positions the readers to align with the point of view Paul puts forward in the supervening disclaim + counter pair: *so, too, nobody knows the [deep] things of God* (DISCLAIM: DENY) *except the Spirit of God* (DISCLAIM: COUNTER).

At v. 12, Paul returns to the idea that he and the mature ones have received this Spirit of God that gives them the ability to know the *secret/hidden wisdom of God.* With another deny + counter pair, Paul reasserts how it is that he preaches wisdom among the mature. The instance of DISCLAIM: DENY rejects the voice of anyone who might claim that Paul and the mature ones have received the πνεῦμα τοῦ κόσμου (spirit of the world), and the DISCLAIM: COUNTER replaces those potential alternative voices with the single claim that Paul and the mature ones have received τὸ πνεῦμα τὸ ἐκ τοῦ θεου (the Spirit that is from God). The final clause in v. 12 states the reason (ἵνα) why Paul and the mature ones received the Spirit from God: *so that we could/can understand the things freely given to us by God* (CONSIDER). The Subjunctive Mood signals modality (in this context, likely MODULATION: OBLIGATION [*so that we* could/can *understand*]), which leaves open semiotic space around the proposition for negotiation; hence it is tagged CONSIDER.

Having established that because he has received the Spirit of God he is able to discern the *deep things of God* and to *understand the things freely given to us by God,* Paul now shifts his attention back to that which he *speaks* (v. 13). He rejects (DISCLAIM: DENY) the notion that he speaks about what God has freely given (i.e., salvation through a crucified Messiah) with *words taught by human wisdom* (ἐν διδακτοῖς ἀνθρωπίνης σοφίας λόγοις). Rather (DISCLAIM: COUNTER), he speaks of salvation with words *taught by the Spirit [of God].* Again, Paul calls upon a deny + counter pair to align the readers to the point of view that what he speaks is the *hidden/secret wisdom of God* that he only knows because it was revealed to him through the Spirit of God.

---

198   See Thiselton, *First Corinthians,* 256.

144   CHAPTER 3

The engagement strategies in vv. 14–15 work together to create a contrast between two newly-introduced participants, the *world-oriented person* (ψυχι-κὸς ἄνθρωπος) (v. 14) and the *spiritual person* (ὁ πνευματικός) (v. 15). As noted above, Paul sets up these "straw men" as reference individuals for the readers to use as standards for self-evaluation. Perhaps not surprisingly, Paul shifts to monogloss as he describes each character. Paul says *the world-oriented person does not receive the things of the Spirit of God.*[199] This is because (γάρ) *it is foolishness to such a person.* This categorical assertion presents both the action of the ψυχικὸς ἄνθρωπος and the reason for the action as though they are givens. They function to create a negative attitudinal disposition through the lens of which one is to interpret the ensuing instance of DISCLAIM: DENY: καὶ οὐ δύναται γνῶναι (thus he is not able to understand [God's wisdom]).[200] With this denial Paul rejects any view that a person who operates by the ideology of the world can know the things of the Spirit or, by extension, the hidden wisdom of God expressed in the crucified Messiah. These engagement strategies make it obvious that Paul does not want the readers to view the *world-oriented person* as a character to be imitated. By beating this "straw man" Paul is clearly attempting to align the readers to the view that one simply cannot live by the ideology and values of the world and still grasp the wisdom of God.

By contrast, Paul asserts (again monoglossically) that the πνευματικός, the *spiritual person* (v. 15),[201] *discerns all things* (i.e., the things of the Spirit). Moreover such a person *is examined* (i.e., judged) *by no one.* Here Paul denies (DISCLAIM: DENY) the notion that any *world-oriented* person is able to make appropriate judgment about what the *spiritual person* proclaims.[202] This strongly positions the implied audience to the view that judging others on the basis of the dominant ideology and values of the world is to exhibit *unspiritual* behavior—and there is no other way to look at it.

3.5.3   Summary

The patterns of ATTITUDE realized in 2:6–9 help Paul to construe the distinction between the wisdom of God that he speaks over against the wisdom of the world. More importantly, these patterns construct attitudinal postures or

---

199   The negative particle οὐ does not signal a denial here (HETEROGLOSS); Paul is simply asserting (MONOGLOSS) that the ψυχικὸς ἄνθρωπος does not accept the things of the Spirit of God.

200   Καί introduces a clause stating the results of not accepting the things of the Spirit of God ("thus") (see *ANLEX*, s.v. καί and BDAG, s.v. καί).

201   In light of co-text, "spiritual" here refers to someone who has received the Spirit from God and accepts the things of the Spirit.

202   See Fee, *First Epistle*, 117. See 1 Cor 4:3–4; 9:3.

stances toward each kind of wisdom, a positive disposition toward the wisdom of God that Paul proclaims and a negative disposition toward the wisdom of the world shown wielded by the so-called *rulers of this age*. Coupled with these attitudes are repeating instances of deny + counter pairs. These serve first to reject points of view that Paul deems wrong or misguided and then to replace those points of view with those he considers correct. In 2:10–13, the attitudinal patterns create a positive disposition toward Paul and the message he speaks. Paul is appraised positively because he has received the Spirit of God and, thus, has the capacity to discern the things God has freely given to him and those who are mature. Deny + counter pairs continue in this section, although a couple of pronouncements also occur, as Paul contracts semiotic space around a number of key issues in his argument, especially as it relates to the content of his proclamation: Paul preaches the wisdom of God and there is no room for discussion on this matter. Finally, in 2:14–15 Paul introduces two "straw men" into the text as reference individuals for the assumed readers. In order to position the readers to imitate the *spiritual person*, Paul portrays this character positively but describes the *world-oriented person* in very negative terms. In the last few verses of this unit, Paul shifts to monoglossic text to evaluate these characters with no acknowledgement of any other voice regarding either character.

4   Conclusion

The claim of this study is that Paul's evaluations and engagement strategies reveal the system of values he believes Christians, and particularly the Corinthian Christians, ought to live by. They portray the basic stance (cf. chapter 1) around which the believers at Corinth and elsewhere can and should construct community. A model of appraisal was introduced in chapter two to help analyze the text of 1 Cor 1–4 for Paul's (and others') attitudes and engagement strategies. Although the study is not yet complete, it is beneficial to conclude this chapter with a demonstration of what the model has revealed thus far.

The thanksgiving period of the letter (1 Cor 1:4–9) is quite revealing. In this section Paul's feeling of gratitude for the believers stems from the many ways that God has shown beneficence to the readers, so that they lack nothing. In fact, the thanksgiving closes with a positive evaluation of God's faithfulness as it pertains to the readers' calling into the fellowship of Jesus Christ. This reveals that for Paul, at least, a core value upon which the community of believers is to stand is the beneficence or patronage of God. The community

146   CHAPTER 3

of believers does not—indeed, must not—operate on the basis of human patronage. Such generates pride that results in division and destruction of the community.

First Corinthians 1:10–17 is, overall, quite negative. Here Paul introduces the problem at Corinth. Yet, when a person, particularly someone who is a leader, discusses problems, value statements usually surface, and here Paul does not disappoint. The strong call to unity (1:10) and the negative prosody generated by the language of division in this section reveal very clearly that wholeness (a value related to holiness) is a central value for members of God's ἐκκλησία.

At 1 Cor 1:18–25, Paul introduces the apocalyptic theme of reversal into his argument and it continues to show up in some way or another through the next several sections. Appraisals and engagement strategies play a key role in construing this theme, so not surprisingly core values become apparent. In this section, the "wisdom" of the world, that is, its ideology and system of values by which it operates and evaluates everything and everyone, is itself appraised negatively as powerless, as holding no value. By contrast, God's wisdom, that is, his mode of operation and system of values, are appraised positively. Only by his choice and plan, revealed in a crucified Messiah, can one experience salvation. Thus, a key part of the axiological framework Paul construes is loyalty or allegiance to God (i.e., faith, trust). One must not trust the world's dominant ideology or those who rule by it for salvation; one must trust in God alone.

The reversal theme continues in 1 Cor 1:26–31, where positive and negative appraisals and dialogic expansions and contractions again emphasize worldly wisdom's fundamental lack of power. Paul shifts his gaze toward behavior at the end of this section where he argues that boasting (striving for personal honor) is improper because God, through Christ, is responsible for granting honor to the readers, they have not gained it themselves. Here the key value emphasized is humility. Humility, the opposite of boasting, flouts the competition for honor (particularly bettering oneself at the expense of others) around which the world's "wisdom" operates. Instead, humility is about living in the status that has been granted them by God.

Instances of ATTITUDE and ENGAGEMENT in 1 Cor 2:1–5 emphasize again the fundamental lack of value of the world's so-called wisdom. In fact, Paul argues here that God operates not merely in spite of but *through* weakness to accomplish his purposes. This was exemplified in the crucifixion of the Messiah and in Paul's ministry. Here is exhibited both humility and loyalty. Just as Paul remained loyal to proclaiming nothing among the Corinthians but Jesus Christ and him crucified (loyalty) in spite of the fact that such was considered "foolish" by the world, so too the community must eschew the world's ideology and values and remain faithful to the crucified Messiah. Otherwise, the integrity of the community will be jeopardized.

Finally, 1 Cor 2:6–16 ATTITUDE and ENGAGEMENT draw a thick line of distinction between the wisdom of God and the "wisdom" of the world; the honor of those who discern the wisdom of God, and the shame of those who do not; those who have the Spirit of God and the concomitant ability to discern the wisdom of God, and those who do not; those who speak with Spirit-taught words, and those who speak with human-taught words; those who have the mind of Christ, and those who are *world-oriented*. One significant value for the ἐκκλησία pressed here is that of being Spirit-guided as opposed to being guided by the dominant ideology of the world. Only when the members of the family of God are guided by the Spirit of God can the group *say the same* (cf. 1:10); otherwise, σχίσματα and ἔριδες, natural by-products of the dominant ideology of the world, will persist and will continue to threaten the integrity of the community of believers.

CHAPTER 4

"Tell Us How You Really Feel, Paul!" (Part 2)

An Appraisal Analysis of 1 Cor 3:1–4:21

1   **Is Christ Divided? The Problem of Coteries in Corinth (1 Cor 1:10–4:21) (Part 2)**

1.1   *"Your Actions Prove Otherwise" (1 Cor 3:1–4)*

In this unit, Paul returns to the specific issues of division and strife with which he began his argument (1 Cor 1:10–17). It may seem at first glance that 1:18–2:16 was a digression from Paul's main point, but this is not the case.[1] In that section, broadly speaking, Paul established two points that apply directly to the readers' discordant behavior discussed in the current unit: (1) the crucified Messiah was the means by which God turned the world's wisdom on end so that all boasting—a major source of division and quarreling among the Corinthians—is precluded; and (2) since this wisdom is available to those who have the Spirit, the readers, who lack no spiritual gift (cf. 1:5–7), should have known this and should not have been quarreling and dividing as the result of boasting.[2] Not surprisingly, then, in this unit Paul enacts his role as apostle (or father [cf. 4:14]) with conspicuous vigor to correct the readers' behavior.[3] This is made quite obvious through selections from both ATTITUDE and ENGAGEMENT. With regard to ATTITUDE, the unit is completely saturated with negativity due to Paul's repeated selections of negative judgment. In fact, except for the address ἀδελφοί (t, + JUDGMENT: ESTEEM: normality), every instance of attitude in vv. 1–4 realizes Paul's negative judgment of the readers. As for instances of ENGAGEMENT, dialogue is consistently contracted which strongly suggests Paul's social goal is to provide correction. It appears the readers, at least as Paul portrays them, think of themselves as spiritual, but as Paul makes very clear their divisive behavior says otherwise.[4]

---

1   Contra Wire, *Corinthian Women Prophets*, 39, 47.

2   Fee, *First Epistle*, 128.

3   deSilva ("Honor Discourse," 72) notes how Paul questions the readers' status as "spiritual" people and declares them to be immature in the faith on the basis of the jealousy and discord they exhibit as a way to use the "power of shaming to motivate the Corinthians to pursue the course of action which Paul perceives is in the best interest of the Christian community."

4   In collectivist group-speak, Paul argues the readers are not living and behaving by the norms of the group to which they now belong (i.e., the ἐκκλησία). That is, they do not seem to have

---

© JAMES D. DVORAK, 2021 | DOI:10.1163/9789004453814_005

1.1.1 Attitudinal Analysis

The attitudinal evaluations of the readers in 3:1–2b are based on Paul's recollection from his prior experience with them (cf. 2:1).[5] Recalling that experience he says, *I was not able to speak to you as spiritual, but as fleshly, as immature in Christ* (οὐκ ἠδυνήθην λαλῆσαι ὑμῖν ὡς πνευματικοῖς ἀλλ᾽ ὡς σαρκίνοις, ὡς νηπίοις ἐν Χριστῷ). *Spiritual* (πνευματικοῖς) recalls the ὁ πνευματικός persona constructed at 2:15 and plays off the contrast with ψυχικὸς ἄνθρωπος established at 2:14. Not being able to speak to the readers as spiritual people insinuates that they, similar to the world-oriented person, were thinking and operating by the standards of this age and unable to fully or rightly discern God's wisdom (t, – JUDGMENT: ESTEEM: capacity). This insinuation becomes explicit in the subsequent clause where Paul says he could only speak to them as *fleshly* (σαρκίνοις) and as *immature* (νηπίοις).[6] It appears that Paul used σάρκινος instead of ψυχικός to avoid suggesting the readers were completely devoid of the Spirit, which they clearly are not (cf. 1:5–7 and the use of the word group ἐν Χριστῷ in v. 1).[7] That said, the term aptly describes the readers who Paul maintains continue to operate by the world's ideology and values in spite of the fact that they have the Spirit.[8] At this point it is still unclear whether these are negative judgments of SANCTION or negative judgments of ESTEEM. Collocation with the term νηπίοις may be of some help. *Immature* contrasts with *mature* at 2:6. In that context, the *mature ones* were those who, because they had received the Spirit from God rather than the spirit of this age, were able to discern the wisdom of God. This strongly suggests that *immature* refers not merely to those whose behavior is childish (SANCTION), but to those who, despite having the Spirit, still operate by the wisdom of the age and are, thus, unable to fully discern God's wisdom (ESTEEM). Thus, both σαρκίνοις and νηπίοις are both criticisms of the readers' incapability to rightly discern and apply to their lives the wisdom of God (– JUDGMENT: ESTEEM: capacity).[9]

---

fully converted or transformed their identity to their new group (cf. Nock, *Conversion*, 7; Meeks, *Origins of Christian Morality*, 21–36; Tucker, *You Belong to Christ*, 205–8).

5   Tucker (*You Belong to Christ*, 206) calls this "employing social memory."

6   See James Francis, "As Babes in Christ—Some Proposals Regarding 1 Corinthians 3:1–3," *JSNT* 7 (1980): 41–60; Thiselton, *First Corinthians*, 288–91; Fee, *First Epistle*, 123–24 and sources they cite. Note that the double comparative clauses used here have a scaling effect similar to repetition, increasing Paul's investment in the judgment of the readers (GRADUATION: FORCE: INTENSIFICATION).

7   See Fee, *First Epistle*, 124; Thiselton, *First Corinthians*, 288.

8   See Fee, *First Epistle*, 124; Tucker, *You Belong to Christ*, 206.

9   Fee, *First Epistle*, 125 says νήπιος "refers to thinking or behavior that is not fitting"; in this case their behavior is not fitting for their "adulthood" in Christ. See G. Braumann, "νήπιος," *NIDNTT* 1:282.

150   CHAPTER 4

The references in v. 2 to giving the readers milk (γάλα) and not solid food (βρῶμα) continues the imagery of immaturity.[10] Paul's play on words with δύναμαι confirms that vv. 1 and 2 speak to the readers' inability to understand God's wisdom: Paul was *not able* (οὐκ ἠδυνήθην) to teach them as spiritual or, by analogy, give them anything more than milk, because the readers were *not yet able to receive it* (– JUDGMENT: ESTEEM: capacity). One should not read this text as Paul's self-reflection on his teaching abilities or his effectiveness; nor should it be taken to mean that Paul taught elementary (*milk*) and advanced (*meat*) principles of Christian living.[11] Rather, "the fundamental contrast in Paul's mind is not between two quite different diets which he has to offer, but between the true food of the Gospel with which he has fed them (whether milk or meat) and the synthetic substitutes which the Corinthians have preferred."[12] In this case, the "synthetic substitutes" consisted of the world's way of thinking, being, and operating. Spoiled by this diet of substitutes, the readers had not undergone a full transformation (including what Meeks calls "social relocation")[13] as part of their conversion—at least as Paul perceived them. They continued to struggle with acceptance and application of the message of the cross and the life of humility it demands. So there are two negative judgments of CAPACITY at work here: the analogy of being fed milk and not solid food, which is an ideational token of the readers' inability to discern and accept the wisdom of God when Paul first brought it to them (t, – JUDGMENT: ESTEEM: capacity); and Paul's directly inscribed assessment, *you were not yet able* (– JUDGMENT: ESTEEM: capacity).

Although each of these criticisms would certainly challenge the honor of the readers and would likely be difficult for them to accept, they are softened somewhat by the fact that they describe an earlier point in the readers' spiritual development. However, in a major move in the final clause of v. 3, Paul brings the accusation of immaturity forward to their present situation: *Indeed, even now you are still not able* (ἀλλ᾽ οὐδὲ ἔτι νῦν δύνασθε). This is yet another criticism of the readers' inability to accept and to apply God's wisdom to their lives (– JUDGMENT: ESTEEM: capacity). They have given assent to (cf. Nock's "adhesion")[14] the message of the gospel (cf. *in Christ* [v. 1]), but they have

---

10   Tucker (*You Belong to Christ*, 206) rightly suggests that Paul here employs the resources of social memory to teach the readers.

11   See Garland, *1 Corinthians*, 107–9; Morna D. Hooker, "Hard Sayings: 1 Corinthians 3:2," *Theology* 69 (1966): 19–22.

12   Hooker, "Hard Sayings," 21.

13   Meeks, *Origins of Christian Morality*, 26–32. See Nock, *Conversion*, 7.

14   Nock, *Conversion*, 7.

"TELL US HOW YOU REALLY FEEL, PAUL!" (PART 2)   151

shown no growth, no maturation in their spiritual understanding.[15] Both the emphatic use of ἀλλά (indeed) and the particle ἔτι (even/still) realize instances of GRADUATION: FORCE: INTENSIFICATION. *Indeed* increases Paul's investment in the criticism he levels against the readers, while *yet/still* increases the force of the "semiotic punch" delivered in the temporal shift.[16] Thus, not only is this the last in the chain of criticisms of the readers' capacity, it is the most prominent of those types of judgments.

At v. 3, Paul says the readers are still not able to take *solid food* because they are *still fleshly*. Σαρκικοί in this context refers to behavior that is blameworthy and is, thus, an instance of negative social sanction (– JUDGMENT: SANCTION: propriety).[17] This becomes clear in following compound leading question (see engagement analysis below): ὅπου γὰρ ἐν ὑμῖν ζῆλος καὶ ἔρις, οὐχὶ σαρκικοί ἐστε καὶ κατὰ ἄνθρωπον περιπατεῖτε; (For where jealousy and discord exist among you, are you not fleshly and living in a merely human way?). Two negative behavioral terms, *jealousy* (ζῆλος)[18] and *discord* (ἔρις),[19] are brought into the discourse in the locative clause that sets up the two-pronged rhetorical question. Since the expected answer to the rhetorical question is "yes" (note the

---

15   Not all scholars believe spiritual progress is the issue here because Paul chose the (typically) pejorative term νήπιος rather than τέκνον, which would be expected in contexts discussing growth and maturation (cf. Fee, *First Epistle*, 125; Francis, "Babes in Christ," 42–48). However, there is no reason why the idea of progress should be dismissed. Paul argues here in temporal frames: "When I was with you before, you thought and behaved in ways unbefitting people with the Spirit—and you still act that way even now!" Based on what Paul has heard from Chloe's people, no spiritual maturation or development has occurred among them, and their divisive behavior proves it. Cf. Malina and Pilch, *Letters of Paul*, 73.

16   Robertson and Plummer (*1 Corinthians*, 53) say that ἔτι "adds force to the rebuke" and that ἀλλά "has its strongest 'ascensive' force."

17   Fee (*First Epistle*, 121 n 3), Garland (*1 Corinthians*, 109), and somewhat hesitantly Thiselton (*First Corinthians*, 288–89) make a distinction between σάρκινος and σαρκικός on the basis that the –ινος ending connotes "made of" while the –ικος ending connotes "characterized by." Conzelmann, on the other hand, argues they are synonymous since they both are expressed by human behavior (see Conzelmann, *1 Corinthians*, 72). The sense should be determined from context. Paul used σάρκινος to criticize the readers for their inability to apply the message of the cross to their behavior (negative esteem), but he uses σαρκικός to refer to blameworthy behavior (negative sanction). Thus, although the two overlap in meaning, they have distinct senses in this particular context of situation.

18   On glossing this term as *jealousy* as opposed to *envy*, see John H. Elliott, "God—Zealous or Jealous but Never Envious: The Theological Consequences of Linguistic and Social Distinctions," in *The Social Sciences and Biblical Translation*, ed. Dietmar Neufeld, SBLSS 41 (Atlanta: SBL, 2008), 90. See also, Chris Seeman, "Zeal/Jealousy," *HBSV* 180–82.

19   Jealousy and discord are paired as vices at 2 Cor 12:20. See also Gal 5:20, where they are each listed among works of the flesh.

152   CHAPTER 4

use of οὐχί) it is implied that the readers do, indeed, have a problem with these kinds of behavior. Ζῆλος refers to the implied readers' divisive behavior manifested in the formation of cliques around one or another leader in the church for whatever reason (cf. 1:12; 4:6).[20] This results in ἔρις (discord), for the formation of cliques naturally stems from and propagates an agonistic environment of competition in which one person or group seeks to gain more honor or prestige than another. This is exactly the kind of worldly behavior that results from operating by the so-called "wisdom" of the world, which is precisely why Paul deems it inappropriate (− JUDGMENT: SANCTION: propriety) to bring it into the community of believers.[21]

Σαρκικοί (fleshly) is further defined by the second part of the rhetorical question κατὰ ἄνθρωπον περιπατεῖτε. The NRSV's *behaving according to human inclinations* may be the best rendering of this clause.[22] Contextually, ἄνθρωπον connects back to ψυχικὸς ἄνθρωπος (world-oriented person) at 2:14.[23] Such a person operates solely in accordance with the world's ideology and values without the benefit of the Spirit. Although Paul does not accuse the readers of being completely devoid of the Spirit (see above), he does not back down from drawing a comparison between the readers and the *world-oriented person* to make a poignant if not painful comment about their improper behavior (t, − JUDGMENT: SANCTION: propriety). What kind of behavior demonstrates that one is *fleshly*, living like someone who operates by the world's standards and not those of the Spirit? According to v. 4, it is making claims such as, "I am of Paul" or "I am of Apollos." That is, anyone who divides up the community of believers through the formation of cliques around various people of status are merely ἄνθρωποι (v. 4e) (t, − JUDGMENT: SANCTION: propriety). Fee's comment is apropos: "They are not only *not* giving evidence of life in the Spirit, but far worse, their quarrels and rivalry confirm that their behavior belongs to the present age, with its fallen, twisted values."[24]

1.1.2   Engagement Analysis

The unit kicks off with a deny + counter pair (v. 1) in which Paul denies that he was able to speak to the readers as πνευματικοί (DISCLAIM: DENY); rather (ἀλλ'), he was only able to speak to them as though they were σάρκινοι and νήπιοι (DISCLAIM: COUNTER). The function of this rhetorical pair is to reject

---

20   See Malina and Pilch, *Letters of Paul*, 73, 342–43.

21   See deSilva, "Honor Discourse," 64–67.

22   Unfortunately, they do not carry the gloss through to the final rhetorical question of the unit, where they gloss "are you not merely human?"

23   See Robertson and Plummer, *1 Corinthians*, 54.

24   Fee, *First Epistle*, 126–27. See also deSilva, "Honor Discourse," 72.

the readers' positive self-assessment as *spiritual* and to replace it with Paul's negative appraisal. Because the denial is directed against the readers—and especially because it rejects the positive attitude they had of themselves, even though it is depicted as an attitude they held at a previous time—this deny + counter pair puts writer-reader solidarity at serious risk. This is largely because Paul presents himself as being able to give a more accurate assessment of the readers than they are able to give of themselves (and of him!). Further, the counter portrays Paul as correcting the implied readers' self-assessment, which portrays them as being incorrect in their assessment.

Following the assessment of the readers as *immature* or *infants* (νήπιοι), Paul stays with the analogy and asserts that he gave them *milk* to drink (i.e., he gave them the basics of the gospel) (v. 2). Although this assertion is monoglossic, the ensuing clause construes a heteroglossic backdrop through the realization of DISCLAIM: DENY in which Paul contracts the dialogue and rejects any notion the readers may have that he had fed them *solid food* (i.e., a higher level of teaching) during his prior experience with them. The reason for this is given in a further instance of DISCLAIM: DENY: *for you were not yet able* [*to receive solid food*] (οὔπω γὰρ ἐδύνασθε). As before, the denials depict Paul as one who was better able to judge the level of teaching the readers received. All of this sets up for the next dialogic move.

The clause ἀλλ᾽ οὐδὲ ἔτι νῦν δύνασθε (Indeed, even now you are still not able) (v. 2d) marks the major turning point in the argument in which Paul brings all of the negative appraisals regarding their earlier stage of belief and applies them to their current stage (see attitudinal analysis above). The grammar of this clause makes it challenging to classify in terms of engagement. On the one hand, Paul's use of ἀλλά is emphatic (indeed),[25] indicating the kind of authorial emphasis that marks instances of PROCLAIM: PRONOUNCE. On the other hand, the negative particle οὐδέ signals an instance of DISCLAIM: DENY. In terms of discourse semantics, the difference between these two is slight. Both denials and pronouncements stand diametrically opposed to some other dialogic position, but authors use denials to reject the opposing view outright and pronouncements to resist the alternative view by "speaking over top of" the alternative view. What tips the scale in favor of DISCLAIM: DENY is the use of the negative particle οὐδέ; pronouncements are typically stated positively. Rather than functioning as a strong disjunctive here,[26] the conjunction ἀλλά realizes GRADUATION: FORCE: INTENSIFICATION, which functions to

---

25 See Thiselton, *First Corinthians*, 291; Barrett, *First Epistle*, 81.

26 This reading is preferable because Paul is not here countering the previous assertion; in fact, he is building upon it.

154   CHAPTER 4

scale up the degree of Paul's investment in the denial. What Paul so forcefully
rejects here is the notion that the readers had reached a more mature level of
spirituality since Paul's previous personal experience with them.

Following this strong denial is an instance of PROCLAIM: PRONOUNCE:
ἔτι γὰρ σαρκικοί ἐστε (v. 3). Typically, attributive relational clauses in which
some Attribute is ascribed to a Carrier are monoglossic, stated without any
acknowledgment of other points of view. In this instance, however, the adverb
ἔτι changes things, for it signals an authorial emphasis (GRADUATION: FORCE:
INTENSIFICATION). As mentioned, authors direct pronouncements at some
assumed or directly referenced counter position in order to resist or challenge
it by insisting that the authorial view is correct or more appropriate. Here, Paul
resists the view that the readers are spiritual (or that they are *not* fleshly).

To support (γάρ) this pronouncement, Paul calls on a so-called "rhetorical"
question (v. 3b). The interpersonal structure of the question is interesting. Paul
uses a locative clause to place *jealousy* (ζῆλος) and *discord* (ἔρις) among them,
after which the question proper is asked: οὐχὶ σαρκικοί ἐστε καὶ κατὰ ἄνθρωπον
περιπατεῖτε; (are you not fleshly and living according to human inclinations?).
The negative particle οὐχί creates the expectation of an affirmative answer
("Yes, we are fleshly ...") and, therefore, functions to construe both Paul and the
readers as being in alignment on this point. This realizes PROCLAIM: CONCUR,
which excludes from the colloquy any opposing points of view by positioning those who would advance them as being at odds with what is purportedly
agreed upon by the writer and readers.[27] This is a powerful means by which
Paul brings the readers-in-the-text into alignment with his point of view.

The unit closes with a second "rhetorical" or leading question (v. 4), but the
setup differs slightly from the preceding one. Where a locative clause was used
to create the interpretive context for the previous question, Paul here uses two
instances of reported speech introduced with a temporal clause: ὅταν γὰρ λέγῃ
τις· ἐγὼ μέν εἰμι Παύλου, ἕτερος δέ· ἐγὼ Ἀπολλῶ, οὐκ ἄνθρωποί ἐστε; (For when
someone says, "I am of Paul," and someone else says, "I am of Apollos," are you
not humans?). With the reported speech, Paul overtly and intentionally connects back to his early directive against disunity (cf. 1:12ff.). Once this specific
divisive, clique-forming behavior is reestablished in the discourse, Paul asks
the leading question. Like the previous question, the negative particle οὐκ is
used to create the expectation for an affirmative answer ("Yes, we are human").
Thus, also like the previous question, this one realizes PROCLAIM: CONCUR and
portrays Paul and the readers as in fundamental agreement on the point that

---

27   See Martin and White, *Language of Evaluation*, 124.

the readers are *merely human*. Again, use of leading ("rhetorical") questions is a powerful means of positioning readers to align with Paul's value position.

1.1.3   Summary

As far as attitudinal appraisals are concerned, this section is entirely negative, consisting of negative judgments throughout. The first five of these eleven negative judgments speak to the readers' incapability to discern and then to live by the wisdom of God, both early in their spiritual walk and at the time Paul addresses them with this letter. The remaining six instances of negative JUDGMENT are directed at the implied readers' behavior. Although they are people endowed with the Spirit, their behavior demonstrates that they do not live by the things of the Spirit. Tracing ATTITUDE in this unit reveals Paul's thought pattern: incapability to discern and live by God's wisdom (vv. 1–2) results in impropriety (vv. 3–4), which in turn signals that one is living in a world-oriented manner rather than by the Spirit (cf. 2:6–16).

Paul's selections from ENGAGEMENT function to align the readers-in-the-text with the attitudinal assessments. Paul makes ample use of DISCLAIM: DENY to keep any opposing voices from being heard in this portion of the colloquy. One of these denials occurs at a key turning point in the argument, where Paul carries forward the negative assessments of the "novice" readers and applies them to their current stage of spiritual development. PROCLAIM: PRONOUNCE is called upon for the purpose of social name-calling, in which he insists the implied readers are *fleshly*. Finally, Paul supports this pronouncement with two leading questions, both realizing PROCLAIM: CONCUR for the sole purpose of aligning the readers to agree with him that they are behaving as though they are fleshly.

1.2   *The Great Reversal (Reprise) (1 Cor 3:5–9)*

Paul's goal in this section is to help the readers do what, in the previous section, he chided them for not being able to do, namely to apply the message of the cross to life. The virtue/value in which he is most interested in applying to life is humility, the "socially acknowledged claim to neutrality in the competition of life."[28] Picking up directly from the reported speech in 3:4 (*I am of Paul; I am of Apollos*), Paul demonstrates how a humble attitude ought to direct the way the implied addressees consider both themselves and others in the community of believers regardless of how they measure up by the world's standards. Farming proves to be a helpful analogy for accomplishing this goal, and the social roles of master and farmhand are especially appropriate analogues for the point

---

28   Bruce J. Malina, "Humility," *HBSV* 99–100.

156 CHAPTER 4

Paul wishes to make.[29] As with previous text exhibiting the theme of reversal, attitudinal appraisals aid in constructing the sense of reversal by generating positive prosodies around those things the world typically appraises negatively and by generating negative prosodies around those things the world typically appraises positively. Choices in engagement strategy vary between monoglossic and heteroglossic, but patterns typically trend toward dialogic contraction when heteroglossia is construed.

1.2.1 Attitudinal Analysis

The two open questions with which Paul launches this unit—τί οὖν ἐστιν Ἀπολλῶς; τί δέ ἐστιν Παῦλος; (What is Apollos? And what is Paul?)—invite an appraisal from the readers, but Paul's immediate answer supplies an appraisal for them: διάκονοι (servants).[30] To a *fleshly* audience, such as the addressees as Paul has construed them (vv. 1–5), this epithet would not likely evoke feelings of admiration for Paul or Apollos; in fact, it would likely evoke a negative appraisal (– JUDGMENT: ESTEEM: normality).[31] Yet, this is exactly the feeling Paul is likely hoping to evoke in order to make salient the topic of humility— the polar opposite of boasting (i.e., self-aggrandizement) in which the readers were involved (cf. 1:29–31; 3:21; 4:7).[32] In naming himself and Apollos *servants* Paul implies that they are not "masters" to which anyone may belong.[33] It is *through* them (δι' ὧν), not *in* them (ἐν οἷς) that the implied readers believed. Neither Apollos nor Paul were seeking honor and prestige for themselves by winning disciples with their teaching as the sophists do;[34] rather, they were seeking disciples and honor for their master, *the Lord* (ὁ κύριος) (t, + JUDGMENT: SANCTION: propriety).

As is proper for good servants to do, both Paul and Apollos fulfill their duties as assigned to them by their divine Master (v. 6). Drawing on the farming analogy, Paul says he was given the task of planting, so he planted (t, + JUDGMENT:

---

29 See D. A. Carson, *The Cross and Christian Ministry* (Grand Rapids: Baker, 1993), 75–77.

30 See Robertson and Plummer, *1 Corinthians*, 56.

31 See Martin, *Corinthian Body*, 102; Garland, *1 Corinthians*, 111.

32 Clarke, *Secular and Christian Leadership*, 119–20; Tucker, *You Belong to Christ*, 211–12. Eckhard J. Schnabel, "The Objectives of Change, Factors of Transformation, and the Causes of Results: The Evidence of Paul's Corinthian Correspondence," *TJ* 26 (2005): 180: "Paul's identification of preachers and teachers as 'servants' turns the frame of reference of Greco-Roman society and its notion of social prestige upside down."

33 Fee, *First Epistle*, 129. Wire, *Corinthian Women Prophets*, 43: "The point of the farming analogy and the following one from building is to undermine any tendency of the Corinthians to choose between leaders, since all workers have distinct roles that are strictly functional and complementary."

34 See now Winter, *After Paul Left Corinth*, 31–43.

SANCTION: propriety); Apollos was given the task of watering, so he watered (t, + JUDGMENT: SANCTION: propriety). Yet, as the analogy goes, neither the one who plants nor the one who waters has anything to do with the actual growth of the crops (v. 7); that is the work of God (ὁ θεὸς ηὔξανεν [God makes grow] [v. 6]; ὁ αὐξάνων θεός [God is the one who makes grow] [v. 7]). Therefore, Paul concludes, ὥστε οὔτε ὁ φυτεύων ἐστίν τι οὔτε ὁ ποτίζων ἀλλ᾽ ὁ αὐξάνων θεός (So then, neither the one who plants nor the one who waters is anything, but God who makes growth [is something]).[35] Here, the planter and waterer are appraised as not being all that special (– JUDGMENT: ESTEEM: normality), but by contrast God is evaluated as being very special (+ JUDGMENT: ESTEEM: normality). As Conzelmann puts it, "Although Paul and Apollos are God's 'fellow-workers' (v. 9), they have no special merit. Their work is incommensurable with God's work."[36] Although the planter and the waterer act appropriately by fulfilling their tasks, they have no right to boast in their efforts (i.e., claim honor for themselves); rather, they must give all honor to God—they must "boast in the Lord" (1:31)—who is ultimately responsible for the fruit of their efforts.

What Paul has said so far is only half of the application he wishes to make. At v. 8, he asserts ὁ φυτεύων δὲ καὶ ὁ ποτίζων ἕν εἰσιν (The one who plants and the one who waters are one). In the context of the analogy, *one* most likely speaks to the *unity of purpose* shared by the workers despite the difference in their tasks.[37] This description of oneness reflects the value of wholeness or completeness that Paul prizes;[38] not surprisingly, such singleness of purpose is viewed in positive light (+ JUDGMENT: SANCTION: propriety).[39] Emphasis is placed on the mutuality of the planter and waterer, of Paul and Apollos; neither of them boasts in the results of their individual tasks, for doing so would destroy their singleness of purpose and hinder the growth God can bring. As Garland puts it, "[A] rivalry between a planter and a waterer is absurd. The farmer's field is not a battlefield where workers vie with one another for

---

35   The assertion of the first clause that neither the planter nor the waterer is anything (or perhaps neither is anybody [special]) is countered and supplanted by the assertion of the second clause that God who makes growth is something (or somebody [special]). In a context where boasting and self-glorying is a problem, the point seems to be that God is "everything," so that only he is to receive glory/honor. Note, too, that τι is an expression of GRADUATION: FOCUS: soften.

36   Conzelmann, *1 Corinthians*, 74.

37   Witherington, *Conflict & Community*, 132. See Carson, *The Cross and Christian Ministry*, 76; Thiselton, *First Corinthians*, 303.

38   See Neyrey, *Paul*, 112–14.

39   This judgment operates on the assumption that the planter and waterer both have the end result of all the work in view, not just the end goal of their own task.

158 CHAPTER 4

supremacy. It is a farmstead to be brought under cultivation so as to produce fruit. If the farmhands do not work cooperatively, the crop will be ruined."[40] Because the workers' unity of purpose stands in such stark contrast to the divisiveness of the readers (cf. 1:12; 3:4; 4:6), the readers are indirectly implicated in hindering, if not ruining, the work of God (t, –JUDGMENT: SANCTION: propriety). They should heed the reminder that *each will receive their own reward according to their own labor*. If the planter and the waterer both do their part so the whole lot benefits (unity for the benefit of the whole),[41] then each worker involved will reap these benefits along with all the other workers. However, if either the planter or the waterer fails to do their part so the whole lot suffers (disunity negatively impacting the whole), then the worker not doing their part will forfeit their share to any benefits that might still have been gleaned.[42]

To conclude the unit (v. 9), Paul claims *we* (i.e., Paul the planter and Apollos the waterer) *are fellow workers belonging to God*. Paul is not here suggesting that he and Apollos are fellow workers *with God*; for he has already established that they are servants of God, and in ancient culture servants are not coworkers with masters.[43] Rather, he reiterates his main point: he and Apollos, planter and waterer, both *belong* to God and are jointly commissioned (though each with his own task) to work for the common cause of planting and watering God's field (t, +JUDGMENT: SANCTION: propriety)[44]—and the readers are that field (v. 9b) (t, +JUDGMENT: ESTEEM: normality).

1.2.2 Engagement Analysis

Each of the two open questions leading off this unit (v. 5) are instances of CONSIDER. As expository questions they introduce the topic into the colloquy and thereby open space for discussion. However, Paul immediately contracts the

---

40 Garland, *1 Corinthians*, 112. See Hays, *First Corinthians*, 52; Oster, *1 Corinthians*, 94.

41 Behaving in ways that support and build up the entire group is an important theme in the Pauline epistles. See, e.g., Rom 14:19; 15:2; 1 Cor 8:1; 10:23–24; 12:7; 14:12, 26–33; Eph 4:12, 29; 1 Thess 5:11.

42 This interpretation takes into account the collectivist (group-oriented) culture shared by Paul and the readers. On group-orientation, see Malina, *New Testament World*, 60–67; Neyrey, "Group Orientation," 80–83. There is debate as to whether or not μισθός is used in reference to eschatological reward (i.e., eternal life) (see D. W. Kuck, *Judgment and Community Conflict: Paul's Use of Apocalyptic Judgment Language in 1 Corinthians 3:5–4:5*, NovTSup 66 [Leiden: Brill, 1998], 167; K. L. Yinger, *Paul, Judaism, and Judgment According to Deeds* [Cambridge: Cambridge University Press, 1999], 212). Many contemporary interpreters think the point here is that the *reward*, whatever it may be, will come from God (see Thiselton, *First Corinthians*, 304; Tucker, *You Belong to Christ*, 215).

43 See Garland, *1 Corinthians*, 113; Carson, *The Cross and Christian Ministry*, 76. Contra Witherington, *Conflict & Community*, 132–33.

44 Cf. Fee, *First Epistle*, 133.

"TELL US HOW YOU REALLY FEEL, PAUL!" (PART 2)   159

dialogue by answering both of these questions with back-to-back instances of
PROCLAIM: PRONOUNCE:[45] *servants through whom you believed* and *to each as
the Lord gave a task.* By insisting in the first clause that both he and Apollos are
nothing more than διάκονοι, Paul directly challenges the view that either one
or both of them are to be venerated in some way based on worldly standards.
The second clause insists that although each of them were commissioned
by the Lord with different tasks, they both serve the same master and thus a
single purpose.

At v. 6, both *I planted* and *Apollos watered* are monoglossic, presenting propositions that are givens or "taken-for-granted." That said, they generate a certain expectation among the readers-in-the-text that because Paul planted and
Apollos watered the two were also responsible for growth. Paul counters that
expectation with ἀλλ᾿ ὁ θεὸς ηὔξανεν (but God gave the increase). The "axiological paradigm"[46] Paul projects onto the readers with this counter is that one
ought to understand that God provides the growth, not God's workers.

As if the counter in v. 6 was not strong enough to make his point, Paul follows in v. 7 with a deny + counter pair that emphasizes the same point, a realization of GRADUATION: FORCE: INTENSIFICATION along the same lines
as repetition. He concludes ὥστε οὔτε ὁ φυτεύων ἐστίν τι οὔτε ὁ ποτίζων ἀλλ᾿ ὁ
αὐξάνων θεός (so then, neither the one who plants nor the one who waters is
anything, but God who makes grow [is something]). The neither/nor structure
embeds two denials (DISCLAIM: DENY) into this single clause (a realization
of GRADUATION: FORCE) by which Paul rejects the idea that the servants—
the planter and the waterer—have anything to do with the growth of crops
they planted and watered. He replaces this notion in the countering clause,
ἀλλ᾿ ὁ αὐξάνων θεός (but God who makes grow [is everything]). Again, Paul
corrects the readers by supplying them with the value position by which they
ought to appraise Paul and Apollos, or for that matter themselves, namely
that they are servants of God who is ultimately responsible for the growth of
the community.

Like v. 6, v. 8 begins with a monoglossic statement, ὁ φυτεύων δὲ καὶ ὁ ποτίζων
ἕν εἰσιν (the one who plants and the one who waters are one), stating categorically that the two workers, though involved in different tasks, work together
for a unified purpose. Any voice that might argue on the basis of their distinct
tasks that they serve distinct purposes is ignored and thus completely shut out
of the dialogue. Paul treats this proposition as though it is a given, something

---

45   Although these statements appear to be instances of MONOGLOSS, they are not because
      they are obvious responses to the opening questions, serving to squelch (contract) other
      possible answers.
46   Martin and White, *Language of Evaluation*, 121.

160   CHAPTER 4

that both he and the readers may take for granted after having argued the point. In fact, the next proposition uses this "taken-for-granted-ness" as its launching point, countering the expectation generated by [*the workers*] *are one*: ἕκαστος δὲ τὸν ἴδιον μισθὸν λήμψεται κατὰ τὸν ἴδιον κόπον (but each can expect to receive their own reward according to their own labor). Paul does not completely supplant the claim that the workers have a single purpose. He does, however, play off ἕν (one) with ἕκαστος (each) to make the point that, as noted above, the planter and the waterer must both do their part so the entire work is completed and the whole group benefits, otherwise the one that fails to do their part will forfeit their access to any benefits that may still be gleaned.

Paul closes the unit with two clauses that exhibit monoglossia (v. 9). Fee rightly sees these closing comments as a terse yet emphatic summation of the whole paragraph's argument.[47] The main point for which Paul has been arguing is that those who lead in the church—even apostles—are merely servants who work at God's behest. These servants seek honor not for themselves, but for God who has given each of them their own task in his larger plan. Thus, Paul concludes θεοῦ γάρ ἐσμεν συνεργοί, θεοῦ γεώργιον, θεοῦ οἰκοδομή ἐστε (For we are co-workers belonging to God; you are God's field, God's building). These new "slogans"[48] are not braggadocio statements; rather, they emphasize that all belongs to God, whether the work of the servants, the field (i.e., the church at Corinth), or the building (i.e., the church at Corinth). As a result, all boasting is excluded, except that which is in the Lord.

1.2.3   Summary

It was noted at the outset of this section that Paul's intent was to demonstrate to the readers how the message of the cross ought to be applied to life. The first move was to name himself and Apollos as *servants* who work to fulfill the duties the Lord has assigned to them. It was very likely Paul's intention to evoke a negative reaction among the readers by casting himself and Apollos in this role, for with servanthood comes a negative evaluation—"not special." With this the reversal theme that was apparent throughout 1 Cor 1:18–2:5 is reestablished in the present text: the high-status, self-promoting people that the world might expect to lead God's community are rejected by God in favor of humble servants. Thus, Paul and Apollos are evaluated as nothing special, as mere farmhands doing their menial labor for the Master. They do not boast in their own efforts, but give honor to God who is ultimately responsible for growth. Any voices that may have appraised Paul, Apollos, or both as something special are

---

47   Fee, *First Epistle*, 134.
48   Fee (*First Epistle*, 134) sees these as countering the "slogans" back at 1 Cor 1:12.

"TELL US HOW YOU REALLY FEEL, PAUL!" (PART 2)   161

squelched from the colloquy by means of pronouncements, denials, counters, and monoglossic assertions. This indicates that on the point of where honor should be given, Paul stands firm on one position: all glory goes to God.

1.3   Consider Carefully How You Build (1 Cor 3:10–17)

Paul moves now to elaborate on the metaphor of God's *building* (οἰκοδομή) which he introduced quite suddenly at the end of v. 9. His purpose is to urge the readers to consider carefully the how they build the community of God (v. 10). From the previous unit, he picks up the notion of each one receiving a reward in accordance with their labor (v. 8), repurposes it for the building metaphor, and relates it to the materials one uses to build (cf. μισθὸν λήμψεται and ζημιωθήσεται in vv. 14 and 15).[49] If they build with appropriate materials, what they construct can withstand the test of fire on the day of the Lord and result in receiving a reward. Thus, Paul appraises both the builders and the (meta-phorical) building materials in order to position readers to choose that which is appropriate. He also draws heavily on the semantics of expectation—what to expect when a someone builds on the foundation of Christ, what to expect on the day of the Lord, what to expect when one's building remains or burns, what to expect if someone destroys "the temple of God"—so dialogically, there are a number of instances of CONSIDER expanding the dialogue around certain conditions. By this means, Paul attempts to get the readers to think critically about their actions.

1.3.1   Attitudinal Analysis

The unit opens with Paul's appraisal of the first of the builders he evaluates in this text: himself (v. 10). He calls himself a *wise (master) builder* (σοφὸς ἀρχι-τέκτων) (+ JUDGMENT: ESTEEM: capacity).[50] Lest someone think he is guilty of the kind of boasting he proscribed earlier in the letter, Paul precedes his self-assessment with a very important qualification: κατὰ τὴν χάριν τοῦ θεοῦ τὴν δοθεῖσάν μοι (in accordance with the benefaction given to me from God).[51] Echoing the thought of 1 Cor 3:5 (i.e., servants perform the tasks that God assigns [ἔδωκεν] to them), Paul speaks here of the *benefaction* that God gave him

---

49   See Fee, *First Epistle*, 136.

50   While it is appropriate to gloss the adjective σοφός as *skilled* here (L&N 1:335–36; NRSV; NET), it is likely no accident that Paul chose this terminology, relating as it does to his argument that he speaks the wisdom of God (2:6–16). See Garland, *1 Corinthians*, 114.

51   This Adjunct appears in the Prime of the clause so that everything in the clause's Subsequent may be read in light of it (cf. Dvorak, "Thematization," 19–20).

162   CHAPTER 4

to complete his task.[52] Thus, in assessing himself as a *wise builder*, Paul is not involved in the kind of self-aggrandizing boasting he eschews in prior text; rather, he is boasting in the Lord (cf. 1:31). It is God who enables him to function as a *skilled (master) builder*.

There are a number of scholarly opinions regarding the nature of the benefaction Paul received from God, but in this context it likely refers to the *foundation* he put down, namely *Jesus Christ*.[53] This becomes the standard by which the next builder is appraised. Paul says θεμέλιον γὰρ ἄλλον οὐδεὶς δύναται θεῖναι παρὰ τὸν κείμενον, ὅς ἐστιν Ἰησοῦς Χριστός (For nobody is able to put down another foundation other than the one already laid, which is Jesus Christ). Here laying a foundation other than the one Paul has already laid is portrayed as overstepping a major group boundary. Therefore, *nobody*[54] *is able to put down* implicitly appraises as deviant any builder who attempts to do so (t, – JUDGMENT: SANCTION: propriety). Fee sees this verse as an intrusion into the analogy, which focuses upon the structure built *on* the foundation rather than the foundation itself; nevertheless, it functions to "anticipate the following elaboration by insisting that the reason for care in building the superstructure is related to the character of the foundation."[55] This suggestion has merit. In terms of ATTITUDE, the JUDGMENT implicit in Paul's utterance construes an attitudinal disposition of caution that permeates the entire paragraph. Not only is this fitting following the command in v. 10, *take heed how you build*, but it is also important since Paul will use a number of conditional structures in this paragraph (vv. 12–13, 14, 15, 17) that invite the readers to do exactly what he commanded: consider (carefully) how to build.[56]

Having established that there is only one legitimate foundation upon which a person may build, Paul now moves on to appraise both the one who builds and what is built on that foundation (vv. 12–14). Verses 12–13a contain the first conditional structure of the unit. Although Paul's concern lies more with the

---

52   For reasoning behind glossing χάριν as *benefaction* rather than *grace*, see Crook, "Grace as Benefaction," 25–38.

53   See Crook, "Grace as Benefaction," 34–38 (esp. 37).

54   Fee (*First Epistle*, 136) observes the dominance of indefinite pronouns used in this text to refer to those who build. He suggests these pronouns refer specifically to the ones building with wood, hay, straw (i.e., human wisdom) and thus allow Paul to make a "frontal attack" on specific people in the Corinthian church. However, indefinite pronouns refer to items or people as unspecified or representative (Porter, *Idioms*, 135). So to speak of a "frontal attack" is an overstatement. These pronouns are more likely used so Paul can make and ambiguous affront, an indirect challenge to the honor of those who fit the representative form portrayed in the text.

55   Fee, *First Epistle*, 139. See also Garland, *1 Corinthians*, 115–16.

56   In light of this context of caution, it may be more appropriate to gloss βλεπέτω as *consider carefully*.

ones doing the building than the materials, that he lists them indicates they are in some way important to the point he will make. He lists *gold, silver, precious stones, wood, hay, straw* (v. 12). It is far from certain that Paul intends the addressees to read this list in terms of items of descending value, though that may be the case.[57] The conditional structure stretching across vv. 12–13 introduces into the colloquy the expectation that whatever structure anyone builds on the foundation will be tested by fire on the day of the Lord (hence the reason for the cautious disposition of the unit). Thus, it is more likely the building materials listed here are to be considered in two groups, those that fire will not consume (*gold, silver, precious stones*) and those that fire will consume (*wood, hay, straw*).[58] If this is the case, the first three items may be analyzed as + APPRECIATION: valuation and the last three items as – APPRECIATION: valuation—not on the basis of costliness, but on the cultural basis that whatever fire does not consume is more valuable, more honorable. Fee appropriately suggests from context that the first three imperishable items represent what is compatible with the foundation of Jesus Christ, while the latter three perishable items represent human *sophia* in all its forms that passes away with the present age.[59]

The pair of conditional structures in vv. 14–15 are Paul's main conveyors of the reason why one is to carefully consider how/what they build on the foundation. These conditions introduce the possible results of the testing by fire. In v. 14 Paul says that *if someone's work that was built will remain,*[60] *that person will receive a reward.* In the event that the builder's work survives the testing by fire, that work by implication is constructed of materials that are imperishable (*gold, silver, precious stones*) and are, therefore, worthy of the foundation (t, + APPRECIATION: valuation). By contrast, in v. 15 Paul says that *if the work of someone does not remain, that person will suffer loss.* Thus, in the event that the builder's work does not survive the fire and she or he suffers loss, by implication that work was constructed of perishable materials (*wood, haw, straw*) and therefore not worthy of the foundation (t, – APPRECIATION: valuation).[61]

---

57 See Fee, *First Epistle*, 140: "Although this is indeed a 'studied scale of descending value' [see BDF, 240–41], Paul's own use of the analogy makes no point of it. Nor does he place emphasis on the 'value' (i.e., costliness) of the first three in contrast to the last three."

58 Fee, *First Epistle*, 140.

59 Fee, *First Epistle*, 140.

60 There is a textual variant here. A number of manuscripts read a present tense μένει, while others read future form μενεῖ, which is maintained here. For an interpretation based on the present tense reading, see Porter, *Verbal Aspect*, 313.

61 It should be noted that implicit in these evaluations of the superstructure are evaluations of behavior. Building a superstructure that burns up implies having chosen materials poorly, a behavior worthy of sanction (t, – JUDGMENT: SANCTION: propriety).

164   CHAPTER 4

At v. 16 Paul asks the readers οὐκ οἴδατε ὅτι ναὸς θεοῦ ἐστε καὶ τὸ πνεῦμα τοῦ θεοῦ οἰκεῖ ἐν ὑμῖν; (Do you not know that you are the temple of God and the Spirit of God dwells among you?).[62] Thiselton suggests that οὐκ οἴδατε ὅτι indicates Paul's "intensity of feeling" and that the proposition to follow is "axiomatic for the Christian and should not have escaped attention as a cardinal element in the community's thinking."[63] The readers' haughty behavior (not to mention that Paul is compelled even to ask this question) implies that the readers somehow "forgot" this point. Thus, negative JUDGMENT: ESTEEM: capacity of the readers is betokened here, even as Paul establishes the fact that they are the temple of God as evidenced by the fact that the Spirit dwells among them. This raises the question of what is to become of those who destroy the temple of God by forming cliques. Paul uses a conditional structure (v. 17) to explain what a person can expect if they are responsible for desecrating the temple in this way: *If someone destroys the temple of God, God will destroy that person.* Herein, that "someone" is condemned for their impropriety (t, – JUDGMENT: SANCTION: propriety).

The end of v. 17 packs quite an interpersonal semiotic punch. What was insinuated in v. 16 ("You know you are the temple of God, right?") is made clear at the end of v. 17: οἵτινές ἐστε ὑμεῖς (you are that temple)[64] (t, + JUDGMENT: ESTEEM: normality).[65] The punch of this appraisal hinges on Paul's evaluation of the temple of God just prior to equating the readers to the temple. The temple, Paul says, is *holy* (+ APPRECIATION: valuation).[66] The reason the *temple of God* is holy is by virtue of the fact that the Holy God "occupies" this "space." Herein lies the interpersonal punch: if the temple of God is holy because God dwells in it, then the readers—now called the temple of God where God dwells (t, + JUDGMENT: ESTEEM: normality)—are expected to exhibit holiness in their behavior so as not to "corrupt" this temple.[67] This means unholy behavior such as the divisive, clique-forming activities of the readers is inappropriate and potentially destructive to the community of God. These behaviors are to be avoided. In this way, selections from ATTITUDE aid in the construal of the axiological paradigm by which Paul wants the readers to live.

---

62   This may also be glossed "You know you are the temple of God and the Spirit dwells among you, right?"

63   Thiselton, *First Corinthians*, 316. Thiselton also fails to note the stative aspect of the verb (οἴδατε), which would provide support for his claim that the saying is axiomatic.

64   Or, *which temple you are.* See Robertson and Plummer, *1 Corinthians*, 68.

65   See Malina, *New Testament World*, 192.

66   See deSilva, *Honor, Patronage, Kinship & Purity*, 246–49; Malina, *New Testament World*, 161–64; Neyrey, "Wholeness," *HBSV* 175–78; Neyrey, "Idea of Purity," 93–94.

67   Fee, *First Epistle*, 149.

1.3.2 Engagement Analysis

This unit starts off "single-voiced"; none of the utterances in v. 10 acknowledge other voices. The first two clauses in this stretch, κατὰ τὴν χάριν τοῦ θεοῦ τὴν δοθεῖσάν μοι ὡς σοφὸς ἀρχιτέκτων θεμέλιον ἔθηκα, ἄλλος δὲ ἐποικοδομεῖ, assert what Paul sees as beyond doubt: he laid down the foundation of Jesus Christ and another is building on it. These two statements create the contextual frame for the remainder of the unit. The third clause is monoglossic by virtue of the imperative βλεπέτω, since, as noted earlier, imperatives neither reference nor allow alternative actions in a text. The point of the imperative is to position the readers such that they will comply by engaging with Paul in the remainder of this paragraph in actually thinking carefully about how they build on the foundation he has established. As will be shown, Paul engages them through a series of conditional structures, all of which, as instances of CONSIDER, construe heteroglossia and expand the dialogue.

Verse 11 construes a heteroglossic backdrop, but the dialogue is contracted by means of a denial: θεμέλιον γὰρ ἄλλον οὐδεὶς δύναται θεῖναι παρὰ τὸν κείμενον (for no one is able to lay another foundation other than the one already laid). The denial is realized through word negation (οὐδεὶς) instead of clause negation (i.e., negation of the verb); as a result, emphasis is placed on the fact that *nobody*—not Paul, not Apollos, not anyone—is able to lay a foundation other than the one Paul has already laid down, namely Jesus Christ and him crucified. Paul is not necessarily suggesting that anyone is attempting to lay a different foundation; rather, it reflects the apparent situation among the readers that they were dividing into cliques around various people.

Verse 12 begins a series of four conditional structures that stretch through to the end of the unit at v. 17. Every one of these structures is a realization of CONSIDER and, thus, expands dialogue. This reflects the interpersonal goal of getting the readers to consider how they build on the foundation of Christ, for the conditional structures invite the readers into dialogue (i.e., invites them to consider) about the specific propositions they offer regarding how to build. The syntax of the first conditional structure is somewhat convoluted, but may be summarized as follows: assuming for the sake of argument that someone builds on the foundation (first class condition), Paul fully expects the kind of the work (ὁποῖον) of each builder, which depends upon the materials they use (*gold, silver, precious stones, wood, hay, straw*), to be made manifest on the Day of the Lord, through the testing of fire with which the day of the Lord is revealed (v. 13).[68] Because the future tense-forms used in this structure (i.e.,

---

68   The clause ὅτι ἐν πυρὶ ἀποκαλύπτεται (*for [the day] is revealed with fire*) is monoglossic, stating the cause/reason as a "given." On reading ἡμέρα as subject of ἀποκαλύπτεται, see Fee, *First Epistle*, 142.

γενήσεται, δηλώσει, and δοκιμάσει) grammaticalize Paul's subjective "emphatic expectation" toward the processes represented,[69] the propositions they present are grounded in Paul's contingent group-shaped and group-oriented subjectivity and therefore construe each proposition as but one of many propositions available in the current communicative context. It is for this reason they are classified as instances of CONSIDER. Paul stops short of categorical statements with regard to any of these propositions, which, in terms of his purpose, opens and even invites "consideration."

With the second and third conditional structures (vv. 14–15), Paul leads the readers to consider the consequences of work that survives the test of fire and work that does not. In both cases, Paul employs a conditional structure with εἴ + future in protasis.[70] These conditional constructions are akin to the Subjunctive Mood and seem to take on a slight hypothetical sense ("If it so happens that ..."). They also, like the Subjunctive Mood, modalize the processes and ground the proposition in Paul's subjectivity. Thus, in the first instance (v. 14), the text may be glossed *if someone's work happens to remain ... he can expect to receive a reward.* It is Paul's strong opinion ("emphatic expectation")— an opinion based on prior argument, the Scriptures, and God's activity in the world, but an opinion nonetheless—that one whose building survives the test of fire will receive a reward. On the contrary, in his opinion—again, a strong opinion based on prior argument, the Scriptures, and God's activity in the world, but still an opinion—the builder whose work *burns up* can expect to *suffer loss* (v. 15). Although open for further debate, these positive and negative expectations are strong moves for positioning the readers to build with what will endure the fire of testing.

With οὐκ οἴδατε (v. 16) Paul again contracts dialogic space, but only for a brief moment in the colloquy. The entire question—*You know you are the temple of God and that the Spirit dwells among you, right?*—is a leading question that expects an affirmative answer ("Yes, we know"). This is an instance of PROCLAIM: CONCUR in which Paul and the readers are construed as being in agreement on the point that the readers are, indeed, the temple of God, which functions as a set up for the final conditional structure (and last heteroglossic element of the unit) in v. 17. In the protasis of this structure, Paul introduces the question of what would happen if someone destroys (φθείρει) the group of believers at Corinth, presumably through boasting, discord, and

---

69   Porter, *Verbal Aspect*, 414.

70   See Porter, *Idioms*, 264–65.

"TELL US HOW YOU REALLY FEEL, PAUL!" (PART 2)   167

the formation of cliques.[71] His response to this scenario, given in the apodosis, is quite stern: *I/you expect that God will destroy* (φθερεῖ) *that person.* Again Paul uses a future form which by grammaticalizing expectation modalizes the process and grounds the proposition in his own subjectivity and construes the proposition as one among many that are available in the current communicative context. Like the previous instances, it is intended to invite dialogue and careful consideration of the issue. Even though it is open to resistance, the strong language of destruction is quite powerful at positioning the readers to avoid dividing the temple of God.

1.3.3   Summary

Both attitudinal evaluations and linguistic engagement clearly serve Paul's main goal of this unit, namely to invoke the readers to careful consideration of how they "build" the community of believers. The dominant engagement strategy was to open the dialogue and invite the readers to consideration of a number of propositions through a chain of instances of CONSIDER realized as conditional structures. Attitudinally speaking, in Paul's view there are appropriate (imperishable materials that survive the fire of testing) and inappropriate materials (perishable materials that are consumed by the fire of testing) with which to build. The point of Paul's assessments is to position the readers such that they avoid building with inappropriate materials and build with those that are appropriate. If Fee's interpretation is correct that the imperishable materials represent God's wisdom and the perishable represents the world's wisdom, then Paul's point to the readers is that they must not be involved in boasting and self-aggrandizement—both "perishable" because they stem from the ideology by which the world operates. Such things do not build, they destroy; and destruction of God's building/temple results in the destruction of the one(s) who destroy it.

1.4   *"All Things Belong to the Wise" (1 Cor 3:18–23)*

In this unit, Paul brings the entire wisdom/foolishness (wise/foolish) dialectic to application for the lives of the readers.[72] The theme of reversal appears again as Paul tells the readers that instead of presuming to be wise by the standards of the world, they are to become foolish by those standards so that they would be considered wise before God. Clearly, as the adjectives "wise" and "foolish"

---

71   In the context of holiness as is the case here, the idea is that of destroying wholeness by corrupting what is holy/sacred.

72   After the close of this section, lexical items on the *σοφ- stem and the *μωρ- stems no longer appear, except for μωροί at 4:10.

168   CHAPTER 4

indicate, attitudinal appraisals play a significant role in construing this reversal. It is also not surprising in light of the unit's social goal that the majority of
Paul's language is monoglossic.

1.4.1   Attitudinal Analysis

The pattern of Paul's attitudinal selections in v. 18 clearly construes the theme
of reversal.[73] The notion of deception is introduced into the discourse via the
third person imperative that opens the clause, μηδεὶς ἑαυτὸν ἐξαπατάτω (No
one is to deceive herself or himself).[74] Deceiving oneself here refers to thinking of oneself as wiser than she or he really is, which is an inappropriate attitude (t, – JUDGMENT: SANCTION: propriety).[75] The protasis of the ensuing
conditional structure makes this explicit: εἴ τις δοκεῖ σοφὸς εἶναι ἐν ὑμῖν ἐν τῷ
αἰῶνι τούτῳ (If anyone among you presumes to be wise in this age). *Presumes
to be wise* stands on par with deceiving oneself in the prior clause, thus Paul
views it as inappropriate behavior (t, – JUDGMENT: SANCTION: propriety).
In contrast to deceiving oneself and presuming to be wise, in the apodosis of the conditional structure Paul says this person μωρὸς γενέσθω (she or
he is to become foolish). This describes behavior in which one forsakes the
world's system of values and adopts those God demonstrated at the cross and
which Paul preaches (t, + JUDGMENT: SANCTION: propriety). Finally, one is to
become foolish ἵνα γένηται σοφός (so that she or he would become [truly] wise).
Wise in this latter use describes someone who has rightly forsaken the wisdom of this age and has accepted the "foolishness" of God that Paul preaches
(+ JUDGMENT: SANCTION: propriety). Thus, the pattern of appraisal aids in
construing reversal as follows: deceiving oneself and presuming to be wise is
to – JUDGMENT: SANCTION: propriety as becoming foolish in order to become
wise is to + JUDGMENT: SANCTION: propriety.

   At v. 19a, Paul further appraises the wisdom of the world as *foolishness before
God* (ἡ γὰρ σοφία τοῦ κόσμου τούτου μωρία παρὰ τῷ θεῷ ἐστιν), a negative appreciation with regard to its value (t, – APPRECIATION: valuation). This is not a
new point in the argument (cf. 1:18–25), but is a point he wishes to reestablish
as he closes the discussion on wisdom and foolishness. The reminders of v. 19
and v. 20 provide endorsement for this point from the Scriptures (Job 5:13 and
Psa 93:11 LXX). Paul uses the first text because its use of πανουργίᾳ (cunning,

---

73   See Witherington, *Conflict & Community*, 135; E. Bernard Allo, *Saint Paul: Première Épitre
      aux Corinthiens*, 2nd ed. (Paris: Gabalda, 1956), 64; Schrage, *Der erste Brief*, 1:311.

74   Imperatives are tokens of a writer's positive AFFECT: inclination: desire (*I want*); prohibi-
      tions are tokens of negative AFFECT: inclination: desire (*I do not want*).

75   See Jerome Neyrey, "Deception," *HBSV* 36–39; Gerd Theissen, *Psychological Aspects of
      Pauline Theology*, trans. John P. Galvin (Philadelphia: Fortress, 1987), 59–66 and 57–114.

"TELL US HOW YOU REALLY FEEL, PAUL!" (PART 2)   169

trickery) supports his view that the wise of the world are deceitful (cf. v. 18) (t, – APPRECIATION: valuation). The second supports Paul's point because it portrays God as appraising the *thoughts*[76] *of the wise* as μάταιοι (futile) (– APPRECIATION: valuation).

Having given scriptural endorsement for his utterly negative evaluation of the world's wisdom and the social entrepreneurs who perpetuate it, Paul turns to his final point of application in v. 21: ὥστε μηδεὶς καυχάσθω ἐν ἀνθρώποις (so then, no one is to boast in a person). This reflects 1:29 (so that all people could not boast before God) and its positive corollary at 1:31 (the one who boasts is to boast in the Lord). Boasting in oneself or in another person for self-aggrandizing purposes is clearly behavior Paul appraises negatively (t, – JUDGMENT: SANCTION: propriety).

When Paul provides explanation (γάρ) for why no one should boast in a person, namely that *all things are yours ...* (vv. 21b–22),[77] he appears to draw upon a Stoic maxim that states, "all things belong to the wise person."[78] The language recalls the readers' "slogans" (cf. 1:12) and flips them on end. According to Paul, if the readers spurn the world's wisdom in favor of God's wisdom, then "I belong to ..." is supplanted by "all things belong to me," which, in light of the Stoic maxim, is a way for Paul to say the readers are truly wise (t, + JUDGMENT: ESTEEM: normality). In similar fashion, in v. 23 *you belong to Christ* portrays Christ as wise (t, + JUDGMENT: ESTEEM: normality) and *Christ belongs to God* portrays God as wise (t, + JUDGMENT: ESTEEM: normality) (cf. 1:21, 24, 30). The readers are only wise if they accept God's wisdom of Jesus Christ and him crucified.

1.4.2   Engagement Analysis

Discussion here is circumscribed by the fact that much of Paul's language in this unit is monoglossic. This is not all that surprising because Paul is concluding his discussion of wisdom/foolishness and now wishes to present a number of propositions as givens (based on previous argument) as well as make a number of commands.

The first clause in v. 18 is a command (*no one is to deceive herself/himself*). As mentioned several times above, imperatives are monoglossic since, textually, they do not acknowledge any action other than compliance. The protasis of the conditional structure in v. 18b briefly construes heteroglossia, in that it introduces into the colloquy the notion of someone presuming to be wise in

---

76   Διαλογισμός may refer not merely to thoughts but also to motives.

77   The repetition of πάντα ὑμῶν realizes GRADUATION: FORCE: INTENSIFICATION.

78   Conzelmann, *1 Corinthians*, 80.

this age (CONSIDER), but Paul immediately returns to monogloss in the apodosis (v. 18c), invoking again an imperative (*she/he must become foolish*). The purpose (ἵνα) for becoming foolish is heteroglossic; the Subjunctive Mood of γένηται (she/he would become) signals modality, which leaves semiotic space open for negotiating other points of view (CONSIDER).

Verse 19 commences with monogloss with which Paul asserts as a given that *the wisdom of this world is foolishness before God.* Immediately following this are two quotations from Scripture intended to provide warrantability for this claim. Thus, each of these two quoted texts is an instance of PROCLAIM: ENDORSE. Hence, the proposition *the wisdom of the world is foolishness before God* is grounded not in Paul, but in God. To take up an alternative position, then, would bring one into disagreement with God.

The remainder of the unit (vv. 21–22) is monoglossic. Verse 21 records another imperative and likely the final point of application of Paul's dialectic on wisdom and foolishness: *So then, no one is to boast in a person.* As mentioned above, this recalls and reiterates 1:29 and 1:31 where all boasting is excluded except boasting in the Lord (i.e., giving honor to God).[79] Verses 21b–23 are entirely monoglossic; no other voices or alternative views are acknowledged. This has the effect of construing Paul and the readers as completely aligned on the points that all things belong to them, they belong to Christ, and Christ belongs to God (i.e., they are wise, Christ is wise, and God is wise [see above]).

1.4.3 Summary

Selections from ATTITUDE and ENGAGEMENT throughout this unit aid in construing the reversal theme. Paul negatively appraises behavior associated with buying into the world's ideology (i.e., self-deception, presuming to be wise when one really is not, boasting). He also negatively appraises worldly wisdom itself. Alternatively, accepting God's wisdom (i.e., becoming foolish) is positively appraised, as is the result of accepting it (i.e., "all things are yours"). In this way, Paul discursively constructs an attitudinal disposition that favors the acceptance of God's wisdom and disapproves the world's. Selections from ENGAGEMENT reflect the fact that Paul is wrapping up the dialectic about wisdom/foolishness (wise/foolish). Much of the text consists of instances of MONOGLOSS; those brief instances of HETEROGLOSS serve to introduce notions into the colloquy or support monoglossic statements.

---

79   This is reminiscent of Rom 3:27: ποῦ οὖν ἡ καύχησις; ἐξεκλείσθη (*Where then is boasting? It is excluded/eliminated*).

"TELL US HOW YOU REALLY FEEL, PAUL!" (PART 2)   171

1.5   *"Only My Master Judges Me" (1 Cor 4:1–5)*

Having just reiterated the directive *no one is to boast in a person* (3:21; cf. 1:29, 31), the culmination of the discussion on σοφία and μωρία, Paul's goal in this unit is to explain how the readers ought to understand his and, secondarily, Apollos's (or any other leader's)[80] roles as *servants* and *stewards*. The spike in the language of "judgment"[81] in this section may betray a concern for how the readers ought to behave toward Paul, though not necessarily since Paul uses himself (with Apollos) as for illustrative purposes. Regardless, judgments of behavior play an important role in the negotiation of values. Much of the text is construed as heteroglossic, though dialogue is limited through a number of contractive engagement techniques.

1.5.1   Attitudinal Analysis

At v. 1, Paul returns to the notion that he and Apollos are servants: οὕτως ἡμᾶς λογιζέσθω ἄνθρωπος ὡς ὑπηρέτας Χριστοῦ καὶ οἰκονόμους μυστηρίων θεοῦ (A person is to consider us as Christ's servants and stewards of God's mysteries).[82] Whereas διάκονοι at 3:5 was likely intended to evoke a negative appraisal for the purpose of redefining the role of leaders (see above), here ὑπηρέτας and οἰκονόμους are positively charged because of the way they are qualified. Because Paul and Apollos are servants *of Christ* and stewards of *God's mysteries*,[83] both ὑπηρέτας and οἰκονόμους stand as tokens of esteem (t, + JUDGMENT: ESTEEM: normality).[84]

At v. 2, Paul stays with the role of οἰκονόμος and adds that it is expected (ζητεῖται, *demanded, strongly desired*)[85] that such a servant should be found *trustworthy* (πιστός). *Trustworthy* directly inscribes feelings of esteem regarding

---

80   Because the theme of being a servant harks back to 3:5 where Paul and Apollos are named and because coming up at 4:6 Paul speaks of applying his teachings to himself and Apollos for the benefit of the readers, the "us" (ἡμᾶς) here likely refers to Paul and Apollos (although other leaders are not necessarily excluded).

81   Terms used are λογίζομαι, κρίνω, ἀνακρίνω (3×), ἀνθρωπίνης ἡμέρα, and δεδικαίωμαι.

82   The term ὑπηρέτας is a broad term that refers generally to a person who renders service for another. Thus, Louw and Nida rightly say, "… it is important to avoid a term which would be too specific.… It may, in fact, be necessary to use an expression which means essentially 'helper'" (L&N 1:460–1). Οἰκονόμος, on the other hand, is more specific; it typically refers to the servant who is in charge of running a household, the household manager, but occasionally, as here, simply means one who has authority and responsibility for something (L&N 1:477; 1:521).

83   *God's mysteries* connects back to 2:7.

84   Secondarily, the second person imperative λογιζέσθω betokens Paul's desire; he wants the readers to consider him and Apollos as servants (t, + AFFECT: INCLINATION [desideration]).

85   See L&N 1:408.

172   CHAPTER 4

the steward's dependability (+ JUDGMENT: ESTEEM: tenacity), which is the
"chief criterion by which stewards are judged."[86] No explicit agent is named in
the passive structure regarding who is the head of household that examines
the steward's trustworthiness. In fact, this vagueness may be by design, since at
v. 3 Paul addresses the readers as though they have assumed that role.

At v. 3, Paul writes, ἐμοὶ δὲ εἰς ἐλάχιστόν ἐστιν, ἵνα ὑφ᾽ ὑμῶν ἀνακριθῶ ἢ ὑπὸ
ἀνθρωπίνης ἡμέρας (It is quite insignificant to me that I am examined by you or
by any human court).[87] The superlative ἐλάχιστόν[88] inscribes a negative attitudinal assessment of sanction (– JUDGMENT: SANCTION: propriety), which can
only be determined when it is read with the ensuing content clause. The content clause makes it clear that what Paul considers *quite insignificant* is that the
readers or the "court of public opinion" would examine him (i.e., their behavior
of examining, not any particular verdict they may have reached). Exactly why
Paul considers this improper behavior becomes clear at the end of v. 4: ὁ δὲ
ἀνακρίνων με κύριός ἐστιν (the one who examines me is the Lord). "The assumption is that since the criterion is faithfulness to a committed trust, only the one
from whom he had received the trust can judge him—not his fellow servants
nor in this case those who might be 'under him,' the Corinthians themselves."[89]
Thus, he considers it improper behavior (– JUDGMENT: SANCTION: propriety) for the readers or the court of public opinion to examine him—it is even
improper for Paul to judge himself by the standards of the world (3c).

Thus, the unit comes to a close with a prohibition ὥστε μὴ πρὸ καιροῦ τι κρίνετε ἕως ἂν ἔλθῃ ὁ κύριος (so then, do not judge anything before the time when
the Lord happens to come). In this context, the readers are not to be involved
in measuring others with the world's measuring stick for two reasons: first
because it is not their place to do so, it is the Lord's; and second, because the
world's standards are not capable of shining light on the hidden things of darkness nor of revealing the motives of hearts, as the Lord's examination can and
will do (v. 5b). Those who would judge Paul's or Apollos's motives, then, would
be involved in improper behavior (t, – JUDGMENT: SANCTION: propriety). Yet,
when the Lord comes and the motives of each servant[90] are made manifest,

---

86   Garland, *1 Corinthians*, 126.

87   On ἀνθρωπίνης ἡμέρας as *human court*, see L&N 1:552. See also Thiselton, *First
      Corinthians*, 338.

88   This term is used in an elative sense here and thus realizes GRADUATION: FORCE:
      INTENSIFICATION (hence, *quite insignificant*). Intensification is infused in this lexical
      item (see Martin and White, *Language of Evaluation*, 143–44).

89   Fee, *First Epistle*, 161. See also Martin, *Corinthian Body*, 65.

90   Contextually, Paul is speaking of each servant, not each person including the readers
      (contra Fee, *First Epistle*, 164).

"TELL US HOW YOU REALLY FEEL, PAUL!" (PART 2)   173

God is expected to grant appropriate commendation[91] to each of them on the basis of the faithful discharge of their duties.

1.5.2   Engagement Analysis

The unit opens with monogloss realized by the third person imperative λογι-ζέσθω, leaving the readers-in-the-text no choice (in the text, that is) but to *consider us* (presumably Paul and Apollos) as *servants of Christ and stewards of God's mysteries*. Staying with οἰκονόμος as the analogue of their task, Paul expands dialogue around the notion that *among stewards it is expected that one should/must be found trustworthy* (v. 2). The Subjunctive Mood form (εὑρεθῇ) grammaticalizes modality (in this context is likely obligation, hence *should/must be found*), which sounds like a strong directive but it is not as strongly directive as the third person imperative *is to be found*. For this reason it is classified as CONSIDER.

With the idea that a steward should be *trustworthy*—where *trustworthy* is a matter of judgment/examination (appraisal)—now introduced into the colloquy, Paul makes the pronouncement *it is quite insignificant to me that I might be examined by you or by a human court* (v. 3). That this is an instance of PROCLAIM: PRONOUNCE is signaled by a couple of grammatical cues. First, the personal pronoun ἐμοί (*to me*) occupies the prime position in the clause, making "me" (i.e., Paul) the focal point of the clause. Second is the use of a matrix clause (*it is quite insignificant to me*) to encode Paul's modal assessment regarding the proposition in the following content clause (*that I might be examined*[92]). With this pronouncement, Paul resists the notion that he should be concerned with how he is judged by the readers or that their judgment even matters. In fact, Paul even rejects the notion that he examines himself (ἀλλ' οὐδὲ ἐμαυτὸν ἀνακρίνω; DISCLAIM: DENY) (v. 3c); that is, he does not judge his own trustworthiness by the worldly standards the readers appear to use. Even by those standards Paul says he knows of nothing in himself that would make him think he is unfaithful (οὐδὲν γὰρ ἐμαυτῷ σύνοιδα; DISCLAIM: deny) (v. 4a), but such a self-assessment matters little because *I am not justified by this* (οὐκ ἐν τούτῳ δεδικαίωμαι; DISCLAIM: COUNTER + DISCLAIM: DENY).[93]

---

91   See Thiselton, *First Corinthians*, 344 on glossing ἔπαινος and why it needs to be glossed somewhat ambiguously in terms of attitude.

92   Martin and White (*Language of Evaluation*, 130–32) refer to this as an explicitly subjective pronouncement. In this case, ἐμοί makes it subjective and that the modal assessment is given prominence in a matrix clause makes it explicit.

93   The perfect passive verb δεδικαίωμαι is not intended to speak of Paul's justification in terms of eternal salvation. Rather, it emphatically (stative aspect) points out that his self-assessment of being trustworthy neither contributes to nor trumps what his master will

174   CHAPTER 4

The reason why neither the readers' assessment nor his own self-assessment matters—and why they should not even be involved in making these kinds of judgments—is revealed in the monoglossic statement in v. 4c: ὁ δὲ ἀνακρίνων με κύριός ἐστιν (now the one who judges/examines me is the Lord). By stating categorically that it is the Lord who examines him, Paul insinuates that it is inappropriate for the readers to be passing judgment on him (cf. appraisal analysis above).[94] This is confirmed by the imperative (which is also monoglossic) that immediately follows, with which Paul proscribes the kind of worldly evaluation in which the readers were involved: *so then do not judge anything* (ὥστε μὴ … κρίνετε). Of course, what Paul teaches them in the remainder of the letter requires the readers to make judgments (cf. e.g., 1 Cor 5:5), but those judgments are of a different kind because they arise from what Fee refers to as a genuine eschatological perspective.[95] That is, rather than examining and passing down judgments on the basis of worldly standards, the implied readers are to make decisions on the basis of the things of the Spirit (cf. πνευματικοῖς πνευματικὰ συγκρίνοντες back at 2:13). Hence, Paul prohibits judging *before the time when the Lord would come* (πρὸ καιροῦ … ἕως ἂν ἔλθῃ ὁ κύριος).

The remainder of the unit consists of a description of the Lord who will act as judge. In the description, Paul uses a number of future forms to construct an appropriate vision of what the reader can expect from the Lord. One can expect that God will *bring to light the things hidden in darkness and will make manifest the intentions of hearts*—presumably the intentions and hearts of the servants—after which, *the appropriate commendation will be given to each [servant] from God*. Both of these clauses are instances of CONSIDER given the use of the future form, which like the Subjunctive Mood modalizes each process depicted. Paul does not speak of any of these processes categorically; instead, he leaves open the possibility for other points of view.

1.5.3   Summary

The key attitudinal pattern in this unit consists of realizations of negative JUDGMENT: SANCTION: propriety. They generate a negative prosody with regard to the readers' behavior: that they are passing judgment (presumably from a worldly perspective) on Paul and other servants of the Lord and stewards of God's wisdom is depicted very negatively. In terms of ENGAGEMENT,

---

say. Colloquially, "Just because I think I am faithfully discharging my duties does not mean anything; what ultimately matters is how my Master assesses me."

94   See Fee, *First Epistle*, 162–63.

95   Fee, *First Epistle*, 163. Note the stated purpose in 1 Cor 5:5: *for the destruction of the flesh so that his spirit may be saved on the day of the Lord*.

"TELL US HOW YOU REALLY FEEL, PAUL!" (PART 2) 175

Paul selects MONOGLOSS, which is grammaticalized through the Imperative Mood form, in order to rule out any other view of himself or of Apollos as anything but servants of Christ and stewards of God's mysteries. He closes the unit with more monoglossic text to prohibit the readers from judging the servants. Between these two instances of monogloss, lies a number of dialogue-contracting moves that serve the purpose squelching from the colloquy any voices that would support examining the servants with worldly standards.

1.6 *True Humility Exemplified by the Apostles (1 Cor 4:6–13)*

In this section Paul addresses the readers with a level of directness and candor similar to that exhibited in 1:10–17 and 3:1–4. His goal in this unit is to apply the teachings recorded between 3:5 and 4:5 for the specific purpose of curbing their excessive pride. A major feature of this passage is the biting irony Paul employs as part of his strategy not only to chide the readers for their hubris but as a means of realigning them to a proper (i.e., humble) perspective of themselves and their leaders. Recognizing the use of irony in this text is crucial for arriving at an appropriate interpretation of the attitudinal tokens in this unit. In most cases, when Paul evaluates the readers positively, he actually intends a negative evaluation. Regardless, the positive and negative attitudes expressed in this unit are used to create a positive disposition for the humility exemplified in the lives of Paul and Apollos (and other apostles) and to create a negative disposition for the haughty lives the readers are living.

1.6.1 Attitudinal Analysis

At v. 6, Paul says he applied the preceding figures (cf. 3:5–4:5) to himself and Apollos[96] for the purpose of teaching the readers the lesson of "*Not beyond what is written*,"[97] which, itself, should result in none of them *taking pride in one person over against another.* Yet context indicates that the readers, being motivated by pride and jealousy, were showing undue allegiance to certain leaders in the community of believers to the point that it was causing discord (cf. 1:10–13; 3:1–4). Paul considers this improper behavior (t, JUDGMENT: SANCTION: propriety), and the readers should already know this, but need to be taught again (t, – JUDGMENT: ESTEEM: capacity).

Verse 7 consists of three expository questions designed to draw the readers' attention to the fact that "the roots of their conflict lie deep in the human desire to distinguish oneself from others and to rise higher on an imagined social

---

96   See Garland, *1 Corinthians*, 132–33.

97   On the possible ways this can be unpacked, see Garland, *1 Corinthians*, 133–36; Fee, *First Epistle*, 168–69; Thiselton, *First Corinthians*, 352–55.

ladder."[98] The first question, τίς γάρ σε διακρίνει; (For who distinguishes you?), may be interpreted "positively" in that if the implied answer is God, then Paul means that the readers are, indeed, "distinguished" (t, + JUDGMENT: ESTEEM: normality).[99] Alternatively, the question may be read negatively ("Who in the world sees anything special in you?"),[100] but this is unlikely because Paul wants to show the inconsistency of boasting for something that was given as a gift. The second question, τί δὲ ἔχεις ὃ οὐκ ἔλαβες; (And what do you have that you did not receive?), follows the logic of the first question, reminding the implied readers that everything they have is a gift from God, which indicates that they are deemed special by him (t, + JUDGMENT: ESTEEM: normality): he saved them (1:18), chose them (1:27–28), and revealed his secret wisdom (2:10–12), with the result that all boasting is excluded (1:30; 3:21).[101] The positive prosody generated by these first two questions is contrasted in the third:[102] εἰ δὲ καὶ ἔλα-βες, τί καυχᾶσαι ὡς μὴ λαβών; (But even though[103] you receive, why do you boast as though[104] you are not receiving?). The question assumes boasting on the part of the addressees, which in prior text Paul clearly denounced as improper (t, – JUDGMENT: SANCTION: propriety). The incongruity of boasting about something they received as a gift serves as the launch pad into the biting irony Paul uses in the remainder of the section to make the crucial point that God's gracious gifts "must be forever humbling, for they finally lead to a discipleship that goes the way of the cross, not the way of false triumphalism."[105]

In staccato-like fashion, Paul rattles off a series of statements that are at once true and false and, thus, ironic. On the one hand *You are already full* (ἤδη κεκο-ρεσμένοι ἐστέ), *You are already rich* (ἤδη ἐπλουτήσατε), and *You reign as kings* (ἐβασιλεύσατε) all reflect the truth that God has filled the readers, made them rich, and made them to reign (cf. 1:4–9). On the other hand, these statements reflect the readers' boasting (v. 7) which flows from their tendency to operate by the world's standards like people who are σάρκινοι/σαρκικοί (cf. 3:1–5). In this regard the terms are to be read as ironic, betokening Paul's negative appraisal of the readers (t, – JUDGMENT: ESTEEM: normality [3×]).[106]

---

98   Garland, *1 Corinthians*, 136.
99   See Garland, *1 Corinthians*, 136–37; Thiselton, *First Corinthians*, 356.
100   See James Moffatt, *The First Epistle to the Corinthians*, MNTC 7 (London: Hodder & Stoughton, 1938), 48.
101   Garland, *1 Corinthians*, 137.
102   The suddenness of the shift from positive to negative judgment and from normality (JUDGMENT: ESTEEM) to propriety (JUDGMENT: SANCTION) construes prominence on the third question (GRADUATION: FORCE: INTENSIFICATION).
103   Concession is grammaticalized by εἰ καί.
104   Concession is grammaticalized by the participle.
105   Fee, *First Epistle*, 172.
106   See Martin, *Corinthian Body*, 65.

"TELL US HOW YOU REALLY FEEL, PAUL!" (PART 2) 177

With regard to the readers' "reign," Paul says they do so *without us* (χωρὶς ἡμῶν); that is, they reign without the apostles having a share in it.[107] The irony of this statement is made clear by Paul's exclamation of an unfulfillable wish:[108] *Would that you did, indeed, reign so that we might reign with you* (καὶ ὄφελόν γε ἐβασιλεύσατε, ἵνα καὶ ἡμεῖς ὑμῖν συμβασιλεύσωμεν).[109] Contra Thiselton and others who claim Paul here combats an overrealized eschatology,[110] it is more contextually sound to understand this statement as opposing the readers' egotism and hubristic boasting.[111] Thus, Paul's wish ironically betokens a negative appraisal—"I wish you really did reign (though you don't) ..." (t, – JUDGMENT: ESTEEM: normality).

Verses 9–13 offer the apostles' way of life as a model of how the cross is to direct the lives of believers, including leaders such as apostles. Again, one must interpret Paul's assessments as ironic; he reconstrues what the world considers "bad" or negative as something that is "good" or positive (Table 13). The dominance of JUDGMENT: ESTEEM: normality is obvious.[112] With these judgments, Paul redefines the standards by which a person is considered "special" in the ἐκκλησία. The reversal theme is conspicuous: what the world considers signs that something or someone is wrong or bad, Paul, through the lens of the cross, reconstrues as signs of being right or good. Thus, *fools because of Christ* (v. 10), a negative judgment from the world's point of view, is for Paul a positive judgment indicating that he and the other apostles are rightly living cross-directed lives. Similarly, working with one's own hands (v. 12; cf. 3:5–9), considered disgraceful by the social elite, is for Paul a positive illustration of a cross-centered life of humility.[113]

---

107   See Fee, *First Epistle*, 173; Garland, *1 Corinthians*, 138.

108   Cf. *ANLEX*; BDAG.

109   *Would that* (ὄφελον) is a modal element that grounds the (ironic) wish in Paul's subjectivity. See L&N 1:671 on ὄφελον: "that which ought to be if one only had one's wish."

110   See Fee, *First Epistle*, 172–73; Anthony C. Thiselton, "Realized Eschatology at Corinth," *NTS* 24 (1977–78): 510–26 (although he has since changed his view [see now his *First Corinthians*, 40–41]).

111   See Garland, *1 Corinthians*, 138 and sources there.

112   Although a number of the ideational tokens in vv. 9–13 (e.g., *insulted*) could be read as implied – JUDGMENT: SANCTION: propriety, they are best taken as tokens of the apostles' lot since Paul addresses the life of an apostle and not those actions specifically. *We bless/praise, we endure* (v. 12), *we encourage* (v. 13) are not interpreted ironically; these are proper behaviors, even in light of insult, persecution, and slander (cf. Matt 5:38–39).

113   See Winter, *After Paul Left Corinth*, 42. Philo, *Det.*, 34 spoke of the social elite as those whose "hands knew no labor."

TABLE 13   Attitudinal analysis of 1 Cor 4:9–13

Vs	Appraiser	Appraised	Appraisal	Congruent (ironic)
9	Paul	us apostles	displayed as last, condemned to die	t, – JUDGMENT: ESTEEM: normality (t, + JUDGMENT: ESTEEM: normality)
9	Paul	us apostles	become a spectacle	t, – JUDGMENT: ESTEEM: normality (t, + JUDGMENT: ESTEEM: normality)
10	Paul	we (apostles)	fools because of Christ	t, – JUDGMENT: ESTEEM: normality (t, + JUDGMENT: ESTEEM: normality)
10	Paul	you (readers)	wise in Christ	+ JUDGMENT: ESTEEM: normality (– JUDGMENT: ESTEEM: normality)
10	Paul	we	are weak	– JUDGMENT: ESTEEM: normality (+ JUDGMENT: ESTEEM: normality)
10	Paul	you	are strong	+ JUDGMENT: ESTEEM: normality (– JUDGMENT: ESTEEM: normality)
10	Paul	you	honored	+ JUDGMENT: ESTEEM: normality (– JUDGMENT: ESTEEM: normality)
10	Paul	we	shamed/dishonored	– JUDGMENT: ESTEEM: normality (+ JUDGMENT: esteem: normality)
11	Paul	we	hunger	– JUDGMENT: ESTEEM: normality (+ JUDGMENT: ESTEEM: normality)

"TELL US HOW YOU REALLY FEEL, PAUL!" (PART 2)

TABLE 13   Attitudinal analysis of 1 Cor 4:9–13 (*cont.*)

Vs	Appraiser	Appraised	Appraisal	Congruent (ironic)
11	Paul	we	thirst	– JUDGMENT: ESTEEM: normality
				(+ JUDGMENT: ESTEEM: normality)
11	Paul	we	poorly clothed	– JUDGMENT: ESTEEM: normality
				(+ JUDGMENT: ESTEEM: normality)
11	Paul	we	beaten	– JUDGMENT: ESTEEM: normality
				(+ JUDGMENT: ESTEEM: normality)
11	Paul	we	homeless	– JUDGMENT: ESTEEM: normality
				(+ JUDGMENT: ESTEEM: normality)
12	Paul	we	work with hands	– JUDGMENT: ESTEEM: normality
				(+ JUDGMENT: ESTEEM: normality)
12	Paul	we	insulted	– JUDGMENT: ESTEEM: normality
				(+ JUDGMENT: ESTEEM: normality)
12	Paul	we	bless/praise	t, + JUDGMENT: SANCTION: propriety
12	Paul	we	persecuted	t, – JUDGMENT: ESTEEM: normality
				(t, + JUDGMENT: ESTEEM: normality)
12	Paul	we	endure	t, + JUDGMENT: SANCTION: propriety
13	Paul	we	slandered	t, – JUDGMENT: ESTEEM: normality
				(t, + JUDGMENT: ESTEEM: normality)

180   CHAPTER 4

TABLE 13   Attitudinal analysis of 1 Cor 4:9–13 (*cont.*)

Vs	Appraiser	Appraised	Appraisal	Congruent (ironic)
13	Paul	we	encourage	t, + JUDGMENT: SANCTION: propriety
13	Paul	we	made like refuse/filth	t, – JUDGMENT: ESTEEM: normality (t, + JUDGMENT: ESTEEM: normality)

1.6.2   Engagement Analysis

Verse 6 opens the monoglossic statement that Paul applies the foregoing figures to himself and Apollos for the sake of the implied readers. This is followed
by back-to-back instances of CONSIDER, each realized in their own purpose
clause: *so that you would learn "Not beyond what is written"* and *lest each of you
are puffed up with pride for one against another.* Both purpose clauses introduce
Paul's opinion that the readers still need to learn that boasting is inconsistent
with the message of the crucified Messiah. Both claims are grounded in Paul's
subjective point of view on the readers' behavior as had been reported to him
by those from Chloe (v. 1:11).

Verse 7 contains three more instances of CONSIDER and an instance of
PROCLAIM: CONCUR. The instances of CONSIDER are realized by three open,
expository questions. None of these signals an expected answer (i.e., there are
no grammatical markers signaling an expectation of either affirmative or negative responses); they are asked to entertain possible propositions. *Who distinguishes you?* raises at least the possibilities that someone does distinguish them
or no one distinguishes them. *What do you have that you did not receive?* raises
at least the possibility that nothing they have was received as a gift or that
everything they have was received as a gift. The concessive clause *although you
did receive* realizes PROCLAIM: CONCUR which functions to contract the possible answers to the second question as well as to set up the interpretive context for the third question in that with it Paul portrays himself and the readers
as agreeing that what they have they had, indeed, received as a gift. Assuming,
then, that the implied audience has received what they have as a gift, then the
third question, *Why do you boast as though you are not receiving?*, is open for
dialogue not around whether or not they have received but around whether or
not they are boasting with regard to what they have received.

"TELL US HOW YOU REALLY FEEL, PAUL!" (PART 2)   181

The next three clauses (v. 8)—*Already you are full, already you are rich*, and *you reign apart from us*—are each realizations of MONOGLOSS. Of course, each of these is still very much a focal point in the argument; thus, although they are declared categorically, they are not "givens." Although they construe Paul as taking them as "givens," they construe the readers as not necessarily in agreement with what they propose (ironically, "you are not full by the world's standards," "you are not rich by the world's standards," and "you do not reign according to the world"). Rather, they are construed as perhaps anticipating further argumentation related to these (implied) propositions.

Paul's own response to these categorical statements (v. 8d) takes the form of a wish that is considered unattainable or unfulfillable: *Would that you were indeed reigning.* In a sense, the verbal particle ὄφελον[114] modalizes ἐβασιλεύσατε along the lines of *I wish that you did reign* (cf. NRSV, NET, NIV), although in Greek there is no hypotactic clause structure expressing the wish as if it was a mental verb/attribute projection.[115] Nevertheless, ὄφελον appears to ground the proposition in Paul's contingent, individual subjectivity making it one among many possible propositions available in the current communicative context. Thus, it realizes CONSIDER. The purpose clause following Paul's fruitless wish, *so that we could reign with you*, is also an instance of CONSIDER by virtue of the Subjunctive Mood of the verb (συμβασιλεύσωμεν). As emphasized on a number of occasions above, the Subjunctive Mood projects the proposition as but one of any number of other propositions that may be appropriate for the current context. For this reason, it expands dialogic space and acknowledges that those alternative voices exist.

Verse 9ab consists of an explicitly subjective modality metaphor realized as a mental verb/attribute projection nexus, where δοκῶ γάρ (For I think) is the projecting clause and ὁ θεὸς ἡμᾶς τοὺς ἀποστόλους ἐσχάτους ἀπέδειξεν ὡς ἐπιθανατίους (that God has exhibited us apostles as last, as condemned to die) is the projected clause. In the Appraisal model, such structures are considered modal/interpersonal rather than experiential/informational in their function. *I think* expresses an assessment of probability (i.e., *I think it is probable*) that gets mapped onto the proposition in the reported clause, thus modalizing it. Thus, the proposition *God has exhibited us apostles as last* states Paul's opinion on the matter of where God has exhibited the apostles in the mix with other possible voices on the matter (CONSIDER).

---

114   Though it is not certain, ὄφελον may be the second aorist participle of ὀφείλω (*ANLEX*).
115   I.e., the structure here is not made up of a reporting clause ^ reported clause.

182   CHAPTER 4

The reason why Paul thinks God has exhibited the apostles last as condemned to die is *because we have become a spectacle to the world and to angels and to people* (ὅτι θέατρον ἐγενήθημεν τῷ κόσμῳ καὶ ἀγγέλοις καὶ ἀνθρώποις [v. 9c]). As causal clauses typically are, the proposition of this clause is stated categorically (MONOGLOSS). Paul assumes it as a given, hence it serves as the basis (cause) for his opinion. However, as with previous monoglossic statements in this unit, the disposition of the text is such that this bare assertion may not be accepted as a given by all (if any) of the readers. Thus, it is still in a sense arguable. In fact, what follows in vv. 10–13 is a series of descriptions (most of which occur in concede + counter pairs) that back this assertion. So, although monoglossically declared and although Paul accepts it as a given, this bare assertion is not formulated as "taken-for-granted" by everyone in the communicative context.

Verse 10 consists of three concede + counter pairs (Table 14). These are interesting to interpret because they occur in a discursive environment of irony or sarcasm. When Paul concedes, for example, that the apostles are *fools because of Christ* (ἡμεῖς μωροὶ διὰ Χριστόν), on the one hand he concedes that those who operate by the standards of the world are bound to evaluate them as "fools" as defined by worldly standards. Yet, throughout his argument he has called the readers to become fools in order to be wise (cf. 3:18). Thus, on the other hand, he "covertly" makes the claim that the apostles are, indeed, fools because of Christ—and that is the way it should be!

When he counters by saying *but you are wise in Christ*, on the one hand, he claims that, again by the world's standards, the readers may in some way be

TABLE 14   Concede (CONCUR) + counter pairs in 1 Cor 4:10

ἡμεῖς μωροὶ διὰ Χριστόν	ὑμεῖς δὲ φρόνιμοι ἐν Χριστῷ
(We are fools because of Christ)	(but you are wise in Christ)
[PROCLAIM: CONCUR]	[DISCLAIM: COUNTER]
ἡμεῖς ἀσθενεῖς	ὑμεῖς δὲ ἰσχυροί
(We are weak)	(but you are strong)
[PROCLAIM: CONCUR]	[DISCLAIM: COUNTER]
ὑμεῖς ἔνδοξοι	ἡμεῖς δὲ ἄτιμοι
(You are honored)	(but we are without honor)
[PROCLAIM: CONCUR]	[DISCLAIM: COUNTER]

"TELL US HOW YOU REALLY FEEL, PAUL!" (PART 2)   183

wise,[116] yet Paul has previously described them as less than "sensible" in that they were not able to discern the things of the Spirit (cf. 2:6–16). Thus, he sarcastically claims in his counter that they are wise, when he means that they are not. Thus, each of these concede + counter pairs packages a double-entendre: we apostles may be fools, weak, and dishonored by the world, but that is what a cruciform life looks like. You readers may be wise, mighty, and honored by the world, but that is not what a cruciform life looks like. Thus, each pair positions the readers to align with the view that they are not living in a way that reflects the values of God, but the values of the world.

In vv. 11–13, Paul abandons irony and speaks plainly. In these verses he describes the life of an apostle, much of which likely comes from his own catalog of experiences. Verses 11–12a are monoglossic; with each clause Paul states categorically and emphatically that *even to the present time we hunger and thirst, we are poorly clothed and beaten and homeless and we labor as we work with our own hands.* By the world's reckoning, each of these experiences would result in dishonor; some of them (e.g., beaten) may refer to public shaming. From v. 12c to the end of the unit, Paul shifts back into using concede + counter pairs (Table 15). Each concession is grammaticalized as a present participle and each counter a finite verb with present tense-form. This changes in the very last clause of the catalog where Paul closes with monoglossic assertion that *we have become refuse of the world, the filth of all things.* In all of these, Paul portrays the kind of humble life members of the community of believers, whether "leaders" or "laypersons," ought to live in light of the crucified Messiah.

TABLE 15   Concede (CONCUR) + counter pairs in 1 Cor 4:12c–13

λοιδορούμενοι	εὐλογοῦμεν
(Although insulted)	(we bless/praise)
διωκόμενοι	ἀνεχόμεθα
(Although persecuted)	(we endure)
δυσφημούμενοι	παρακαλοῦμεν
(Although slandered)	(we encourage)

---

116   The term φρόνιμος is used here instead of σόφοι. Fee (*First Epistle*, 176 n 60) says that φρόνιμος is typically pejorative in Paul (cf. 2 Cor 11:19; Rom 11:25; 12:16).

184 CHAPTER 4

1.6.3 Summary

Instances of JUDGMENT dominate this unit and most of them are personal judgments of ESTEEM, although a handful of moral judgments of SANCTION (propriety) appear as well. A key to interpreting these judgments is recognizing that they appear in a section where irony is thick. The result is that many of the positive judgments are to be interpreted as negative and many of the negative judgments are to be interpreted as positive. These judgments, especially because they are ironic, create strong attitudinal dispositions opposed to measuring and being measured by the world's standards that results in boasting even for gifts, while at the same time generating a positive disposition for living a humble life as dictated by the cross. As far as engagement goes, to support these attitudinal dispositions Paul opts for a number of concede + counter pairs, but in the ironic context, what Paul "concedes" actually supports his value position as do each of the counters. In this way, Paul makes a strong bid to align the readers to his value position.

1.7 *Maintain the Family's Honor by Imitating Me* (*1 Cor 4:14–21*)

Paul begins the final section of 1 Cor 1–4 with an attempt to rebuild solidarity with the readers, for he certainly risked and perhaps damaged writer-reader solidarity in the previous sections. To do this he reminds the readers that he is their father in the faith, and as a father is supposed to do, he has been providing correction to his beloved children so they do not bring shame upon the family. By the close of the section, however, he returns to using bold speech and risks solidarity with the readers by engaging in social "name calling" (*some are puffed up*) and even in threatening to come to Corinth with a rod (i.e., the rod of correction used by fathers). The chief concern of the section is with the readers' behavior, and Paul's central purpose is to direct the readers to become his imitators and so apply the lesson of the cross to their lives as he has done in his. The positive and negative inscribed and implied judgments of SANCTION (propriety) correspond respectively to the behaviors he wants to promote and those he wishes to suppress. Most of the text is construed as heteroglossic as Paul dialogues with the readers-in-the-text regarding his purpose for writing in such a bold tone and how he might come to come to them when the Lord allows him to visit. However, the key point of the paragraph—the directive to become his imitators—is, not surprisingly, monoglossic and categorical.

1.7.1 Attitudinal Analysis

Paul opens the final unit with an account for the bold language he has used in the first four chapters. He explains that he writes not to shame them (οὐκ ἐντρέπων) but to correct their behavior (νουθετῶν).[117] This stated purpose obviously implies the readers have been behaving improperly as Paul sees it and is therefore an ideational token of negative sanction (t, – JUDGMENT: SANCTION: propriety). Yet Paul balances this implied judgment by enacting the father-child relationship, calling the readers his *beloved children* (τέκνα μου ἀγαπητά), which betokens a positive judgment of esteem (+ JUDGMENT: ESTEEM: normality).[118] Taken together, these appraisals aid in portraying Paul as a loving father who, as fathers in the ancient circum-Mediterranean world did,[119] corrects his misbehaving children in order to protect the family's honor (t, + JUDGMENT: SANCTION: propriety). He continues this depiction into v. 15, where he reminds the readers that if they happen to have myriad[120] guardians (παιδαγωγούς) in Christ,[121] only he is their father in Christ, which he became when he preached the gospel to them and they believed (ἐν γὰρ Χριστῷ Ἰησοῦ διὰ τοῦ εὐαγγελίου ἐγὼ ὑμᾶς ἐγέννησα [For I became your father in Christ Jesus through the gospel]). Thus, only he inhabits this special relationship with them (t, + JUDGMENT: ESTEEM: normality).

Based on his role of father, Paul urges the readers to imitate him (μιμηταί μου γίνεσθε [Be imitators of me]) (v. 16).[122] Castelli points out that in the ancient Greco-Roman world, sameness was valued above difference at least in part because it affected other core values such as unity, harmony, and order.[123]

---

117 The verb νουθετέω refers to instruction and/or rebuke with regard to belief or behavior (cf. *ANLEX*) and may refer to correction which fits the current context.

118 *Beloved children*, together, is a positive judgment of normality; the readers are Paul's (fictive) kin and are therefore special. The definer ἀγαπητά realizes + AFFECT: happiness (affection).

119 In the ancient circum-Mediterranean world (ca. 300 BCE to 300 CE), fathers commanded uncompromised respect and obedience from their children (unequal status) (see McVann, "Family-Centeredness," *HBSV* 64–67), and were also responsible for passing on and establishing the tradition among them (cf. Deut 6:6–7; Prov 22:6; 1 Cor 15:1–8) as well as providing correction for the sake of family honor should their children become involved in foolish, shameless, or deviant behavior (cf. Prov 19:18; 23:13–14; 29:17). This appears to be the kind of role Paul takes up with respect to the readers. See also Castelli, *Imitating Paul*, 101–2.

120 *Myriad* realizes GRADUATION: FORCE: QUANTIFICATION.

121 It is possible that Paul implies here that the readers are still in need of a παιδαγωγός, insinuating that they are still immature, unlearned children. However, this cannot be certain since the portrayal is hypothetical (third class condition) and Paul's speech is hyperbolic (*myriad of guardians*). It seems the point has more to do with emphasizing Paul's role as the readers' father.

122 See D. M. Stanley, "'Become Imitators of Me': The Pauline Conception of Apostolic Tradition," *Bib* 40 (1959): 872–73; Fee, *First Epistle*, 186.

123 Castelli, *Imitating Paul*, 86. But see the critiques of Castelli in Witherington, *Conflict & Community*, 144–46 and Thiselton, *First Corinthians*, 371–73.

Moreover, change and novelty met sometimes quite violent rejection because they put tradition and its values at risk.[124] Thus, as a father urges his children,[125] Paul urges the readers to become imitators of him so that by applying the message of the cross, a lesson in humility, as Paul had, the readers would maintain the integrity of both the ἐκκλησία (i.e., the fictive family of believers) at Corinth and the gospel itself that Paul had passed down to them. The integrity of neither can be maintained if the readers do not apply to their lives the lesson of humility taught through the cross. In a way, then, calling the readers to imitate him implies that they have not applied the lesson of the cross and have been acting in ways incompatible with the message of the cross (t, – JUDGMENT: SANCTION: propriety).

Since Paul could not immediately travel back to Corinth to teach the readers in person, he sent Timothy to facilitate their imitation of Paul (v. 17). Timothy is appraised quite positively, likely so the Corinthians would give him a hearing upon his arrival. As Fee says,

> This verse implies that Timothy is going in Paul's stead, and therefore that he is to be regarded by them as though Paul himself were present among them.... Paul's point, then, is not to inform the Corinthians about someone they already know, but to reinforce Timothy's own relationship to Paul so that they will pay attention to what he says.[126]

Paul calls him his *beloved and loyal child in the Lord* (μου τέκνον ἀγαπητὸν καὶ πιστὸν ἐν κυρίῳ) (17b). This language is very similar to that used to appraise the readers in v. 14. Just as *beloved children* there realized a positive judgment of esteem for the readers, so too here it realizes positive esteem for Timothy (+ JUDGMENT: ESTEEM: normality).[127]

Garland says that this puts Timothy on the same level as the readers,[128] in that they are all Paul's children (i.e., converts to Christ through his preaching). However, that Paul adds the additional definer *loyal* (+ JUDGMENT: ESTEEM: tenacity) to Timothy realizes + GRADUATION: FOCUS, which sets Timothy apart from the readers, who have not, as co-text and context indicate, demonstrated

---

124 McVann, "Change/Novelty Orientation," *HBSV* 14–16.

125 See deSilva, *Honor, Patronage, Kinship & Purity*, 185–88.

126 Fee, *First Epistle*, 189.

127 As noted with regard to the readers, *beloved and faithful child* taken together is a positive judgment of normality; Timothy is Paul's (fictive) kin in Christ and is therefore special. Additionally, the definer ἀγαπητόν realizes + AFFECT: happiness (affection).

128 Garland, *1 Corinthians*, 147.

the same level of tenacity and therefore do not fit as well the expectation that comes with being a son in the ancient world or a fictive son in the fictive family of believers. Timothy is sent as a model for the readers to follow—not that they are necessarily to imitate *him*, but to imitate how he imitates Paul. This is what Paul means when he says Timothy will *remind you of all my ways in Christ Jesus* (v. 17c). Of course, as Garland points out, this need not mean the readers had forgotten all that Paul had taught while he was among them,[129] but given Paul's heavy emphasis on the readers' inability to apply what he had taught as demonstrated by their fleshly behavior (cf., e.g., 3:1–5), it implies quite strongly that Paul doubted their ability to imitate him and to apply the lesson of humility taught by the cross (t, – JUDGMENT: ESTEEM: capacity) without someone like Timothy acting as a facilitator.

Having just established that he sent Timothy in his stead because he cannot immediately go to Corinth in person, at v. 18 Paul fixes his gaze on some (τινες [GRADUATION: FOCUS: soften]) who assume that the father, Paul, is not going to come "home" to Corinth any time soon and, thus, as Garland colloquially states it, act like "little children who have the house to themselves when the parents have slipped out for a minute."[130] These "children" talk like they have the authority of the head of household, but upon his next visit to Corinth Paul will see if they have any ability (δύναμις) to back up their talk (τὸν λόγον) (v. 19). That he refers to these people as *puffed up* (– JUDGMENT: SANCTION: propriety) and that he asserts *the kingdom of God is not exhibited in speech, but in power* (v. 20) strongly implies that he does not regard these people as all that powerful (t, – JUDGMENT: ESTEEM: capacity).

In the final verse (v. 21), the salience of Paul's role as father is renewed when he asks them if he should come with a *rod* (i.e., severe discipline) or with *love and a gentle spirit*. The question itself implies Paul's belief that the readers were at the time of writing behaving badly (t, – JUDGMENT: SANCTION: propriety) and they had to choose whether they would change their behavior to reflect the humility demonstrated by a crucified Messiah (resulting in Paul coming in love and with a gentle spirit) or continue in their world-oriented, boastful arrogance (which would require Paul to come with a spirit of discipline). By juxtaposing the rod (negative) with a spirit of love and gentleness (positive), Paul hopes to position the readers to align with his value position and to modify their behavior.

---

129   Garland, *1 Corinthians*, 147.
130   Garland, *1 Corinthians*, 148.

1.7.2   Engagement Analysis

Paul adopts a deny + counter pair for his first move in rebuilding solidarity with the readers (v. 14). The denial *I do not write these things to shame you* construes Paul as being aware that at least some of the readers may feel as though he has addressed them too harshly. However, as is the nature of denials, Paul acknowledges this voice only to reject it. He supplants the rejected notion with more appropriate description of the situation: he was not writing to bring shame, but the exact opposite, *to correct you*,[131] in order to protect the "family name" from shame like any honorable father would do in his culture. So then, the deny + counter strategy functions to reject a misguided notion and to supplant it with one Paul deems to be more appropriate.

The realizations of ENGAGEMENT in the three clauses comprising v. 15 all function together to position the readers to view Paul—and only Paul— as inhabiting the social role of father of the implied readers. The first clause is the protasis of a third class conditional structure, portraying a hypothetical situation for consideration. In doing so, it opens the dialogue to the idea that its proposition might possibly hold (CONSIDER): *If you happen to have a myriad of guardians in Christ....*[132] The apodosis, however, contracts the dialogue with a counter: *at least*[133] [*you will*] *not have many fathers*.[134] This counter contracts dialogue around the notion of the number of fathers the readers will have compared to the number of guardians they may have. This sets up for the final clause in the verse in which Paul asserts *For I myself became your father in Christ Jesus through the gospel*. The use of ἐγώ realizes Paul's subjective interpolation into the text and signals that this clause is an instance of PROCLAIM: PRONOUNCE. Paul overtly resists the view that anyone else could be their father in Christ. He and only he brought the gospel to them; they had believed in Christ through his service to God (cf. 3:5).

Like 1 Cor 1:10, παρακαλῶ in v. 16 is an interpersonal modality metaphor, but with the significant difference that here the semiotic space opened by the modality metaphor for interpersonal negotiation is overridden by the

---

131   The participles ἐντρέπων and νουθετῶν both express purpose (on this use of the participle, see Porter, *Idioms*, 192–93).

132   In order to make sense of the relationship between the first two clauses, most English versions transform the conditional protasis into a concession (*For though you have a myriad ...*), but doing so changes the semantics of the structure. A third class condition signifies an indefinite or unfulfilled hypothesis, but a concession signifies that the proposition holds and that both writer and reader stand in agreement on the point. Paul intends the former, not the latter.

133   See Turner, *Syntax*, 330 on glossing ἀλλά following a conditional protasis.

134   See Robertson, *Grammar*, 1018.

"TELL US HOW YOU REALLY FEEL, PAUL!" (PART 2)   189

ensuing imperative μιμηταί μου γίνεσθε. On the one hand, the modality meta-phor grounds the command in the subjectivity of Paul's desire[135] for the read-ers, which is generally something that is open for negotiation (CONSIDER); on the other hand, however, Paul closes up space for negotiation and, in fact, does not even acknowledge the possibility of resistance, by using the imperative (MONOGLOSS). It is as though he says, "As your father, I want you to do this: be my imitators."

As noted above, Paul sent Timothy, his *beloved and loyal child in the Lord* (MONOGLOSS) to Corinth as his emissary (v. 17). He *will remind* the readers of the ways Paul applies the message of the cross in his ministry to all the churches everywhere. The future form ἀναμνήσει realizes CONSIDER in that it modal-izes the process because it grammaticalizes expectation. Thus the proposition *I expect that he will remind you* is grounded in Paul's contingent subjectivity and presents what he believes Timothy will accomplish during his time in Corinth.

At v. 18, Paul references the apparent attitude of *some* (τινες) of the read-ers, that they have become arrogant (*puffed up*) thinking that Paul will not be visiting them any time soon (ATTRIBUTE: DISTANCE). In response (v. 19), Paul opens the possibility that he will come to (ἐλεύσομαι [I expect to come]) the addressees relatively soon, if the Lord will it (CONSIDER). Upon his arrival, assuming he does visit them, he expects to find out (γνώσομαι) whether or not these people have any power (δύναμιν) backing their talk (λόγον) (CONSIDER). For to Paul, the kingdom of God is not exhibited merely in talk (DISCLAIM: DENY), but in power (DISCLAIM: COUNTER) (v. 20). To think otherwise, as the deny + counter pair signifies, is wrong and must be corrected.

The unit closes, indeed the entire argument contained in chapter 1–4 closes, with two open, expository questions. The first, *What do you want?* is dialogi-cally expansive in that it invites the readers to enter into the dialogue with a response. The second question, *Shall I come with a rod or with love and a spirit of gentleness?* although not quite as wide open as the first since it limits answers to two possibilities, is still dialogically expansive, which is signaled by the use of the Subjunctive Mood form (ἔλθω) and the fact that the choice is left open to the readers (i.e., Paul does not contract dialogue by answering the question for them) (CONSIDER).

1.7.3   Summary
The attitudinal evaluations in this closing unit aid in accomplishing several things. First, Paul uses ATTITUDE to create a positive disposition toward the way

---

135   Urging someone toward (or away from) a certain attitude, belief, or behavior stems from that person's desire (t, + AFFECT: inclination [desire]).

he has engaged the readers in the text thus far. He portrays himself as acting appropriately toward them, not shaming them but correcting them as a father corrects his beloved children. This is Paul's attempt to restore any solidarity that may have been damaged or lost thus far in the argument. Second, Paul's command to the readers to imitate him implies that his ways are worthy of being imitated. This is a betokened attitude, but crucial nonetheless. Third, appraisal is used to portray Timothy as the model child whom the implied readers can trust to remind them of Paul's ways and teachings. Of course, ATTITUDE is also used to portray the readers as needing to be reminded of Paul's ways. Finally, Paul uses attitude to generate a negative disposition toward those who have become haughty in Paul's absence. The indirect threat to come with a rod signifies that Paul, as their father, is quite displeased with their behavior.

The two main engagement strategies adopted in this section are CONSIDER and, as a rhetorical pair, DISCLAIM: DENY and DISCLAIM: COUNTER. With these Paul engages the readers in dialogue, positioning them to reach certain conclusions. He denies shaming them, countering with the proposition that his intent is to correct them as his beloved children. He entertains the notion that they may have a myriad of guardians, but they only have him as their father. He considers the expectation that he will visit them and learn if the puffed-up ones have any power or if they are all talk. And he opens the possibility that when he does visit, he may need to come with the rod of correction—if they do not change their ways. Together Paul's selections from ATTITUDE and ENGAGEMENT, as has been the case throughout the argument in 1 Cor 1–4, have been to bring the readers into alignment with the controlling ideology (i.e., theology) and system of values that direct Paul's way of life, namely those expressed through a crucified Messiah.

2 Conclusion

At the conclusion of the previous chapter, it was noted by way of reminder that a main claim of this study is that Paul's attitudinal evaluations and engagement strategies reveal the values by which he believes the Corinthian believers (really, all believers everywhere [cf. 1:2; 4:16]) ought to live and those by which the ought *not* live. Although a number of these will be revisited in the conclusion in the subsequent chapter, it is nonetheless instructive to conclude this chapter by highlighting the key values that surface as 1 Cor 3–4 unfolds.

Paul's language in 1 Cor 3:1–5 is exacting; he steps into the lives of the readers to point out what they have *wrong* and how they ought *not* to live, hence the repeated negative judgments regarding their capacity to discern what is proper and to behave properly. It becomes clear through the social name calling and rhetorical questioning in this unit that Paul stands quite opposed to the formation of cliques around people in the church who are people of status by the world's standards. Such behavior reveals the readers have not grown in their faith but are still as *fleshly* and *immature* as they were when Paul first brought them the gospel. Paul rebukes them because their divisive behavior is inconsistent with the fact that they are *in Christ* (3:1) and presumably have the Spirit of God (cf. 1:1–9). When the readers involve themselves in clique formation (*I am of Paul ... I am of Apollos*) they *behave according to human inclinations* (3:4), mirroring the ψυχικὸς ἄνθρωπος (world-oriented person) constructed at 1 Cor 2:14 rather than the πνευματικός (spiritual person) (2:15)—not the reference person they should emulate. Clearly, then, the value at issue here is that of wholeness. Wholeness is concerned with the integrity of belief (faith) and behavior and by extension the integrity of the group of believers.[136] For Paul, to lack wholeness is to be unholy; to act like *mere humans* undermines the "set-apartness" that distinguishes the community of believers from an unholy society.

The farming analogy in 1 Cor 3:5–9 allows Paul to teach the readers the proper way to view people in the family of God. Using himself and Apollos as representatives of people who are presumably "important" in the church, Paul destroys any notion of self-aggrandizement and social self-betterment ("boasting") by defining them as διάκονοι (*servants*). He explains in the language of the analogy that both he and Apollos were each given a specific task—planting and watering, respectively (3:6)—but that these tasks served a single purpose. Neither he nor Apollos completed their distinctive tasks for their own self-promotion or honor; rather, they discharged their duties to the glory of their Master, God who makes the crop grow. The value propagated here is humility. As a social value, humility directs a person to remain in their inherited social status, to remain neutral in the social competition of life.[137] To humble oneself is "to declare oneself powerless to defend one's status" and then to act accordingly either factually or ritually by renouncing one's status, setting aside the use of power, or eschewing boastful, self-promoting behavior.[138] Paul and Apollos exemplify humility in this text by fulfilling the tasks to which God has commissioned them without seeking more honor for themselves by "moving up" to a more honorable task. This is a lesson the boastful Corinthians need to learn

---

136   See Neyrey, "Wholeness," *HBSV* 175.

137   Malina, "Humility," *HBSV* 99.

138   Malina, "Humility," *HBSV* 99.

192   CHAPTER 4

and apply, hence the use of ATTITUDE and ENGAGEMENT to position the reader to live an "upside-down" life (upside-down in the eyes of the world, that is).

At 3:10–17, Paul changes metaphors rather abruptly from the world of farming to the world of building, and, specifically, to building the temple of God. As noted above, at the outset of this section, Paul issues a directive to the readers to carefully consider how and with what they build the temple (3:10). For Paul, God's temple was no longer a specific designated area of sacred space; rather, "temple" referred to the groups of believers among whom the Spirit of God dwelled (3:16–17).[139] Thus, as one builds on the foundation of Jesus, she or he must take care not to build with materials that are perishable—things of the present age—that would corrupt (φθείρει) God's temple (3:17). By this analogy Paul emphasizes holiness which is related to wholeness. If the believers at Corinth constitute the temple of God, which Paul assumes (3:16), then they must exhibit holy behavior. Dividedness (i.e., the lack of wholeness) is considered indicative of defilement and corruption;[140] thus, the one who causes division among the group of believers is guilty of defiling the very temple of God. Such a one would be seen as violating the "purity law" of keeping the ἐκκλησία free from behavior that did not fit "in Christ,"[141] and would thus be in danger of being *destroyed* (φθερεῖ) by God (3:17). Holiness (wholeness) is, once again, revealed as a core value undergirding Christian morality.

1 Corinthians 3:18–23 perpetuates the value of humility. It does so by suggesting that one who presumes to be wise by the standards of the world has fallen prey to self-deception, thinking they are something when they are not (v. 18). Further, wisdom as the world defines it is cast as foolishness before God (vv. 19–20), thus *no one is to boast in a person* (v. 22). In fact, those who avoid being self-deceived and become "fools" as the world sees it are described as having everything belonging to them (v. 22), apparently a play on the Stoic saying "all things belong to the wise person." In this, the reversal theme is reestablished: what the world considers wise, God considers foolish, and what the world considers foolish, God considers wise. The readers are directed to humble themselves, to "become foolish," in order to be wise before God.

Paul continues to propagate the value of humility in 1 Cor 4:1–5. Here he positively portrays servanthood as well as the faithful discharging of the duties that God has assigned to each (vv. 1–2). Another facet of humility appears in this passage as Paul negatively appraises the readers for judging him (presumably by the standards of the world). A humble person does not take on roles

---

139   See Malina, *New Testament World*, 192.
140   See deSilva, *Honor, Patronage, Kinship & Purity*, 247–48.
141   See Malina, *New Testament World*, 194.

"TELL US HOW YOU REALLY FEEL, PAUL!" (PART 2)

higher than what they have been allotted. In this instance, the readers are depicted as improperly having taken on the role of the master and are judging Paul and, assuming Paul is representative of other important people, others. This is inappropriate, haughty behavior, for as Paul says, *the one who judges me is the Lord* (v. 10). In this way Paul again emphasizes humility as a core value of the ἐκκλησία τοῦ θεοῦ, and it is a value that contributes to the wholeness/holiness of the community in that it does not encourage divisive behavior.

Perhaps the most poignant yet powerful depiction of humility applied to one's life appears in 1 Cor 4:6–13. Ironically, Paul holds up the defamed life of *us apostles* as the quintessence of humility lived out. It is so, Paul argues, because God wanted to demonstrate in the apostles the lesson of the cross applied. The apostles are considered fools because of the message of a crucified Messiah they preach, dishonored, hungry, thirsty, poorly clothed, beaten, homeless, and having to work with their own hands (vv. 10–12). Yet, despite the shame heaped on them by the world, they humbly respond to the difficulties they face. When they are insulted, they respond with blessing/praise; when they are persecuted, they endure; when they are slandered, they encourage (vv. 12–13). In these descriptions, the negativity of humiliation is supplanted with positivity, so that humility becomes honorable before God.[142]

Finally, in 1 Cor 4:14–21 at least two key values surface in Paul's language. The first is honor. In reality, honor undergirds the entire argument surfacing at various times in the text where it becomes an explicit issue. Such is the case at the beginning of this text where Paul must defend the appropriateness of the challenging, if not harsh, language he has used to address the readers. He claims to have acted in an honorable way toward the implied readers because his intent was not to shame them but to provide correction. In describing his use of language as corrective, he not only protects his own honor, but more importantly he construes himself as protecting the honor of the ἐκκλησία τοῦ θεοῦ that exists at Corinth and beyond. If, as the father of the Corinthians, he allows their improper behavior to fragment the church, he would thereby invite shame not only upon himself but also upon the fictive kin group, which could ultimately end up bringing dishonor to God. The idea that God's name might be defamed motivates him to respond to the readers with frankness, even if it might risk solidarity between them.

A second value that appears in 1 Cor 4:14–21 is that of respect. As their father in Christ (not to mention the apostle to their church), Paul commands the respect of the readers. That is, Paul expects the readers to change their behavior

---

142   See now deSilva, *Honor, Patronage, Kinship & Purity*, 65–70 under the heading "When Dishonor is No Dishonor."

because he, as their father, has directed them to do so. Most of the time in this and other of his letters, Paul does not play the authoritarian as if all ἐξουσία (*power, authority*) resided in him. Rather, the authority with which he speaks derives from God. This being the case, it is quite interesting that at 4:16 Paul would command the readers to imitate him. Contra to Castelli's notion[143] that Paul makes this command as some sort of self-aggrandizing political power play—which would contradict a staple teaching in 1 Cor 1–4—it appears that the command is a call to the readers to appropriate the kind of humility exemplified in 4:6–13, namely seeking what station God has called them to in Christ and humbly taking it up for God's glory. If they respect Paul as their father, they will imitate him in this way, and he will not have to bring the rod of correction when he comes for a visit.

143 Castelli, *Imitating Paul*, 98–111.

CHAPTER 5

Conclusion

The purpose of this work has been to examine the role of Paul's language in the resocialization of the assumed readers of 1 Corinthians 1–4. Since resocialization is about convincing people to replace certain beliefs, values, and behaviors with new or modified ones—a social task accomplished primarily through language—a sociolinguistic model of interpersonal discourse analysis called Appraisal Theory was adopted for text analysis. This model operates on the supposition that people negotiate values and ideologies through the negotiation of attitudes. If one's goal is to convince an arrogant person to be humble, she or he will adopt a negative stance or attitudinal disposition toward arrogance and arrogant behavior while taking up a positive stance toward humility and humble behavior. These stances are encoded in text and exchanged with the person to be convinced as positive or negative evaluations or appraisals. The model of APPRAISAL identifies these evaluations and the strategies of engagement that together attempt to impress an axiological paradigm (i.e., a framework of what is "right" and what is "wrong") upon the person to be convinced. This model is used to analyze 1 Cor 1–4 to see what stances Paul took up vis-à-vis the readers to get a sense for the core values, the axiological paradigm, he wished to impress upon them as believers in Christ and members of the ἐκκλησία τοῦ θεοῦ.

Applying the model to 1 Cor 1–4 brings several things to light. First, the attitudinal appraisals and engagement strategies do, indeed, reflect Paul's social goals in each unit of the text, the major moves of which I recount here in broad strokes. It has long been argued that the letter opening and thanksgiving serve to build writer-reader solidarity. This is reflected in the dominance of positive judgments of ESTEEM in regards to normality (those that bespeak how unique or special a person is) of the readers. Moreover, these judgments are stated matter-of-factly, almost entirely in monoglossic text. There is a major shift to the dominance of negative judgment of the readers' behavior (SANCTION) and heteroglossic text in 1 Cor 1:10–17, which corresponds to Paul's statement of the problem and the beginning of his argument against that problem that occurs in the letter body. Alternation between positive and negative appreciations appear in 1 Cor 1:18–25 as Paul invokes the thematic formation of reversal in his attempt to align the readers to an appropriate view of the message of the cross. First Corinthians 1:26–31 and 2:1–5 offer more alternations between positive and negative APPRECIATION continuing the reversal theme, although here

© JAMES D. DVORAK, 2021 | DOI:10.1163/9789004453814_006

they are applied to the readers' transformative experience and to the power of God's message despite Paul's weaknesses. The goal, it appears, is to convince the implied readers that God has put them in the position they enjoy, so they must give God honor, not seek it for themselves.

The goal in 1 Cor 2:6–16 is still primarily to establish that what Paul preaches is, indeed, wisdom from God. Thus, the engagement strategies and positive appreciations continue to function to this end. However, starting in this section, there are an increasing number of negative judgments regarding the readers' capacity to discern what Paul preaches as God's wisdom. These mark the beginning of the shift in the argument from teaching about God's wisdom to applying it directly to the readers' lives. This transition is made in 1 Cor 3:1–4 where there is a definite spike in negative judgments regarding the readers' behavior, which dominate through 1 Cor 4:5. Clearly, Paul's goal in these sections (i.e., 3:1–4, 5–9, 10–17, 18–23; 4:1–5) is to emphasize the implied readers' bad behavior and, through positive evaluations, point out the kind of good behavior with which they ought to replace it. The appraisals and engagement techniques used in 1 Cor 4:6–13 strongly suggest that Paul is about the business of correction. The reversal theme is clearly invoked as Paul appraises positively those things the world appraises negatively and vice versa. In terms of ENGAGEMENT, this section is dominated by concede + counter pairs in which, ironically, the points Paul concedes ultimately support his value position, as do the counter points. This is a powerful section of text in terms of reader alignment. The final section, 1 Cor 4:14–21, sees positive appraisals of Paul as he seeks to rebuild solidarity with the readers in order that he might command them to imitate him. Yet, he ends the unit on a mixed note designed to move the readers to his value position: if they remain puffed up, he threatens the rod; however, if they humble themselves and change their ways, he will come with love and a gentle spirit. So then, the model of appraisal can help interpreters trace Paul's social goals through the text.

A second observation that comes into focus through the application of the model is that the core values that Paul wishes to impose upon the readers become apparent. As the model was applied to the thirteen units of text comprising chapters 1–4, the evaluations and reader alignments through engagement began to project a pattern with regard to values Paul wanted the readers to accept. In six of the thirteen units (cf. 1:26–31; 2:1–5; 3:5–9; 3:18–23; 4:1–5; and 4:6–13), the value of humility clearly rose to the top.[1] This value was communicated though negative appraisals of boasting and the readers' hubristic behavior, positive appraisals of Paul completing his task of preaching the "foolish"

---

1   See Malina, "Humility," *HBSV* 99–100.

CONCLUSION

message of the cross with less than impressive speech and stature (according to the world), positive appraisals of the role of servant, negative appraisals of overstepping one's bounds to judge another's servant, and the reconstrual of what the world considers shameful as what God considers honorable. Another value that is foregrounded several times (cf. 1:10–17; 3:1–4; 3:10–17) is that of wholeness/holiness.[2] This value is propagated mainly through positive evaluations of unity and behavior that results in unity and negative evaluations of division and divisive behavior. Other values that surface throughout Paul's argument include: loyalty (faithfulness), respect, sameness (i.e., resistance to diverting from the tradition Paul has handed down to them), patronage/beneficence of God, and, of course honor and (positive) shame.[3] This is a significant observation because it demonstrates that the model was able to aid in successfully accomplishing the goal of the study.

This study opens a number of avenues for future research. One of the hallmarks of the current study is that it focuses its gaze on interpersonal meaning in text, but much more work with this emphasis needs to be done in nearly every area of biblical studies. In the area of Greek grammar, for example, the vast majority of Greek grammars—beginning, intermediate, and advanced— privilege ideational meanings in their definitions of grammatical concepts. For example, one specific grammatical topic that could benefit from the insights of interpersonal analysis is that of verbal mood. Even those who rightly emphasize the role played by the language user's subjective view still often define mood in terms of the language user's view of the action *in relation to reality*. This favors ideational meaning. There is little to no discussion of the interpersonal semantics of mood/modality (e.g., the dialogic expansiveness of the Subjunctive Mood).

Another area of linguistic analysis that could benefit from Appraisal Theory is paragraphing. Debates continue to swirl around the definition of paragraph and how units of text should be marked off. Many contemporary discourse analyses, especially those arising from within the SFL paradigm, tend to focus on features related to the textual metafunction. This is certainly the most appropriate approach, but perhaps attitudinal appraisals could be added to the number of features analyzed when determining paragraph or unit breaks. For example, most scholars would place a break at 1 Cor 2:6, and there are good

---

2 See Neyrey, "Wholeness," *HBSV* 175–78.

3 See Malina, "Faith/Faithfulness," *HBSV* 61–63; Malina, *New Testament World*, 30 (respect); McVann, "Change/Novelty Orientation," *HBSV* 14–16; deSilva, *Honor, Patronage, Kinship & Purity*, 95–156 (patronage); deSilva, *Honor, Patronage, Kinship & Purity*, 23–93 (honor); and Plevnik, "Honor/Shame," *HBSV* 89–96 (honor).

textual reasons for doing so, such as the change of aspect and person, and the introduction of new participants. One other key indicator is the shift from negative evaluation of σοφία to a positive one. This is helpful since Paul continues to use a lexical item from prior text, but in spite of this the semantic link to the previous uses has been broken on account of the shift in ATTITUDE.

Another area in biblical studies that could benefit from the kind of discourse analysis modeled in this study is the area of exegetical methodology. Even a cursory perusal of commentaries in the major series (e.g., NIGTC, NICNT) reveals the privileging of ideational and textual meanings. Commentators exert great effort (and in many cases use a lot of ink!) in describing the meaning of a text in terms of what the text is *about* (i.e., text as representation [ideational]) and, to a fair extent, the "stylistic" features a writer uses to convey their message (i.e., text as message [textual meaning]). Often very little space is given to the interpersonal question of what the writers are attempting to *do* to their assumed audiences through the texts that they have produced (i.e., text as exchange [interpersonal meaning]). As a result, important features of texts, such as the creation and maintenance of social relations and value systems, are often left completely out of the discussion even though, as argued in this study, these are often (if not always) the main reason the New Testament documents were penned in the first place.

Finally, in the broader field of biblical criticism and hermeneutics, it would be especially interesting to see the kind of discourse analysis modeled here adopted by practitioners of social-scientific criticism. In many cases, those who practice this approach adopt rhetorical or socio-rhetorical criticism as the main tool for analyzing text, but rhetorical-critical models often stall out on matters of generic form and content and fail to deal adequately with the formal and semantic features (i.e., the *linguistic* features) of the language in use. It would be refreshing to see practitioners of social-scientific criticism utilize a SFL-based model of interpersonal discourse analysis to study again ancient documents, both biblical and non-biblical, in order to revise as necessary the description of the social landscape of the ancient circum-Mediterranean world and the axiological paradigm(s) of the early Christians.

APPENDIX

Survey of the Literature on the Study of 1 Corinthians

This appendix contains a brief survey of the key works related to the analysis presented above. In this survey, one will find works from a broad spectrum of approaches to the interpretation of 1 Corinthians. All of the works included in this survey deal with the interpretation of 1 Corinthians to some degree; some deal specifically with 1 Cor 1–4, others with specific texts in 1 Corinthians but outside chapters 1–4, still others with issues related to 1 Corinthians as a whole. The spectrum of approaches includes but is not limited to: linguistic criticism and discourse analysis; rhetorical and socio-rhetorical criticism; social-scientific criticism; and social identity theory. The works are treated in order of their year of publication (if more than one work exists for a single publication year, they are ordered alphabetically by last name).

In 1990, Antoinette Clark Wire published *The Corinthian Women Prophets*, in which she attempts to reconstruct the social and theological location of the women prophets at Corinth. Her stated interest in these women is "their behavior, daily and occasional, their position in society and the church, and their values and theology."[1] To accomplish her task, Wire adopts for her analytical framework a model built on the New Rhetoric espoused by Perelman and Olbrechts-Tyteca. What attracts her to such a model is its emphasis on the point that persuaders like Paul must be keenly aware of the audience with whom they share the rhetorical situation. On the basis of this audience and the situation they share, persuaders shape their arguments in ways they believe will have the greatest persuasive impact on that audience in that situation. Moreover, as Wire points out, "because to argue is to gauge your audience as accurately as you can at every point, to use their language, to work from where they are toward where you want them to be,"[2] an argumentative text such as 1 Corinthians will contain both Paul's point of view as well as, to some extent, the alternative and/or opposing points of view that Paul sets out to argue against to which at least some of the audience holds. If this is the case, as Wire argues, then rhetorical analysis of the text ought to produce enough data to reconstruct a social and theological profile not only of the whole group to which Paul writes but even of a subgroup, such as the women prophets in Corinth.[3]

---

1   Wire, *Corinthian Women Prophets*, 1.
2   Wire, *Corinthians Women Prophets*, 3.
3   Wire draws on an eclectic array of social models to help with her task, including those of Gerd Theissen, Victor Turner, Bruce Malina, Mary Douglas, Wayne Meeks, and Elisabeth Schüssler Fiorenza (cf. *Corinthian Women Prophets*, 5).

© JAMES D. DVORAK, 2021 | DOI:10.1163/9789004453814_007

Procedurally, Wire categorizes Paul's key arguments according to Perelman and Olbrechts-Tyteca's four kinds of argument (i.e., quasi-logical arguments, arguments from the structure of reality, arguments to establish the structure of reality, and dissociation of concepts),[4] and then she "factors" for the role of the women prophets within the argumentative situation. Wire borrows the term "factoring" from the world of algebra on the analogy that in an algebraic equation one may determine the unknown value of variable x on the basis of its relationship with the other variables in the equation that have known values. The variables that have a known value include: (1) Paul's intent is to persuade the audience with the letter; (2) everything Paul says about human beings, Corinthians, believers in Christ, women, and prophets—if it serves his goal of persuasion—is a possible resource for understanding the women prophets in Corinth; and (3) the points upon which Paul is most insistent and intense reveal the opposing point of view. The variable to "solve for" through "factoring" is the social location of the Corinthian women prophets in the Corinthian church and, concomitantly, their role in the rhetorical situation of 1 Corinthians.[5]

Wire concludes that these women were very much caught up in the wider social changes occurring in first-century Corinth. Due to the collapse of the Roman republican system about a century before Paul, achieved honor status began to bypass attributed honor status in importance and competition for honor status/power increased.[6] In terms of religion, Wire claims, "established Jews and Jewish Christians were more interested in recovering the stability and respect traditionally theirs by alliance with Rome."[7] Thus, as traditional social and religious mores were faltering in this changing social environment, the Corinthian women prophets were taking advantage of the potential for "upward mobility" both in the church and in society at large. However, Paul, having come from the "class among Jews with education, family influence, and Roman citizenship,"[8] rejects this social trend at least as it impacts the church. Self-aggrandizing competition for honor status (i.e., "boasting") is rejected in favor of humility. Paul "makes virtue out of the losses he has taken to keep his integrity in and unstable world, first as a Jew and even more as a servant of Christ."[9] He does this in an effort to "strengthen 'group' boundaries and secure discipline and group order modeled

---

4   Wire, *Corinthian Women Prophets*, 6–7; see Perelman and Olbrechts-Tyteca, *New Rhetoric*, 190–92; Chaim Perelman, *The Realm of Rhetoric*, trans. William Kluback (Notre Dame: University of Notre Dame Press, 1982), 48–53.

5   Wire, *Corinthian Women Prophets*, 8–9.

6   Wire, *Corinthian Women Prophets*, 191.

7   Wire, *Corinthian Women Prophets*, 191.

8   Wire, *Corinthian Women Prophets*, 192.

9   Wire, *Corinthian Women Prophets*, 192.

SURVEY OF THE LITERATURE ON THE STUDY OF 1 CORINTHIANS   201

after his own apostolic sacrifices in the name of the cross of Christ."[10] Paul does not advocate a return to Torah, but, according to Wire, he does try to limit the Corinthians' loss of traditional privileges at the expense of rising groups in society (e.g., the women prophets) "by calling all believers to remain in the positions they had when called."[11]

Wire's work was helpful for the present study for several reasons. First, she rightly approves and applies New Rhetoric as a tool for historical inquiry. She correctly observes that persuasive/argumentative texts do not only give one side of an argument; they provide a window through which one may see opposing points of view. Second, her use of Douglas's (and Neyrey's) grid/group framework for reconstructing the social situation of the Corinthians is both apropos and enlightening, particularly as she uses the tool to reconstruct the social boundary that existed between the church at Corinth and Corinthians society. Finally, her perspective on how to understand Paul's (and the Bible's) authority is compelling:

> Two appropriate standards for determining a text's authority are the way it claims authority and the authority it actively exercises with the receptive reader. Paul claims a hearing on the basis of insistent arguments from God's calling, from revelation, from hard work, and from modeling Christ. The letters do not claim to be authoritative in their own right or this argument would be redundant. For Paul, such intrinsic authority belongs to God alone. Paul's letters' authority depends upon free assent to Paul's arguments because they are convincing.[12]

The work's major weakness, however, lies in the fact that Wire reads the women prophets in so many sections of 1 Corinthians. As Scroggs asks, "Are they as pervasive in Paul's mind and thus, at least covertly, in his statements as Wire thinks?"[13] The perspective on Wire's work taken up in the present study is that she has not convincingly argued for the appropriateness of singling out and reconstructing the social and theological location of the women prophets from among Paul's intended audience. At best, her findings would apply to the more general audience that Paul has in mind.

Elizabeth Castelli's 1991 work *Imitating Paul* is an analysis of Paul's discourse of power. Although this monograph is a discourse analysis in the vein of Michel Foucault and not a linguistic discourse analysis *per se*, the work does take into account the use of language for the construction and perpetuation of ideologies. Castelli's thesis is that

---

10   Wire, *Corinthian Women Prophets*, 192.
11   Wire, *Corinthian Women Prophets*, 192.
12   Wire, *Corinthian Women Prophets*, 10.
13   Robin Scroggs, "Review of *The Corinthian Women Prophets* by Antoinette Clark Wire," *JBL* 111 (1992): 547.

Paul uses the notion of mimesis as a strategy of power to articulate and naturalize a particular set of power relations in the social formation of the early Christian communities for which he is responsible.[14] She argues on the basis of a survey of mimesis in Greco-Roman antiquity that (1) mimesis is always articulated in terms of a hierarchical relationship in which the "copy" is always a derivation of the "model" (and can never reach the "privileged status" of the model); (2) mimesis perpetuates sameness over against difference; (3) the "model" in a mimetic relationship is generally seen as authoritative.[15] When Paul commands the putative readers to become his imitators (1 Cor 4:16), argues Castelli, he evokes among them these three associations so that he puts himself in the privileged position of "model," he perpetuates sameness by "erasing" discursive space for difference, and, by construing himself as father, he assumes total authority over his children.

Castelli's work offers a number of helpful insights for interpreting Paul's directive for the readers to become his imitators. First, her point that mimesis in Greco-Roman antiquity reflects a positive value for sameness over against difference is essentially correct. Change and novelty, especially in religious contexts, were often met with sometimes fierce resistance because they challenged the traditions that were supposed to bring stability and constancy to life.[16] Second, in her discussion of 1 Cor 4:16, she rightly argues that the paternal imagery Paul adopts must be interpreted in light of cultural context as a role that possesses total authority over children.[17] Fathers in the first-century Greco-Roman world, including Jewish subculture, demanded utmost respect and loyalty from their children.[18] Finally, her engagement with Foucault has led her to the worthy conclusion that discourse, whether in Foucault's broader sense of social practice or in the narrower sense of written or spoken text (which is a form of social action), never functions "disinterestedly" and "is an active constructor of ideology."[19] As it applies to 1 Cor 1–4, this means that Paul wrote the text in order to "do something" to the readers; namely, he aimed to dissuade the readers that the dominant ideology of the world was an appropriate guide for life in the church of God and to persuade them to adopt instead the ideology (theology) of the cross.

However, Castelli's main claim that Paul uses mimesis as a means of executing a political (i.e., coercive) power move to establish himself at the top of a hierarchical relationship with the putative readers is problematic. If she is correct, then Paul acts in a way contrary to the very teaching he has given the putative readers in 1 Cor 1–4, namely to avoid the kind of haughty behavior encouraged by the dominant

---

14   Castelli, *Imitating Paul*, 15.

15   Castelli, *Imitating Paul*, 16.

16   See McVann, "Change/Novelty Orientation," *HBSV* 14–16.

17   Castelli, *Imitating Paul*, 101.

18   See deSilva, *Honor, Patronage, Kinship & Purity*, 185–88.

19   Castelli, *Imitating Paul*, 53.

SURVEY OF THE LITERATURE ON THE STUDY OF 1 CORINTHIANS 203

ideology of the world. This would mean Paul was dishonest, encouraging the readers to humble themselves so that *he* might be exalted! Although Paul does claim status in 1 Corinthians, both as apostle and as fictive father, he does not do so in self-interest. He fills these roles because God has granted it. Thus, in the end, although Castelli's work does offer a number of helpful insights into interpreting Paul's relation to the putative readers, her work is only of modest value for the present study. Because her Foucaultian perspective is not tempered by other social theories or social-scientific perspectives or sociolinguistic theories, she arrives at a conclusion that does not fully take into consideration genre, register, and the text of 1 Corinthians.

Margaret Mitchell's *Paul and the Rhetoric of Reconciliation*, published in 1991, seems to have captured and maintained the attention of scholars. The purpose of her work is not to offer a rhetorical-critical commentary of canonical 1 Corinthians, but to use rhetorical criticism (of the Betz school) to determine if the letter is, indeed, a unitary composition. Her basic methodology is to determine the overall genre of the letter and to see if the *topoi* (topics) and *taxis* (arrangement of arguments) support the genre throughout the entire text. If so, according to Mitchell, it is reasonable to insist the current literary form of the letter is a compositional whole rather than a series of other letters "sewn together" into its current form.[20]

Mitchell's basic argument is that 1 Corinthians is deliberative (i.e., political) rhetoric, which, she says, is supported by the fact that the majority of the letter's content (i.e., 1:18–15:57) provide "proofs" (advice) as to why the readers ought to be unified as called for in the letters thesis at 1 Cor 1:10. Mitchell is quick to deduce these proofs from 1 Cor 1:18–4:21, which she says as a unit has the purpose of censuring the readers for their factions.[21] In this section she offers several very helpful insights. She correctly identifies the wisdom of the world as "the norms and values of human politics" (i.e., power struggles) that the believers were mirroring in the church which resulted in boasting and ultimately in division.[22] In the end, she says, the main point of 1 Cor 1:18–4:21 is to highlight the implied readers' blameworthiness for the purpose of reprimanding them and persuading them back to unity.

The major shortcoming of Mitchell's work here is that she interprets the entire section of 1 Cor 1:18–4:21 through a lens of negativity. She only sees rebuke, censure, and vituperation. Because of this she fails to recognize any of the positive values Paul put forward as replacements for the negative. A closer look at Paul's engagement strategies, particularly the way he uses deny + counter and concede + counter pairs, would have brought many of these positives to light. Although *Rhetoric of Reconciliation* offers a

---

20 See Anderson, *Ancient Rhetorical theory and Paul*, 254–65 for a critical review of whether or not Mitchell achieved her goal.

21 Mitchell, *Rhetoric of Reconciliation*, 209–10.

22 Mitchell, *Rhetoric of Reconciliation*, 211–12.

number of helpful insights and interpretations, because its purpose and scope are much broader than 1 Cor 1–4, its overall aid for the current study is limited.

Kathleen Callow's 1992 essay, "Patterns of Thematic Development in 1 Corinthians 5:1–13," although it does not pertain directly to 1 Cor 1–4, does introduce a number of issues pertinent to the present study. As its title suggests, the purpose of her paper is to demonstrate how discourse analysis (SIL school) enables interpreters to see patterns of thematic development in a text as it unfolds. She starts with the assumption that a communicator always communicates about something and for some purpose with text that is coherent (this is similar to SFL's ideational, interpersonal, and textual functions).[23] The topic of 1 Cor 5:1–13 (what it is about) is "the immoral man." Callow discovers this by identifying lexical/semantic chains related to πορνεία (5:1), which she argues in this context is a reference to the person committing the sin, not the sin in the abstract. She goes on to emphasize that "all the references [to this person] are unequivocally negative," which factors into Paul's final command to expulse the man, an action which is "an inherently negative evaluation."[24] Here is where Callow makes a number of points relevant to the present study. First, "all willed action" (e.g., the expulsion of the man) "is based on some evaluation, and it is therefore common in volitional messages that at least some of the supporting material is evaluative, presenting certain situations and actions as good, others as bad."[25] Callow's point here is valid but too restrictive. Her claim makes it appear as though attitudinal evaluations only impact the meaning of a discourse in volitive (hortatory) contexts. While attitudinal evaluations may be more *prominent* in such contexts, they are always present in every text type. *Every* text—even those we often think are strictly "informational"—is intended to "do something" to the reader, to fulfill some social task; thus, evaluation is always present.

Another point that she makes that has some merit is that "special devices" such as exclamations or rhetorical questions are used by a writer to "express or arouse emotion," and as such they gain "special prominence" constituting a separate "thematic strand" that intertwines with the "structural theme" of the text.[26] What Callow seems to be trying to put her finger on here is, in SFL terms, the fact that both ideational and interpersonal meaning are encoded in text simultaneously. But this occurs in every clause of every text type, not just in hortatory or volitive contexts, as Callow's point implies.

---

23 Kathleen Callow, "Patterns of Thematic Development in 1 Corinthians 5:1–13," in *Linguistics and New Testament Interpretation: Essays on Discourse Analysis*, ed. David Alan Black, Katherine Barnwell, and Stephen Levinsohn (Nashville: Broadman, 1992), 194–95.

24 Callow, "Patterns," 196.

25 Callow, "Patterns," 196.

26 Callow, "Patterns," 199.

SURVEY OF THE LITERATURE ON THE STUDY OF 1 CORINTHIANS   205

The key points from Callow's article of value for the present study are, first, that texts are not just ideational, they are interpersonal—they try to do something to the reader. Second, ATTITUDE (what she refers to as emotion) plays a significant role in the identification and interpretation of thematic material in texts. The shortcomings of the article revolve around her limited applications of these ideas, restricting, for example, the meaningfulness of emotion/attitude to hortatory textual environments.

Stephen M. Pogoloff's 1992 monograph entitled *Logos and Sophia: The Rhetorical Situation of 1 Corinthians*, sets out, as its subtitle suggests, to define the rhetorical exigence of canonical 1 Corinthians. The work is not really interested in rhetorical theory *per se*; rather, it is mainly interested in the recreation of the rhetorical environment in which Paul writes—not just the exigence of the letter, but the environment of Paul himself—and specifically the role that environment plays in determining the manner in which it is written. He is particularly interested in defining what Paul means by οὐκ ἐν σοφίᾳ λόγου (not in wisdom of speech) at 1 Cor 1:17. Much of the work is spent making a case for reading the phrase as a reference to rhetoric ("cleverness of speech").[27]

Pogoloff's next move is to show how rhetoric has attached to it high social value,[28] and if one was good at it, that person would gain not only the adulation of the people but also actual followers. In fact, Pogoloff argues that Paul's rhetoric was good enough that the presumed audience of 1 Corinthians perceived him "as a Hellenistic σοφός suitable for divisive allegiance,"[29] hence the "slogan" *I am of Paul* at 1 Cor 1:12. This causes a problem for Paul, for the message of the cross that he preaches opposes the cultural sources of power and status. So, Paul, in this environment, must "defend himself as a credible orator" yet reject the status that comes with this role.[30] To accomplish this he must remind the readers that although his speech may have been persuasive and "wise" he only used this speech "to draw the readers into a world in which the 'champion' is crucified."[31] Pogoloff's approach and argument are certainly very interesting, and his creative (though speculative) narrative of the exigence is intriguing.

However, an important lynchpin in his argument is too weak to hold up his claim. Pogoloff accepts BAGD's gloss of 1 Cor 2:1, "I have not come as a superior person in speech or (human) wisdom,"[32] but he seems to miss the point of both 1 Cor 2:1 and BAGD's gloss. He sees this as evidence that Paul is dealing not only with rhetoric but with the social status that comes with it.[33] Yet, as Anderson has also noticed,[34] the

---

27   See Pogoloff, *Logos and Sophia*, 111.
28   See Pogoloff, *Logos and Sophia*, 129–72.
29   Pogoloff, *Logos and Sophia*, 153.
30   See Pogoloff, *Logos and Sophia*, 153.
31   Pogoloff, *Logos and Sophia*, 119.
32   Pogoloff, *Logos and Sophia*, 131 (cf. 108–9); BAGD, 841.
33   Pogoloff, *Logos and Sophia*, 132, 134.
34   Anderson, *Ancient Rhetorical Theory and Paul*, 271.

point of the text, reflected in BAGD, is that Paul is not a superior person with regard to speech or wisdom, not that he does not have superior social status as such. Thus, the foundation of Pogoloff's argument is quite badly fractured, making his overall claim unattractive. That said, his work does emphasize that social status is a factor in the exigence of 1 Corinthians. Certainly, the putative readers are concerned about gaining honor and status for themselves, to which Paul responds with the directive to humility. Overall, although *Logos and Sophia* delivers a handful of significant insights into the exigence of the letter, it is of minimal value for the current study.

In 1994, Duane Litfin published a study of 1 Cor 1–4 (focusing specifically on 1:17–2:5) entitled *St. Paul's Theology of Proclamation*. The work does not offer a rhetorical-critical analysis of this text *per se*; rather, it investigates Paul's conception of his own preaching—his "philosophy of rhetoric" or "theology of preaching."[35] To accomplish this, Litfin argues, one must examine Paul's comments at 1 Cor 1:17–2:5 against the backdrop of Greco-Roman rhetorical-philosophical tradition prominent in his day (i.e., "Isocratean-Aristotelian tradition" of rhetoric as exemplified by Cicero and Quintilian).[36] Litfin's interpretation of the available data portrays a philosophy of rhetoric that placed very high value upon eloquence of speech, associating such eloquence with fame, power, status, and wealth. This, according to Litfin, is this kind of "dynamic rhetoric" that Paul disavows as inappropriate (cf. 1 Cor 1:17–2:5) "because ... the results would have been rooted in his own facility as an orator, his own ability to adapt malleably to the rhetorical demands, his own capacity to manipulate the persuasive possibilities of the rhetorical situation so as to engender belief ... in his audience."[37] This approach, says Litfin, is what Paul believed would void the cross's own power to create belief.[38]

Although insightful at times, there are two major issues that curtail the usefulness of Litfin's work for the current work. First, Litfin's separation of proclamation from persuasion is unjustifiable.[39] Because the message of the cross is value-laden and ideologically (i.e., theologically) shaped and because it is a message that Paul himself believes, one may presume he would proclaim the message in a manner that privileges it over competing messages so that his hearers, too, might believe it.[40] Second, even if Paul eschews the rhetorical practices of his day as self-aggrandizing and potentially damaging to the message of the cross, to claim that he avoids persuasive strategies altogether

---

35   Litfin, *Theology of Proclamation*, 2, 17.

36   Litfin, *Theology of Proclamation*, 11.

37   Litfin, *Theology of Proclamation*, 192.

38   Litfin, *Theology of Proclamation*, 192.

39   See Litfin, *Theology of Proclamation*, 247–48.

40   Consider Paul's claim at 1 Cor 9:20–23.

SURVEY OF THE LITERATURE ON THE STUDY OF 1 CORINTHIANS   207

and that he does not adapt them based on audience is a *non sequitur* and does not do justice to the textual evidence.[41]

In his 1995 monograph, *The Corinthian Body*, Dale B. Martin set out "to sketch the logic underlying [the] ancient discourses about body and see how the different Greco-Roman concepts of the body and its components relate to one another."[42] He does this in an effort to access and to interpret the clashing ideologies represented in the text of 1 Corinthians. Martin argues that "the theological differences reflected in 1 Corinthians all resulted from conflicts between various groups in the local church rooted in different ideological constructions of the body."[43] This assumes the body was viewed as a microcosm of the universe at large and, more specifically, the social world in which the first-century people lived.[44] On the basis of how Paul treats the issues of rhetoric and philosophy, eating meat that had been sacrificed to idols, prostitution, sexual desire, marriage, speaking in tongues, and bodily resurrection,[45] Martin argues that "Whereas Paul and (probably) the majority of the Corinthian Christians saw the body as a dangerously permeable entity threatened by polluting agents, a minority in the Corinthian church ... stressed the hierarchical arrangement of the body and the proper balance of its constituents, without evincing much concern over body boundaries or pollution."[46]

To support this claim, Martin turns to an investigation of ancient "medical and other upper-class discourses,"[47] which he rightly says reflect and the dominant ideology and system of values of the elite and privileges a hierarchical view of society with "those who to a great extent controlled their own economic destiny" at the top of the hierarchy and those who did not control their own economic destiny at various points below them.[48] With regard to 1 Cor 1–4, Paul's primary concern is with the social body as it pertains to both the church and to the world. More specifically, Paul is concerned

---

41   If the record of Paul's ministry and proclamation in Acts is to be considered (see F. F. Bruce, "Is the Paul of Acts the Real Paul?," *BJRL* 58 [1976]: 282–305), the account of Paul's speech before the Areopagus (Acts 17:18–33) clearly illustrates his willingness to adapt his strategies depending upon audience.

42   Martin, *Corinthian Body*, xiii.

43   Martin, *Corinthian Body*, xv.

44   Martin, *Corinthian Body*, 3–37. See also Jerome H. Neyrey, "Body Language in 1 Corinthians: The Use of Anthropological Models for Understanding Paul and His Opponents," *Semeia* 35 (1986): 131–38.

45   See Neyrey, "Body Language," 138–64.

46   Martin, *Corinthian Body*, xv.

47   Martin, *Corinthian Body*, xiii.

48   Martin, *Corinthian Body*, xvii. It is important to note that Martin's "guess is that the more affluent members of Paul's churches were in that middle area between the true elite and the poor" and that the Corinthian church did not contain anyone from the highest levels of Greco-Roman culture (*Corinthian Body*, xvii).

with the *hierarchy* of the social body. Martin points out that although Paul's purpose is to promote unity in the Corinthian church, he neither attacks social hierarchy nor preaches equality. "Instead, he appropriates the terminology of status ('wisdom,' 'power') and claims it for the oppositional realm apocalyptic discourse."[49] Hierarchies are not dissolved into equality in the apocalyptic world, but "are acknowledged but then turned on their heads. The apocalyptic gospel reveals the instability of the values assumed by Greco-Roman culture, replacing them with a mirror world in which top is bottom and bottom top."[50] Thus, what the world views as foolish, weak, and shameful, God, from the perspective of an apocalyptic world view, views as wise, strong, and honorable.

Although Martin's engagement with the ancient sources on body and their reflection of the social "body politic" is both intriguing and quite enlightening, it is this discussion about Paul's apocalyptic worldview and concomitant use of apocalyptic thematic formations that has the most impact on the present study. This is especially insightful with regard to interpreting 1 Cor 1:18–2:5 and 1 Cor 3:5–9 where the theme of reversal is, perhaps, at its most prominent. On a number of occasions in the former stretch of text, Paul calls on the Jewish Scriptures to oppose the hierarchical ideology and value system by replacing it with the view that the humble downtrodden would be exalted by God above those who are currently exalted.[51] In the latter text, Paul uses the analogy of the farmer (i.e., planter and waterer) to supplant the dominant ideology that privileges the elite with one that exalts the servant. Martin argues that in neither case is Paul suggesting the those of high status must evacuate their standing; rather, according to Martin, they "can retain the high position assigned to them only by avoiding the schisms that would destroy the house of God."[52]

In 1995 Ralph Bruce Terry published *A Discourse Analysis of First Corinthians*. The stated purpose of the work is "to discover discourse-linguistic features that are used in the Greek text of ... 1 Corinthians."[53] Terry's model is built upon the tagmemic theories of Pike and especially Longacre.[54] His methodology reflects the strong emphasis

---

49   Martin, *Corinthian Body*, 59.

50   Martin, *Corinthian Body*, 60.

51   See Martin, *Corinthian Body*, 60.

52   Martin, *Corinthian Body*, 65.

53   Ralph B. Terry, *A Discourse Analysis of First Corinthians*, SIL Publications in Linguistics 120 (Dallas: SIL, 1995), 1.

54   See Terry, *Discourse Analysis*, xi. On tagmemic theory, see K. L. Pike, *Language in Relation to a Unified Theory of the Structure of Human Behavior*, Janua Linguarum Series Major 24 (The Hague: Mouton, 1967); Longacre, *Grammar of Discourse*; Robert de Beaugrande, *Linguistic Theory: The Discourse of Fundamental Works*, Longman Linguistics Library (New York: Longman, 1991), 187–222.

SURVEY OF THE LITERATURE ON THE STUDY OF 1 CORINTHIANS

209

upon sentence grammar typical of tagmemic discourse analyses,[55] though the model does contain parameters for identifying and interpreting larger structures such as paragraphs.[56] Perhaps the most important portion of Terry's book relative to the current project is his discussion of "peak." Following Longacre, Terry defines peak as "a zone of grammatical or stylistic turbulence within a discourse that corresponds to its climax and/or denouement."[57] "Turbulence" is indicated by changes in a text's surface structure, particularly in the form of deviations from "routine features."[58] Common manifestations include increases or decreases in lexical density, changes in the nominal/verbal balance, and various other shifts in grammar and/or syntax.[59] At one point in his analysis, Terry correlates peak with emotion: "... it can be said that the peak area in 1 Corinthians does indicate topics about which Paul felt and showed a marked increase in emotion and wanted to convey that emotion to his intended audience."[60] From the perspective of the present study, Terry is correct to make this correlation; however, his model lacks a framework for defining how emotion gets encoded in text and what kinds of linguistic realizations of these encodings would be considered "grammatically turbulent." Nevertheless, the correlation is an important one, and the current project addresses it by tying inscribed attitude (AFFECT, JUDGMENT, APPRECIATION) to the notion of prominence and grounding.[61]

In the end, Terry's *Discourse Analysis* is of limited value to the current project for one major reason: the model makes no explicit connection between the *structure(s)* of 1 Corinthians and its *social function(s)* (i.e., the social action Paul tries to accomplish with the text).[62] Consequently, the model lacks the ability to formulate the interactional semantics of 1 Corinthians—how it contributes to the creation and/or maintenance of social relations and value systems. Because of this, Terry's book comes

---

55 See Porter's critique of this kind of approach in his, "Discourse Analysis and New Testament Studies," 24–27 (reiterated in Porter and Pitts, "New Testament Greek Language and Linguistics," 236–7). See also, Stanley E. Porter, "Linguistics and Rhetorical Criticism," in *Linguistics and the New Testament: Critical Junctures*, ed. Stanley E. Porter and Christopher D. Stanley, SBLSS 50 (Atlanta: SBL, 2008), 73–77.

56 See Terry, *Discourse Analysis*, 65–69.

57 Terry, *Discourse Analysis*, 9. See Longacre, *Grammar of Discourse*, 37–48.

58 See Terry, *Discourse Analysis*, 3; Longacre, *Grammar of Discourse*, 38.

59 See especially Longacre, *Grammar of Discourse*, 38–48.

60 Terry, *Discourse Analysis*, 124.

61 On prominence and grounding, see Halliday, *Explorations*, 112–21; Porter, *Verbal Aspect*, 92–3; Porter, "Prominence," 45–74; Cynthia Long Westfall, "A Method for the Analysis of Prominence in Hellenistic Greek," in *The Linguist as Pedagogue*, ed. Stanley E. Porter and Matthew Brook O'Donnell, NTM 11 (Sheffield: Sheffield Phoenix, 2009), 75–94; Westfall, *Hebrews*, 35; Porter and O'Donnell, *Discourse Analysis*, 119–60.

62 Terry's model, like other tagmemic models, is concerned with *function*, but only in terms of grammatical or syntactic function. It is not directly concerned with the *social functions* of language. See Halliday, *Explorations*, 104.

across more as a textbook on tagmemic-based discourse analysis that uses texts from 1 Corinthians to illustrate methodology than the application of a model and method for the purpose of explicating the text of 1 Corinthians.

John Paul Heil's 2005 monograph *The Rhetorical Role of Scripture in 1 Corinthians* addresses the rhetorical or instrumental effects of the use of scripture (i.e., "scriptural quotations" and "other explicit references and allusions to scripture")[63] in 1 Corinthians. Methodologically, Heil adopts a rhetorical-critical approach, though his model is eclectic, drawing upon classical rhetorical criticism,[64] New Rhetoric, and speech-act theory.[65] The main concern of the work is to determine how Paul's use of scripture plays into the persuasive force of each "rhetorical demonstration"[66] (i.e., major unit) in 1 Corinthians.

For the current study, the most influential notion from Heil's work is the recognition that most often Paul cites or alludes to scripture in order to advance his rhetorical or argumentative agenda[67] as he seeks to convince readers to believe and/or behave in a certain way. Beneficially, this centers the discussion on the *function* of these scriptures in making meaning with text. Despite Heil's care to place each use of scripture into its argumentative context and despite his effort to draw out implications of each, the significance of his work for the current study is limited in that, due to methodological limitations, his insights rarely amount to anything more than the point that a scriptural citation is "persuasive" or that it enjoins the readers to do or to think (or not) a certain thing. There are no linguistic or semiotic explanations as to why a scripture citation is considered to be persuasive or how it contributes to the persuasiveness of a given "rhetorical demonstration."

In his 2010 monograph *You Belong to Christ: Paul and the Formation of Social Identity in 1 Corinthians 1–4*, J. Brian Tucker utilizes Social Identity Theory (SIT)[68] and Self-Categorization Theory (SCT) in his attempt to demonstrate that "some in Corinth were continuing to identify primarily with key aspects of their Roman social identity rather than their identity 'in Christ' and that this confusion over identity positions

---

63 See Heil, *Rhetorical Role of Scripture*, 2.

64 Heil refers to this as "historical-critical" rhetorical criticism (*Rhetorical Role of Scripture*, 4).

65 Heil, *Rhetorical Role of Scripture*, 4–5. Here one may see the influence of Stanley's articles, "Rhetoric of Quotations" and "Paul's 'Use' of Scripture."

66 Heil adopts Collins's terminology here. See Heil, *Rhetorical Role of Scripture*, 10 n 25; Collins, *First Corinthians*, 86–87.

67 See Stanley, "Rhetoric of Quotations," 50, 55.

68 See Philip F. Esler, "Group Boundaries and Intergroup Conflict in Galatians: A New Reading of Galatians 5:13–6:10," in *Ethnicity and the Bible*, ed. Mark G. Brett (Leiden: Brill, 1996), 215–40. Tucker (*You Belong to Christ*, 41) credits Esler as the first to apply SIT in New Testament Studies.

contributed to the problems within the community."[69] These problems manifest themselves in various forms of division and discordant behavior among the believers, such as identification with certain sub-groups for the purpose of self-enhancement, boasting, and a general over-reliance on the world's wisdom and power. In language very similar to Meeks's "resocialization,"[70] Tucker argues that Paul writes 1 Corinthians to "realign the positions within the Corinthians' identity hierarchy in order to produce an alternative community with a distinct ethos,"[71] namely an "in Christ" social identity. Stated generally, SIT and SCT theories argue that social identity is formed through social comparisons in which individuals find similarities and differences in values and ideologies that can then be used to form "in-groups" and "out-groups."[72] In this equation, ideology and values play a central formative role in group formation, and Tucker argues that the problem reflected in the text of 1 Corinthians is that the putative readers were basing their group identities on the values and ideology of the Roman world in which Corinth was situated.[73]

In chapters 5–9 of his book, Tucker methodically analyzes the text of 1 Cor 1–4, carefully applying his hybrid SIT/SCT model. His work elucidates a number of important ideas regarding both the problem at Corinth Paul addresses and how Paul attempts to realign the readers. In his discussion of 1 Cor 1:10, Tucker (citing Tajfel) says that group definition realizes three features: a sense of knowing that one belongs to a group (cognitive dimension); a sense that the notion of the group may have a positive or negative value (evaluative dimension); and a sense that the cognitive and evaluative aspects may be accompanied by emotions (affective or emotional dimension).[74] The problem within the Christ-movement in Corinth was that none of these components was functioning adequately. As a result, the community of believers exemplified instability as a group and experienced conflict within. Tucker identifies as the root of the problem that some of the believers were relating to other believers on the basis of worldly values rather than the values exemplified and demanded by the cross. So then, Paul sets out to reshape the identity of the group by providing them with a distinct "in Christ" identity, as Tucker calls it.

One of the main tactics Paul uses to accomplish this is social categorization in which Paul categorizes certain desired kinds of thinking and behavior as appropriate for those who are in Christ and categorizing undesired thinking and behavior as

---

69   Tucker, *You Belong to Christ*, 2.

70   See Meeks, *Origins of Christian Morality*, 8–11.

71   Tucker, *You Belong to Christ*, 2.

72   See Tucker, *You Belong to Christ*, 42.

73   See Tucker, *You Belong to Christ*, 89–128 on the impact of Roman civic identity on the Corinthian addressees.

74   Tucker, *You Belong to Christ*, 152.

belonging to those who are not in Christ.[75] It is here where Tucker's work has bearing on the present study. Tucker is certainly right to say that Paul attempts to realign the putative readers in this way, and that is one of the basic premises of the present study. Where Tucker's work falls short is in describing how this realignment tactic is encoded into language. Tucker promises to draw on the tools of discourse analysis to explain how the language of the text functions in forming meaning,[76] but nowhere does he really engage with the language beyond what most traditional commentaries and grammars have to offer. For this reason, Tucker's work, although quite insightful in terms of the formation of social identity among groups, is limited in its ability to help the present study fulfill its purpose.

75   See Tucker, *You Belong to Christ*, 167.
76   Tucker, *You Belong to Christ*, 32. He even cites Martin and Rose, *Working with Discourse*, as a model of discourse analysis.

Bibliography

Aageson, James W. "Written Also for Our Sake: Paul's Use of Scripture in the Four Major Epistles, with a Study of 1 Corinthians 10." Pages 152–81 in *Hearing the Old Testament in the New Testament*. Edited by Stanley E. Porter. Grand Rapids: Eerdmans, 2006.

Abasciano, Brian J. "Diamonds in the Rough: A Reply to Christopher Stanley Concerning the Reader Competency of Paul's Original Audiences." *NovT* (2007): 153–83.

Adams, Sean A. "A Linguistic Approach for Detecting Paragraph Divisions in Narrative Greek Discourse: With Application to Mark 14–16." Paper presented at the annual meeting of the Society for Textual Studies. New York, NY, 03-March-2007.

Adams, Sean A. "Paul's Letter Opening and Greek Epistolography." Pages 33–55 in *Paul and the Ancient Letter Form*. Edited by Stanley E. Porter and Sean A. Adams. PAST 6. Leiden: Brill, 2010.

Agnew, Francis H. "The Origin of the NT Apostle-Concept: A Review of Research." *JBL* 105 (1986): 75–96.

Allo, E. Bernard. *Saint Paul: Première Épitre aux Corinthiens*. 2nd ed. Paris: Gabalda, 1956.

Althusser, Louis. "Ideology and Ideological State Apparatuses (Notes Towards an Investigation)." Pages 1–60 in *Essays on Ideology*. New York: Verso, 1984.

Anderson, Margaret L., and Howard F. Taylor. *Sociology: The Essentials*. 7th ed. Belmont, CA: Wadsworth Cengage, 2013.

Anderson, R. Dean, Jr. *Ancient Rhetorical Theory and Paul*. Rev. ed. Contributions to Biblical Exegesis & Theology 18. Leuven: Peeters, 1999.

Arzt-Grabner, Peter. "Paul's Letter Thanksgiving." Pages 129–58 in *Paul and the Ancient Letter Form*. Edited by Stanley E. Porter and Sean A. Adams. PAST 6. Leiden: Brill, 2010.

Aune, David E. "Apocalypticism." Pages 25–35 in *Dictionary of Paul and His Letters*. Edited by Gerald F. Hawthorne, Ralph P. Martin, and Daniel G. Reid. Downers Grove: InterVarsity Press, 1993.

Aune, David E. *Revelation 1–5*. WBC 52A. Nashville: Thomas Nelson, 1997.

Aune, David E. *The New Testament in Its Literary Environment*. LEC 8. Philadelphia: Westminster, 1987.

Aune, David E., Timothy J. Geddert, and Craig A. Evans. "Apocalypticism." Pages 45–58 in *Dictionary of New Testament Background*. Edited by Craig A. Evans and Stanley E. Porter. Downers Grove: InterVarsity Press, 2000.

Austin, John L. *How to Do Things With Words*. 2nd ed. Cambridge: Harvard University Press, 1975.

Bakhtin, Mikhail M. "The Problem of Speech Genres." Pages 60–102 in *Speech Genres & Other Late Essays*. Edited by Caryl Emerson and Michael Holquist. Translated by Vern W. McGee. Austin: University of Texas Press, 1986.

Bakhtin, Mikhail M. "Discourse in the Novel." Pages 259–422 in *The Dialogic Imagination: Four Essays*. Edited by Michael Holquist. Translated by Caryl Emerson and Michael Holquist. Austin: University of Texas Press, 1981.

Barclay, John M. G. "Mirror-Reading a Polemical Letter: Galatians as a Test Case." *JSNT* 31 (1987): 73–93.

Barrett, C. K. *The First Epistle to the Corinthians*. HNTC. New York: Harper and Row, 1968.

Bauer, Walter, Fredrick W. Danker, W. F. Arndt, and F. W. Gingrich. *Greek-English Lexicon of the New Testament and Other Early Christian Literature*. 2nd ed. Chicago: University of Chicago Press, 1979.

Bauer, Walter, Fredrick W. Danker, W. F. Arndt, and F. W. Gingrich. *Greek-English Lexicon of the New Testament and Other Early Christian Literature*. 3rd ed. Chicago: University of Chicago Press, 2000.

Beasley-Murray, George R. *Baptism in the New Testament*. Grand Rapids: Eerdmans, 1962.

Bednarek, Monika. *Emotion Talk Across Corpora*. New York: Palgrave, 2008.

Bellous, Joyce E. "Foucault, Michel." Pages 120–21 in *Dictionary of Biblical Criticism and Interpretation*. Edited by Stanley E. Porter. New York: Routledge, 2007.

Berger, Peter L., and Thomas Luckmann. *The Social Construction of Reality: A Treatise in the Sociology of Knowledge*. Garden City, NY: Doubleday, 1966. Reprint New York: Anchor, 1967.

Bernard, J. H. *A Critical and Exegetical Commentary on the Gospel According to John*. 2 vols. ICC. Edinburgh: T & T Clark, 1999.

Bernstein, Basil. *Class, Codes, and Control*. 2 vols. London: Routledge, 1971–1973.

Best, Ernest. "Paul's Apostolic Authority—?" *JSNT* 27 (1986): 3–25.

Betz, Hans Dieter. "The Problem of Rhetoric and Theology According to the Apostle Paul." Pages 16–48 in *L'apôtre Paul: Personalité, Style et Conception du Ministère*. Edited by A. Vanhoye. BETL 17. Leuven: Leuven University Press, 1986.

Betz, Hans Dieter, and Margaret M. Mitchell. "Corinthians, First Letter to the." *ABD* 1:1139–48.

Biber, Douglas. "An Analytical Framework for Register Studies." Pages 31–56 in *Sociolinguistic Perspectives on Register*. Edited by Douglas Biber and Edward Finegan. Oxford Studies in Sociolinguistics. Oxford: Oxford University Press, 1994.

Bjerkelund, Carl J. *Parakalō: Form, Funktion, und Sinn der parakalō-Sätze in den paulinischen Briefen*. Biblioteca Theologica Norvegica 1. Oslo: Universitetsforlaget, 1967.

Black, Stephanie L. *Sentence Conjunctions in the Gospel of Matthew: καί, δέ, τότε, γάρ, οὖν, and Asyndeton in Narrative Discourse*. JSNTSup 216. Sheffield: Sheffield Academic, 2002.

BIBLIOGRAPHY

Blass, Friedrich, and Albert DeBrunner. *A Greek Grammar of the New Testament and Other Early Christian Literature*. Translated and revised by Robert W. Funk. Chicago: University of Chicago Press, 1961.

Bock, Darrell L. *Luke 1:1–9:50*. BECNT. Grand Rapids: Baker, 1994.

Bourdieu, Pierre. *Outline of a Theory of Practice*. Translated by Richard Nice. Cambridge Studies in Social and Cultural Anthropology 16. Cambridge: Cambridge University Press, 1977.

Bourdieu, Pierre. *The Logic of Practice*. Translated by Richard Nice. Stanford, CA: Stanford University Press, 1990.

Braumann, G. "νήπιος." *NIDNTT* 1:281–83.

Brim, Orville G. "Adult Socialization." In *International Encyclopedia of Social Sciences*, edited by David L. Sills, 14:555–61. New York: Macmillan, 1968.

Brown, Colin, ed. *New International Dictionary of New Testament Theology*. 4 vols. Grand Rapids: Zondervan, 1975–1985.

Brown, Gillian, and George Yule. *Discourse Analysis*. CTL. Cambridge: Cambridge University Press, 1983.

Brown, Raymond E. *The Epistles of John*. AB 30. New York: Doubleday, 1982.

Brown, Roger, and Albert Gilman. "The Pronouns of Power and Solidarity." Pages 156–76 in *Sociolinguistics: The Essential Readings*. Edited by Christina Bratt Paulston and G. Richard Tucker. Malden, MA: Blackwell, 2003.

Bruce, F. F. "Is the Paul of Acts the Real Paul?" *BJRL* 58 (1976): 282–305.

Bultmann, Rudolf. "Is Exegesis Without Presuppositions Possible?" Pages 145–53 in *New Testament & Mythology and Other Basic Writings*. Edited and translated by Schubert M. Ogden. Philadelphia: Fortress, 1984.

Bultmann, Rudolf. *The History of the Synoptic Tradition*. Translated by John Marsh. Oxford: Basil Blackwell, 1968.

Caldas-Coulthard, Carmen R. "On Reporting Reporting: The Representation of Speech in Factual and Factional Narratives." Pages 295–308 in *Advances in Written Text Analysis*. Edited by Malcolm Coulthard. London: Routledge, 1994.

Callow, Kathleen. "Patterns of Thematic Development in 1 Corinthians 5.1–13." Pages 194–206 in *Linguistics and New Testament Interpretation: Essays on Discourse Analysis*. Edited by David Alan Black, Katharine Barnwell and Stephen Levinsohn. Nashville: Broadman, 1992.

Calvin, John. *First Epistle of Paul the Apostle to the Corinthians*. Calvin's New Testament Commentaries 9. Translated by J. W. Fraser. Edited by D. W. Torrance and T. F. Torrance. Grand Rapids: Eerdmans, 1960.

Carney, Thomas F. *The Shape of the Past: Models and Antiquity*. Lawrence, KS: Coronado Press, 1975.

Carson, Donald A. *The Cross and Christian Ministry*. Grand Rapids: Baker, 1993.

Carson, Donald A. *The Gospel According to John*. PNTC. Grand Rapids: Eerdmans, 1991.

Castelli, Elizabeth A. *Imitating Paul: A Discourse of Power*. Literary Currents in Biblical Interpretation. Louisville: Westminster John Knox, 1991.

Cen, Esther G. "The Metaphor of Leaven in 1 Corinthians 5." *Dialogismos* 3 (2019): 1–26.

Chafe, Wallace L. "Evidentiality in English Conversation and Academic Writing." Pages 261–72 in *Evidentiality: The Linguistic Coding of Epistemology*. Edited by W. L. Chafe and J. Nichols. Advances in Discourse Processes 20. Norwood, NJ: Ablex, 1986.

Channell, Joanna. *Vague Language*. Oxford: Oxford University Press, 1994.

Charles, Maggie. "Construction of Stance in Reporting Clauses: A Cross-Disciplinary Study of Theses." *Applied Linguistics* 27 (2006): 492–518.

Chomsky, Noam. *Language and the Mind*. 3rd ed. Cambridge: Cambridge University Press, 2006.

Chow, John K. *Patronage and Power: A Study of Social Networks in Corinth*. JSNTSup 75. Sheffield: Sheffield Academic, 1992.

Ciampa, Roy E. "Scriptural Language and Ideas." Pages 41–57 in *As It Is Written: Studying Paul's Use of Scripture*. Edited by Stanley E. Porter and Christopher D. Stanley. SBLSS 50. Atlanta: Society of Biblical Literature, 2008.

Clarke, Andrew D. *Secular and Christian Leadership at Corinth: A Socio-Historical and Exegetical Study of 1 Corinthians 1–6*. Leiden: Brill, 1993.

Coenen, Lothar. "καλέω." *NIDNTT* 1:271–76.

Coffin, Caroline, Jim Donohue, and Sarah North. *Exploring English Grammar: From Formal to Functional*. New York: Routledge, 2009.

Collins, Raymond F. "A Significant Decade: The Trajectory of the Hellenistic Epistolary Thanksgiving." Pages 159–84 in *Paul and the Ancient Letter Form*. Edited by Stanley E. Porter and Sean A. Adams. PAST 6. Leiden: Brill, 2010.

Collins, Raymond F. *First Corinthians*. Sacra Pagina 7. Collegeville, MN: Liturgical Press, 1999.

Conzelmann, Hans. *1 Corinthians: A Commentary on the First Epistle to the Corinthians*. Edited by George W. MacRae. Translated by James W. Dunkly. Hermeneia. Philadelphia: Fortress, 1975.

Cortazzi, Martin, and Lixian Jin. "Evaluating Evaluation in Narrative." Pages 102–20 in *Evaluation in Text: Authorial Stance and the Construction of Discourse*. Edited by Susan Hunston and Geoff Thompson. Oxford: Oxford University Press, 1999.

Coulthard, Malcolm. *An Introduction to Discourse Analysis*. 2nd ed. Applied Linguistics and Language Study. London: Longman, 1985.

Crook, Zeba A. "Grace as Benefaction in Galatians 2:9, 1 Corinthians 3:10, and Romans 12:3; 15:15." Pages 25–38 in *The Social Sciences and Biblical Translation*. Edited by Dietmar Neufeld. SBLSS 41. Atlanta: Society of Biblical Literature, 2008.

Cross, Anthony R. "Baptism among Baptists." Pages 136–55 in *Baptism: Historical, Theological, and Pastoral Perspectives*. Edited by Gordon L. Heath and James D. Dvorak. MTSS. Eugene, OR: Pickwick, 2011.

Dahl, Nils A. "Anamnesis: Memory and Commemoration in Early Christianity." Pages 11–29 in *Jesus in the Memory of the Early Church*. Minneapolis: Augsburg, 1976.

de Beaugrande, Robert. *Linguistic Theory: The Discourse of Fundamental Works*. LLL. New York: Longman, 1991. http://beaugrande.com/LINGTHERLinguistic%20 Theory%20Title.htm.

de Saussure, Ferdinand. *Course in General Linguistics*. Open Court Classics. Translated and annotated by Roy Harris. Chicago: Open Court, 1986.

deSilva, David A. *Honor, Patronage, Kinship & Purity*. Downers Grove: InterVarsity Press, 2000.

deSilva, David A. "'Let the One Who Claims Honor Establish That Claim in the Lord': Honor Discourse in the Corinthian Correspondence." *BTB* 28 (1998): 61–74.

Dibelius, Martin. *From Tradition to Gospel*. Translated by Bertram L. Woolf. 2nd ed. London: Ivor Nicholson and Watson, 1934.

Dibelius, Martin, and Hans Conzelmann. *The Pastoral Epistles*. Hermeneia. Philadelphia: Fortress, 1972.

Douglas, Mary. *Natural Symbols*. Routledge Classics. New York: Routledge, 2003.

Douglas, Mary. *Purity and Danger: An Analysis of Concept of Pollution and Taboo*. Routledge Classics. New York: Routledge, 2002.

Dunn, James D. G. *The Epistles to the Colossians and to Philemon*. NIGTC. Grand Rapids: Eerdmans, 1996.

Dunn, James D. G. *Romans 1–8*. WBC 38A. Dallas: Word, 1988.

Dutch, Robert S. *The Educated Elite in 1 Corinthians: Education and Community Conflict in Graeco-Roman Context*. JSNTSup 271. London: T & T Clark, 2005.

Dvorak, James D. "Ask and Ye Shall Position the Readers: James's Use of Questions to (Re-) Align His Readers." Pages 196–245 in *The Epistle of James: Linguistic Exegesis of an Early Christian Letter*. Edited by James D. Dvorak and Zachary K. Dawson. LENT 1. Eugene: Pickwick, 2019.

Dvorak, James D. "'Evidence that Commands a Verdict': Determining the Semantics of Imperatives in the New Testament." *BAGL* 7 (2018): 201–23.

Dvorak, James D. "John H. Elliott's Social-Scientific Criticism." *TJ* 28 (2007): 251–78.

Dvorak, James D. "'Prodding with Prosody': Persuasion and Social Influence through the Lens of Appraisal Theory." *BAGL* 4 (2015): 85–120.

Dvorak, James D. "Thematization, Topic, and Information Flow." *JLIABG* 1 (2008): 17–37.

Dvorak, James D. "To Incline Another's Heart: The Role of Attitude in Reader Positioning." Pages 599–624 in *The Language and Literature of the New Testament: Essays in Honor of Stanley E. Porter's 60th Birthday*. Edited by Lois K. Fuller Dow, Craig A. Evans, and Andrew W. Pitts. BibInt 150. Leiden: Brill, 2016.

218 BIBLIOGRAPHY

Dvorak, James D., and Ryder Dale Walton. "Clause as Message: Theme, Topic, and Information Flow in Mark 2:1–12 and Jude." *BAGL* 3 (2014): 31–85.

Eastman, Susan. "The Evil Eye and the Curse of the Law: Galatians 3.1 Revisited." *JSNT* 83 (2001): 69–87.

Eckert, Jost. "καλέω." *EDNT* 2:240–44.

Edwards, Thomas C. *A Commentary on the First Epistle to the Corinthians*. 2nd ed. London: Hodder and Stoughton, 1885.

Eggins, Suzanne. *An Introduction to Functional Linguistics*. 2nd ed. London: Continuum, 2004.

Eggins, Suzanne, and J. R. Martin. "Genres and Registers of Discourse." Pages 230–56 in *Discourse as Structure and Process*. Edited by Teun A. van Dijk. Discourse Studies 1. London: Sage, 1997.

Elliott, John H. "God—Zealous or Jealous but Never Envious: The Theological Consequences of Linguistic and Social Distinctions." Pages 79–90 in *The Social Sciences and Biblical Translation*. Edited by Dietmar Neufeld. SBLSS 41. Atlanta: Society of Biblical Literature, 2008.

Elliott, John H. "Patronage and Clientism in Early Christian Society." *FFF* 3 (1987): 39–48.

Elliott, John H. "Paul, Galatians, and the Evil Eye." *CurTM* 17 (1990): 262–73.

Elliott, John H. "Social-Scientific Criticism of the New Testament: More on Methods and Models." *Semeia* 35 (1986): 1–33.

Elliott, John H. *What is Social-Scientific Criticism?* GBS. Minneapolis: Fortress, 1993.

Engberg-Pedersen, Troels. "The Gospel and Social Practice According to 1 Corinthians." *NTS* 33 (1987): 557–84.

Esler, Philip F. "Group Boundaries and Intergroup Conflict in Galatians: A New Reading of Galatians 5:13–6:10." Pages 215–40 in *Ethnicity and the Bible*. Edited by Mark G. Brett. Leiden: Brill, 1996.

Exler, Francis X. J. *The Form of the Ancient Greek Letter of the Epistolary Papyri (3rd c. B.C.–3rd c. A.D.)*. Chicago: Ares, 1976.

Fairclough, Norman. *Analysing Discourse: Textual Analysis for Social Research*. London: Routledge, 2003.

Fairclough, Norman. *Discourse and Social Change*. Cambridge: Polity Press, 1992.

Fee, Gordon D. *The First Epistle to the Corinthians*. NICNT. Grand Rapids: Eerdmans, 1987.

Ferguson, Everett. *Baptism in the Early Church: History, Theology, and Liturgy in the First Five Centuries*. Grand Rapids: Eerdmans, 2009.

Fiore, Benjamin. "'Covert Allusion' in 1 Corinthians 1–4." *CBQ* 47 (1985): 85–102.

Firth, John R. "Personality and Language in Society." Pages 177–89 in *Papers in Linguistics 1934–1951*. London: Oxford University Press, 1957.

Fitzmyer, Joseph A. *First Corinthians*. AB 32. New Haven: Yale University Press, 2008.

BIBLIOGRAPHY

Foucault, Michel. *The Archaeology of Knowledge*. Translated by Alan Sheridan. New York: Pantheon, 1972.

Foucault, Michel. "The Subject and Power." Pages 208–26 in *Michel Foucault: Beyond Structuralism and Hermeneutics*. Edited by H. Dreyfus and P. Rabinow. Chicago: University of Chicago Press, 1982.

France, Richard T. *The Gospel of Mark*. NIGTC. Grand Rapids: Eerdmans, 2002.

France, Richard T. *The Gospel of Matthew*. NICNT. Grand Rapids: Eerdmans, 2007.

France, Richard T. "Herod and the Children of Bethlehem." *NovT* 21 (1979): 98–120.

France, Richard T. *Jesus and the Old Testament*. Vancouver: Regent College Publishing, 1998.

Francis, James. "As Babes in Christ—Some Proposals Regarding 1 Corinthians 3:1–3." *JSNT* 7 (1980): 41–60.

Furnish, Victor Paul. *II Corinthians*. AB 32A. Garden City, NY: Doubleday, 1984.

Gaertner, Dennis. *Acts*. CPNIVC. Joplin, MO: College Press, 1993.

Garland, David E. *1 Corinthians*. BECNT. Grand Rapids: Baker, 2003.

Gill, Ann M., and Karen Whedbee. "Rhetoric." Pages 157–84 in *Discourse as Structure and Process*. Edited by Teun A. van Dijk. Discourse Studies 1. London: Sage, 1997.

Gillmayr-Bucher, Susanne. "Intertextuality: Between Literary Theory and Text Analysis." Pages 13–23 in *The Intertextuality of the Epistles: Explorations of Theory and Practice*. Edited by Thomas L. Brodie, Dennis R. MacDonald, and Stanley E. Porter. NTM 16. Sheffield: Sheffield Phoenix, 2006.

Goatly, Andrew. *Critical Reading and Writing*. New York: Routledge, 2000.

Godet, Frederic L. *Commentary on First Corinthians*. Translated by A. Cusin. Edinburgh: T & T Clark, 1889. Reprint, Grand Rapids: Kregel, 1977.

Gonda, Jan. *The Character of the Indo-European Moods with Special Regard to Greek and Sanskrit*. Wiesbaden: Otto Harrassowitz, 1956.

Goodacre, Mark. "NT Pod 18: Was Jesus a Carpenter?" http://podacre.blogspot.com/2009/11/nt-pod-18-was-jesus-carpenter.html.

Green, Gene L. *The Letters to the Thessalonians*. PNTC. Grand Rapids: Eerdmans, 2002.

Green, Joel B. *The Gospel of Luke*. NICNT. Grand Rapids: Eerdmans, 1997.

Gundry, Robert H. *Matthew: A Commentary on His Handbook for a Mixed Church under Persecution*. 2nd ed. Grand Rapids: Eerdmans, 1994.

Hafemann, Scott J. "Corinthians, Letters to the." Pages 164–79 in *Dictionary of Paul and His Letters*. Edited by Gerald F. Hawthorne, Ralph P. Martin, and Daniel G. Reid. Downers Grove: InterVarsity Press, 1993.

Hahn, H. C. "παρρησία." *NIDNTT* 2:734–37.

Halliday, M. A. K. "Categories of the Theory of Grammar." Pages 37–94 in *On Grammar*. Edited by Jonathan Webster. CWMAKH 1. London: Continuum, 2002.

Halliday, M. A. K. "Context of Situation." Pages 3–14 in *Language, Context, and Text: Aspects of Language in a Social-Semiotic Perspective*. 2nd ed. Oxford: Oxford University Press, 1989.

Halliday, M. A. K. *Explorations in the Functions of Language*. Explorations in Language Study. London: Arnold, 1973.

Halliday, M. A. K. "Functions of Language." Pages 15–28 in *Language, Context, and Text: Aspects of Language in a Social-Semiotic Perspective*. Oxford: Oxford University Press, 1989.

Halliday, M. A. K. "Introduction: On the 'Architecture' of Human Language." Pages 1–29 in *On Language and Linguistics*. Edited by Jonathan Webster. CWMAKH 3. London: Continuum, 2003.

Halliday, M. A. K. *An Introduction to Functional Grammar*. 2nd ed. London: Edward Arnold, 1994.

Halliday, M. A. K. "Language as Code and Language as Behaviour: A Systemic-Functional Interpretation of the Nature and Ontogenesis of Dialogue." Pages 3–35 in *The Semiotics of Culture and Language, Volume 1, Language as Social Semiotic*. Edited by Robin P. Fawcett, M. A. K. Halliday, Sydney M. Lamb, and Adam Makkai. Open Linguistics Series. London: Frances Pinter, 1984.

Halliday, M. A. K. *Language as Social Semiotic*. Baltimore: University Park Press, 1978.

Halliday, M. A. K. "Language in a Social Perspective." Pages 43–64 in *Language and Society*. Edited by Jonathan Webster. CWMAKH 10. London: Continuum, 2007.

Halliday, M. A. K. "Language Structure and Language Function." Pages 173–95 in *On Grammar*. Edited by Jonathan Webster. CWMAKH 1. London: Continuum, 2002.

Halliday, M. A. K. "Modes of Meaning and Modes of Expression: Types of Grammatical Structure and Their Determination by Different Semantic Functions." Pages 196–218 in *On Grammar*. Edited by Jonathan Webster. CWMAKH 1. London: Continuum, 2002.

Halliday, M. A. K. "On the 'Architecture' of Human Language." Pages 1–29 in *On Language and Linguistics*. Edited by Jonathan Webster. CWMAKH 3. London: Continuum, 2003.

Halliday, M. A. K. "Register Variation." Pages 29–43 in *Language, Context, and Text: Aspects of Language in a Social-Semiotic Perspective*. 2nd ed. Oxford: Oxford University Press, 1989.

Halliday, M. A. K., and Ruqaiya Hasan. *Cohesion in English*. English Language Series 9. London: Longman, 1976.

Halliday, M. A. K., and Christian M. I. M. Matthiessen. *An Introduction to Functional Grammar*. 3rd ed. London: Arnold, 2004.

Hanson, K. C. "How Honorable! How Shameful! A Cultural Analysis of Matthew's *Makarisms* and Reproaches." *Semeia* 68 (1994): 81–111.

Harré, Rom, and Luk van Langenhove. *Positioning Theory: Moral Contexts of Intentional Action*. Oxford: Blackwell, 1999.

Harris, Murray J. *Colossians and Philemon*. EGGNT. Nashville: Broadman & Holman, 2010.

Hasan, Ruqaiya. "The Identity of the Text." Pages 97–116 in *Language, Context, and Text: Aspects of Language in a Social-Semiotic Perspective*. 2nd ed. Oxford: Oxford University Press, 1989.

Hasan, Ruqaiya. "The Place of Context in a Systemic Functional Model." Pages 166–89 in *Continuum Companion to Systemic Functional Linguistics*. Edited by M. A. K. Halliday and Jonathan J. Webster, 166–89. London: Continuum, 2009.

Hasan, Ruqaiya. "The Structure of a Text." Pages 52–69 in *Language, Context, and Text: Aspects of Language in a Social-Semiotic Perspective*. 2nd ed. Oxford: Oxford University Press, 1989.

Hasan, Ruqaiya. "Text in the Systemic-Functional Model." Pages 228–46 in *Current Trends in Textlinguistics*. Edited by Wolfgang Dressler. Berlin: Walter de Gruyter, 1977.

Hawthorne, Gerald F. *Philippians*. Revised and expanded by Ralph P. Martin. WBC 43. Nashville: Thomas Nelson, 2004.

Hays, Richard B. *First Corinthians*. Interpretation. Louisville, KY: John Knox, 1997.

Hayes, John H., and Carl R. Holladay. *Biblical Exegesis*. 3rd ed. Louisville: Westminster John Knox, 2007.

Heil, John P. *The Rhetorical Role of Scripture in 1 Corinthians*. Studies in Biblical Literature 15. Atlanta: SBL, 2005.

Hellerman, Joseph H. *The Ancient Church as Family*. Minneapolis: Augsburg Fortress, 2001.

Hjelmslev, Louis. *Prolegomena to a Theory of Language*. Translated by Francis J. Whitfield. Madison: University of Wisconsin Press, 1963.

Holquist, Michael. *Dialogism: Bakhtin and His World*. 2nd ed. New York: Routledge, 2002.

Hood, Susan. "The Persuasive Power of Prosodies: Radiating Values in Academic Writing." *JEAP* 5 (2006): 37–49.

Hood, Susan, and J. R. Martin. "Invoking Attitude: The Play of Graduation in Appraising Discourse." Pages 739–64 in Vol. 2 of *Continuing Discourse on Language: A Functional Perspective*. Edited by Ruqaiya Hasan, Christian Matthiessen, and Jonathan Webster. London: Equinox, 2007.

Hooker, Morna D. "Hard Sayings: I Corinthians 3:2." *Theology* 69 (1966): 19–22.

Hudson, Richard A. *Sociolinguistics*. CTL. Cambridge: Cambridge University Press, 1980.

Hunston, Susan. "Evaluation and Ideology in Scientific Writing." Pages 57–73 in *Register Analysis: Theory and Practice*. Edited by Mohsen Ghadessy. Open Linguistics Series. London: Pinter, 1993.

Hunston, Susan. "Evaluation and the Planes of Discourse." Pages 176–207 in *Evaluation in Text*. Edited by Susan Hunston and Geoff Thompson. Oxford: Oxford University Press, 1999.

Hunston, Susan, and Geoff Thompson. *Evaluation in Text: Authorial Stance and Construction of Discourse*. Oxford: Oxford University Press, 1999.

Hyland, Ken. *Hedging in Scientific Research Articles*. Pragmatics & Beyond 54. Amsterdam: Benjamins, 1998.

Jenkins, Richard. "Categorization: Identity, Social Process, and Epistemology." *Current Sociology* 48 (2000): 7–25.

Johnson, Luke Timothy. *The Acts of the Apostles*. SP 5. Collegeville, MN: Liturgical Press, 1992.

Judge, Edwin A. "The Social Pattern of the Christian Groups in the First Century." Pages 1–56 in *Social Distinctives of the Christians in the First Century: Pivotal Essays by E. A. Judge*. Edited by David M. Scholer. Peabody: Hendrickson, 2008.

Keck, Leander E. "The Function of Romans 3:10–18—Observations and Suggestions." Page 141–57 in *God's Christ and His People: Studies in Honor of Nils Alstrup Dahl*. Edited by Jacob Jervell and Wayne A. Meeks. Oslo: Universitetsforlaget, 1977.

Keck, Leander E. "On the Ethos of Early Christians." *JAAR* 42 (1974): 435–52.

Keener, Craig S. *Revelation*. NIVAC. Grand Rapids: Zondervan, 2000.

Kelly, J. N. D. *The Pastoral Epistles*. BNTC XIV. Peabody: Hendrickson, 1960.

Kennedy, George. *The Art of Persuasion in Greece*. Princeton: Princeton University Press, 1963.

Kirk, John Andrew. "Apostleship since Rengstorff: Toward a Synthesis." *NTS* 21 (1975): 249–64.

Klein, William W., Craig L. Blomberg, and Robert L. Hubbard, Jr. *Introduction to Biblical Interpretation*. Dallas: Word, 1993.

Knight, George W., III. *The Pastoral Epistles*. NIGTC. Grand Rapids: Eerdmans, 1992.

Kroeber, A. L., and Clyde Kluckhohn. *Culture: A Critical Review of Concepts and Definitions*. Cambridge: Peabody Museum, 1952.

Kruse, Colin G. *The Letters of John*. PNTC. Grand Rapids: Eerdmans, 2000.

Kuck, D. W. *Judgment and Community Conflict: Paul's Use of Apocalyptic Judgment Language in 1 Corinthians 3:5–4:5*. NovTSup 66. Leiden: Brill, 1998.

Kuhn, Thomas S. *The Structure of Scientific Revolutions*. 3rd ed. Chicago: University of Chicago Press, 1996.

Labov, William. "Intensity." Pages 43–70 in *Meaning, Form and Use in Context*. Edited by Deborah Schiffrin. Washington, DC: Georgetown University Press, 1984.

BIBLIOGRAPHY

Labov, William, and Joshua Waletsky. "Narrative Analysis: Oral Versions of Personal Experience." Pages 12–44 in *Essays on the Verbal and Visual Arts*. Edited by J. Helm. Seattle, WA: American Ethnological Society, 1967.

Lakoff, George. "Hedges: A Study in Meaning Criteria and the Logic of Fuzzy Concepts." *Journal of Philosophic Logic* 2 (1973): 458–508.

Lane, William L. *Hebrews 1–8*. WBC 47A. Waco: Word, 1991. Repr., Nashville: Thomas Nelson, 2003.

Lang, Friedrich. "σκύβαλον." *TDNT* 7:445–7.

Lea, Thomas D., and Hayne P. Griffin, Jr. *1, 2 Timothy, Titus*. NAC 34. Nashville: Broadman, 1992.

Lee, Sook Hee. "An Integrative Framework for the Analyses of Argumentative/ Persuasive Essays from an Interpersonal Perspective." *Text & Talk* 28 (2008): 239–70.

Lemke, Jay L. "Discourse, Dynamics, and Social Change." *Cultural Dynamics* 6 (1993): 243–75.

Lemke, Jay L. "Interpersonal Meaning in Discourse: Value Orientations." Pages 82–104 in *Advances in Systemic Linguistics: Recent Theory and Practice*. Edited by Martin Davies and Louise Ravelli. Open Linguistics Series. London: Pinter, 1992.

Lemke, Jay L. "Semantics and Social Values." *Word* 40 (1989): 37–50.

Lemke, Jay L. *Textual Politics*. Critical Perspectives on Literacy and Education. London: Taylor & Francis, 1995.

Lightfoot, Joseph B. *The Epistle of St. Paul to the Galatians*. London: Macmillan, 1890. Reprint, Grand Rapids: Zondervan, 1974.

Lightfoot, Joseph B. *Notes on the Epistles of St. Paul*. London: Macmillan, 1895. Reprint, Grand Rapids: Zondervan, 1957.

Litfin, A. Duane. *St. Paul's Theology of Proclamation: 1 Corinthians 1–4 and Greco-Roman Rhetoric*. SNTSMS 83. Cambridge: Cambridge University Press, 1994.

Longacre, Robert E. *The Grammar of Discourse*. 2nd ed. Topics in Language and Linguistics. New York: Plenum, 1996.

Longenecker, Richard N. *Galatians*. WBC 41. Waco: Word, 1990.

Louw, Johannes P. "Discourse Analysis and the Greek New Testament." *BT* 24 (1973): 101–18.

Louw, Johannes P., and Eugene A. Nida, eds. *Greek-English Lexicon of the New Testament: Based on Semantic Domains*. 2nd ed. 2 vols. New York: United Bible Societies, 1989.

Lyons, John. *Semantics*. 2 vols. Cambridge: Cambridge University Press, 1977.

Malherbe, Abraham J. *The Letters to the Thessalonians*. AB 32B. New York: Doubleday, 2000.

Malherbe, Abraham J. *Social Aspects of Early Christianity*. 2nd ed. Eugene, OR: Wipf and Stock, 2003.

Malina, Bruce J. "Authoritarianism," *HBSV* 9–14.

Malina, Bruce J. *Christian Origins and Cultural Anthropology: Practical Models for Biblical Interpretation*. Atlanta: John Knox, 1986.

Malina, Bruce J. "Collectivism in Mediterranean Culture." Pages 17–28 in *Understanding the Social World of the New Testament*. Edited by Dietmar Neufeld and Richard E. DeMaris. London: Routledge, 2010.

Malina, Bruce J. "Faith/Faithfulness." *HBSV* 61–63.

Malina, Bruce J. "Grace/Favor." *HBSV* 75–78.

Malina, Bruce J. "Humility." *HBSV* 99–100.

Malina, Bruce J. "Love." *HBSV* 106–9.

Malina, Bruce J. *New Testament World: Insights from Cultural Anthropology*. 3rd ed. Louisville: Westminster John Knox, 2001.

Malina, Bruce J. "Patronage." *HBSV* 131–34.

Malina, Bruce J. "Reading Theory Perspective: Reading Luke-Acts." Pages 3–23 in *The Social World of Luke-Acts: Models for Interpretation*. Edited by Jerome H. Neyrey. Peabody: Hendrickson, 1991.

Malina, Bruce J. "Honor and Shame in Luke-Acts: Pivotal Values in the Mediterranean World." Pages 25–65 in *The Social World of Luke-Acts: Models for Interpretation*. Edited by Jerome H. Neyrey. Peabody, MA: Hendrickson, 1991.

Malina, Bruce J. *Portraits of Paul: An Archaeology of Ancient Personality*. Louisville: Westminster John Knox, 1996.

Malina, Bruce J. *Social-Science Commentary on the Letters of Paul*. Minneapolis: Fortress, 2006.

Malina, Bruce J., and Jerome H. Neyrey. "Conflict in Luke-Acts: Labelling and Deviance Theory." Pages 97–122 in *The Social World of Luke-Acts: Models for Interpretation*. Edited by Jerome H. Neyrey. Peabody, MA: Hendrickson, 1991.

Malina, Bruce J., and John J. Pilch. *Social-Science Commentary on the Book of Acts*. Minneapolis: Fortress, 2008.

Malinowski, Bronislaw. "The Problem of Meaning in Primitive Languages." Pages 296–336 in *The Meaning of Meaning*. Edited by C. K. Ogden and I. A. Richards. 8th ed. New York: Harcourt, Brace and World, 1923.

Marcus, Joel. *Mark 1–8*. AB 27. New York: Doubleday, 1999.

Marcus, Joel. "Mark and Isaiah." Pages 449–66 in *Fortunate the Eyes That See*. Edited by Astrid B. Beck. Grand Rapids: Eerdmans, 1995.

Marshall, I. Howard. "The Meaning of the Verb 'Baptize.'" Pages 8–24 in *Dimensions of Baptism: Biblical and Theological Studies*. Edited by Stanley E. Porter and Anthony R. Cross. JSNTSup 234. London: Sheffield Academic, 2002.

Martin, Dale B. *The Corinthian Body*. New Haven: Yale University Press, 1995.

Martin, James R. "Analysing Genre: Functional Parameters." Pages 3–39 in *Genre and Institutions: Social Processes in the Workplace and School*. Edited by F. Christie and J. R. Martin. London: Cassell, 1997.

Martin, James R. "Beyond Exchange: Appraisal Systems in English." Pages 142–75 in *Evaluation in Text: Authorial Stance and the Construction of Discourse*. Edited by Susan Hunston and Geoff Thompson. Oxford: Oxford University Press, 1999.

Martin, James R. "Cohesion and Texture." Pages 35–53 in *The Handbook of Discourse Analysis*. Edited by Deborah Schiffrin, Deborah Tannen, and Heidi E. Hamilton. Malden, MA: Blackwell, 2003.

Martin, James R. "The Discourse Semantics of Attitudinal Relations: Continuing the Study of Lexis." *Russian Journal of Linguistics* (2017): 22–47.

Martin, James R. *English Text: System and Structure*. Amsterdam: Benjamins, 1992.

Martin, James R. "Factoring Out Exchange: Types of Structure." Pages 19–40 in *Dialogue Analysis VII: Working with Dialogue*. Edited by Malcolm Coulthard, Janet Cotterill, and Frances Rock. Tübingen: Max Niemeyer Verlag, 2000.

Martin, James R. "Interpersonal Meaning, Persuasion and Public Discourse." *Australian Journal of Linguistics* 15 (1995): 33–67.

Martin, James R. "Negotiating Difference: Ideology and Reconciliation." Pages 85–118 in *Communicating Ideologies*. Edited by Martin Pütz, JoAnne Neff-van Aertselaer, and Teun A. van Dijk. DASK 53. Frankfurt: Peter Lang, 2004.

Martin, James R. "Process and Text: Two Aspects of Semiosis." Pages 248–74 in *Systemic Perspectives on Discourse, Vol. 1: Selected Theoretical Papers from the 9th Annual International Systemic Workshop*. Edited by J. D. Benson and W. S. Greaves. Norwood, NJ: Ablex, 1985.

Martin, James R. "Reading Positions/Positioning Readers." *Prospect* 10 (1995): 27–37.

Martin, James R. "Text and Clause: Fractal Resonance." *Text* 15 (1995): 5–42.

Martin, James R., and David Rose. *Genre Relations: Mapping Culture*. Equinox Textbooks and Surveys in Linguistics. London: Equinox, 2008.

Martin, James R., and David Rose. *Working with Discourse: Meaning beyond the Clause*. 2nd ed. London: Continuum, 2007.

Martin, James R., and Peter R. R. White. *The Language of Evaluation: Appraisal in English*. New York: Palgrave, 2005.

Martin, Ralph P. *2 Corinthians*. WBC 40. Waco: Word, 1986.

Martin, Ralph P. *Mark: Evangelist & Theologian*. Exeter: Paternoster, 1972.

Matthiessen, Christian M. I. M., Kazuhiro Teruya, and Marvin Lam. *Key Terms in Systemic Functional Linguistics*. Key Terms Series. London: Continuum, 2010.

McVann, Mark. "Change/Novelty Orientation." *HBSV* 14–16.

McVann, Mark. "Family-Centeredness." *HBSV* 64–67.

McVann, Mark. "Rituals of Status Transformation in Luke-Acts: The Case of Jesus the Prophet." Pages 333–60 in *The Social World of Luke-Acts*. Edited by Jerome H. Neyrey. Peabody: Hendrickson, 1991.

Meeks, Wayne A. "The Circle of Reference in Pauline Morality." Pages 305–17 in *Greeks, Romans, and Christians: Essays in Honor of Abraham J. Malherbe*. Edited by David Balch, Everett Ferguson, and Wayne A. Meeks. Minneapolis: Fortress, 1990.

Meeks, Wayne A. *First Urban Christians: The Social World of the Apostle Paul*. New Haven: Yale University Press, 1983.

Meeks, Wayne A. *The Moral World of the First Christians*. LEC 6. Philadelphia: Westminster, 1986.

Meeks, Wayne A. *The Origins of Christian Morality: The First Two Centuries*. New Haven: Yale University Press, 1993.

Merton, Robert K. *Social Theory and Social Structure*. New York: Free Press, 1968.

Metzger, Bruce M. *A Textual Commentary on the Greek New Testament*. 2nd ed. Stuttgart: United Bible Societies, 1994.

Mey, Jacob L. "Literary Pragmatics." Pages 778–97 in *The Handbook of Discourse Analysis*. Edited by Deborah Schiffrin, Deborah Tannen, and Heidi E. Hamilton. Malden, MA: Blackwell, 2003.

Meyer, Heinrich A. W. *Critical and Exegetical Handbook to the Epistles to the Corinthians*. Translated by D. Douglas Bannerman. New York: Funk & Wagnalls, 1884.

Mitchell, Margaret M. "The Corinthian Correspondence and the Birth of Pauline Hermeneutics." Pages 17–53 in *Paul and the Corinthians: Studies on a Community in Conflict, Essays in Honor of Margaret Thrall*. Edited by Trevor J. Burke and J. Keith Elliott. Boston: Brill, 2003.

Mitchell, Margaret M. *Paul and the Rhetoric of Reconciliation: An Exegetical Investigation of the Language and Composition of 1 Corinthians*. Tübingen: Mohr Siebeck, 1991. Repr., Louisville: Westminster John Knox, 1993.

Moffatt, James. *The First Epistle to the Corinthians*. MNTC 7. London: Hodder & Stoughton, 1938.

Moo, Douglas J. *The Epistle to the Romans*. NICNT. Grand Rapids: Eerdmans, 1996.

Moo, Douglas J. *The Letter of James*. PNTC. Grand Rapids: Eerdmans, 2000.

Morson, Gary S., and Caryl Emerson. *Mikhail Bakhtin: Creation of a Prosaics*. Stanford, CA: Stanford University Press, 1990.

Moule, C. F. D. *An Idiom Book of New Testament Greek*. 2nd ed. Cambridge: Cambridge University Press, 1959.

Mounce, William D. *Pastoral Epistles*. WBC 46. Nashville: Thomas Nelson, 2000.

Moyise, Steve. "Quotations." Pages 15–28 in *As It Is Written: Studying Paul's Use of Scripture*. Edited by Stanley E. Porter and Christopher D. Stanley. SBLSS 50. Atlanta: Society of Biblical Literature, 2008.

Müller, Dietrich. "ἀποστέλλω." *NIDNTT* 1:128–35.

Mullins, Terence Y. "Petition as a Literary Form." *NovT* 5 (1962): 46–54.

Nash, Robert S. *1 Corinthians*. SHBC. Macon, GA: Smyth & Helwys, 2009.

Neville, Robert C. *Reconstruction of Thinking*. Axiology of Thinking 1. New York: SUNY, 1981.

Neyrey, Jerome H. "Bewitched in Galatia: Paul and Cultural Anthropology." *CBQ* 50 (1988): 72–100.

Neyrey, Jerome H. "Body Language in 1 Corinthians: The Use of Anthropological Models for Understanding Paul and His Opponents." *Semeia* 35 (1986): 129–70.

Neyrey, Jerome H. "Deception." *HBSV* 36–39.

Neyrey, Jerome H. "Dyadism." *HBSV* 46–49.

Neyrey, Jerome H. "God, Benefactor and Patron: The Major Cultural Model for Interpreting the Deity in Greco-Roman Antiquity." *JSNT* 27 (2005): 465–92.

Neyrey, Jerome H. "Group Orientation." *HBSV* 80–83.

Neyrey, Jerome H. *Honor and Shame in the Gospel of Matthew*. Louisville: Westminster John Knox, 1998.

Neyrey, Jerome H. "The Idea of Purity in Mark's Gospel." *Semeia* 35 (1986): 91–128.

Neyrey, Jerome H. *Paul in Other Words: A Cultural Reading of His Letters*. Louisville: Westminster John Knox, 1990.

Neyrey, Jerome H. "Wholeness." *HBSV* 175–78.

Niccum, Curt. "Baptism in the Restoration Movement." Pages 174–200 in *Baptism: Historical, Theological, and Pastoral Perspectives*. Edited by Gordon L. Heath and James D. Dvorak. MTSS. Eugene, OR: Pickwick, 2011.

Nock, Arthur D. *Conversion: The Old and the New in Religion from Alexander the Great to Augustine of Hippo*. Baltimore: John Hopkins, 1998.

Nystrom, David P. *James*. NIVAC. Grand Rapids: Zondervan, 1997.

O'Brien, Peter T. *Colossians, Philemon*. WBC 44. Waco: Word, 1982.

O'Brien, Peter T. *The Epistle to the Philippians*. NIGTC. Grand Rapids: Eerdmans, 1991.

O'Brien, Peter T. *Introductory Thanksgivings in the Letters of Paul*. NovTSup 49. Leiden: Brill, 1977.

O'Brien, Peter T. "Letters, Letter Forms." Pages 550–53 in *Dictionary of Paul and His Letters*. Edited by G. F. Hawthorne, R. P. Martin, D. G. Reid. Downers Grove: InterVarsity Press, 1993.

O'Brien, Peter T. "Thanksgiving in Pauline Theology." Pages 50–66 in *Pauline Studies: Essays Presented to Professor F. F. Bruce on his 70th Birthday*. Edited by Donald A. Hagner and Murray J. Harris. Exeter: Paternoster, 1980.

Ochs, Elinor. "Socialization through Language and Interaction." *Issues in Applied Linguistics* 2 (1991): 143–47.

Ochs, Elinor, and Bambi Schiefflen. "Language Has a Heart." *Text* 9 (1989): 7–25.

O'Donnell, Matthew Brook, Stanley E. Porter, Jeffrey T. Reed, Robert Picirilli, Catherine J. Smith, and Randall K. Tan. "Clause Level Annotation Specification." http://www.opentext.org/model/guidelines/clause/0-2.html.

Osborne, Grant R. *The Hermeneutical Spiral*. Rev. ed. Downers Grove: InterVarsity Press, 2006.

Oster, Richard E., Jr. *1 Corinthians*. CPNIVC. Joplin, MO: College Press, 1995.

Oswalt, John N. *Isaiah*. NIVAC. Grand Rapids: Zondervan, 2003.

Oswalt, John N. *Isaiah 1–39*. NICOT. Grand Rapids: Eerdmans, 1986.

Packer, J. I. "σκύβαλον." *NIDNTT* 1:480.

Painter, Clare. *Learning through Language in Early Childhood*. Open Linguistics Series. London: Cassell, 1999.

Palmer, Frank R. *Mood and Modality*. 2nd ed. CTL. Cambridge: Cambridge University Press, 2001.

Pao, David W. "Constraints of an Epistolary Form: Pauline Introductory Thanksgivings and Paul's Theology of Thanksgiving." Pages 101–27 in *Paul and the Ancient Letter Form*. Edited by Stanley E. Porter and Sean A. Adams. PAST 6. Leiden: Brill, 2010.

Peirce, Charles S. "Letters to Samuel P. Langley, and 'Hume on Miracles and Laws of Nature.'" Pages 275–457 in *Values in a Universe of Chance*. Edited by P. P. Wiener. Garden City, NY: Doubleday, 1958.

Peirce, Charles S. "What is a Sign?" Pages 4–10 in Vol. 2 of *The Essential Peirce: Selected Philosophical Writings*. Edited by Nathan Houser and Christian J. W. Kloesel. Bloomington, IN: Indiana University Press, 1992.

Perelman, Chaim. *The Realm of Rhetoric*. Translated by William Kluback. Notre Dame: University of Notre Dame Press, 1982.

Perelman, Chaim, and Lucie Olbrechts-Tyteca. *The New Rhetoric: A Treatise on Argumentation*. Edited and translated by John Wilkinson and Purcell Weaver. Notre Dame: University Press, 1969.

Peterson, Brian K. *Eloquence and the Proclamation of the Gospel at Corinth*. SBLDS 163. Atlanta: Scholars Press, 1998.

Pike, K. L. *Language in Relation to a Unified Theory of the Structure of Human Behavior*. Janua Linguarum Series Major 24. The Hague: Mouton, 1967.

Pike, K. L. *Linguistic Concepts: An Introduction to Tagmemics*. Lincoln, NE: University of Nebraska Press, 1982.

Pilch, John J. "Domination Orientation." *HBSV* 42–43.

Pilch, John J. "Power." *HBSV* 137–39.

Pilch, John J. and Bruce J. Malina. "Introduction." *HBSV* xix–xxxviii.

Plevnik, Joseph. "Honor/Shame." *HBSV* 89–96.

Pogoloff, Stephen M. *Logos and Sophia: The Rhetorical Situation of 1 Corinthians*. SBLDS 134. Atlanta: Scholars Press, 1992.

Porter, Stanley E. "The Adjectival Attributive Genitive in the NT: A Grammatical Study." *TJ* 4 (1983): 3–17.

Porter, Stanley E. "Allusions and Echoes." Pages 29–40 in *As It Is Written: Studying Paul's Use of Scripture*. Edited by Stanley E. Porter and Christopher D. Stanley. SBLSS 50. Atlanta: Society of Biblical Literature, 2008.

Porter, Stanley E. "Dialect and Register in the Greek of the New Testament." Pages 190–208 in *Rethinking Contexts, Rereading Texts: Contributions from the Social Sciences to Biblical Interpretation*. Edited by M. Daniel Carroll R. JSOTSup 299. Sheffield: Sheffield Academic, 2000.

Porter, Stanley E. "Discourse Analysis and New Testament Studies: An Introductory Survey." Pages 14–35 in *Discourse Analysis and Other Topics in Biblical Greek*. Edited by Stanley E. Porter and D. A. Carson. JSNTSup 113. Sheffield: Sheffield Academic, 1995.

Porter, Stanley E. "Exegesis of the Pauline Letters, Including the Deutero-Pauline Letters." Pages 503–53 in *A Handbook to the Exegesis of the New Testament*. Edited by Stanley E. Porter. Leiden: Brill, 2002.

Porter, Stanley E. "Further Comments on the Use of the Old Testament in the New Testament." Pages 98–113 in *The Intertextuality of the Epistles: Explorations of Theory and Practice*. Edited by Thomas L. Brodie, Dennis R. MacDonald, and Stanley E. Porter. NTM 16. Sheffield: Sheffield Phoenix, 2006.

Porter, Stanley E. "Holiness, Sanctification." Pages 397–402 in *Dictionary of Paul and His Letters*. Edited by Gerald F. Hawthorne, Ralph P. Martin, and Daniel G. Reid. Downers Grove: InterVarsity Press, 1993.

Porter, Stanley E. *Idioms of the Greek New Testament*. 2nd ed. BLG 2. London: Sheffield Academic, 1999.

Porter, Stanley E. "Linguistics and Rhetorical Criticism." Pages 73–77 in *Linguistics and the New Testament: Critical Junctures*. Edited by Stanley E. Porter and D. A. Carson. Sheffield: Sheffield Academic, 1999.

Porter, Stanley E. "Paul and His Bible: His Education and Access to the Scriptures of Israel." Pages 97–124 in *As It Is Written: Studying Paul's Use of Scripture*. Edited by Stanley E. Porter and Christopher D. Stanley. SBLSS 50. Atlanta: Society of Biblical Literature, 2008.

Porter, Stanley E. "Peace, Reconciliation." Pages 695–99 in *Dictionary of Paul and His Letters*. Edited by Gerald F. Hawthorne, Ralph P. Martin, and Daniel G. Reid. Downers Grove: InterVarsity Press, 1993.

Porter, Stanley E. "Pericope Markers and the Paragraph: Textual and Linguistic Considerations." Pages 175–95 in *The Impact of Unit Delimitation on Exegesis*. Edited by Raymond de Hoop, Marjo C. A. Korpel, and Stanley E. Porter. Leiden: Brill, 2008.

Porter, Stanley E. "Prominence: A Theoretical Overview." Pages 45–74 in *The Linguist as Pedagogue*. Edited by Stanley E. Porter and Matthew Brook O'Donnell. NTM 11. Sheffield: Sheffield Phoenix, 2009.

Porter, Stanley E. "Register in the Greek of the New Testament: Application with Reference to Mark's Gospel." Pages 209–29 in *Rethinking Contexts, Rereading Texts: Contributions from the Social Sciences to Biblical Interpretation*. Edited by M. Daniel Carroll R. JSOTSup 299. Sheffield: Sheffield Academic, 2000.

Porter, Stanley E. "Θαυμάζω in Mark 6:6 and Luke 11:38: A Note on Monosemy." *BAGL* 2 (2013): 75–79.

Porter, Stanley E. "The Use of the Old Testament in the New Testament: A Brief Comment on Method and Terminology." Pages 79–96 in *Early Christian Interpretation of the Scriptures of Israel: Investigations and Proposals*. Edited by Craig A. Evans and James A. Sanders. JSNTSup 148. Sheffield: Sheffield Academic, 1997.

Porter, Stanley E. *Verbal Aspect in the Greek of the New Testament, with Reference to Tense and Mood*. SBG 1. New York: Peter Lang, 1993.

Porter, Stanley E., and Andrew W. Pitts. "New Testament Greek Language and Linguistics in Recent Research." *CBR* 6 (2008): 214–55.

Porter, Stanley E., and Kent D. Clarke. "What is Exegesis?" Pages 3–21 in *A Handbook to the Exegesis of the New Testament*. Edited by Stanley E. Porter. Leiden: Brill, 2002.

Porter, Stanley E., and Matthew Brook O'Donnell. *Discourse Analysis*. Unpublished manuscript. Forthcoming.

Poynton, Cate. "Address and the Semiotics of Social Relations." PhD. diss., University of Sydney, 1990.

Poynton, Cate. *Language and Gender: Making the Difference*. 2nd ed. Oxford: Oxford University Press, 1989.

Quinn, Jerome D., and William C. Wacker. *The First and Second Letters to Timothy*. ECC. Grand Rapids: Eerdmans, 2000.

Ravelli, L. J. "Grammatical Metaphor: An Initial Analysis." Pages 133–47 in *Pragmatics, Discourse and Text: Some Systemically-Inspired Approaches*. Edited by E. H. Steiner and Robert Veltman. London: Pinter, 1988.

Reed, Jeffrey T. "Are Paul's Thanksgivings 'Epistolary'?" *JSNT* 61 (1996): 87–99.

Reed, Jeffrey T. "The Cohesiveness of Discourse: Towards a Model of Linguistic Criteria for Analyzing New Testament Discourse." Pages 28–46 in *Discourse Analysis and the New Testament*. Edited by Stanley E. Porter and Jeffrey T. Reed. JSNTSup 170. Sheffield: Sheffield Academic, 1999.

Reed, Jeffrey T. "Discourse Analysis." Pages 189–217 in *A Handbook to the Exegesis of the New Testament*. Edited by Stanley E. Porter. Leiden: Brill, 2002.

Reed, Jeffrey T. *A Discourse Analysis of Philippians: Method and Rhetoric in the Debate over Literary Integrity*. JSNTSup 136. Sheffield: Sheffield Academic, 1997.

Rengstorf, Karl H. "ἀπόστολος." *TDNT* 1:407–47.

Robertson, A. T. *A Grammar of the Greek New Testament in Light of Historical Research*. Nashville: Broadman, 1934.

BIBLIOGRAPHY

Robertson, A. T., and Alfred Plummer. *A Critical and Exegetical Commentary on The First Epistle of St. Paul to the Corinthians*. ICC. Edinburgh: T & T Clark, 1999.

Robins, R. H. "The Contributions of John Rupert Firth to Linguistics in the First Fifty Years of *Lingua*." *Lingua* 100 (1997): 205–22.

Runge, Steven E. *Discourse Grammar of the Greek New Testament*. LBRS. Peabody: Hendrickson, 2010.

Sampley, J. Paul. "Paul and Frank Speech." Pages 293–318 in *Paul in the Greco-Roman World: A Handbook*. Edited by J. Paul Sampley. Harrisburg, PA: Trinity Press International, 2003.

Sanders, Jack T. "The Transition from Opening Epistolary Thanksgiving to the Body in the Letters of the Pauline Corpus." *JBL* 81 (1962): 348–62.

Schaefer, Robert T., and Robert P. Lamm. *Sociology*. 4th ed. New York: McGraw Hill, 1992.

Schnabel, Eckhard J. *Der erste Brief des Paulus an die Korinther*. Historisch Theologische Auslegung. Wuppertal: R. Brockhaus, 2006.

Schnabel, Eckhard J. "The Objectives of Change, Factors of Transformation, and the Causes of Results: The Evidence of Paul's Corinthian Correspondence." *TJ* 26 (2005): 179–204.

Schnackenburg, Rudolf. "Apostles Before and During Paul's Time." Pages 287–303 in *Apostolic History and the Gospel*. Edited by W. Ward Gasque and Ralph P. Martin. Grand Rapids: Eerdmans, 1970.

Schrage, Wolfgang. *Der erste Brief an die Korinther*. 4 vols. EKKNT 7. Düsseldorf: Benziger Verlag, 1991–1999.

Schubert, Paul. *Form and Function of the Pauline Thanksgivings*. BZNW 20. Berlin: Töpelmann, 1939.

Schüssler Fiorenza, Elisabeth. "Rhetorical Situation and Historical Reconstruction in 1 Corinthians." *NTS* 33 (1987): 386–403.

Schütz, John H. *Paul and the Anatomy of Apostolic Authority*. NTL. Loiusville: Westminster John Knox, 2007.

Scroggs, Robin. Review of *The Corinthian Women Prophets*, by Antoinette Clark Wire. *JBL* 111 (1992): 546–48.

Searle, John R. *Speech Acts: An Essay in the Philosophy of Language*. Cambridge: Cambridge University Press, 1969.

Seebass, Horst. "ἅγιος." *NIDNTT* 2:224–32.

Seeman, Chris. "Zeal/Jealousy." *HBSV* 180–82.

Silva, Moisés. *Philippians*. BECNT. Grand Rapids: Baker, 1992.

Simon-Vandenbergen, Anne-Marie. "Lexical Metaphor and Interpersonal Meaning." Pages 223–55 in *Grammatical Metaphor: Views from Systemic Functional Linguistics*.

Edited by Anne-Marie Simon-Vandenbergen, Miriam Taverniers, and Louise Ravelli. Amsterdam: John Benjamins, 2003.

Simon-Vandenbergen, Anne-Marie, P. R. R. White, and Karin Aijmer. "Presupposition and 'Taking-for-Granted' in Mass Communicated Political Argument." Pages 31–74 in *Political Discourse in the Media*. Edited by Anita Fetzer and Gerda Eva Lauerbach. Amsterdam: John Benjamins, 2007.

Smith, Jay E. "1 Thessalonians 4:4: Breaking the Impasse." *BBR* 11 (2001): 65–105.

Spicq, Ceslas. "σκύβαλον." *TLNT* 3:263–5.

Stamps, Dennis L. "A Literary-Rhetorical Reading of the Opening and Closing of 1 Corinthians." PhD. diss., University of Durham, 1994.

Stamps, Dennis L. "Rhetorical Criticism of the New Testament." Pages 129–69 in *Approaches to New Testament Study*. Edited by Stanley E. Porter and David Tombs. JSNTSup 120. Sheffield: Sheffield Academic, 1995.

Stamps, Dennis L. "The Use of the Old Testament in the New Testament as a Rhetorical Device: A Methodological Proposal." Pages 9–37 in *Hearing the Old Testament in the New Testament*. Edited by Stanley E. Porter. Grand Rapids: Eerdmans, 2006.

Stanley, Christopher D. *Arguing with Scripture: The Rhetoric of Quotations in the Letters of Paul*. New York: T & T Clark, 2004.

Stanley, Christopher D. "Paul's 'Use' of Scripture: Why the Audience Matters." Pages 125–55 in *As It Is Written: Studying Paul's Use of Scripture*. Edited by Stanley E. Porter and Christopher D. Stanley. Atlanta: Society of Biblical Literature, 2008.

Stanley, Christopher D. "'Pearls Before Swine': Did Paul's Audiences Understand His Biblical Quotations?" *NovT* 41 (1999): 124–44.

Stanley, Christopher D. "The Rhetoric of Quotations: An Essay on Method." Pages 44–58 in *Early Christian Interpretation of the Scriptures of Israel: Investigations and Proposals*. Edited by Craig A. Evans and James A. Sanders. JSNTSup 148. SSEJC 5. Sheffield: Sheffield Academic, 1997.

Stanley, D. M. "'Become Imitators of Me': The Pauline Conception of Apostolic Tradition." *Biblica* 40 (1959): 859–77.

Stowers, Stanley K. *Letter Writing in Greco-Roman Antiquity*. LEC 5. Philadelphia: Westminster, 1986.

Stowers, Stanley K. *A Rereading of Romans: Justice, Jews, and Gentiles*. New Haven: Yale University Press, 1994.

Stowers, Stanley K. "Romans 7.7–25 as a Speech-in-Character (προσωποποιΐα)." Pages 180–202 in *Paul in His Hellenistic Context*. Edited by Troels Engbert-Pedersen. Minneapolis: Fortress, 1995.

Stubbs, Michael. "'A Matter of Prolonged Field Work': Notes Towards a Modal Grammar of English." *Applied Linguistics* 7 (1987): 1–25.

BIBLIOGRAPHY

Stubbs, Michael. *Text and Corpus Analysis: Computer-Assisted Studies of Language and Culture*. Cambridge, MA: Blackwell, 1996.

Sumney, Jerry L. "Studying Paul's Opponents: Advances and Challenges." Pages 7–58 in *Paul's Opponents*. Edited by Stanley E. Porter. PAST 2. Leiden: Brill, 2005. Repr., Atlanta: Society of Biblical Literature, 2009.

Tajfel, Henri. "Social Categorization, Social Identity, and Social Comparison." Pages 61–76 in *Differentiation between Social Groups: Studies in Social Psychology of Intergroup Relations*. Edited by Henri Tajfel. European Monographs in Social Psychology 14. London: Academic Press, 1978.

Tannen, Deborah. *Talking Voices*. Studies in Interactional Sociolinguistics. 2nd ed. Cambridge: Cambridge University Press, 2007.

Tate, W. Randolph. "Point of View." Pages 268–69 in *Interpreting the Bible: A Handbook of Terms and Methods*. Edited by W. Randolph Tate. Peabody: Hendrickson, 2006.

Taylor, Nicholas H. "Apostolic Identity and the Conflicts in Corinth and Galatia." Pages 99–127 in *Paul and His Opponents*. Edited by Stanley E. Porter. PAST 2. Leiden: Brill, 2005. Repr., Atlanta: Society of Biblical Literature, 2009.

Taylor, Nicholas H. "Conflict as Context for Defining Identity: A Study of Apostleship in the Galatian and Corinthian Letters." *HTS* 59 (2003): 915–45.

Terry, Ralph B. *A Discourse Analysis of First Corinthians*. SIL Publications in Linguistics 120. Dallas: SIL, 1995.

Theissen, Gerd. *Psychological Aspects of Pauline Theology*. Translated by John P. Galvin. Philadelphia: Fortress, 1987.

Theissen, Gerd. "Social Stratification in the Corinthian Community: A Contribution to the Sociology of Early Hellenistic Christianity." Pages 69–119 in *The Social Setting of Pauline Christianity*. Edited and translated by John H. Schütz. Philadelphia: Fortress, 1982.

Thibault, Paul J. "An Interview with Michael Halliday." Pages 599–627 in *Language Topics: Essays in Honour of Michael Halliday*. Edited by Ross Steele and Terry Threadgold. Amsterdam: Benjamins, 1987.

Thiselton, Anthony C. *The First Epistle to the Corinthians*. NIGTC. Grand Rapids: Eerdmans, 2000.

Thiselton, Anthony C. "The Logical Role of the Liar Paradox in Titus 1:12, 13: A Dissent from the Commentaries in the Light of Philosophical and Logical Analysis." *Biblical Interpretation* 2 (1994): 207–23.

Thiselton, Anthony C. "Realized Eschatology at Corinth." *NTS* 24 (1977–78): 510–26.

Thiselton, Anthony C. "The Supposed Power of Words in the Biblical Writings." *JTS* 25 (1974): 283–99.

Thompson, Geoff. *Introducing Functional Grammar*. 2nd ed. London: Arnold, 2004.

Thompson, Geoff, and Ye Yiyun. "Evaluation in the Reporting Verbs Used in Academic Papers." *Applied Linguistics* 12 (1991): 365–82.

Thompson, Geoff, and Jianglin Zhou. "Evaluation and Organization in Text: The Structuring Role of Evaluative Disjuncts." Pages 121–41 in *Evaluation in Text: Authorial Stance and the Construction of Discourse*. Edited by Susan Hunston and Geoff Thompson. Oxford: Oxford University Press, 1999.

Tite, Philip L. "The Compositional Function of the Petrine Prescript: A Look at 1 Pet 1:1–3." *JETS* 39 (1996): 47–56.

Tite, Philip L. "How to Begin and Why?" Pages 57–99 in *Paul and the Ancient Letter Form*. Edited by Stanley E. Porter and Sean A. Adams. PAST 6. Leiden: Brill, 2010.

Trew, Tony. "Theory and Ideology at Work." Pages 94–116 in *Language and Control*. Edited by Roger Fowler, Bob Hodge, Gunther Kress, and Tony Trew. London: Routledge & Kegan Paul, 1979.

Tucker, J. Brian. *You Belong to Christ: Paul and the Formation of Social Identity in 1 Corinthians 1–4*. Eugene, OR: Pickwick, 2010.

Tuckett, Christopher M. "Mark." Pages 84–134 in *The Gospels*. Edited by John Muddiman and John Barton. OBC. Oxford: Oxford University Press, 2001.

Tull, Patricia K. "Rhetorical Criticism and Intertextuality." Pages 156–80 in *To Each Its Own Meaning: An Introduction to Biblical Criticisms and Their Application*. Edited by Steven L. McKenzie and Stephen R. Haynes. Rev. ed. Louisville: Westminster John Knox, 1999.

Turner, Nigel. *Syntax*. Vol. 3 of *A Grammar of New Testament Greek* by James H. Moulton. 4 vols. Edinburgh: T & T Clark, 1908–1976.

van Dijk, Teun A. *Studies in the Pragmatics of Discourse*. The Hague: Mouton, 1981.

van Langenhove, Luk, and Rom Harré. "Introducing Positioning Theory." Pages 14–31 in *Positioning Theory*. Edited by Luk van Langenhove and Rom Harré. Oxford: Blackwell, 1999.

Vološinov, Valentin N. *Marxism and the Philosophy of Language*. Translated by Ladislav Matejka and I. R. Titunik. Studies in Language 1. New York: Seminar Press, 1973.

Wallace, Daniel B. *Greek Grammar Beyond the Basics*. Grand Rapids: Zondervan, 1996.

Wanamaker, Charles A. *The Epistles to the Thessalonians*. NIGTC. Grand Rapids: Eerdmans, 1990.

Wanamaker, Charles A. "A Rhetoric of Power: Ideology and 1 Cor 1–4." Pages 115–37 in *Paul and the Corinthians: Studies on a Community in Conflict. Essays in Honor of Margaret Thrall*. Edited by Trevor J. Burke and J. Keith Elliott. Leiden: Brill, 2003.

Wedderburn, Alexander J. M. "ἐν τῇ σοφίᾳ τοῦ θεοῦ—1 Kor 1:21." *ZNW* 64 (1973): 132–4.

Weiss, Johannes. *Der erste Korintherbrief*. KEK. 9th ed. Göttingen: Vandenhoeck & Ruprecht, 1910.

Welborn, L. L. "On the Discord in Corinth: 1 Corinthians 1–4 and Ancient Politics." *JBL* 106 (1987): 85–111.

BIBLIOGRAPHY

Welborn, L. *Politics and Rhetoric in the Corinthian Epistles*. Macon, GA: Mercer University Press, 1997.

Westfall, Cynthia Long. "Blessed Be the Ties that Bind: Semantic Domains and Cohesive Chains in Hebrews 1.1–2.4 and 12.5–8." *JGRChJ* 6 (2009): 199–216.

Westfall, Cynthia Long. *A Discourse Analysis of the Letter to the Hebrews*. LNTS 297; SNTG 11. London: T & T Clark, 2005.

Westfall, Cynthia Long. "A Method for the Analysis of Prominence in Hellenistic Greek." Pages 75–94 in *The Linguist as Pedagogue*. Edited by Stanley E. Porter and Matthew Brook O'Donnell. NTM 11. Sheffield: Sheffield Phoenix, 2009.

White, John L. "Introductory Formulae in the Body of the Pauline Letter." *JBL* 90 (1971): 91–7.

White, John L. *Light from Ancient Letters*. FF. Philadelphia: Fortress, 1986.

White, Peter R. R. "Appraisal: An Overview." http://www.grammatics.com/appraisal/appraisalguide/framed/frame.htm.

White, Peter R. R. "Beyond Modality and Hedging." *Text* 23 (2003): 259–84.

White, Peter R. R. "Dialogue and Inter-Subjectivity: Reinterpreting the Semantics of Modality and Hedging." Pages 67–80 in *Dialogue Analysis VII: Working with Dialogue*. Edited by Malcolm Coulthard, Janet Cotterill, and Frances Rock. Tübingen: Max Niemeyer Verlag, 2000.

White, Peter R. R. "Evaluative Semantics and Ideological Positioning in Journalistic Discourse: A New Framework for Analysis." Pages 37–67 in *Mediating Ideology in Text and Image*. Edited by Inger Lassen, Jeanne Strunck, and Torben Vestergaard. Amsterdam: John Benjamins, 2006.

White, Peter R. R. "An Introductory Tour Through Appraisal Theory." http://grammatics.com/appraisal/AppraisalOutline/AppraisalOutlineWPFiles.html.

Wiles, Gordon P. *Paul's Intercessory Prayers: The Significance of the Intercessory Prayer Passages in the Letters of St. Paul*. SNTSMS 24. Cambridge: Cambridge University Press, 1974.

Winer, G. B. *A Treatise on the Grammar of NT Greek*. Translated by W. F. Moulton. Edinburgh: T & T Clark, 1882.

Winter, Bruce W. *After Paul Left Corinth: The Influence of Secular Ethics and Social Change*. Grand Rapids: Eerdmans, 2001.

Winter, Bruce W. *Philo and Paul among the Sophists*. SNTSMS 96. Cambridge: Cambridge University Press, 1997.

Wire, Antoinette Clark. *The Corinthian Women Prophets*. Eugene, OR: Wipf & Stock, 2003.

Witherington, Ben, III. *The Acts of the Apostles: A Socio-Rhetorical Commentary*. Grand Rapids: Eerdmans, 1998.

236   BIBLIOGRAPHY

Witherington, Ben, III. *Conflict and Community in Corinth: A Socio-Rhetorical Commentary on 1 and 2 Corinthians*. Grand Rapids: Eerdmans, 1995.

Woodson, Linda. *A Handbook of Modern Rhetorical Terms*. Urbana, IL: National Council of Teachers of English, 1979.

Wright, J. Stafford. "μαγεία." *NIDNTT* 2:556–59.

Wuellner, Wilhelm. "Paul as Pastor: The Function of Rhetorical Questions in First Corinthians." Pages 49–77 in *L'Apôtre Paul: Personnalité, Style, et Conception du Ministère*. Edited by A. Vanhoye. BETL 73. Leuven: University Press, 1986.

Wuellner, Wilhelm. "Rhetorical Criticism in Biblical Studies." *Jian Dao* 4 (1995): 73–96.

Wuellner, Wilhelm. "The Sociological Implications of I Corinthians 1:26–28 Reconsidered." *SE* 4 (1973): 666–72 (= TUGAL 112; Berlin: Akadmie-Verlag, 1973).

Wuellner, Wilhelm. "Where is Rhetorical Criticism Taking Us?" *CBQ* 49 (1987): 448–63.

Yarbrough, Robert W. "Sexual Gratification in 1 Thess 4.1–8." *TJ* 20 (1999): 215–32.

Yinger, K. L. *Paul, Judaism, and Judgment According to Deeds*. Cambridge: Cambridge University Press, 1999.

Young, Richard A. *Intermediate New Testament Greek*. Nashville: Broadman and Holman, 1994.

Yule, George. *The Study of Language*. 2nd ed. Cambridge: Cambridge University Press, 1996.

Name Index

Aageson, James W.   123
Abasciano, Brian J.   124
Adams, Sean A.   18, 96, 99
Agnew, Francis H.   100
Aijmer, Karin   100
Allo, E. Bernard   168
Althusser, Louis   38, 39
Anderson, Margaret L.   3
Anderson, R. Dean, Jr.   106, 203, 205
Arzt-Grabner, Peter   104
Aune, David E.   34, 89, 103, 109, 113, 119
Austin, John L.   115

Bakhtin, Mikhail M.   22, 23, 30, 32, 36, 37, 67, 69, 82
Barclay, John M. G.   43
Barrett, C. K.   60, 103, 121, 127, 153
Beasley-Murray, George R.   111, 113
Beaugrande, Robert de   208
Bednarek, Monika   62
Bellous, Joyce E.   100
Berger, Peter L.   1, 2, 3, 31, 32
Bernard, J. H.   53
Bernstein, Basil   36
Best, Ernest   100
Betz, Hans Dieter   45, 109, 203
Biber, Douglas   26
Bjerkelund, Carl J.   113
Black, Stephanie L.   142
Blomberg, Craig L.   43
Bock, Darrell L.   77
Bourdieu, Pierre   2, 6
Braumann, G.   149
Brim, Orville G.   1
Brown, Colin   54
Brown, Gillian   18
Brown, Raymond E.   74
Brown, Roger   25
Bruce, F. F.   207
Bultmann, Rudolf   8, 34

Caldas-Coulthard, Carmen R.   79
Callow, Kathleen   204, 205
Calvin, John   134

Carney, Thomas F.   6
Carson, D. A.   53, 156, 157, 158
Castelli, Elizabeth A.   2, 100, 185, 194, 201, 202, 203
Cen, Esther G.   49
Chafe, Wallace L.   5
Channell, Joanna   5
Charles, Maggie   78
Chomsky, Noam   8, 9
Chow, John K.   97
Chrysostom, John   97
Ciampa, Roy E.   123
Clarke, Andrew D.   106, 156
Clarke, Kent D.   42
Coenen, Lothar   96
Coffin, Caroline   30
Collins, Raymond F.   97, 104, 123, 210
Conzelmann, Hans   51, 61, 98, 105, 111, 112, 113, 114, 124, 151, 157, 169
Cortazzi, Martin   52
Coulthard, Malcolm   18
Crook, Zeba A.   102, 103, 162
Cross, Anthony R.   111

Dahl, Nils A.   112
Demetrius of Phalerum   44
deSilva, David A.   29, 61, 85, 96, 97, 118, 119, 121, 127, 129, 130, 148, 152, 164, 186, 192, 193, 197, 202
Dibelius, Martin   34, 51, 61
Donohue, Jim   30
Douglas, Mary   39, 110, 199, 201
Dunn, J. D. G.   50, 75
Dutch, Robert S.   97
Dvorak, James D.   9, 11, 15, 17, 18, 19, 22, 43, 46, 63, 65, 70, 71, 76, 116, 124, 125, 142, 161

Eastman, Susan   76
Eckert, Jost   96
Edwards, Thomas C.   109
Eggins, Suzanne   11, 15, 20, 22, 24, 30, 31, 32, 34, 40, 41, 42, 43, 113, 114
Elliott, John H.   3, 6, 8, 22, 35, 42, 43, 76, 103, 151
Emerson, Caryl   100

NAME INDEX

Engberg-Pedersen, Troels 129
Esler, Philip F. 210
Evans, Craig A. 103, 119
Exler, Francis X. J. 99

Fairclough, Norman 2, 5, 7, 35, 37, 40, 76, 100, 103, 113
Fee, Gordon D. 95, 96, 98, 99, 105, 106, 111, 112, 113, 114, 115, 119, 123, 124, 127, 138, 139, 140, 142, 144, 148, 149, 151, 152, 156, 158, 161, 162, 163, 164, 165, 167, 172, 174, 175, 176, 177, 183, 185, 186
Ferguson, Everett 111
Fiore, Benjamin 116
Fiorenza, Elisabeth Schüssler 109, 199
Firth, John R. 20
Fitzmyer, Joseph A. 98, 99, 105, 113, 121, 123, 139
Foucault, Michel 2, 100, 201, 202
France, Richard T. 66, 72
Francis, James 149, 151
Furnish, Victor Paul 61, 75, 86

Gaertner, Dennis 59
Garland, David E. 96, 97, 98, 100, 106, 111, 113, 117, 119, 121, 127, 129, 138, 139, 142, 151, 151, 156, 157, 158, 161, 162, 172, 175, 176, 177, 186, 187
Geddert, Timothy J. 103, 119
Gill, Ann M. 49
Gillmayr-Bucher, Susanne 36, 37
Gilman, Albert 25
Goatly, Andrew 25, 38, 40, 69, 76, 101, 103, 116, 124
Goodacre, Mark 28
Godet, Frederic L. 96
Gonda, Jan 104
Green, Gene L. 79
Green, Joel B. 77
Griffin, Hayne P., Jr. 51
Gundry, Robert H. 66

Hafemann, Scott J. 95, 99
Hahn, H. C. 57
Halliday, M. A. K. 2, 7, 8, 9, 10, 11, 14, 15, 16, 19, 20, 21, 22, 23, 24, 31, 36, 39, 40, 41, 49, 65, 76, 89, 94, 105, 113, 114, 125, 128, 131, 209
Hanson, K. C. 60
Harré, Rom 95

Harris, Murray, J. 81
Hasan, Ruqaiya 26, 31, 33, 40, 41
Hawthorne, Gerald F. 49
Hayes, John H. 42
Hays, Richard B. 110, 115, 117, 119, 124, 125, 158
Heil, John Paul 123, 210
Hellerman, Joseph H. 96, 113
Hjelmslev, Louis 12
Holladay, Carl R. 42
Holquist, Michael 37
Hood, Susan 49, 65, 83, 136
Hooker, Morna D. 150
Hubbard, Robert L. Jr., 43
Hudson, Richard A. 2
Hunston, Susan 3, 100
Hyland, Ken 5

Jenkins, Richard 120
Jin, Lixian 52
Johnson, Luke Timothy 74
Judge, Edwin A. 97

Keck, Leander 19, 31
Keener, Craig S. 89
Kelly, J. N. D. 51
Kennedy, George 45
Kim, Chan-Hie 43
Kirk, John Andrew 100
Klein, William W. 42
Kluckhohn, Clyde 22
Knight, George W. III 51, 52
Kroeber, A. L. 22
Kruse, Colin G. 74
Kuck, D. W. 158
Kuhn, Thomas S. 6

Labov, William 5, 52
Lakoff, George 5, 38
Lam, Marvin 16, 19
Lamm, Robert P. 1
Lane, William L. 70
Lang, Friedrich 49
Langenhove, Luk van 95
Lea, Thomas D. 51
Lee, Sook Hee 100
Lemke, Jay L. 2, 4, 6, 7, 12, 14, 15, 16, 23, 30, 35, 36, 37, 67, 123
Lightfoot, Joseph B. 105, 111, 114, 116, 132
Litfin, A. Duane 106, 206

NAME INDEX

Longacre, Robert E.   110, 208, 209
Longenecker, Richard N.   73
Louw, Johannes P.   6
Luckmann, Thomas   1, 2, 3, 31, 32
Lyons, John   5, 10, 38, 80

Malherbe, Abraham J.   39, 97
Malina, Bruce J.   3, 11, 22, 25, 26, 36, 37, 39,
    44, 47, 52, 71, 80, 81, 85, 100, 103, 108,
    110, 112, 120, 121, 129, 140, 151, 152, 155,
    158, 164, 191, 192, 196, 197, 199
Malinowski, Bronislaw   20
Marcus, Joel   72
Marshall, I. H.   111
Martin, Dale B.   35, 97, 106, 113, 118, 119, 156,
    172, 176, 207, 208
Martin, James R.   3, 4, 5, 7, 11, 12, 13, 14, 14,
    15, 16, 17, 19, 20, 21, 22, 23, 24, 25, 26, 27,
    30, 31, 32, 33, 34, 35, 36, 37, 38, 40, 41,
    42, 46, 47, 48, 49, 50, 53, 54, 55, 57, 59,
    63, 65, 67, 68, 69, 70, 71, 72, 73, 74, 75,
    76, 78, 79, 82, 83, 84, 85, 86, 87, 88, 89,
    90, 93, 99, 100, 105, 109, 113, 114, 122, 123,
    124, 125, 131, 136, 154, 159, 172,
    173, 212
Martin, Ralph P.   49, 61, 72, 75
Matthiessen, Christian M. I. M.   8, 14, 15, 16,
    19, 24, 39, 76, 89, 94, 105, 113, 114, 125,
    128, 131
McVann, Mark   25, 96, 185, 186, 197, 202
Meeks, Wayne A.   1, 2, 89, 95, 96, 97, 98, 100,
    103, 112, 113, 119, 123, 139, 149, 150,
    199, 211
Metzger, Bruce M.   142
Mey, Jacob L.   52
Meyer, Heinrich A.   105
Mitchell, Margaret M.   97, 108, 109, 110, 114,
    203
Moffatt, James   176
Moo, Douglas J.   54, 75, 79, 96
Morson, Gary S.   100
Moule, C. F. D.   96, 102
Mounce, William D.   51, 52, 61
Moyise, Steve   123
Müller, Dietrich   95, 100
Mullins, Terence Y.   113

Nash, Robert S.   97
Neville, Robert C.   4

Neyrey, Jerome H.   4, 25, 39, 52, 61, 72, 76,
    80, 97, 103, 109, 110, 112, 120, 121, 129, 157,
    158, 164, 168, 191, 197, 201, 207
Niccum, Curt   111
Nock, Arthur D.   1, 149, 150
North, Sarah   30
Nystrom, David P.   54

O'Brien, Peter T.   49, 50, 77, 94, 99, 104, 105
Ochs, Elinor   2, 4
O'Donnell, Matthew Brook   7, 8, 17, 18, 93,
    209
Olbrechts-Tyteca, Lucie   46, 100, 123, 199, 200
Osborne, Grant R.   52
Oster, Richard E.   60, 95, 158
Oswalt, John N.   54

Packer, J. I.   49
Palmer, Frank R.   5
Pao, David W.   104
Peirce, Charles S.   10, 43
Perelman, Chaim   46, 100, 123,199, 200
Peterson, Brian K.   106
Pike, K. L.   15, 16, 208
Pilch, John J.   3, 39, 80, 100, 110, 140, 151, 152
Pitts, Andrew W.   6, 8
Plevnik, Joseph   197
Plummer, Alfred   96, 97, 109, 114, 121, 151, 152,
    156, 164
Pogoloff, Stephen M.   97, 106, 120, 127, 205,
    206
Porter, Stanley, E.   6, 7, 8, 11, 17, 18, 19, 28, 29,
    33, 39, 42, 43, 48, 59, 65, 70, 71, 75, 76,
    80, 81, 93, 98, 99, 104, 105, 111, 116, 123,
    124, 125, 162, 163, 166, 188, 209
Poynton, Cate   2, 25, 26, 99, 100

Quinn, Jerome D.   61

Ravelli, L. J.   49
Reed, Jeffrey T.   7, 41, 89, 93, 104, 114, 128
Rengstorf, Karl H.   100
Robertson, A. T.   96, 97, 109, 114, 121, 151, 152,
    156, 164, 188
Robins, R. H.   20
Rose, David   7, 11, 12, 13, 14, 21, 22, 24, 25, 26,
    27, 30, 31, 32, 33, 34, 35, 41, 42, 53, 54, 55,
    59, 65, 82, 86, 88, 125, 131, 212
Runge, Steven E.   142

240 NAME INDEX

Sampley, J. Paul 57
Sanders, Jack T. 103, 113
Saussure, Ferdinand de 9, 10
Schieffelin, Bambi 4
Schnabel, Eckhard J. 112, 156
Schnackenburg, Rudolf 100
Schrage, Wolfgang 105, 168
Schubert, Paul 104
Schütz, John H. 100, 118
Scroggs, Robin 201
Searle, John R. 115
Seebass, Horst 98
Seeman, Chris 151
Shaefer, Robert T. 1
Silva, Moisés 49
Simon-Vandenbergen, Anne-Marie 49, 100
Smith, Jay E. 39
Spicq, Ceslas 49
Stamps, Dennis L. 45, 71, 95, 97, 99, 109, 123, 124
Stanley, Christopher D. 71, 78, 109, 120, 123, 124, 210
Stanley, D. M. 185
Stowers, Stanley K. 34, 43, 44, 109
Stubbs, Michael 5, 37, 76
Sumney, Jerry L. 95

Tajfel, Henri 120, 211
Tannen, Deborah 99, 109, 110
Tate, W. Randolph 52
Taylor, Howard F. 3
Taylor, Nicholas H. 85, 95, 100
Terry, Ralph Bruce 208, 209
Teruya, Kazuhiro 16, 19
Theissen, Gerd 97, 127, 129, 168, 199
Thibault, Paul J. 22, 36
Thiselton, Anthony C. 51, 96, 97, 98, 99, 100, 105, 106, 109, 110, 111, 112, 113, 115, 116, 118, 119, 121, 122, 123, 127, 129, 132, 138, 139, 142, 143, 149, 151, 151, 153, 157, 158, 164, 172, 173, 175, 176, 177, 185
Thompson, Geoff 3, 15, 16, 39, 41, 42, 78, 89, 114
Tite, Philip L. 95, 99
Trew, Tony 65, 103
Tucker, J. Brian 1, 2, 96, 109, 110, 113, 118, 120, 128, 129, 130, 149, 150, 156, 158, 210, 211, 212

Tuckett, Christopher M. 72
Tull, Patricia K. 45
Turner, Nigel 114, 188
Turner, Victor 199

Vološinov, Valentin N. 10, 37

Wacker, William C. 61
Waletsky, Joshua 52
Wallace, Daniel B. 70, 80, 114
Walton, Ryder Dale 15, 17, 18
Wanamaker, Charles A. 39, 79, 100
Wedderburn, Alexander J. M. 121
Weiss, Johannes 122
Welborn, L. L. 108, 109
Westfall, Cynthia Long 6, 7, 18, 41, 93, 118, 209
Whedbee, Karen 49
White, John L. 93, 113
White, Peter R. R. 3, 4, 5, 15, 16, 17, 30, 37, 38, 46, 47, 48, 49, 50, 53, 54, 55, 57, 59, 61, 63, 65, 67, 68, 69, 70, 71, 72, 73, 74, 75, 76, 78, 79, 82, 83, 84, 85, 86, 87, 88, 89, 90, 93, 99, 100, 102, 105, 107, 109, 113, 115, 122, 123, 124, 136, 154, 159, 172, 173
Wiles, Gordon P. 99
Winer, G. G. 80
Winter, Bruce W. 100, 109, 156, 177
Wire, Antoinette Clark 99, 100, 113, 148, 156, 199, 200, 201
Witherington, Ben, III 59, 74, 97, 98, 106, 113, 115, 127, 157, 158, 168, 185
Woodson, Linda 43
Wright, J. Stafford 76
Wuellner, Wilhelm 45, 69, 116, 128

Yarbrough, Robert W. 39
Yinger, K. L. 158
Yiyun, Ye 78
Young, Richard A. 39, 75
Yule, George 18, 63

Zhou, Jianglin 89

Scripture Index

Old Testament

Deuteronomy
6:6–7   185

Judges
16:15   57

Job
5:13   168

Psalms
93:11   168
95:7–11   70

Proverbs
19:18   185
22:6   185
23:13–14   185
29:17   185

Isaiah
29   120
29:14   123
33:14–16   54
56:1   54

Jeremiah
9:22–23   132
31:15   66

Deuterocanonical Books
Wis 19:17   58

Ancient Jewish Writers

Philo
Det. 34   177

New Testament

Matthew
2:16   65, 83
2:18   66
5:34   87
5:38–39   177
6:6   58
7:15–20   110
10:11   61
10:38   61, 62
11:28   53
17:6   88
19:17   48
23:16   50, 52
23:17   50, 52
23:28   87
26:38   88
27:23   87

Mark
1:4–6   18
1:8   16
1:21–22   29
1:45   88
6:1–6   27, 28
6:4   29
7:5   71
7:6–7   71, 72
7:36   87
7:37   87
12:27   86

Luke
1:47   88
3:22   48
4:28   54
6:11   55
6:23   53
6:43–45   110
7:40–41   77
7:42   77
7:43   77
10:41   48
12:32   54
13:16   90
15:5   48
18:23   87
24:52   48, 89

John

11:13	78
11:35	48
15:1–2	41
16:20	53
17:3	85
19:28–29	63
21:11	89

Acts

5:28	59
5:29–32	59
5:41–42	59
6:7	88
11:3	80
11:12	80
11:15	80
12:20	48
13:1–3	63, 64
17:18	34
17:18–33	207
18	97
18:8	112
18:27	88
19	34
19:26	84
20:9	58
20:37–38	57
21:27–36	74
22:30	74
23:6	74
23:9	74
27:16	85
27:29	55

Romans

1:8	112
1:11	85
1:22	75
3:10–18	19, 20
3:27	132
3:27	170
5:7	88
6:4	111
6:8	111
7:7–25	109
7:14–25	59
7:25	112

9:7	96
9:25	96
9:26	96
11:25	183
12:16	183
14:19	158
15:2	158

1 Corinthians

1–4	46, 75, 90, 93, 94, 107, 117, 123, 131, 145, 184, 189, 190, 194, 195, 199, 202, 204, 206, 207, 211
1:1–3	94, 99, 101
1:1–9	94, 191
1:1–2:16	94
1:2	111, 190
1:3	99
1:4	102, 103, 104, 112
1:4–8	103
1:4–9	101, 145, 176
1:5	102, 103, 104, 106, 107
1:5–7	148, 149
1:6	102, 103, 104
1:7	102, 103, 105, 106, 107
1:8	101, 102, 103, 104, 105, 106
1:9	60, 92, 102, 103, 104
1:10	107, 108, 110, 113, 114, 115, 131, 146, 147, 188, 203, 211
1:10–13	175
1:10–17	108, 109, 117, 146, 148, 175, 195, 197
1:10–4:21	107, 148
1:11	108, 113, 180
1:12	109, 152, 154, 158, 160, 169, 205
1:13	111, 115, 116
1:13–17	111
1:14	112, 117
1:15	112
1:16	112, 117
1:17	205
1:17–2:5	206

SCRIPTURE INDEX

1:18	120, 121, 122, 125, 176	2:10–16	138
		2:10–21:16	108
1:18–25	108, 117, 129, 133, 146, 168, 195	2:11	139
		2:12	138, 139, 143
1:18–2:5	160, 208	2:13	143, 174
1:18–2:16	148	2:14	136, 139, 144, 149, 152, 191
1:18–4:21	203		
1:18–15:57	203	2:14–15	138, 144, 145
1:19	120, 121, 123, 125, 127	2:15	136, 139, 144, 149, 191
1:20	123, 124	2:15–16	108
1:21	121, 125, 126, 127, 129	2:16	140
		3–4	190
1:22	122, 124, 125	3:1	149, 150, 152, 191
1:22–23	122, 126, 127	3:1–2	149, 150, 155
1:23	108, 118, 121, 126	3:1–4	148, 175, 196, 196, 197
1:24	122, 126		
1:25	122, 126	3:1–5	156, 176, 187, 190
1:26	128, 129, 130, 131	3:1–4:21	148
1:26–28	131, 138	3:2	150, 153
1:26–31	92, 104, 108, 127, 146, 195, 196	3:3	59, 150, 151, 154
		3:3–4	155
1:27–28	130, 131, 176	3:4	152, 154, 155, 158, 191
1:29	130, 169, 170, 171		
1:29–31	156	3:5	103, 158, 161, 171, 175, 188
1:30	130, 176		
1:30–31	131	3:5–8	108
1:31	123, 130, 157, 162, 169, 170	3:5–9	25, 155, 177, 191, 196, 208
2:1	134, 141, 149, 205	3:6	97, 156, 157, 159, 191
2:1–5	133, 140, 146, 195, 196	3:7	157, 159
		3:8	157, 159, 161
2:2	108, 133, 135	3:9	158, 160, 161
2:3	57, 133	3:10	97, 161, 162, 192
2:4	133	3:10–17	161, 192, 196, 197
2:5	134, 135	3:11	165
2:6	119, 136, 138, 140, 141, 149, 197	3:12	163, 165
		3:12–13	162, 163
2:6–9	138, 144	3:12–14	162
2:6–16	136, 147, 155, 161, 183, 196	3:13	165
		3:14	162, 163, 166
2:7	108, 133, 136, 142, 171	3:14–15	161, 163, 166
		3:15	162, 163, 166, 166
2:8	141	3:16	192
2:9	123, 138, 142	3:16–17	192
2:10	138, 138, 140, 142	3:17	162, 165, 166, 192, 168
2:10–12	176		
2:10–13	145	3:18	17, 169, 170, 182, 192

1 Corinthians (cont.)

3:18–23	167, 192, 196
3:19	68, 123, 168, 170
3:19–20	192
3:20	168
3:21	156, 169, 170, 171, 176
3:21–22	169, 170
3:21–23	170
3:22	192
3:23	109, 169
3:24	169
3:30	169
4	117
4:1	104, 171
4:1–2	192
4:1–5	171, 192, 196
4:2	171, 173
4:3	172, 173
4:3–4	144
4:4	172, 173, 174
4:5	172, 175, 196
4:6	108, 123, 152, 158, 171, 175, 180
4:6–13	175, 193, 194, 196
4:7	156, 175, 176, 180
4:8	181
4:9	178, 181, 182
4:9–13	177, 178, 179, 180
4:10	167, 177, 178, 182, 193
4:10–12	193
4:10–13	182
4:11	178, 179
4:11–12	183
4:11–13	183
4:12	177, 179, 183
4:12–13	183, 193
4:13	177, 179, 180
4:14	148, 186, 188
4:14–15	113
4:14–21	184, 193, 196
4:15	97, 185, 188
4:16	185, 188, 190, 194, 202
4:17	186, 187, 189
4:18	187, 189
4:19	187, 189
4:20	187, 189
4:21	187
5:1	204
5:1–13	2, 204
5:5	174
6:9–10	98
6:9–11	98
7:15	96
7:31	58
8:1	158
9:1–2	95
9:3	144
9:5	96
9:20–23	206
10:17	132
10:23–24	158
10:27	96
12	111
12:3–11	106
12:7	158
12:12–13	111
13	25
13:4	49
14:1–25	106
14:8	112
14:12	158
14:18	112
14:26–33	158
15:1–8	185
15:9	96
16:15	117

2 Corinthians

6:11	56
9:7	61
11:2	85
11:3	85
11:4	86
11:5	85
11:19	183
12:11	75, 85
12:15	87
12:20	151

Galatians

1:14	86

SCRIPTURE INDEX

2:11	25	5:5	85
2:11–14	34		
2:11–24	34	*2 Timothy*	
3:1	76	2:3	83
3:28	111	4:8	59
5:2–3	73		
5:20	151	*Titus*	
		1:10	51
Ephesians		1:10–11	51
2:5	111	1:12	51, 78
4:12	158	1:12–13	50
4:17	73	1:13	51, 52
4:29	158		
		Philemon	
Philippians		1	43
1:3	112	4	112
2:20	84		
2:25	77	*Hebrews*	
2:26	77	3:10	54
3:8	49	3:15–16	70
4:11	54	3:19	59
Colossians		*James*	
1:3	112	1:2	49
1:24	50	1:20	54
2:11–12	111	1:22	84
2:20	81	1:27	92
3:1	81	2:14	79
3:1–4:5	81	2:14–18	54
3:10	111	3:1	54
3:12–13	89	3:11	54
		3:13	54
1 Thessalonians		5:1	54
1:2	112	5:11	88
2:12	73	5:12	87
2:13	87, 112		
3:6	79	*1 Peter*	
3:13	25	3:14	53
4:1–8	39, 40		
5:11	158	*2 Peter*	
5:16	87	2:22	83
1 Timothy		*1 John*	
1:15	59, 61, 87	2:15	81
1:16	59	2:26	74
5:3	84, 85	2:27	74
5:4–5	85	2:28–3:17	19

1 John (cont.)

3:15	38, 68
4:18	84

2 John

4	84

Revelation

2:4	51
2:6	50–51

2:6	55
4:8	89

Early Christian Writings

Diognetus

12:8	86

Printed in the United States
by Baker & Taylor Publisher Services